LOCATIONS TO SURVIVE
AN
ECONOMIC DEPRESSION

LOCATIONS TO SURVIVE
AN
ECONOMIC DEPRESSION

THE ULTIMATE GUIDE TO THE SAFEST
PLACES OF THE COMING DEPRESSION

by TIGRAN MANDALIAN

PALMETTO
PUBLISHING
Charleston, SC
www.PalmettoPublishing.com

Paperback ISBN: 9798990858626
Hardcover ISBN: 9798990858633

Contents

Acknowledgments

A special thank you to Palmetto Publishing for designing an exceptional book cover and for beautifully formatting this book. I also want to extend my gratitude to the following organizations and companies for their invaluable research and tools, which greatly contributed to the creation of this book: U.S. Census Bureau, BEA, USGS, USDA, Mapchart.net, SparkRental, FBI, and Cato Institute. Finally, data graphs were created using Microsoft Excel.

Introduction

Locations to Survive an Economic Depression: Regional Economic and Social Risks in the United States

There is little research or published material on regional economic and social risks in the United States. If there is a considerable economic collapse, which states, regions, and areas would be safer economically and socially? Which regions would suffer the most? It would be very difficult to answer those questions because no books offer a comprehensive and all-encompassing idea of regional economic and social differences. This book provides a unique perspective by considering economic and social risks and probabilistically identifying which locations will suffer most from a depression in terms of economic downturn and various social risks. It concludes by identifying the riskiest and safest places to outlive a depression. Maps visually illustrate each state's characteristics. Based on evidence and objectively defined probabilities, the methods used incorporate creativity and uniqueness, making this book easy to understand and visualize.

After reading this book, readers will gain a new understanding of the desirable locations in the United States. While individual analyses of some of the risks mentioned have been conducted, there has never been a complete summary of all risks combined in a general bird's-eye view and precise intrastate format.

This book will leave readers informed on how a potential economic crash will affect various locations economically and socially. With this knowledge, readers will know the effect on their city, county, and state. Based on this book, an action plan can be developed in case economic depression unfolds. This book will keep readers informed and ahead of everyone else.

I think we are on the verge of an economic downturn. I cannot say when it will start, but I think being prepared right now is vital. This book does not aim to explain why the economy will collapse. It is based on historical evidence and tells readers what to expect from the depression and where to expect its consequences the most and the least.

The book starts by identifying different economic risks. Chapters 1 through 4 analyze a specific industry or risk, including crime. Each chapter has a map with locations that are deemed risky. Chapter 5 summarizes all economic and crime risks. Chapter 6 applies all the findings of the previous chapter on a state basis in an easy-to-visualize format. The book concludes with Chapter 7's analysis of states' agricultural self-sufficiency and Chapter 8's analysis of additional social risks. Chapter 9 identifies the exact U.S. counties that will be much safer and easier to weather and outlive an economic depression.

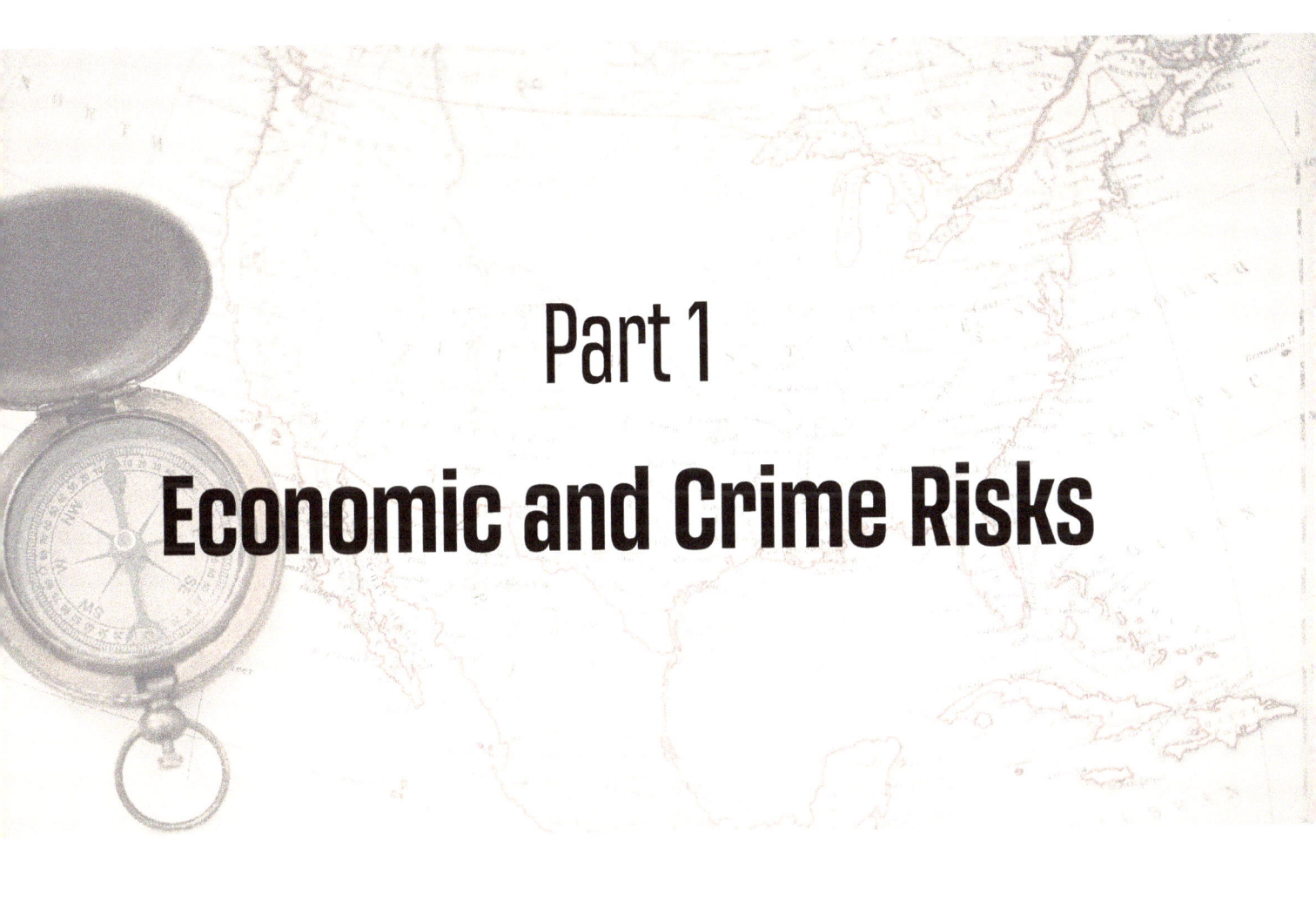

Part 1

Economic and Crime Risks

CHAPTER 1

Durable Goods Manufacturing Risk

Figure 1.1 from the 1940 U.S. census presents data on U.S. national income by industrial divisions from 1929 to 1939. Notice that most industries experienced a precipitous decline from 1929, bottoming either in 1932 or 1933. In fact, most industries, except the government, had not yet recovered in 1939. Also, Figure 1.1 shows the census data on the number of employees and their per capita income. The number of employees plunged, as did their income.

Besides contract construction, which often experiences sharp declines in economic recessions, it is difficult to say which industries are riskier because most experienced deep downturns. During a profound downturn, the mining industry might also decline dramatically. Someone might say, "Over 90 years, the U.S. economy has changed. Why would someone look back 90 years and think the same lessons will apply today?" Ironically and tragically, so many people had foreclosures in 2008–2010 and lost their jobs and money in the stock market. Whether it was the depression of the late 1830s–early 1840s, the 1870s, the Great Depression of 1929–39, the 2007–09 recession, or the next big crash, the financial and real estate markets are very susceptible sectors during financial downturns. Sounds logical? Most financial assets, index funds, and real estate decline in tandem or shortly after major stock market drops that lead to depressions. They are not safe. Those who say otherwise argue against historical evidence, and therefore, they are factually wrong. Thus, regions with economies most dependent on these industries will suffer greatly. However, look at something that could be more obvious. What industry famously suffered so much in 2008? Durable goods manufacturing. By nature durable goods last several years and do not wear out quickly. They include machinery and equipment, industrial machinery, automobiles, furniture, appliances, cell phones, laptops, televisions, refrigerators, jewelry, etc. Remember the General Motors bailout or the decline of the famous Detroit? Detroit and many other heavy manufacturing cities in Michigan and Ohio highly depended on industrial plants. Once the economy crashed, those cities suffered more than many others.

Durable goods manufacturing has historically demonstrated excessive sensitivity to economic downturns. During bad times, consumers hold off purchasing durable goods because of pessimism, uncertainty about the future, and a lack of money. For example, one would choose to use their current old car rather than buy a new one or use a laptop for many more years rather than replace it with a brand-new one. Individuals are unlikely to splurge on expensive fancy appliances rather adopting a more conservative, frugal approach of saving and using the old as long as possible. On top of that, many people simply do not have money to buy expensive goods, as their finances tighten.

Conversely, there is a nondurable goods industry. Nondurable goods require imminent consumption, such as food, cigarettes, cosmetics, cleaning products, soaps, medication, clothing, gasoline, or other items with a short lifespan. Certain nondurable goods are a necessity for physical existence. Also, they are relatively inexpensive. Nondurable goods manufacturing slows down as consumption declines almost everywhere, but it does so at a much slower rate than the durable goods industry. People will eat less food, buy less new underwear, consume less gasoline, and save on cleaning products, but they will still buy those products.

Is the same the case for 1929 as it was in 2008? Figure 1.2 shows the indexes of employment and payrolls for durable and nondurable goods from 1926 to 1940. Observe 1929–1933. Employment in the durable goods industry yielded an average index of 106.2 in 1929. It crashed, bottoming in March 1933 at 46.8. In the same period, nondurable goods employment had an average index of 105.9 in 1929 and bottomed out at 71.5 in July 1932. Additionally, durable goods payrolls set an average index of 111.2 in 1929 and plunged to a staggering 25.8 in March 1933. In comparison, nondurable goods payrolls set an average index of 109.6 in 1929 and collapsed to 52.4 in March 1933. The difference between declines in the durable goods and nondurable goods industries is very large. The durable goods industry had a much more significant decline in employment and payrolls.

Durable goods have historically underperformed nondurable goods industry in market crashes, not only just during the Great Depression. Besides, the durable goods industry is also riskier than other industries. Payrolls in the durable goods group collapsed from 117.5 in April 1929 to 25.8 in March 1933 (see Figure 1.2), a 78% decline, more than the average industry decline in the 1929–1932(3) crash (see Figure 1.1).

It is clear the durable goods industry is risky. Examine the current regional exposure to durable goods manufacturing in each state. Before that, two things must be noted. First, durable goods manufacturing and the overall manufacturing industry have consistently declined as a percentage of the U.S. total employment since the 1940s. Figure 1.3 shows that employment in the manufacturing sector has declined since the 1940s relative to other industries. In the 1950s, about 30% of total nonfarm employment was in manufacturing; in March 2024, it is 8.2%.

Let us define industries classified into durable goods groups today. According to the U.S. Bureau of Economic Analysis (BEA), durable goods are "Tangible products that can be stored or inventoried and that have an average life of at least three years."[1] Using the North American Industry Classification System (NAICS), durable goods manufacturing includes these industries: wood product manufacturing; nonmetallic mineral product manufacturing; primary metal manufacturing; fabricated metal product manufacturing; machinery manufacturing; computer and electronic product manufacturing; electrical equipment, appliance, and component manufacturing; transportation equipment manufacturing; furniture and related product manufacturing; and miscellaneous manufacturing. The NAICS numbers for the listed industries are 321, 327–339.

Figure 1.1

National Income, By Industrial Divisions; Number of Employees and The Per Capita Income of Employees: 1929–1939. Reprinted from U.S Census Bureau—1940 Census; Bureau of Internal Revenue

NATIONAL INCOME   315

No. 352.—NATIONAL INCOME, BY INDUSTRIAL DIVISIONS: 1929 TO 1939

[In millions of dollars]

	1929	1930	1931	1932	1933	1934[1]	1935	1936	1937	1938	1939
National income	82,885	68,901	54,310	40,074	42,430	50,347	55,870	65,165	71,172	63,610	69,378
Agriculture	7,258	5,622	3,729	2,551	3,419	4,553	5,276	5,970	6,378	5,432	5,635
Mining	1,883	1,327	748	524	590	991	1,028	1,299	1,530	1,072	1,232
Electric light and power and gas	1,425	1,324	1,240	1,096	1,026	1,127	1,152	1,233	1,380	1,365	1,384
Manufacturing	20,308	14,987	10,194	6,009	8,162	10,510	12,402	14,978	16,994	12,359	15,425
Contract construction	3,670	2,759	1,862	906	581	735	964	1,570	1,902	1,749	2,148
Transportation	7,108	6,155	4,946	3,622	3,587	3,817	4,133	4,795	5,088	4,261	4,800
Communication	1,047	1,011	907	722	640	679	723	770	839	808	863
Trade	11,314	9,245	7,415	5,290	6,031	6,971	7,608	8,516	9,131	8,593	9,135
Finance	8,915	7,836	6,441	4,895	4,318	4,630	5,131	5,749	6,199	5,837	5,983
Government, including work-program wages	6,330	6,438	6,518	6,487	6,563	7,632	7,923	9,446	9,153	9,846	9,884
Government, excluding work-program wages	6,330	6,438	6,459	6,355	5,917	6,202	6,584	7,063	7,370	7,701	8,015
Work-program wages	---	---	59	132	646	1,430	1,339	2,383	1,783	2,145	1,869
Service	9,615	8,725	7,343	5,579	5,321	6,181	6,828	7,643	8,477	8,067	8,374
Miscellaneous	4,012	3,472	2,967	2,393	2,192	2,518	2,695	2,897	3,161	3,102	3,319
Social security contribution of employers	---	---	---	---	---	3	7	299	950	1,119	1,196

[1] Data on dividends, interest, and corporate savings by industrial divisions for 1934 and for subsequent years are based on a different industrial classification than are the estimates of these items for earlier years because of a change in the Revenue Act of 1934. Special tabulations of the Bureau of Internal Revenue permitted the making of estimates for 1934 on the earlier basis. For specific items in certain industries the variations are substantial, but for total income the changes were small. The 2 estimates were averaged in compiling this table.

No. 353.—NUMBER OF EMPLOYEES AND THE PER CAPITA INCOME OF EMPLOYEES:[1] 1929 TO 1939

	1929	1930	1931	1932	1933	1934	1935	1936	1937	1938	1939
NUMBER OF EMPLOYEES (thousands)											
All employees	35,563	33,122	29,715	26,222	26,133	28,402	28,725	31,858	33,768	31,239	32,419
Salaried employees (selected industries)[2]	2,478	2,373	2,050	1,693	1,634	1,831	1,922	2,068	2,206	2,064	2,100
Wage earners (selected industries)[2]	10,964	9,649	8,155	6,877	7,430	8,553	9,021	9,765	10,618	8,832	9,404
Salaried employees or wage earners (all other industries)	22,121	21,100	19,510	17,652	17,069	18,018	18,782	20,025	20,944	20,343	20,915
PER CAPITA INCOME OF EMPLOYEES											
All employees	$1,472	$1,433	$1,341	$1,180	$1,092	$1,140	$1,191	$1,240	$1,309	$1,294	$1,329
Salaried employees (selected industries)[2]	2,483	2,511	2,404	2,119	1,995	2,054	2,098	2,113	2,213	2,198	2,215
Wage earners (selected industries)[2]	1,360	1,278	1,149	943	913	996	1,071	1,143	1,231	1,159	1,237
Salaried employees or wage earners (all other industries)	1,414	1,383	1,310	1,183	1,083	1,116	1,155	1,197	1,254	1,261	1,281

[1] Averages for the calendar year. The numbers represent in some industries a full-time equivalent. Unpaid family farm labor and work-relief employees have not been included.
[2] Includes mining, manufacturing, steam railroads, Pullman, railway express, and water transportation.

Source of tables 352 and 353: Department of Commerce, Bureau of Foreign and Domestic Commerce. Annual and current figures are published in "Survey of Current Business" and reprints.

Figure 1.2

Employment and Pay Rolls in Manufacturing Industries—Indexes for Durable Goods and Nondurable Goods Groups, by Months: 1926–1940. Reprinted from U.S. Census Bureau—1940 Census; Department of Labor, Bureau of Labor Statistics

EMPLOYMENT AND PAY ROLLS   341

No. 381.—EMPLOYMENT AND PAY ROLLS IN MANUFACTURING INDUSTRIES—INDEXES FOR DURABLE-GOODS AND NONDURABLE-GOODS GROUPS, BY MONTHS: 1926 TO 1940

NOTE.—Monthly average, 1923–25=100. See headnote, table 379

YEAR	Jan.	Feb.	Mar.	Apr.	May	June	July	Aug.	Sept.	Oct.	Nov.	Dec.	Av.
EMPLOYMENT					DURABLE-GOODS GROUP [1]								
1926	101.3	102.9	103.9	104.3	103.7	103.2	101.8	103.0	103.5	103.0	100.8	98.6	102.5
1927	96.0	97.9	99.1	99.3	99.2	98.2	95.8	96.4	95.9	95.2	92.9	91.5	96.5
1928	90.3	92.8	94.9	96.1	97.7	98.2	97.4	99.0	101.3	101.6	101.0	100.6	97.7
1929	101.0	103.9	105.9	108.0	109.3	109.3	109.2	110.3	109.8	107.7	102.5	97.6	106.2
1930	94.8	95.3	95.1	94.9	93.8	90.8	83.3	83.7	82.3	80.0	78.1	75.7	87.6
1931	72.3	72.4	72.5	72.6	71.9	69.8	67.1	65.8	65.0	62.2	60.6	60.2	67.7
1932	58.1	58.8	57.5	55.5	54.0	52.5	50.1	48.9	49.2	49.6	50.0	49.6	52.8
1933	47.7	48.6	46.8	47.9	50.9	55.3	50.8	65.0	68.3	68.0	66.1	66.8	57.5
1934	65.1	69.4	73.5	76.6	78.3	77.6	75.1	72.9	70.7	69.3	68.8	66.8	72.4
1935	73.5	77.3	79.3	80.2	79.7	77.4	77.3	79.1	79.9	83.8	85.1	84.7	79.8
1936	83.2	83.0	84.7	87.5	89.6	90.5	91.0	91.3	92.5	96.3	98.3	100.4	90.7
1937	97.9	101.2	104.9	107.4	109.1	107.8	108.2	107.6	106.8	107.2	101.4	92.4	104.3
1938	82.4	80.8	80.0	77.7	75.7	76.1	70.9	72.4	75.9	79.7	82.9	83.8	77.9
1939	82.3	83.3	84.1	84.8	84.0	84.6	83.0	83.9	89.8	96.1	98.2	100.0	87.8
1940	97.4	96.6	96.4	96.0	96.5	97.0							
PAY ROLLS													
1926	99.9	106.4	108.6	107.8	106.5	106.1	100.2	104.7	104.6	108.2	103.9	101.1	104.8
1927	98.6	101.8	104.8	104.6	104.7	101.2	94.8	98.5	96.1	97.7	93.7	94.7	98.9
1928	90.1	98.0	101.0	101.6	103.0	99.0	104.5	104.8	109.4	105.8	102.3		102.3
1929	102.2	111.5	114.6	117.5	118.7	115.8	109.8	115.4	114.6	113.4	109.9	97.4	111.2
1930	91.0	96.1	96.8	97.0	94.8	90.3	79.1	76.0	75.4	74.4	68.6	66.1	83.8
1931	59.1	63.7	65.2	64.6	63.7	58.7	53.6	52.2	48.8	47.7	45.3	44.9	55.6
1932	40.7	41.8	39.5	36.9	36.8	32.6	29.4	27.9	27.9	29.8	29.5	29.0	33.4
1933	27.5	27.8	25.8	27.5	32.0	38.4	39.6	45.2	46.0	46.3	43.6	43.8	36.8
1934	43.1	49.6	54.8	59.6	60.9	59.2	51.3	51.7	47.1	48.2	48.1	52.7	52.2
1935	55.1	61.6	63.6	64.9	62.6	60.0	58.2	62.5	64.6	70.4	71.9	73.5	64.1
1936	69.1	68.1	73.2	75.2	81.0	81.6	78.7	79.8	80.1	88.6	92.4	97.8	80.7
1937	90.3	96.8	104.9	112.0	113.3	109.9	106.1	109.2	104.7	107.0	93.8	80.2	102.4
1938	66.5	66.6	66.8	65.0	63.6	61.1	58.1	63.1	68.1	74.6	77.6	79.6	67.0
1939	76.0	77.7	79.4	79.5	78.8	80.7	76.0	81.5	87.8	99.6	100.9	104.6	85.2
1940	98.2	96.7	97.6	97.2	97.5	100.0							
EMPLOYMENT					NONDURABLE-GOODS GROUP [2]								
1926	100.7	101.1	101.2	99.4	98.0	98.5	97.7	100.7	104.4	104.2	102.4	101.9	100.9
1927	101.1	102.3	102.6	101.2	100.0	101.1	101.2	103.3	106.2	104.0	102.8	101.3	102.3
1928	100.1	101.3	101.3	99.4	98.7	99.4	99.4	102.2	105.1	105.4	104.1	103.6	101.6
1929	102.3	104.3	105.0	105.4	103.9	104.4	105.6	108.2	110.8	110.2	106.6	103.6	105.9
1930	101.4	101.2	100.5	99.6	97.4	96.3	94.3	95.3	98.6	96.2	92.3	89.9	96.9
1931	87.5	88.7	89.5	89.4	88.9	87.4	87.5	89.5	90.9	88.1	84.3	83.2	87.9
1932	81.4	83.0	82.1	79.5	75.9	73.4	71.5	75.0	82.2	83.9	81.8	79.8	79.2
1933	78.1	80.1	77.0	79.1	82.0	87.1	91.8	97.0	100.8	100.3	95.6	92.5	88.5
1934	91.8	97.2	100.2	100.4	99.3	97.6	97.0	101.2	95.8	101.8	99.0	99.4	98.4
1935	99.3	101.3	102.2	101.7	99.6	99.6	103.7	107.2	107.2	103.7	103.2		102.2
1936	101.0	102.0	102.7	103.0	102.8	103.1	105.4	110.7	114.5	113.1	111.3	112.2	106.8
1937	111.2	113.7	115.1	115.0	113.5	112.6	113.5	116.8	117.6	113.3	106.7	102.2	112.6
1938	98.5	100.9	100.7	98.7	96.0	94.9	97.8	104.4	107.3	104.6	103.1	103.8	100.9
1939	101.7	103.5	104.0	103.0	101.6	101.8	103.5	108.1	110.2	110.8	109.2	108.0	105.5
1940	105.3	106.1	105.1	103.0	101.4	101.7							
PAY ROLLS													
1926	103.5	105.0	105.6	101.6	100.2	101.1	98.6	102.8	105.6	107.9	104.9	106.3	103.6
1927	104.3	108.2	108.5	105.5	104.9	105.4	103.9	107.0	108.8	108.3	104.7	105.0	106.3
1928	103.8	106.4	106.3	101.2	100.6	102.3	101.5	104.8	107.7	109.7	106.2	108.2	104.9
1929	105.6	110.0	111.2	110.3	108.5	109.2	107.2	111.3	114.2	114.0	107.1	105.4	109.6
1930	102.0	103.3	103.0	100.3	97.6	95.7	91.6	92.6	95.3	92.5	87.0	85.8	95.6
1931	82.8	86.5	87.9	86.0	84.8	82.4	81.1	82.2	80.6	77.7	72.9	72.3	81.4
1932	68.9	70.6	69.3	63.8	59.1	56.1	52.8	56.4	62.1	63.8	59.4	57.4	61.6
1933	54.6	56.6	52.4	54.8	58.3	63.3	67.3	73.5	78.4	77.7	70.8	65.0	65.0
1934	70.7	77.8	81.2	80.9	79.5	76.7	75.7	80.2	76.2	81.6	78.5	81.4	78.4
1935	81.3	85.0	86.4	85.4	82.2	80.9	81.2	86.9	95.8	89.6	86.2	88.4	85.3
1936	85.7	86.1	88.8	87.4	87.3	87.1	89.0	95.8	95.1	97.8	96.6	101.3	91.5
1937	99.4	103.9	107.0	107.0	106.4	105.1	104.1	108.1	105.1	102.5	92.6	89.4	102.6
1938	85.1	89.6	89.6	86.0	84.0	82.3	85.7	93.2	96.7	94.9	92.1	95.4	89.6
1939	92.4	95.3	96.7	92.2	91.0	93.0	93.7	99.0	100.5	103.9	102.4	102.8	97.0
1940	98.4	99.1	99.0	95.4	94.9	95.8							

[1] Iron and steel and their products; machinery; transportation equipment; nonferrous metals and their products; lumber and allied products; and stone, clay, and glass products.
[2] Food and kindred products; textiles and their products; paper and printing; chemical, petroleum, and coal products; leather and its manufactures; rubber products; and tobacco manufactures.

Source: Department of Labor, Bureau of Labor Statistics. See source of table 379 regarding current figures.

Figure 1.3

Employment in Manufacturing Sector Relative to Total U.S. Employment, 1939–2024

Image source: Federal Reserve Bank of St. Louis, U.S. Bureau of Labor Statistics

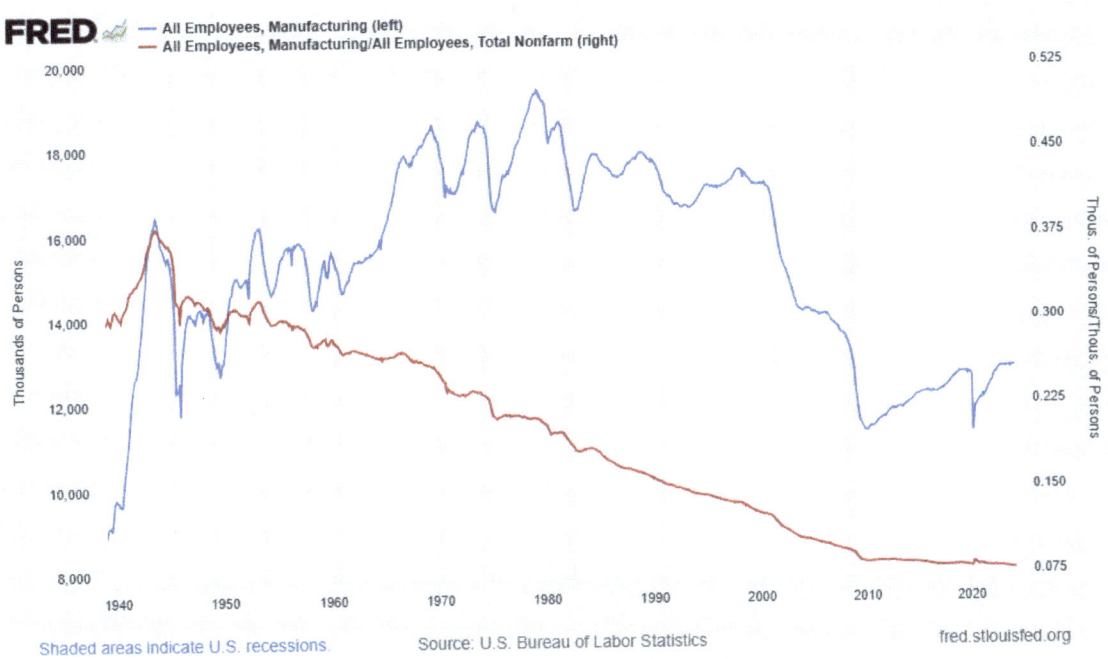

Looking at the state-level picture, the bird's-eye view picture tells us which states might be more susceptible to durable goods overconcentration risk. A county-level map provides even more specifics. Suppose the state has a relatively large durable goods manufacturing sector. However, within those states, the durable goods industry might be concentrated only in a few areas, not the whole state.

Figure 1.4 will be a helpful guide throughout this book. Analyze the regional classification of the U.S. states according to the U.S. census. This classification of regions and divisions will be frequently referenced. A link to the U.S. census website containing the map is in the references section of this chapter.[2]

Figure 1.5 is a U.S. state map showing the percentage of state gross domestic product (GDP) from durable goods manufacturing. Figure 1.6 is a U.S. state map showing the percentage of employment in durable goods manufacturing relative to total state employment. Both maps show all 50 states and Washington, DC. For precise state-by-state data of the calculations for Figures 1.5 and 1.6, additional materials are provided in the Appendix. Note that the data in the Appendix uses a regional division different from the one used here. Durable goods manufacturing is highly concentrated in the East North Central Midwest (Wisconsin, Michigan, Indiana, and Ohio), with the exception of Illinois. Besides the Midwest, a relatively high concentration exists in the East South Central states of Kentucky, Alabama, and Mississippi, with lower concentration in Tennessee. Many of us have heard of the concentration of factories in Ohio and Michigan—notably Detroit—that specialize in automobile manufacturing. We remember the troubles with the auto industry and the consequent economic decline during and after 2008. Alabama also ranks high on this list. History is rhythmic and tragic at times, but the benefit of it is that you can learn from it and save money and trouble. During the Great Depression, Birmingham, a large city in Alabama, had an extensive concentration of iron and steel manufacturing, which is part of the durable goods industry. When the Depression hit, the city had severe unemployment, above the national average of 25%. Then-President Franklin D. Roosevelt called Birmingham "the hardest hit in America."

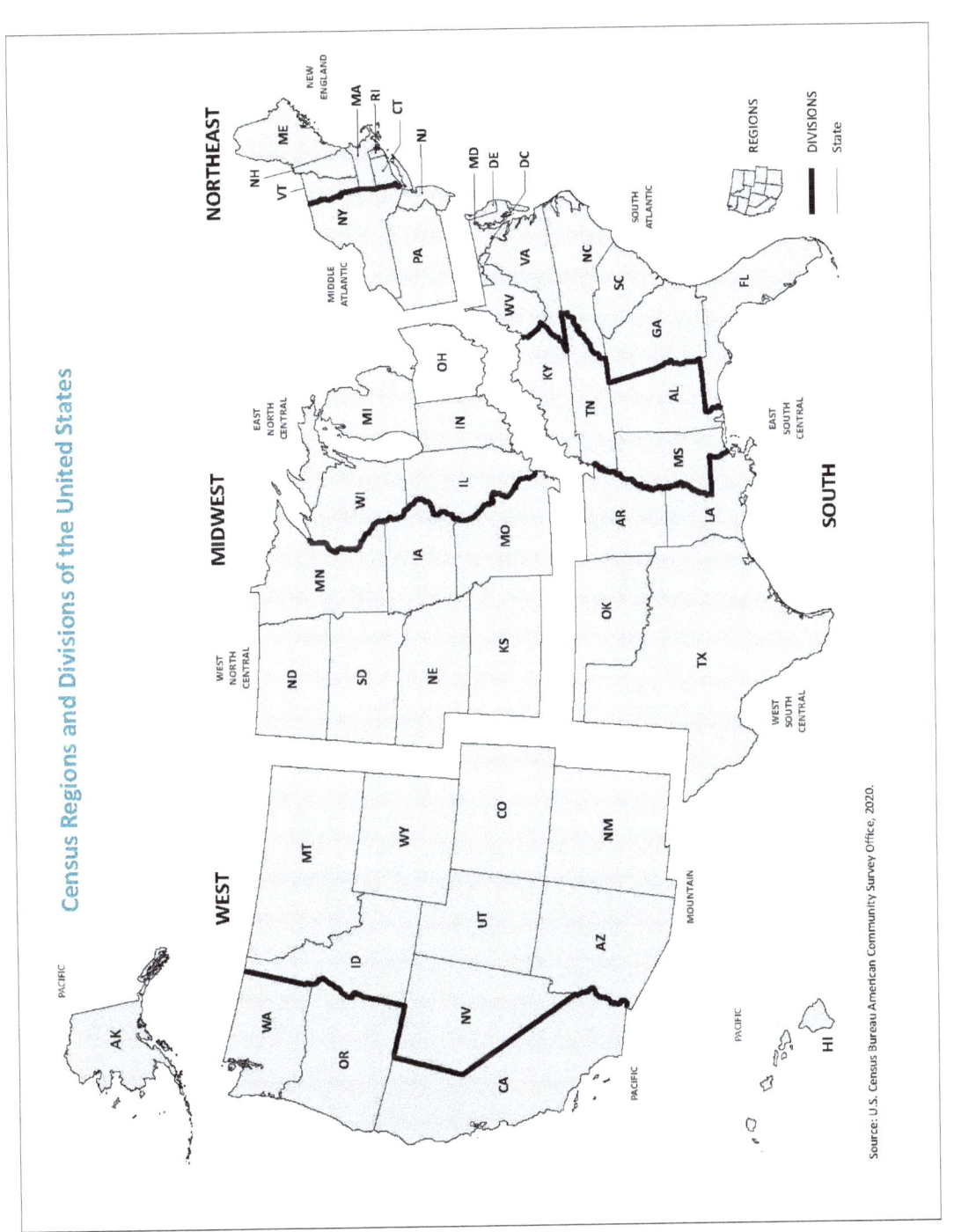

Census Regions and Divisions of the United States

Source: U.S. Census Bureau American Community Survey Office, 2020.

Figure 1.4

Census Regions and Divisions of the United States

Image Source: U.S. Census Bureau and U.S. Census Bureau American Community Survey Office, 2020

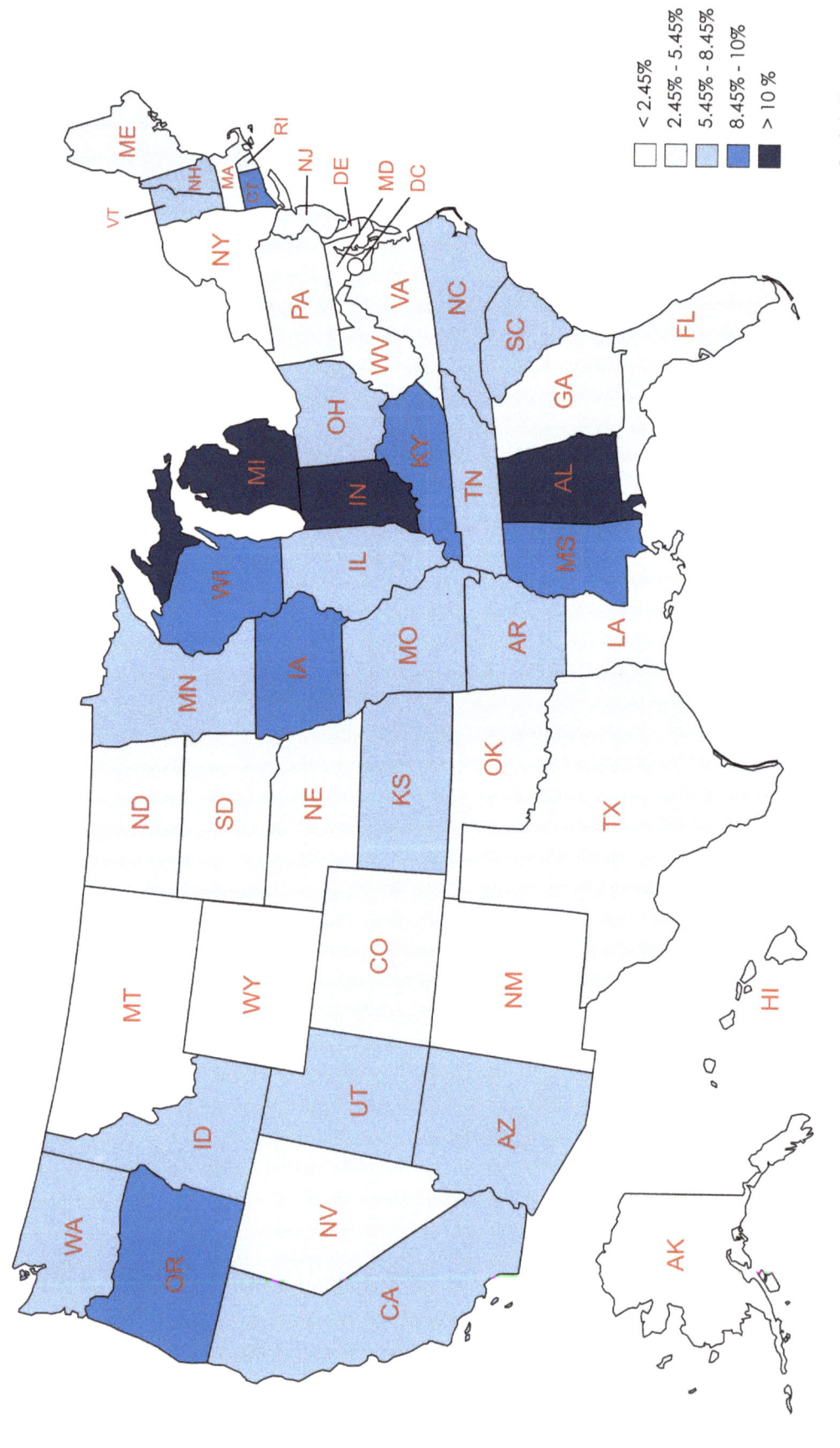

Figure 1.5

Durable Goods Manufacturing as a Percent of Total GDP by State

Data Source: U.S. Bureau of Economic Analysis (BEA). Data is for Second Quarter (Q2) of 2023, For District of Columbia data last updated on September 29, 2023—revised statistics for 2017–2022

Created with Mapchart.net

Legend:
- < 2.45%
- 2.45% - 5.45%
- 5.45% - 8.45%
- 8.45% - 10%
- > 10 %

Created with mapchart.net

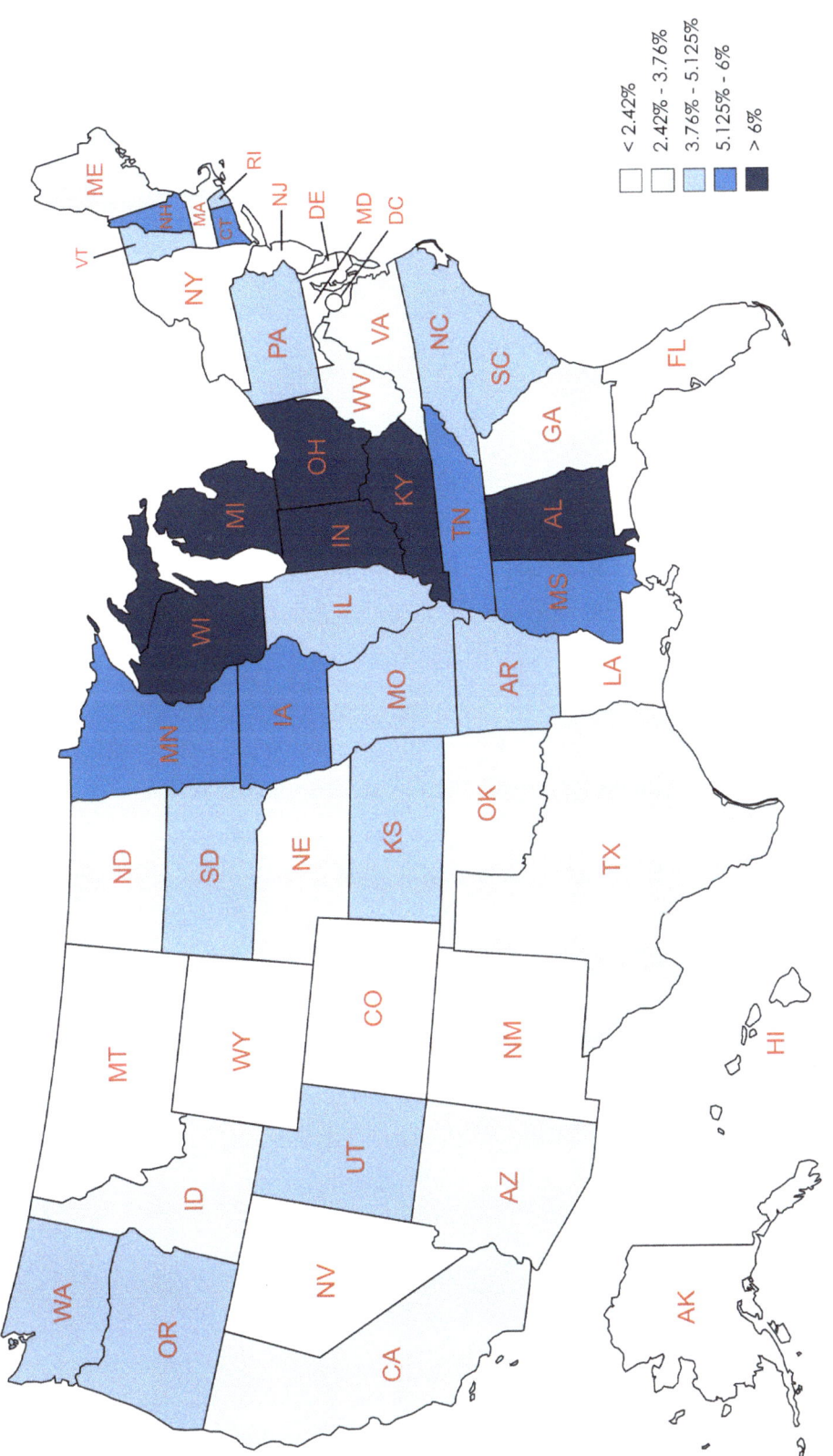

Figure 1.6

Durable Goods Employment as a Percent of Total Employment by State

Data Source: U.S. Bureau of Economic Analysis (BEA), Data last updated on September 29, 2023

Created with Mapchart.net

Legend:
- < 2.42%
- 2.42% - 3.76%
- 3.76% - 5.125%
- 5.125% - 6%
- > 6%

Created with mapchart.net

Figures 1.5 and 1.6 provide a bird's-eye view of durable goods manufacturing in the United States. However, the concentration of the durable goods industry could be only limited to a specific part of the state or spread in little pockets throughout. To get the county-level picture, I have created Figure 1.7 by calculating the durable goods private nonfarm earnings as a percentage of total nonfarm earnings per U.S. county. I have selected only the counties with an industry concentration above 20% and 25% of each county's total nonfarm earnings. Counties with a concentration between 20% and 25% are light purple, and those above 25% are dark purple. Either purple color indicates a durable goods industry overconcentration risk and the dark purple (above 25%) are probabilistically slightly riskier. If the county is not colored, the concentration of the durable goods industry is too low to present much risk. I decided to compare durable goods earnings to total nonfarm earnings because farm earnings can decrease the percentage of concentration of durable goods manufacturing if included and therefore, downplay its risks. In fact, a high concentration of farm industry itself could be very risky because of the lack of diversity of economic production. Chapters 2 and 7 examine the overconcentration of other industries and the overconcentration of the agricultural industry, respectively.

Figure 1.7 shows that Indiana has the highest number of counties engaged in durable goods manufacturing, with 31, which is not surprising because the state is known as the industrial powerhouse of America. Additionally, the East North Central division of the Midwest includes counties that manufacture durable goods in Ohio, Michigan, Wisconsin, and Illinois. Although quite a few counties engage in durable goods manufacturing in Illinois, overall, durable goods manufacturing and employment as a percent of the total state's GDP and total employment are not very high in Illinois. Michigan is known for manufacturing durable goods, but that industry occupies fewer counties than expected. Another noticeable cluster of counties engaged in durable goods is on the Alabama and Mississippi border. Wisconsin also often ranks as a high durable goods manufacturing state and has 10 counties on the list. Kentucky and Tennessee have 15 and 11 counties, respectively. Of interest is the high concentration in Iowa. Iowa is for its agriculture, not its manufacturing. However, as evidenced, there is a high concentration of durable goods manufacturing. See the Appendix for further explanation of counties in Figure 1.7, including information on each county.

We may conclude that the most clustered area of the durable goods industry is the Midwest region, specifically the East North Central division. That area is commonly known as the Rust Belt because of its overconcentration of the manufacturing industry. To some extent, the East South Central region is also a risky territory. Additionally, states like Iowa contain many counties that rely on manufacturing durable goods, which we need to consider. The overconcentration of durable goods makes these areas—and their adjacent counties at risk of spillover—highly undesirable. In other words, adjacent counties next to the Rust Belt will also suffer the effects of the heavy manufacturing decline in that area.

In conclusion, the durable goods industry includes industrial factories. These factories depend on economic growth. In a deep recession, they might close, leading to high unemployment and poverty in their locations and nearby areas. Thus, living in an area with a high concentration of industrial factories and adjacent territories could be risky and force many to abandon their current locations and relocate to places hit relatively less severely by the depression. The picture could be so ugly that small-to-medium-sized industrial factory city populations could be forced to relocate because of unlivable conditions. The benefit of this chapter is that we identified the concentration of one of the riskiest economic sectors on a precise county basis in Figure 1.7. It will later be combined with other maps that reflect the concentration of other industries for further analysis.

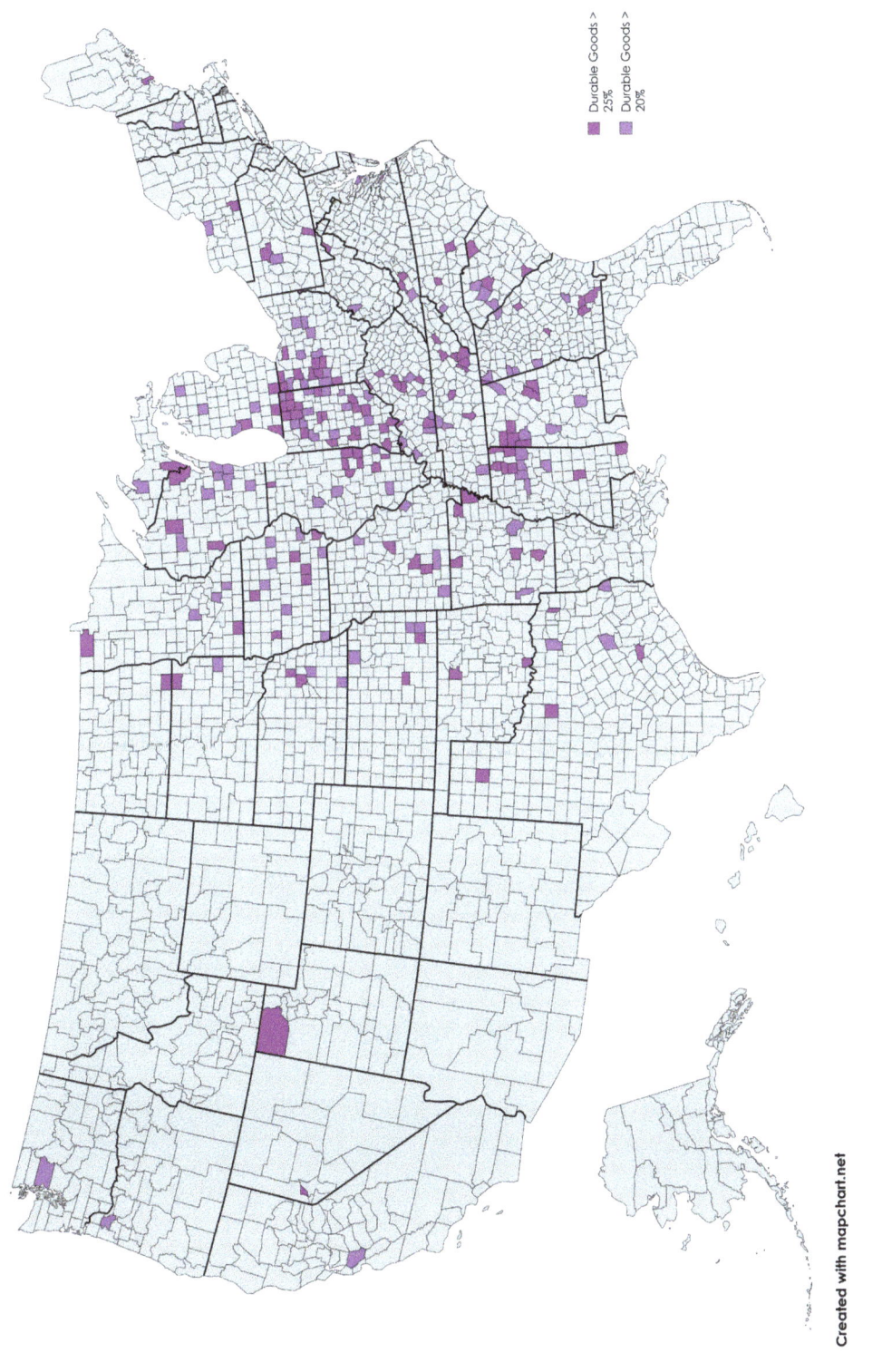

Figure 1.7
Durable Goods Manufacturing Private Nonfarm Earnings as a Percent of Total Private Nonfarm Earnings by County
Data Source: U.S. Bureau of Economic Analysis (BEA), last updated: November 16, 2023—new statistics for 2022

Created with Mapchart.net

References

1. U.S. Bureau of Economic Analysis (BEA). *Glossary*. Retrieved from https://www.bea.gov/help/glossary/durable-goods

2. U.S. Census Bureau. *Census Regions and Divisions of the United States*. Retrieved from https://www2.census.gov/programs-surveys/sahie/reference-maps/2020/us_regdiv.pdf

CHAPTER 2

Industry Overconcentration Risk

The previous chapter analyzed the durable goods industry, which has historically been prone to economic declines. This chapter examines the overconcentration of other industries/sectors. Industry and sector will be used interchangeably. High overconcentration of any industry in a particular geographical area would imply risks associated with the decline of that industry because of the implied lack of industry diversity. Even if the industry is not one of the riskiest industries per se during the economic downturn, the lack of diversity means that the whole area might be very severely affected by a downturn in that industry or location. I plotted the map with an overconcentration of the following industries: construction; farming; government; mining; health; finance and real estate; transportation and warehousing. A later chapter addresses the real estate more in depth. Out of the listed industries, finance and real estate, construction, mining, transportation and warehousing would also likely be riskier than other industries. Besides the mining industry, only a few sectors are regionally clustered, so I decided not to allocate an individual chapter for each industry. Additionally, mining makes up only about 1.3% of U.S. gross domestic product (GDP) and durable goods manufacturing comprises 5.59%.[1] All counties used in Figures 2.1 to 2.6 are listed in the Appendix.

Construction Industry

The construction industry will likely experience a deeper downturn than most industries, as commercial and residential construction is very susceptible to economic activity. I did not allocate a chapter to this industry, as it is not clustered in any obvious way. Figure 2.1 depicts counties with construction private nonfarm earnings above 20% of total private nonfarm earnings. Figure 2.1 has 52 counties. Twenty percent is a highly significant value and a reasonable requirement when estimating an industry overconcentration risk; the average contribution to U.S. GDP from the construction industry is about 4%. Because construction is risky, avoiding the counties shown in Figure 2.1 is advisable. I did not choose a smaller than 20% because it would imply a low concentration and diversification. Thus, if you live in an area highly dependent on construction, it is advisable to avoid working and investing in construction and consider moving to a safer location.

To conclude, there is no further need to analyze this industry as there are only 52 counties spread in various locations.

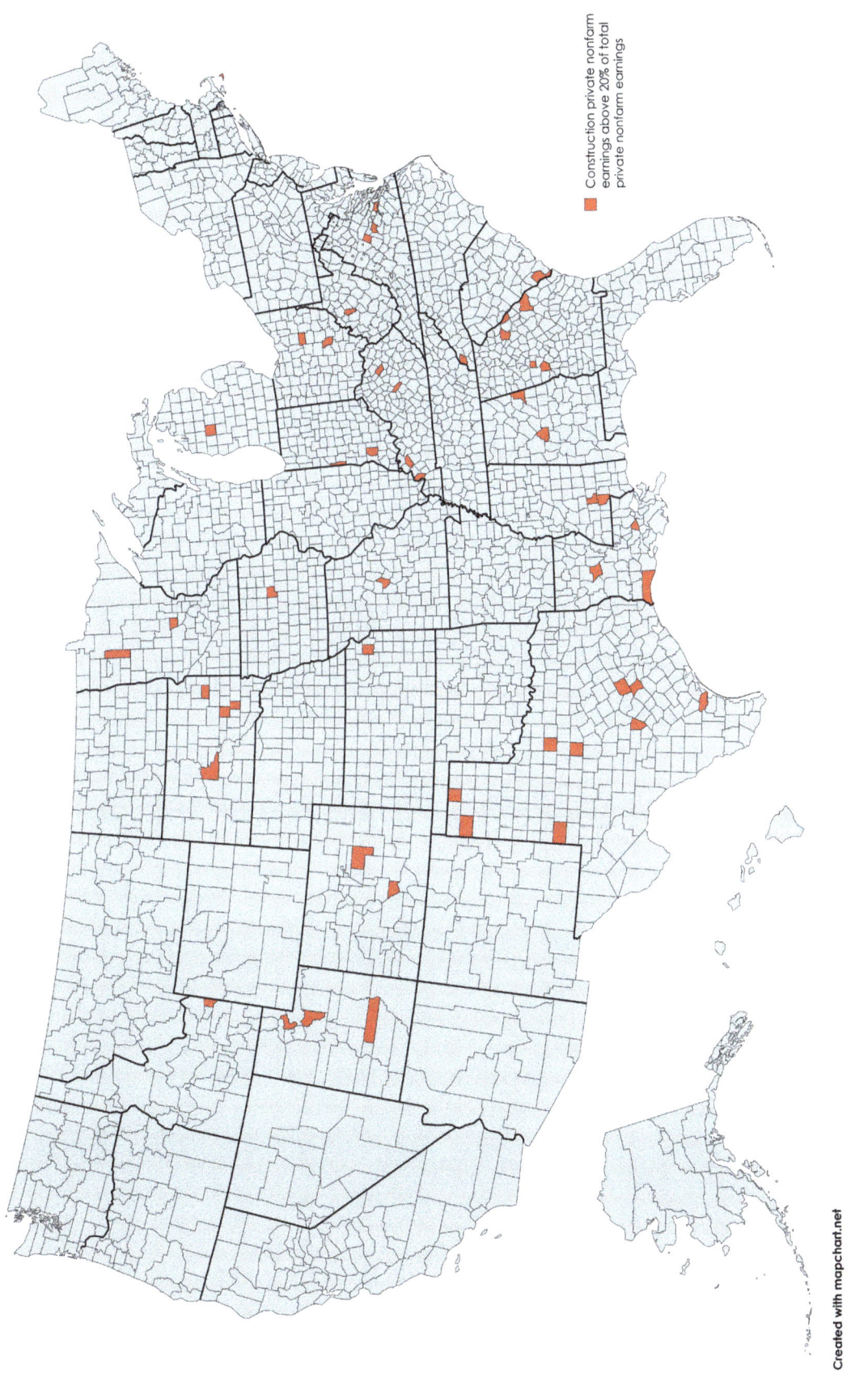

Construction private nonfarm
earnings above 20% of total
private nonfarm earnings

Figure 2.1

Counties with Construction Private Nonfarm Earnings Above 20% of Total Private Nonfarm Earnings

Data Source: U.S. Bureau of Economic Analysis (BEA)

Created with Mapchart.net

PART 2

Farming Industry

Previously, we used only nonfarm earnings as a benchmark. Now, we will use the sum of farm and nonfarm earnings because the industry is farming. The farming industry suffered a lot during the Great Depression. However, it is tough to say if the same will happen. Obviously, it will experience a downturn like every other industry, but it is hard to say if that downturn will be below or above average. Counties that are overly dependent on farming are at risk, as a lack of industry diversity is undesirable during the downturn. I decided to choose a 45% minimum requirement for farm earnings as a percent of the sum of farm and nonfarm earnings. Again, because it is difficult to forecast if this industry will outperform or underperform others, choosing a higher requirement will be a much safer and more logical choice. The results in Figure 2.2 show only 57 counties clustered in North Dakota, South Dakota, and partly in Nebraska. Many other counties and regions specialize in farming but to a lesser degree. The agricultural maps of the U.S. appear in Chapter 7. The counties you see in Figure 2.2 carry the most risk. If you live in North Dakota, South Dakota, or any area marked in Figure 2.2, I recommend protecting your income if it is heavily dependent on farming (e.g., you have farm debt; almost all of your income is agriculture driven; little employment exists in industries besides farming in your living area). Nevertheless, people who depend on farming will be at a lesser risk than, for example, those who depend on construction or durable goods industries. To conclude, the areas in Figure 2.2 will be probabilistically risky during the downturn.

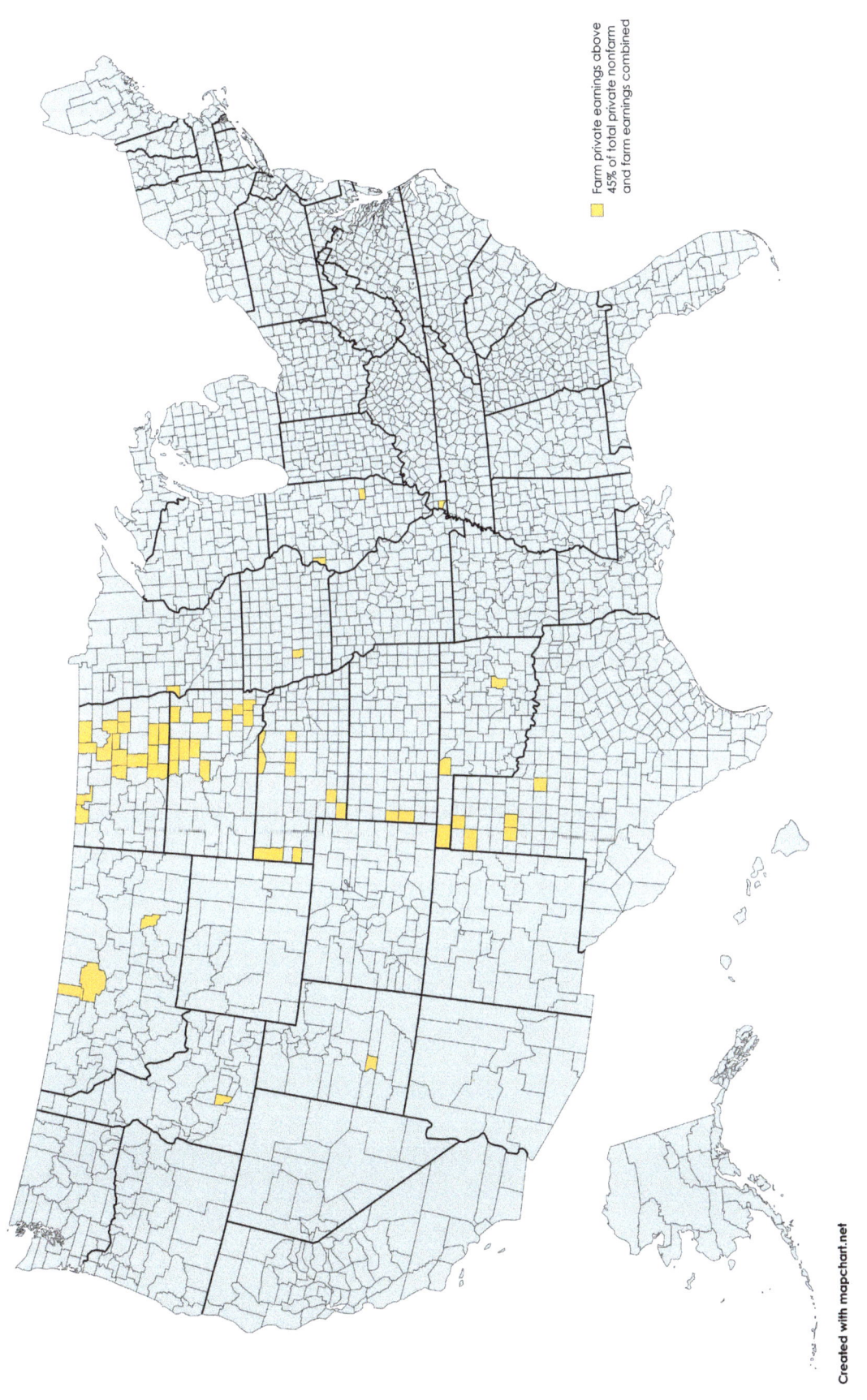

Farm private earnings above
45% of total private nonfarm
and farm earnings combined

Figure 2.2

Counties with Farm Private Earnings Above 45% of Total Private Nonfarm and Farm Earnings Combined

Data Source: U.S. Bureau of Economic Analysis (BEA)

Created with Mapchart.net

PART 3

Government and Government Enterprises

During the Great Depression, the government was in a much better fiscal position than today, measured by the federal debt-to-GDP ratio. In the first quarter of 2024, the federal debt-to-GDP ratio has reached an alarming 97%.[2] Today, the U.S. government, with its extraordinarily high public debt, hardly will be able to spend money in a desperate attempt to help the economy recover or to finance its current obligations. It is a matter of time before the U.S. government faces fiscal issues. Should the economy slow causing tax receipts to fall and incomes to plummet, the government will have to cut its spending. Since 1930s the U.S. economy heavily relies on the U.S. government. Federal government spending as a percentage of GDP is about 23% for 2023, while the annual federal deficit was 6.2% of GDP in 2023.[3] Much more than it should be in a capitalist country. Considering the fiscal state of the U.S. government, the counties that rely on the U.S. government subsidies will be extremely risky during this crash. As government spending plummets, it is unlikely that the government will be able to fully make its promises on Medicare, Medicaid, Social Security, etc., and those dependent on government income will suffer. When it comes to personal finance, avoid dependency on the government, be it state or federal.

I plotted counties with government and government enterprises' private nonfarm earnings above 50% of total private nonfarm earnings. Figure 2.3 maps those 80 counties. When using a 30% minimum requirement for earnings, the number of counties skyrockets to 526. Out of slightly more than 3,100 counties, people in about a sixth of all counties rely on the government for at least 30% of their private nonfarm earnings. When the trouble arrives, it will be difficult, especially for people who live in counties plotted in Figure 2.3.

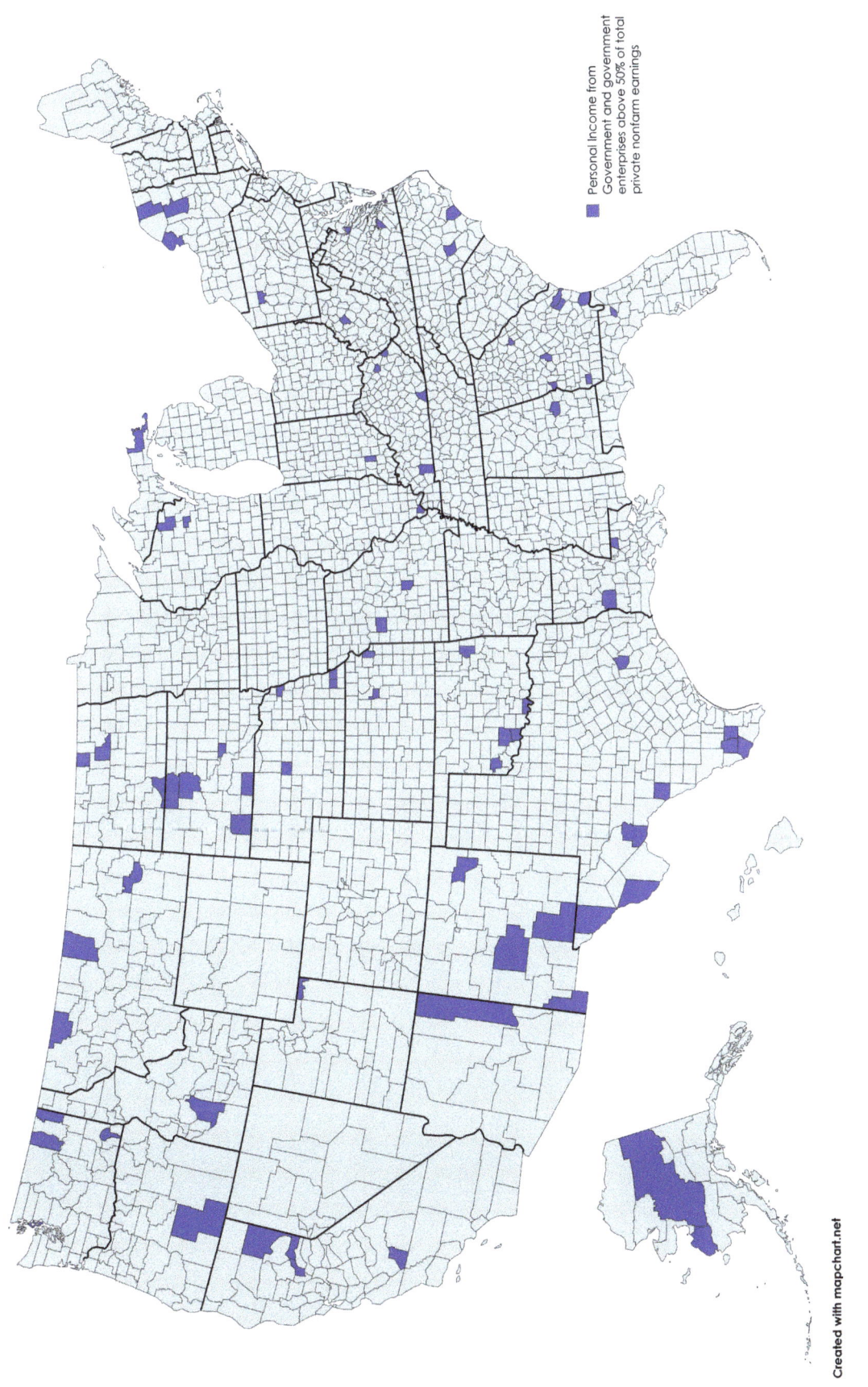

Figure 2.3

Counties with Government and Government Enterprises' Private Nonfarm Earnings Above 50% of Total Private Nonfarm Earnings

Data Source: U.S. Bureau of Economic Analysis (BEA)

Created with Mapchart.net

PART 4

Mining, Quarrying, and Oil and Gas Extraction

Mining is a very risky industry because it is very dependent on economic performance and requires appropriate natural geography, which can lead to clustering. Figure 2.4 illustrates the counties with mining, quarrying, and oil and gas extraction private nonfarm earnings above 20% of total private nonfarm earnings. I chose a 20% requirement similar to that of the durable goods and construction industries. Mining, quarrying, and oil and gas extraction are also industries that likely will crash more than others. Figure 2.4 illustrates a total of 69 counties, with significant clustering within Texas and several smaller clusters within the Mountain Census division. Remember the U.S. regional map (Figure 1.4) in Chapter 1. It would be wise to avoid areas near those clusters, as the deep downturn of the mining industry will significantly affect its nearby counties. Some people refer to copper as "doctor copper" as its price reflects the economy's health because it is used in many industries. If there is a significant market downturn, demand for copper and many other metals will decline because they depend on economic growth. Similarly, oil and gas consumption also is dependent on economic activity.

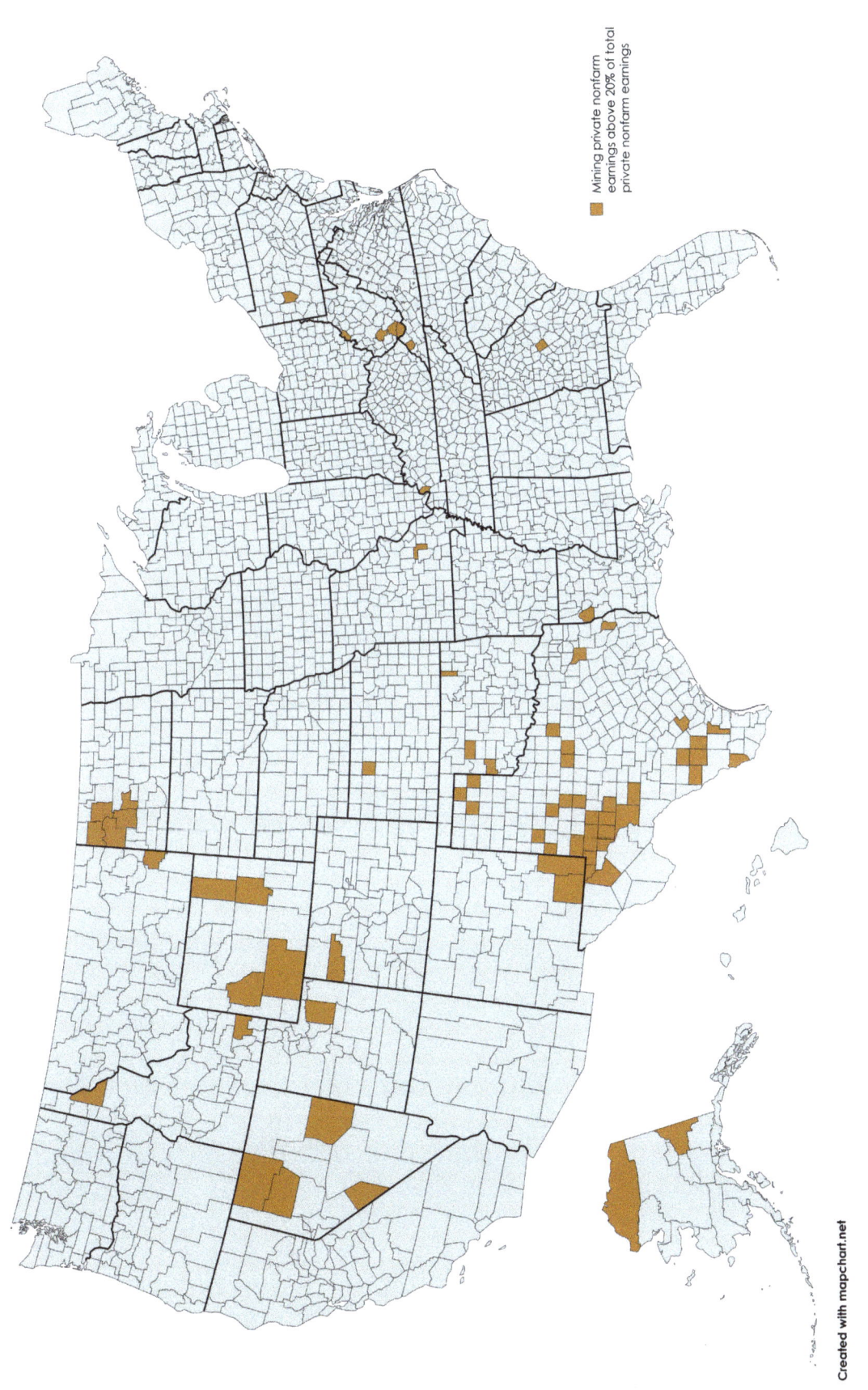

Mining private nonfarm earnings above 20% of total private nonfarm earnings

Figure 2.4

Counties with Mining, Quarrying, and Oil and Gas Extraction Private Nonfarm Earnings Above 20% of Total Private Nonfarm Earnings

Data Source: U.S. Bureau of Economic Analysis (BEA)

Created with Mapchart.net

PART 5

Other Industries

I analyzed a few other industries, namely, health care and social assistance; finance, insurance, real estate, and rental and leasing; and transportation and warehousing. I grouped finance and insurance with real estate and rental and leasing into a single group. Figure 2.5 shows the map with 28 counties from the health care and social assistance industry; four from finance, insurance, real estate, and rental and leasing; and 10 from transportation and warehousing. The earnings percentages were set as 25%, 30%, and 25%. There are so few counties because these industries are not overconcentrated in specific areas—these industries are present almost everywhere. Real estate risk is spread differently in many regions, which will be discussed later, however, the counties in Figure 2.5 still identify the few riskiest among these industries.

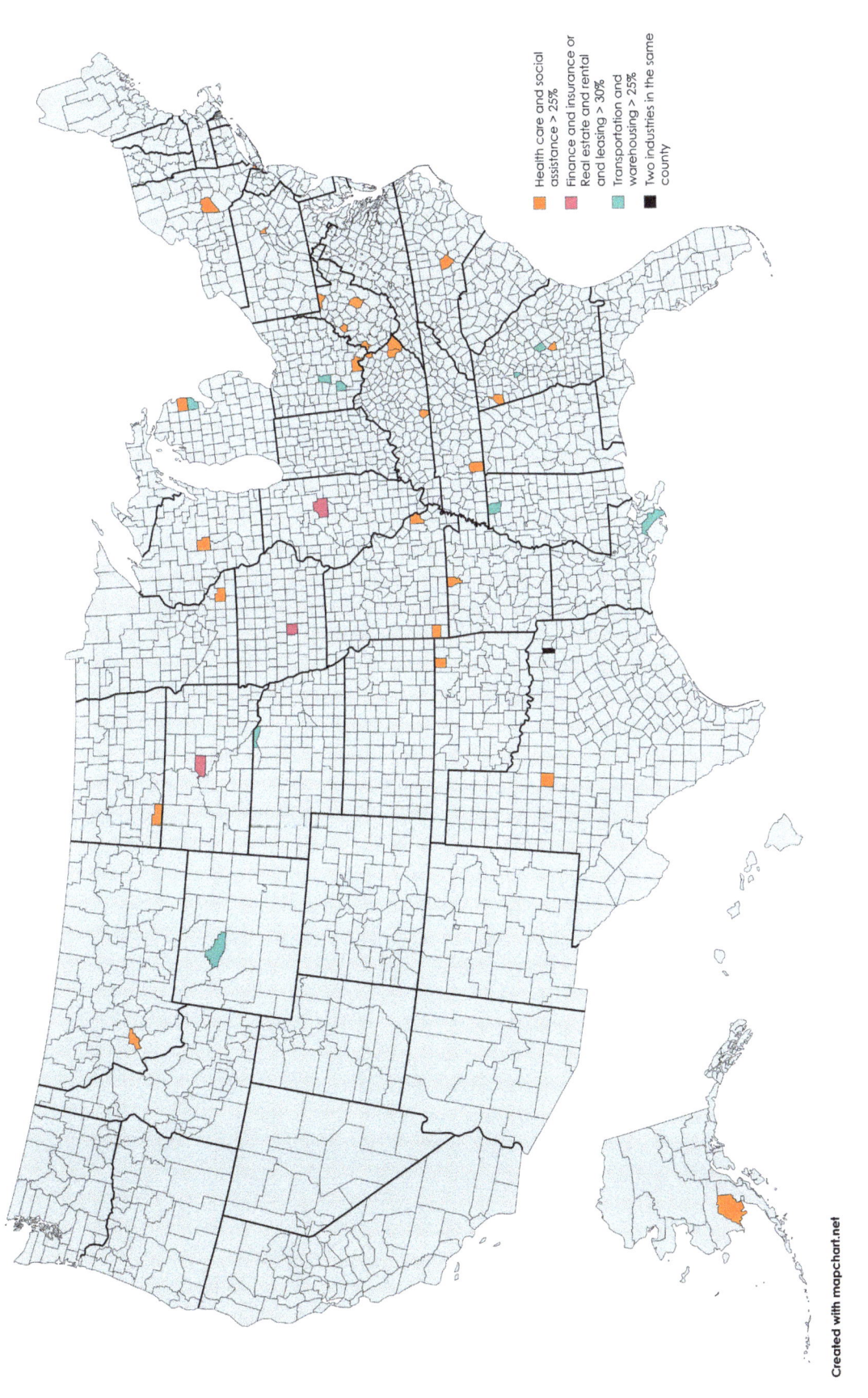

Figure 2.5

Counties with Private Nonfarm Earnings (Industries Mentioned in the Legend) Above a Certain Percentage of Total Private Nonfarm Earnings

See the legend for the exact numbers. Source: U.S. Bureau of Economic Analysis (BEA)

Created with Mapchart.net

PART 6

All Industries Combined

After analyzing eight industries in total, including durable goods manufacturing, I plotted the counties with overconcentrated industries on the same map. There are 11 counties with an overconcentration of two industries simultaneously. Refer to the Appendix for the names of all counties from each industry. Figure 2.6 maps the counties with overconcentrated industries. The next chapter will analyze real estate and metropolitan area risks, and we will conclude with a section on economic risks. We will build future chapters upon the map in Figure 2.6. After that, we will analyze every state using the final economic risk map and identify the areas that are probabilistically less likely to suffer the most from the crash.

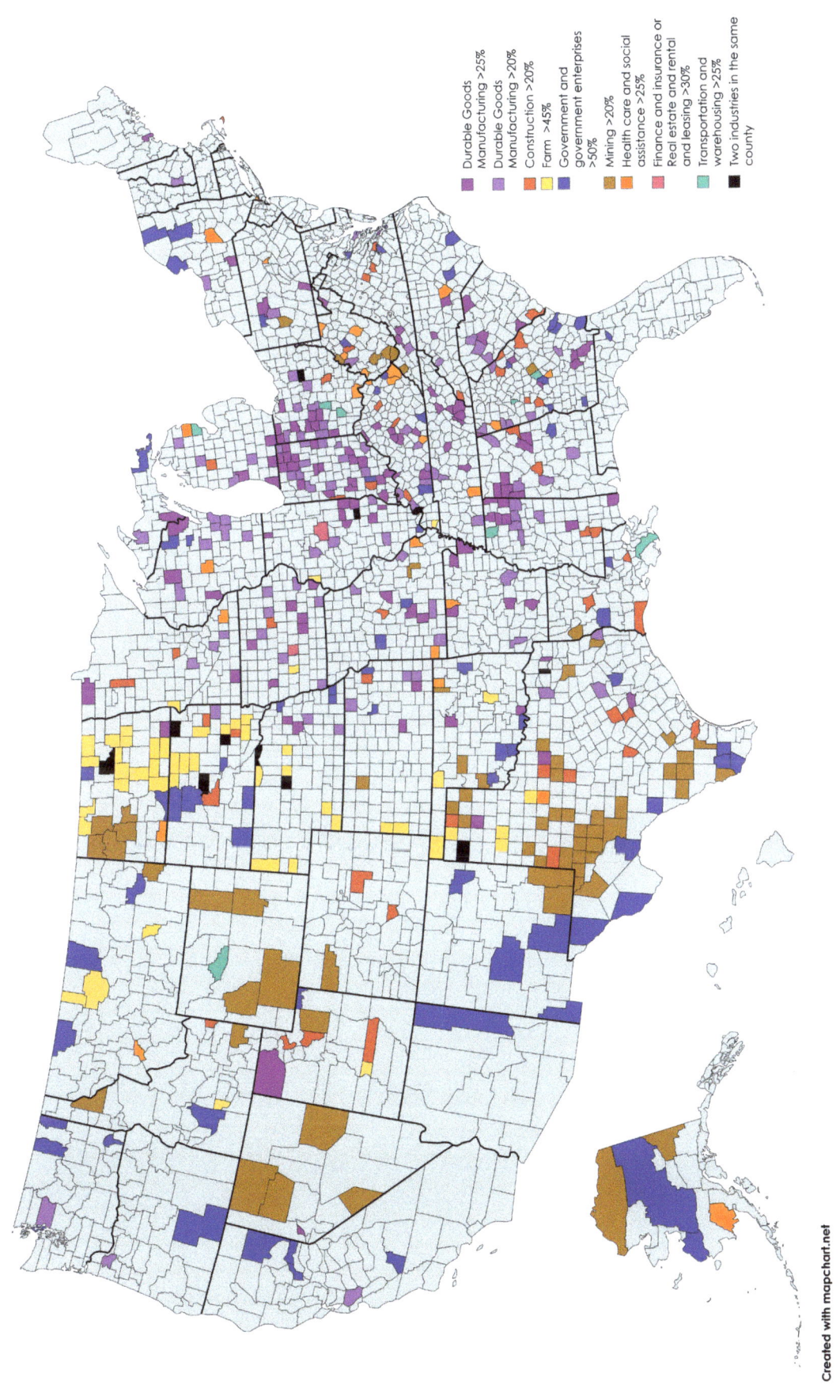

Figure 2.6

Counties with High Economic Risk, Measured by Percentage of Private Nonfarm Earnings Above a Certain Percentage of Total Nonfarm Earnings For each industry percentage, see the legend. Farm private earnings were measured against total private nonfarm and farm earnings combined. Source: U.S. Bureau of Economic Analysis (BEA)

Created with Mapchart.net

Legend:
- Durable Goods Manufacturing >25%
- Durable Goods Manufacturing >20%
- Construction >20%
- Farm >45%
- Government and government enterprises >50%
- Mining >20%
- Health care and social assistance >25%
- Finance and insurance or Real estate and rental and leasing >30%
- Transportation and warehousing >25%
- Two industries in the same county

References

1. U.S. Bureau of Economic Analysis. *"SQGDP2 Gross domestic product (GDP) by state 1"* (accessed March 30, 2024).

2. Federal Reserve Bank of St. Louis. *Federal Debt Held by the Public as Percent of Gross Domestic Product.* Retrieved from https://fred.stlouisfed.org/graph/?g=1bt9Z

3. Federal Reserve Bank of St. Louis. *Federal Surplus or Deficit [-] as Percent of Gross Domestic Product.* Retrieved from https://fred.stlouisfed.org/series/FYFSGDA188S

CHAPTER 3

Real Estate & Metropolitan Area Risks

Residential and commercial real estate markets are often very risky during financial downturns. Commercial real estate gets sold at massive discounts during a recession or depression. The 2007–2009 Great Recession is commonly called the mortgage crisis. Impulsively motivated people have borrowed too much money with little rational concern about their ability to commit to a mortgage for up to 30 years. Numerous people who had mortgages had no excess savings. If they had lost their jobs, they likely would have had to default on their payments. Today, the situation is much worse. Almost every U.S. bank, large or regional, is exposed to commercial and residential real estate. When the subsequent depression occurs and people start defaulting on their mortgages, banks will lose customer deposits, and many of those banks will be insolvent. Real estate markets employ so many people and organizations that the effects of the downturn will cause turmoil. The finance, insurance, real estate, rental, and leasing industries combined contribute more to the U.S. gross domestic product (GDP) than any other industry. Today, they are "very important" industries. Unfortunately, they are the most susceptible to the downturn.

Real estate exposure differs from city to city. By identifying locations less susceptible to real estate price declines, we can find places that will be less severely affected. The real estate industry is spread everywhere. No place is safe from a real estate downturn, but we still need a method to predict relative exposure to real estate. Historically, metropolitan areas (large cities) were more susceptible to real estate declines, as they often had the highest growth in real estate prices during an economic boom. Metropolitan areas are centers of the economic and financial boom. They enjoy the fruits of good times. Similarly, when the bad times come, metros are epicenters of the decline. Metropolitan areas suffer more than smaller cities, suburbs, or rural areas from real estate declines. However, we must still understand the relative effects on different metro areas. Figure 3.1, a map published by sparkrental.com, analyzed how badly the Covid-19 pandemic would impact counties across the United States. The crash during the Covid-19 pandemic did not turn out to be a significant depression, as we speak in 2024. Still, their methodology is relevant as it analyzes the susceptibility of the counties where home prices face the highest risk. Thus, their research will be very useful during the next severe downturn. The methodology "included three risk factors: local affordability, local foreclosure rates pre-coronavirus, and the local percentage of homes underwater on their mortgages." Figure 3.1 is very important as it shows the counties subject to serious real estate price decline risk. Figure 3.2 shows the U.S. density map by county, excluding Alaska and Hawaii. Figures 3.1 and 3.2 illustrate that the areas most sensitive from real estate price drops are usually the densest areas, which are metropolitan areas. In contrast, suburban and rural areas are less susceptible to real estate risk. For example, states such as California, Florida, New York, Illinois, Pennsylvania, Maryland, Delaware, Massachusetts, and Connecticut contain large and famous cities: New York, Miami, Los Angeles, San Francisco, Chicago, Washington DC, Boston, Baltimore, Philadelphia, etc. These cities are the most susceptible to downturns. Suburban areas adjacent to these cities are also at serious risk, as the effects of the real estate downturn will spill over. Later, we will analyze these states individually, using many tools, including density, landscape, economic, crime, and poverty maps, to get the picture on a county basis.

Figure 3.1

Housing Market Risk Measured by Local Affordability, Local Foreclosure Rates Pre–coronavirus, and the Local Percentage of Homes Underwater on their Mortgages

Image Source: G. Brian Davis, SparkRental, ATTOM Data Solutions; created with Datawrapper

County Ranking

- 1-99 Highest Risk
- 100-199 High Risk
- 200-349 Mod. Risk
- 350+ Lower Risk

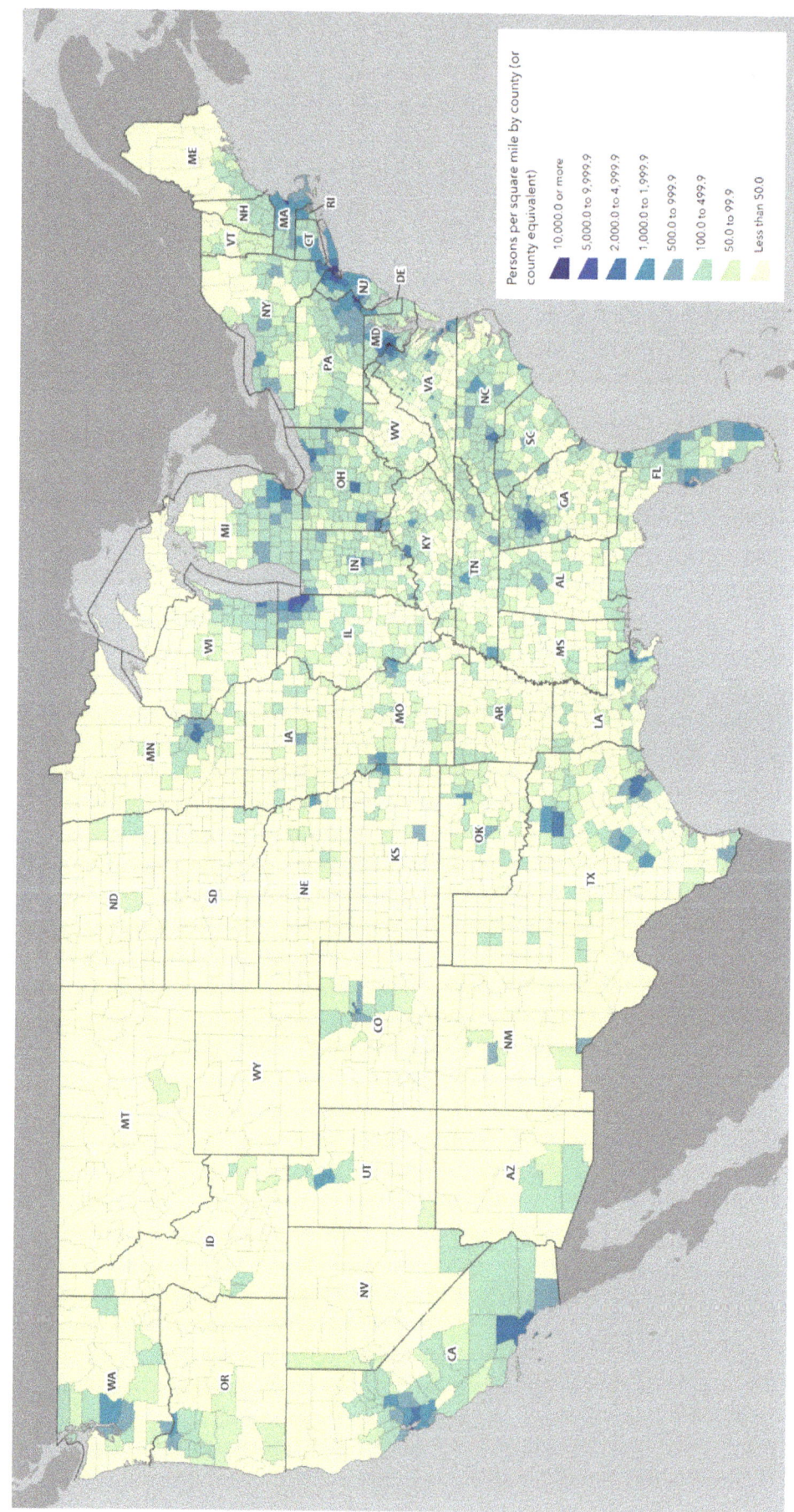

Figure 3.2

U.S. Density Map by County, 2020

Image Source: U.S. Census Bureau 2020 census demographic data map viewer

Metropolitan Area Risk

The highest average unemployment rate during the Great Depression in the United States was about 25%,[1] while in big cities, that number was above the average. Figure 3.3 shows counties included in the 50 largest metropolitan areas.

I have combined the metro area map with our current economic industry risk map. Figure 3.4 illustrates our up-to-date economic risk map of the areas more susceptible to economic decline. All the colored areas are economically risky. Durable goods manufacturing, construction, mining, and metro areas are comparably the riskiest areas. Whenever the county has industry overconcentration and belongs to the metropolitan area, I gave priority to industry overconcentration in Figure 3.4.

Cities that have experienced very high economic growth have also experienced population growth, perhaps both as a cause and a result. Cities that have experienced the largest population inflow have seen increasing prices on commercial and residential real estate and businesses. However, as we know, the higher the growth, the steeper the decline. Thus, I added statistics of the metro areas and cities that have experienced the largest population growth from 2010 to 2024, roughly during the latest economic boom that started after the Great Recession of 2007–2009. Figure 3.5 lists those metro areas. U.S. census defines metropolitan areas as "Metropolitan statistical areas consist of the county or counties (or equivalent entities) associated with at least one urban area of at least 50,000 population, plus adjacent counties having a high degree of social and economic integration with the core as measured through commuting ties."[2]

The five fastest-growing metro areas are in Texas and include Austin, Houston, San Antonio, Dallas-Fort Worth, and McAllen metro areas (see Figure 3.5). That is unsurprising, as Texas has recently become a popular destination for many. Figure 3.1 shows that some of these Texas metro areas are quite risky regarding real estate. However, considering the recent inflow of people in Texas, the relative economic risk is quite high. As businesses and markets have experienced higher growth than in other cities and metros, the likelihood of a pronounced economic downturn increases for these Texas metros. Figure 3.5 also highlights four growing metro areas in Florida. Florida overall also scores very high on real estate risk (see Figure 3.1). That is not surprising, as the state was one of the epicenters of the real estate downturn during the 2008 crash, where housing prices declined more than in most other locations. After housing prices bottomed in 2012, they have grown faster than in most other places, confirming that Florida's real estate market is inherently sensitive to economic fluctuations. Considering the staggeringly high exposure to the real estate market today, the risks of losing so much capital for many people in Florida have increased. Cities such as Miami are fueled by the economic boom. When the music stops, it will suffer more than other locations. I believe most of Florida today is Miami on a larger scale when compared to other states. California is another example.

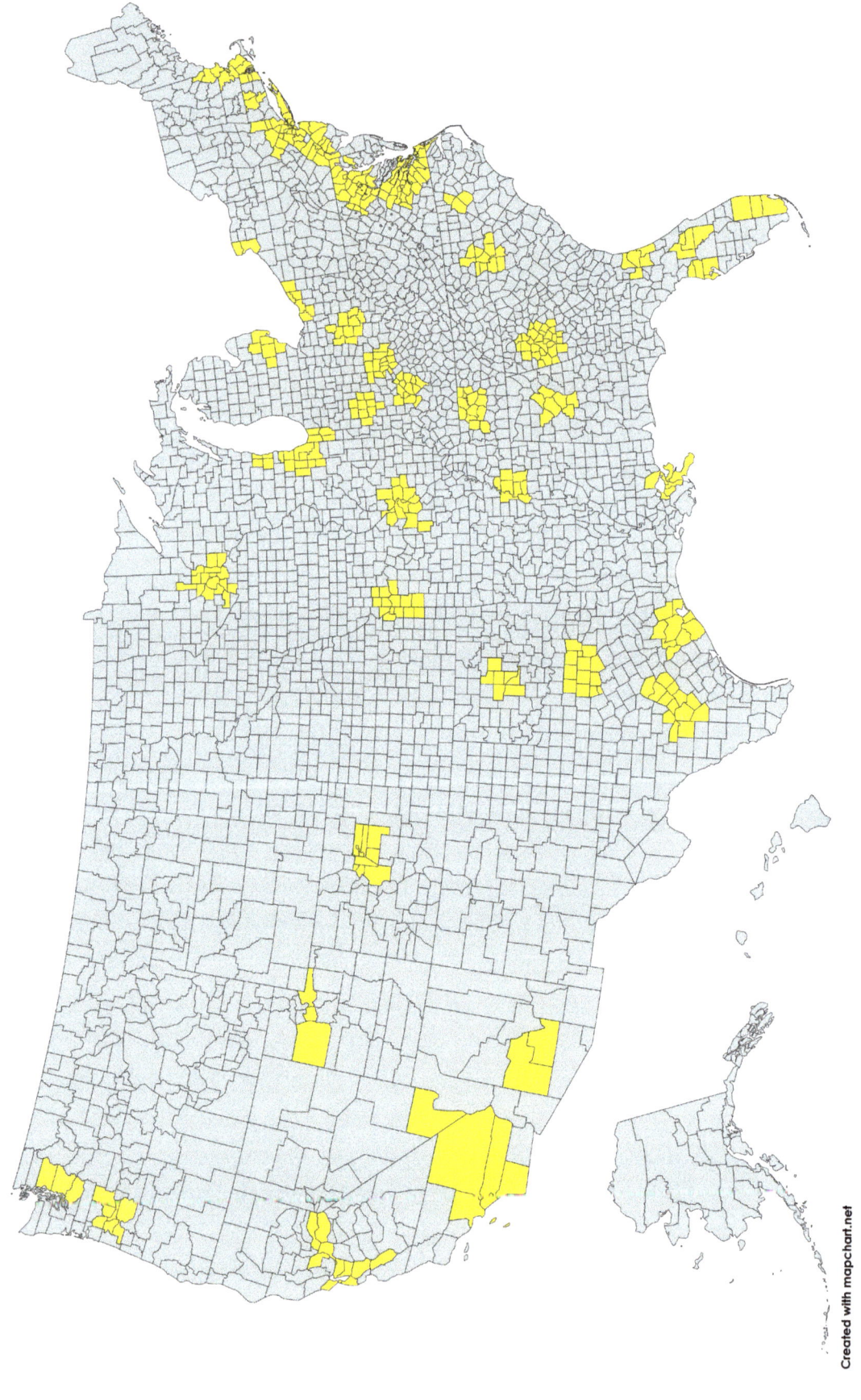

Created with mapchart.net

Figure 3.3

U.S. Counties Included in the 50 Largest Metropolitan Areas

Created with Mapchart.net

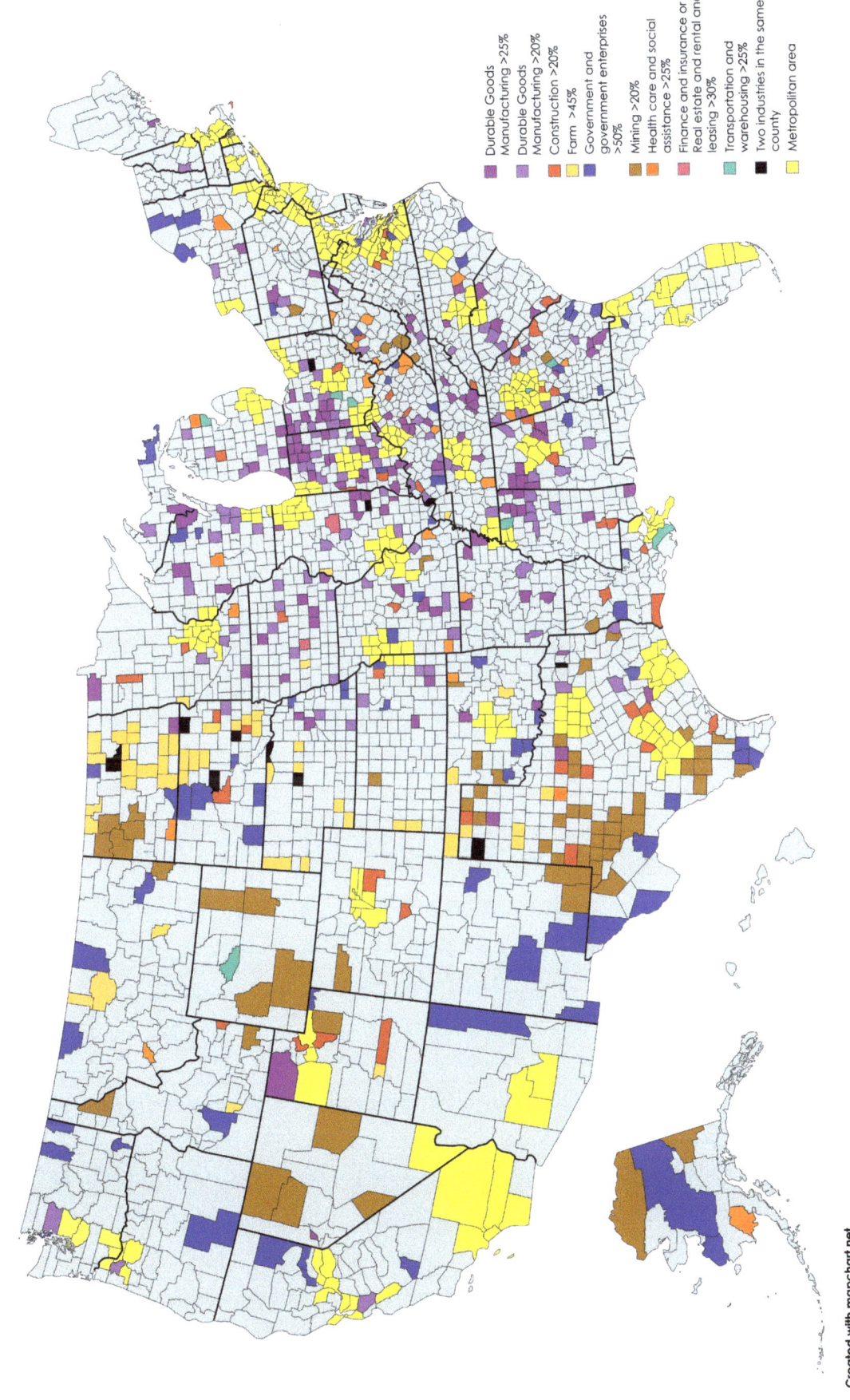

Legend:
- Durable Goods Manufacturing >25%
- Durable Goods Manufacturing >20%
- Construction >20%
- Farm >45%
- Government and government enterprises >50%
- Mining >20%
- Health care and social assistance >25%
- Finance and insurance or Real estate and rental and leasing >30%
- Transportation and warehousing >25%
- Two industries in the same county
- Metropolitan area

Created with mapchart.net

Figure 3.4

Economic Risk by County

Note. Includes risk by industry and metro area

Figure 3.5

The 20 Fastest-Growing U.S. Metro Areas (2010–2024) Measured by Population Growth
Image Source: Josh Howarth, publishing in https://explodingtopics.com/

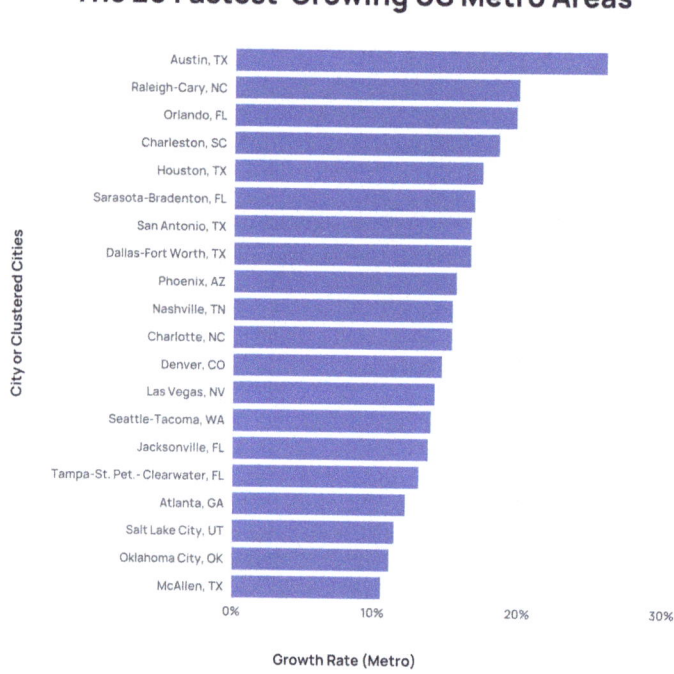

It is highly advisable to adjust life accordingly. High unemployment and economic turmoil are unavoidable, however, it is possible to avoid the largest metro areas before a crisis starts. Before relocating, study other locations and develop a comprehensive plan because other locations also will carry risk. Those too connected to their current location through work or family, and therefore who cannot leave the metro area, must be prepared. Thinking that there will always be enough time to act is wrong. When it comes to social and financial issues, acting in panic is equivalent to self-destruction.

Sparkrental.com hypothesizes that the unemployment rate could be a good indicator of future rent defaults.[3] That is a disputable issue. The areas that already have high unemployment today are those experiencing certain economic problems. Also, high unemployment in good times is often the result of adverse social conditions such as high poverty, crime, or bad demographics, which we will cover in the following chapters. At the same time, low unemployment does not mean a place is devoid of risk. There is no correlation, but I suggest avoiding the areas with the highest unemployment rate. Figure 3.6 shows the U.S. map based on the unemployment created by sparkrental.com using U.S. Bureau of Labor Statistics data from December 2020 to February 2021. The darker the area—the higher the unemployment rate.

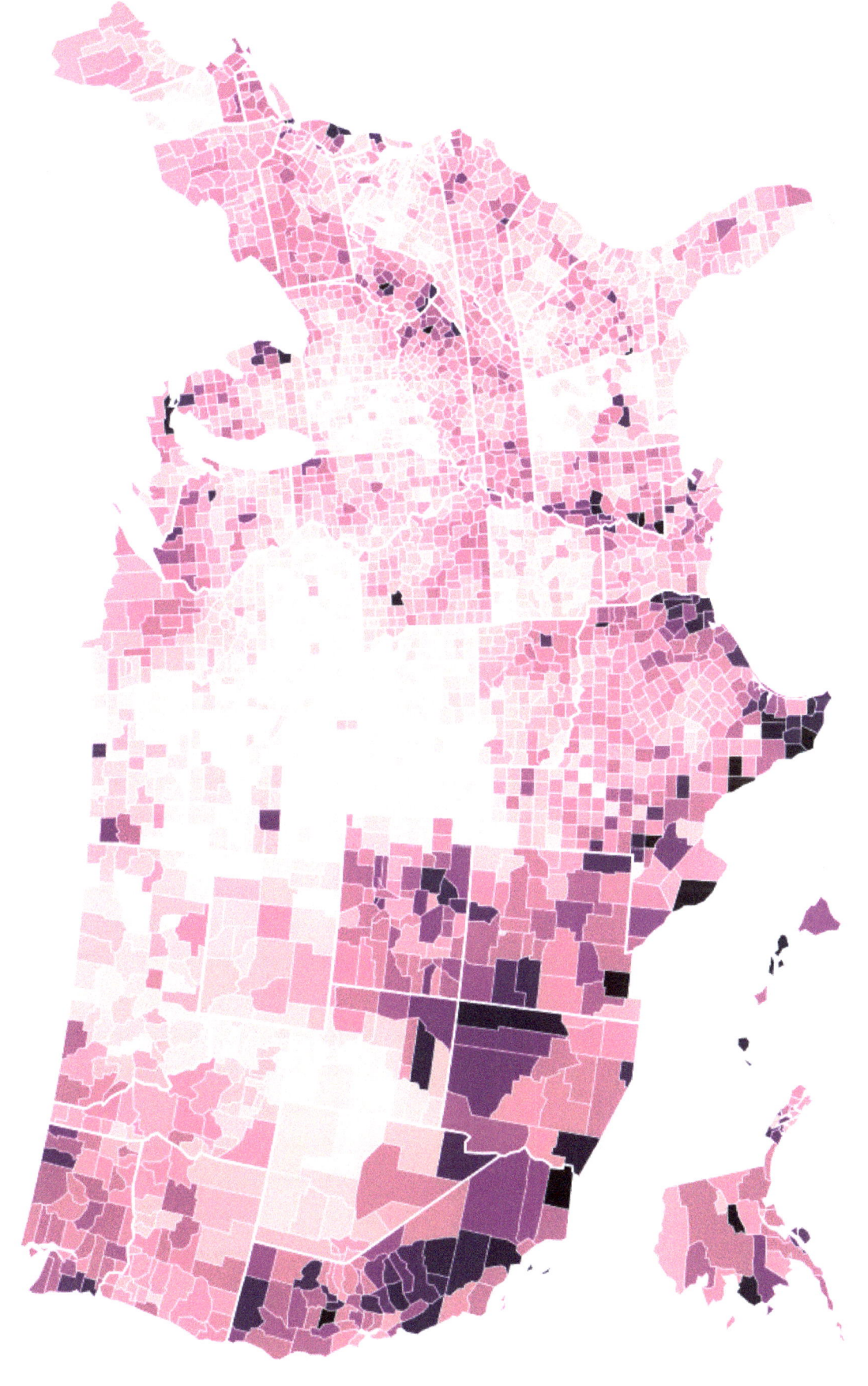

Figure 3.6

U.S. Unemployment Rate by County (December 2020 to February 2021)

Image source: G. Brian Davis, SparkRental. Data source: U.S. Bureau of Labor Statistics. Created with Datawrapper

References

1. Robert S. McElvaine (2004). *Encyclopedia of The Great Depression*. New York. Thomson Gale. Volume 2, page 999.

2. U.S. Census Bureau. *Glossary*. Retrieved from https://www.census.gov/programs-surveys/metro-micro/about/glossary.html

3. Davis, G. Brian. SparkRental. *"Unemployment Rates by County: Interactive Map."* Retrieved from https://sparkrental.com/unemployment-rates-by-county-interactive-map/

CHAPTER 4

Crime Risk

During severe economic depression, crime rates will highly increase. The rise in crime and an economic downturn will have a symbiotic relationship. During economic depression, many people are angry, uncertain, and aggressive. It will be almost impossible to reasonably live in very high crime cities. High violent crime will cause economic trouble for businesses and ordinary people. Remember Los Angeles during the Covid-19 pandemic onset? Businesses were physically raided and businessmen could not defend themselves because of totalitarian anti-self-defense regulations.

This is why this book is so important. First, I will provide statistical data on the violent crime rate by race and ethnicity. Then, we will identify the locations that will likely be more crime prone. I also statistically will illustrate the nature of crime and help readers avoid those areas during the bad times. Later, I will mention states with anti-individual laws.

Scientifically and statistically speaking, there is a correlation between crime and the Black population. In the areas where many Black people live, crime is also high. We must identify areas more prone to crime and, therefore, aim to avoid them in the next economic downturn.

Figure 4.1 shows homicide mortality rate by state and percentage of the Black population by state. Even the untrained eye can see that areas with a high Black population have a high crime rate. A regression analysis yielded a 0.85 correlation between the percentage of Black people and the homicide mortality rate. Statistically speaking, 0.85 is very high, and we can confidently conclude that when there are more Black people present, the violent fatal crime is probabilistically going to be higher. There are additional reasons for high crime: the politics of each state, sociocultural differences among people living in different regions, poverty, the presence of other racial groups, etc. Yet, despite these, a high correlation remains. Even though the conclusion is probabilistic, it is highly probabilistic. If the percentage of the Black population in a particular state is somewhat medium and there are alternating factors or the high presence of white people and lack of other ethnicities, the crime rate might be relatively low. However, betting against the probabilities might be disastrous. The statistical analysis can be reviewed in the Appendix.

There is another generally accepted data on crime by ethnicity. In 2021, the FBI released "Race or ethnicity of the U.S. resident population and of persons arrested for nonfatal violent crimes" data for 2018.[1] In 2018, non-Hispanic White people made up 60.4% of the U.S. population and committed 45.9% of all crimes. Hispanics made up 18.3% of all people and committed 17.6% of all crimes. Black people made up 12.5% of the population and committed 33% of all nonfatal violent crimes, see Figure 4.2. So, on average 1% of the U.S. population consisting of non-Hispanic White people are responsible for 0.76% of crimes. 1% of Hispanics are responsible for 0.96% of crimes, which is about 26.5% higher than for non-Hispanic White people. And 1% of Black people are responsible for 2.64% of all crimes, which is 3.47 times more crimes than for non-Hispanic White people, see Figure 4.3. After these statistics, there should not be any controversy about the facts. When it comes to Asians, they commit fewer nonfatal violent crimes than any other race. At the same time, American Indians make up only 0.7% of the U.S. population but commit 1.9% of all crimes, meaning they are also significantly prone to crime, slightly more than Black people.

Usnews.com provides jail incarceration rates by race and ethnicity from the sentencingproject.org study.[2] It reports that "Black Americans are incarcerated at a state average of 1,240 per 100,000 residents, whereas Latino Americans are imprisoned at a rate of 349 per 100,000 residents. White, non-Latino Americans, meanwhile, are incarcerated at 261 per 100,000 residents." Black Americans are incarcerated at almost 5 times more than non-Latino White people, and Latino Americans 1.3 times, or 30% more than non-Latino White people.

In addition, the FBI provides data on arrests by race and ethnicity in 2019.[3] In total, 7,964 people were arrested for murder and nonnegligent manslaughter. Of that number, 3,650 are White Americans, which includes White Hispanic or Latino, 4,078 are Black American. The percentage of White Americans, including White Hispanic or Latino is 75.5% of the total U.S. population for 2022, according to U.S. Census Quick-Facts data.[4] Black Americans made up 13.6% of the U.S. population for 2022. So, 13.6% of Black Americans commit more murders than 75.5% White Americans (including Hispanic or Latino). And 13.6% of Black Americans contribute to 51.2% of total murders in the United States, while 75.5% White Americans commit 45.83%. Black Americans commit 6.2 times more crime than White Americans (including Hispanic or Latino). Because Hispanics or Latinos are more prone to crime than Whites alone (not Hispanic or Latino), the ratio would be even higher if we compare Blacks to Whites alone (not Hispanic or Latino). The FBI reported that 1,341 people who identified as Hispanic or Latino were arrested for murder and nonnegligent manslaughter. Of the 6,474 arrested who declared their ethnicity, 20.7% declared themselves as Hispanic or Latino, which is more than the percentage of the U.S. population who are Hispanic or Latino at 19.1%. The FBI does not tell what percentage of Hispanics or Latinos were included in the White race category, but we can compute approximate numbers ourselves. The 2022 U.S. Census QuickFacts data identifies that 19.1% of the U.S. population is Hispanic or Latino. And 16.6% of Hispanics or Latinos out of 19.1% of the U.S. population of Hispanics or Latinos is included in the White category.[5] So, 86.9% are identified as White. Thus, we can conclude that about 86.9% of 1,341 Hispanics or Latinos were likely identified as White and 86.9% is 1,165 people. Subtracting 1,165 arrested who identified as Hispanic or Latino from 3,650 White Americans leaves 2,485 White-alone (not Hispanic or Latino) arrestees. In total, the percentage of arrested who belong to the White-alone race (not Hispanic or Latino) is 2,485 divided by 7,964, or 31.2%. In other words, 58.9% of Whites alone (not Hispanic or Latino) conduct only 31.2% of the murder and nonnegligent manslaughter crimes reported. Whereas 13.6% of Blacks commit 51.2% of total murders. This ratio is 7.1 times more than among Whites alone (not Hispanic or Latino). On average White Americans (not Hispanic or Latino) are 7.10 times less likely to commit murder and nonnegligent manslaughter than a Black American. In comparison, 19.1% of U.S. Hispanic or Latino population contributed to 20.7% of total murder and nonnegligent manslaughter crimes. The ratio is slightly 2 times higher than among White alone (not Hispanic or Latino). Figure 4.4 illustrates these ratios.

Figure 4.1

States by Percentage of Black Population and Homicide Mortality Rate
Data Source for percentage Black: worldpopulationreview.com and U.S. Census 2022 ACS 5-Year Survey (Table B02009). Source for homicide mortality (2021): cdc.gov, for DC, NH, VT, and WY: number of homicides divided by population and multiplied by 100,000

State	Blacks %	Homicide mortality per 100,000
Alabama	26.23%	15.9
Alaska	5.07%	6.4
Arizona	5.67%	8.1
Arkansas	15.99%	11.7
California	7.22%	6.4
Colorado	5.23%	6.3
Connecticut	12.58%	4.8
Delaware	22.44%	11.3
District of Columbia	48.49%	33.9
Florida	16.26%	7.4
Georgia	31.40%	11.4
Hawaii	3.58%	2.7
Idaho	1.07%	2.2
Illinois	15.64%	12.3
Indiana	10.68%	9.6
Iowa	4.86%	3.2
Kansas	7.34%	6.4
Kentucky	9.37%	9.6
Louisiana	34.23%	21.3
Maine	1.99%	1.7
Maryland	31.27%	12.2
Massachusetts	9.43%	2.3
Michigan	15.18%	8.7
Minnesota	7.76%	4.3
Mississippi	39.08%	23.7
Missouri	12.62%	12.4
Montana	1.05%	4.4
Nebraska	5.92%	3.6
Nevada	10.52%	8.5
New Hampshire	2.30%	1.1
New Jersey	14.33%	4.8
New Mexico	2.95%	15.3
New York	17.44%	4.8
North Carolina	21.80%	9.7
North Dakota	3.63%	3.4
Ohio	14.17%	9.3
Oklahoma	8.92%	8.9
Oregon	2.95%	4.9

Pennsylvania	12.62%	9.2
Rhode Island	8.34%	3.6
South Carolina	26.04%	13.4
South Dakota	2.80%	5.3
Tennessee	16.85%	12.2
Texas	12.38%	8.2
Utah	1.71%	2.7
Vermont	1.91%	1.5
Virginia	20.57%	7.2
Washington	5.43%	4.5
West Virginia	4.80%	6.9
Wisconsin	7.45%	6.4
Wyoming	1.83%	2.8

Figure 4.2

United States 2018 Racial Makeup vs. Nonfatal Violent Crime by Race and Ethnicity
Data Source: FBI, Race and Ethnicity of Violent Crime Offenders and Arrestees, 2018

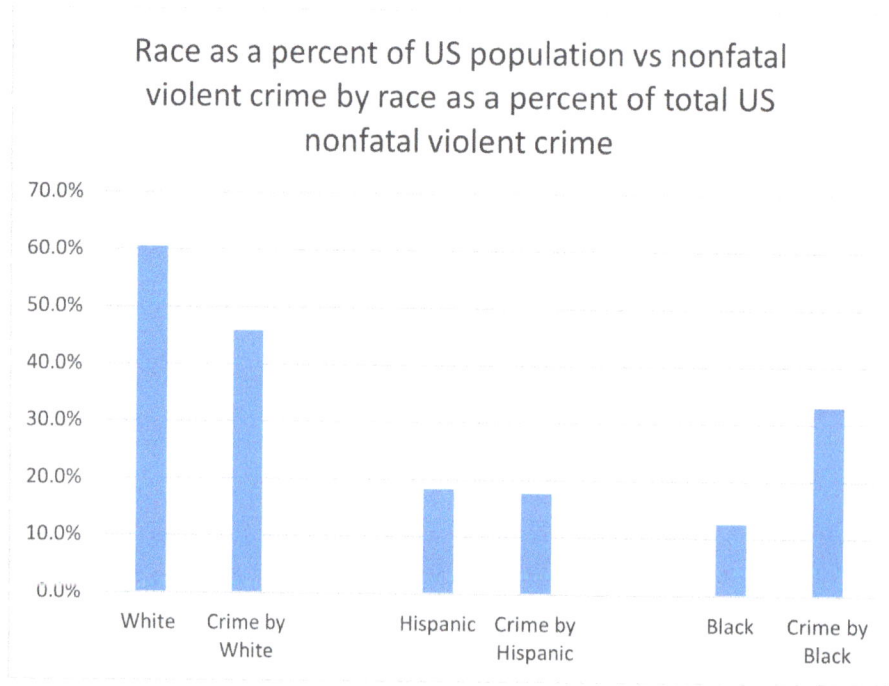

Figure 4.3

Nonfatal Violent Crime Predisposition of the Following Racial Groups and Ethnicities

Data Source: FBI, Race and Ethnicity of Violent Crime Offenders and Arrestees, 2018

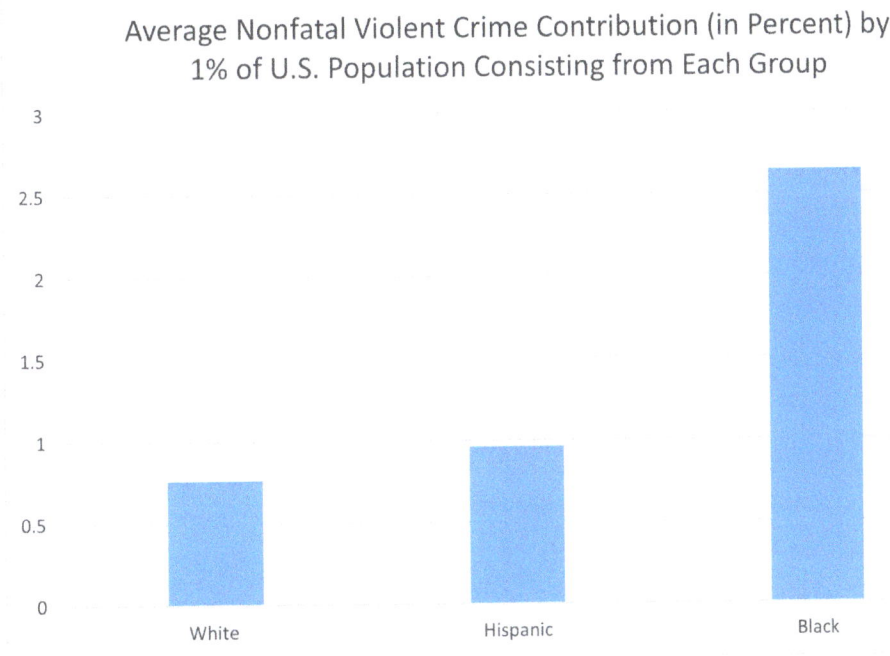

Average Nonfatal Violent Crime Contribution (in Percent) by 1% of U.S. Population Consisting from Each Group

Figure 4.4

Murder and Nonnegligent Manslaughter Predisposition of the Following Racial Groups and Ethnicities

Data Source: FBI, Arrests, by Race and Ethnicity, 2019, Table 43

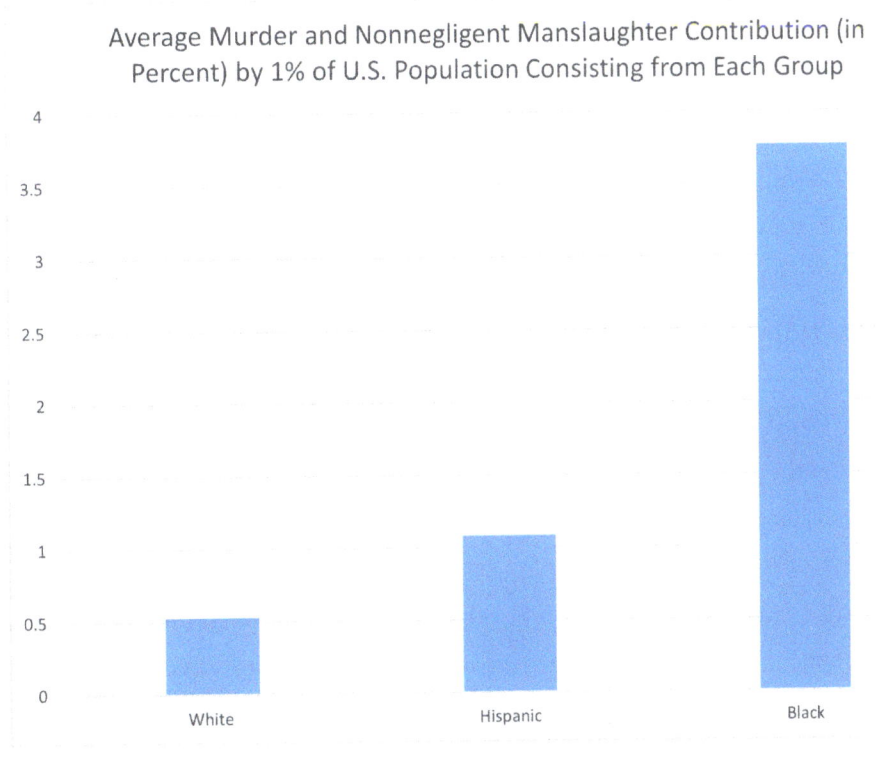

Average Murder and Nonnegligent Manslaughter Contribution (in Percent) by 1% of U.S. Population Consisting from Each Group

We know that Black Americans are 7.1 times more likely to commit murder and nonnegligent manslaughter than Whites alone (not Hispanic or Latino), and Hispanics or Latinos are 2 times more likely to do so. Thus, I have created a U.S. racial demographics map (see Figure 4.5).

I used the State Profiles: 2020 Census Data when creating Figure 4.5.[6] Blue counties are more than 85% White (including Hispanic or Latino). In these statistics, the U.S. census adds additional race categories. These options are absent in the FBI data and previous 2022 U.S. Census QuickFacts data. A significant portion of Hispanics or Latinos are referred to additional non-White categories, such as "White in combination," "Some other Race Alone," "Some other Race in combination," "Two or More Races," etc. So, a smaller percentage than 86.9% of Hispanics or Latinos are considered White. The red counties show where Blacks comprise more than 15% of the total population. Because Black Americans are more prone to crime and poverty and earn lower incomes, they are more likely to be less desirable than other races to live next to. See Figures 4.6 and 4.7 for information on poverty and income. In Figure 4.5, counties with two colors indicate the presence of two minority groups, and black counties have three minorities. Of note, Hispanic or Latino individuals identifying as White are included in both the White and Hispanic or Latino categories, as it is tough to separate those using the U.S. census data. Though rare, it is possible to simultaneously have above 85% White and above 20% Hispanic or Latino. In that case, the county is colored as Hispanic or Latino. Whites (including Hispanic or Latino) are less prone to crime and much less criminally dangerous than other non-White races except Asians.

A bird's-eye view of Figure 4.5 allows the following conclusions:

- Blacks are overrepresented in several states in the South Atlantic and East South Central.
- Hispanics or Latinos are overrepresented in the southern areas of the West census region and west-south of Texas.
- Minorities are overrepresented in urban metropolitan areas.
- Whites (including Hispanics or Latinos) above 85% are overrepresented in northern and non-metropolitan areas, such as suburban and rural.

Comparing Figures 3.2 and 3.3 with Figure 4.5 shows that minorities are overrepresented in metropolitan areas, as illustrated in Figure 4.8.

Pew Research provides demographic data on the percentage of White non-Hispanic Americans living in urban, suburban, and rural areas based on 2012–2016 data.[7] At less than 50% of the population, non-Hispanic Whites are a minority in urban areas. Based on 2012–2016 Pew Research data, the number is 44%, and it declined from 51% based on 2000 data, implying that the non-Hispanic White population steadily declines in urban areas (large cities and metropolitan areas). This is another significant reason why metropolitan areas contain plenty of risk. Those areas will likely become crime epicenters during the depression. Considering the much higher economic risk of metro areas, the metro areas will become surreal and almost unlivable places. Detroit after 2008 is a perfect example. However, such a thing did not happen in the United States during the Great Depression. People were much less collectivist before the Great Depression, and large cities were much Whiter than now. This is a crucial difference. In my opinion, racial risk is the ultimate risk to avoid.

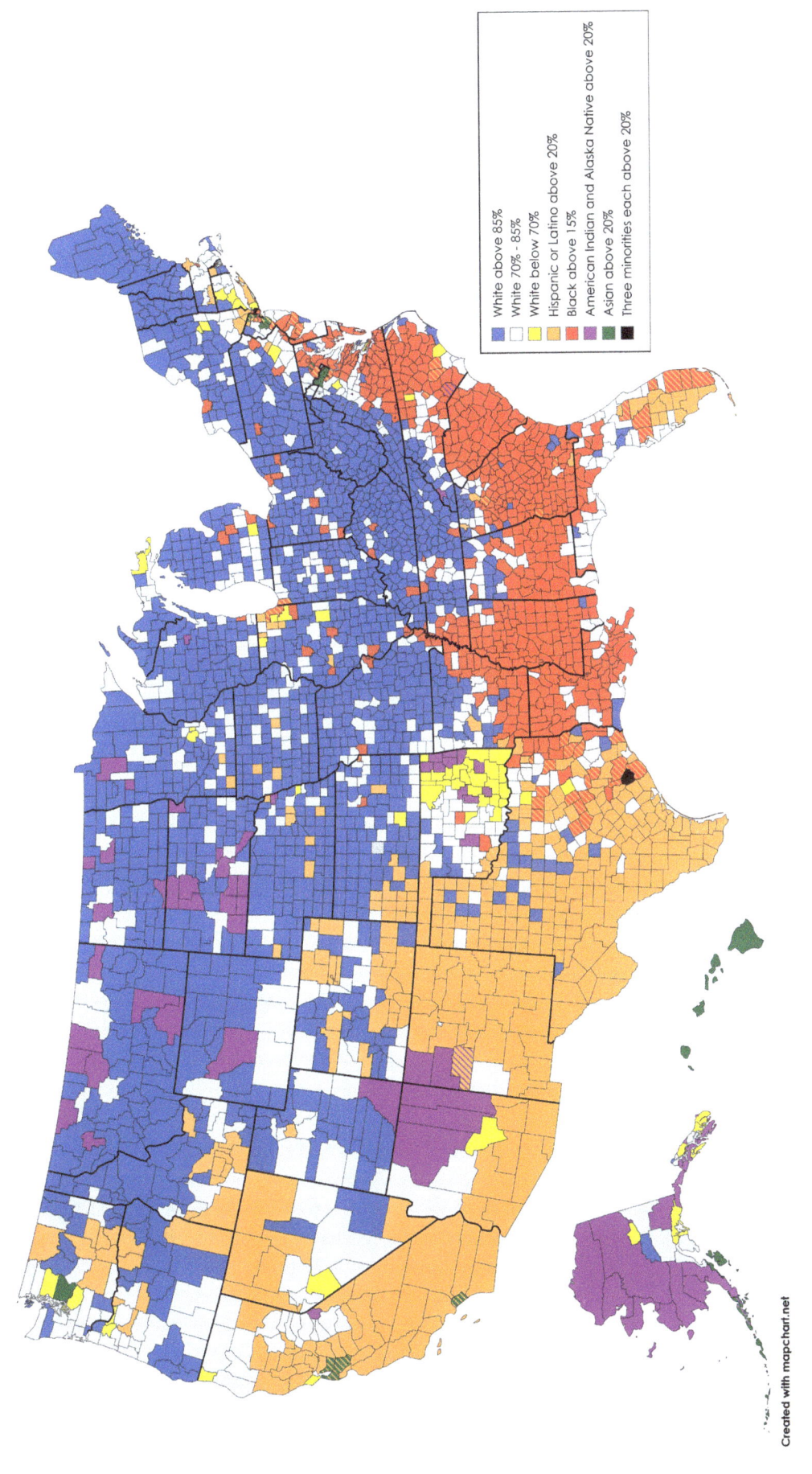

Created with mapchart.net

Figure 4.5

Racial Map of the United States

Data Source: U.S. Census, 2020 census state profiles. Note: The idea for the map was derived from Vivid Maps. Visit vividmaps.com at https://vividmaps.com/

Figure 4.6

Median Household Income in 2020 by Race and Ethnicity

Data Source: U.S. Census, Income and Poverty in the United States: 2020, Table A-2

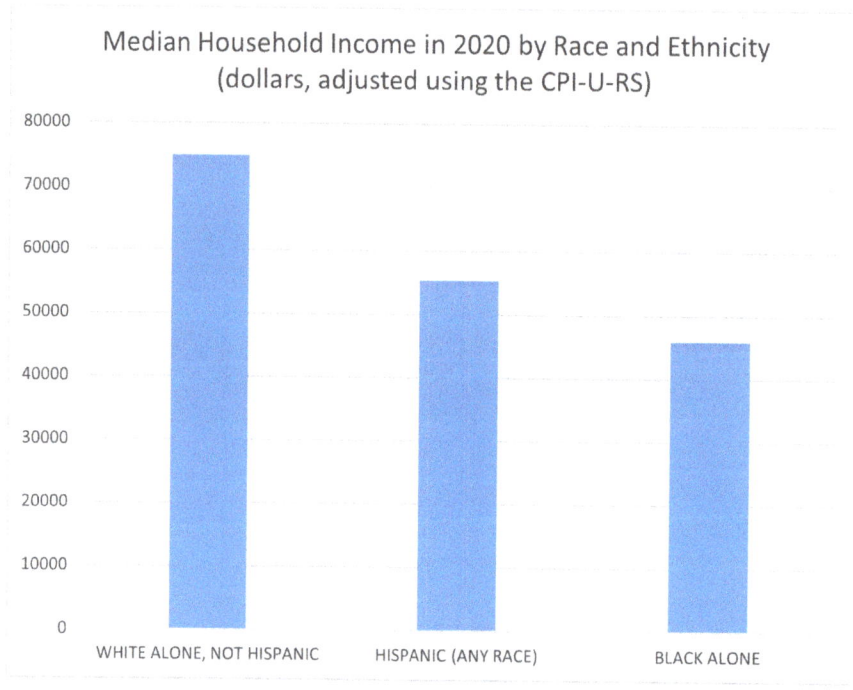

Figure 4.7

Poverty Status of People in 2020 by Race and Ethnicity

Data Source: U.S. Census, Income and Poverty in the United States: 2020, Table B-4

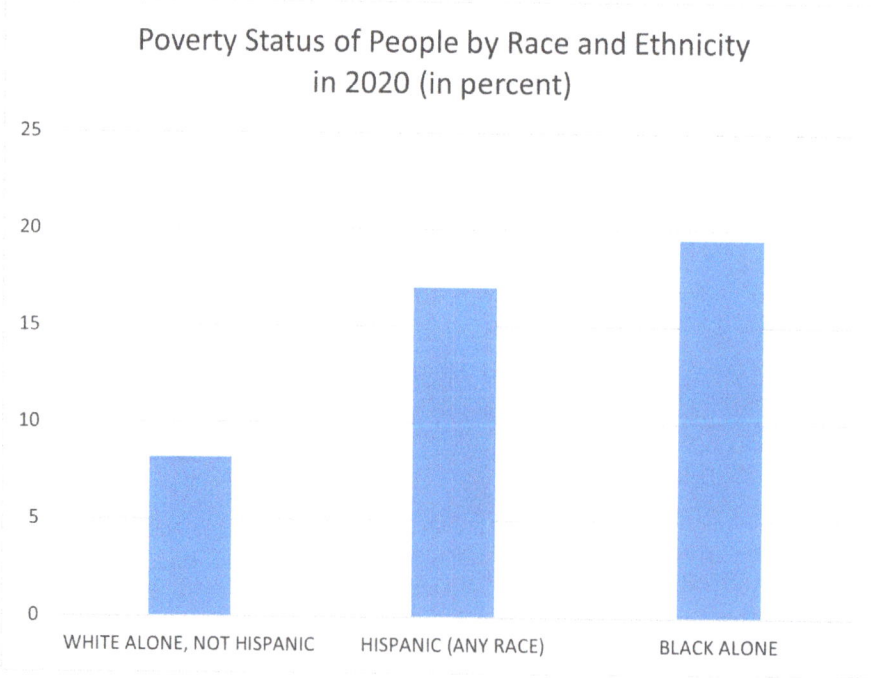

Figure 4.8

Percentage of Non-Hispanic White People Living in Urban, Suburban, and Rural Areas based on 2012–2016 Data

Data Source: pewresearch.org, Demographic and economic trends in urban, suburban and rural communities

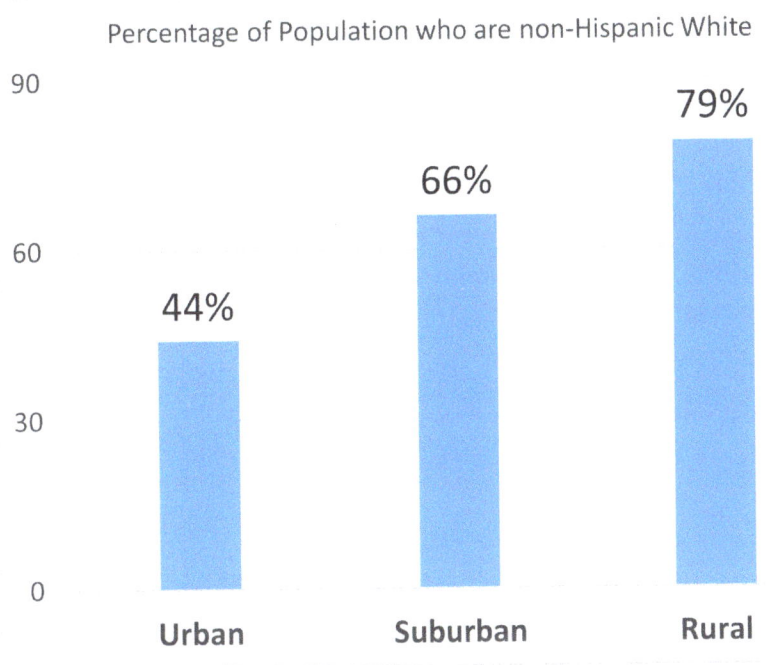

There are opposing opinions regarding the correlation between poverty and crime. I have conducted a statistical regression analysis to check the correlation between poverty and crime. (See the Appendix for a graph with U.S. state poverty and homicide rates and a statistical regression analysis.) The correlation co-efficient is 0.70, a medium strengths correlation between poverty and crime. It does not mean that poverty causes crime. We showed that Black and Hispanic or Latino Americans are much more prone to poverty than White Americans. Therefore, poverty might not necessarily cause high crime but results from differ-ences in the states' racial population, which means poverty and crime tend to result from the same cause. Poverty itself means a relatively negative sociocultural development. It would be said that regions full of poverty have less room for a downturn than prospering locations simply because there is less room for a decline. However, it is tough to probabilistically predict which high-poverty areas would end up better than others. High poverty could also reflect a bad economy. Before the Great Depression, there were areas where the economy worsened in the 1920s, a prelude for the 30s when those areas kept deteriorating, at least as much as the average U.S. region. It is easier to tell that most booming areas will likely be epicenters of economic decline. However, it is difficult to claim that the areas with the highest poverty rates will suf-fer the least. Figure 4.9 reflects the percentage of families living below the poverty level in the continental United States. Similar to the U.S. unemployment map in the previous chapter, the high-poverty regions are concentrated where the percentage of White people is low and the percentage of minorities is high.

This is not surprising at all because the statistics show that non-White Americans tend to have lower incomes and higher poverty levels. This is mainly caused by the difference in racial demographics. I believe those "other" sociocultural reasons are also the results of the fundamental differences in the racial behavior of White and non-White Americans, which statistics prove. The only significant region where the poverty rate is high among White Americans is the Appalachian Mountains. The highest poverty in this region includes the eastern part of Kentucky and the state of West Virginia.

In conclusion, avoid areas that are highly populated by non-White Americans to avoid high crime, high poverty, and likely negative living conditions. An economic depression is often an issue of physical survival. The fact that Black Americans are 7 times more likely to commit murder than White (not Hispanic or Latino) Americans is a significant reason alone to avoid those areas. I would also recommend avoiding counties with very high poverty because there are no objectively good reasons to move there: worse life, incomes, and probabilistically higher crime. However, if the poverty level is above average and the area is populated almost entirely by White Americans, it will not be as terrible as an area that is poor and racially diverse.

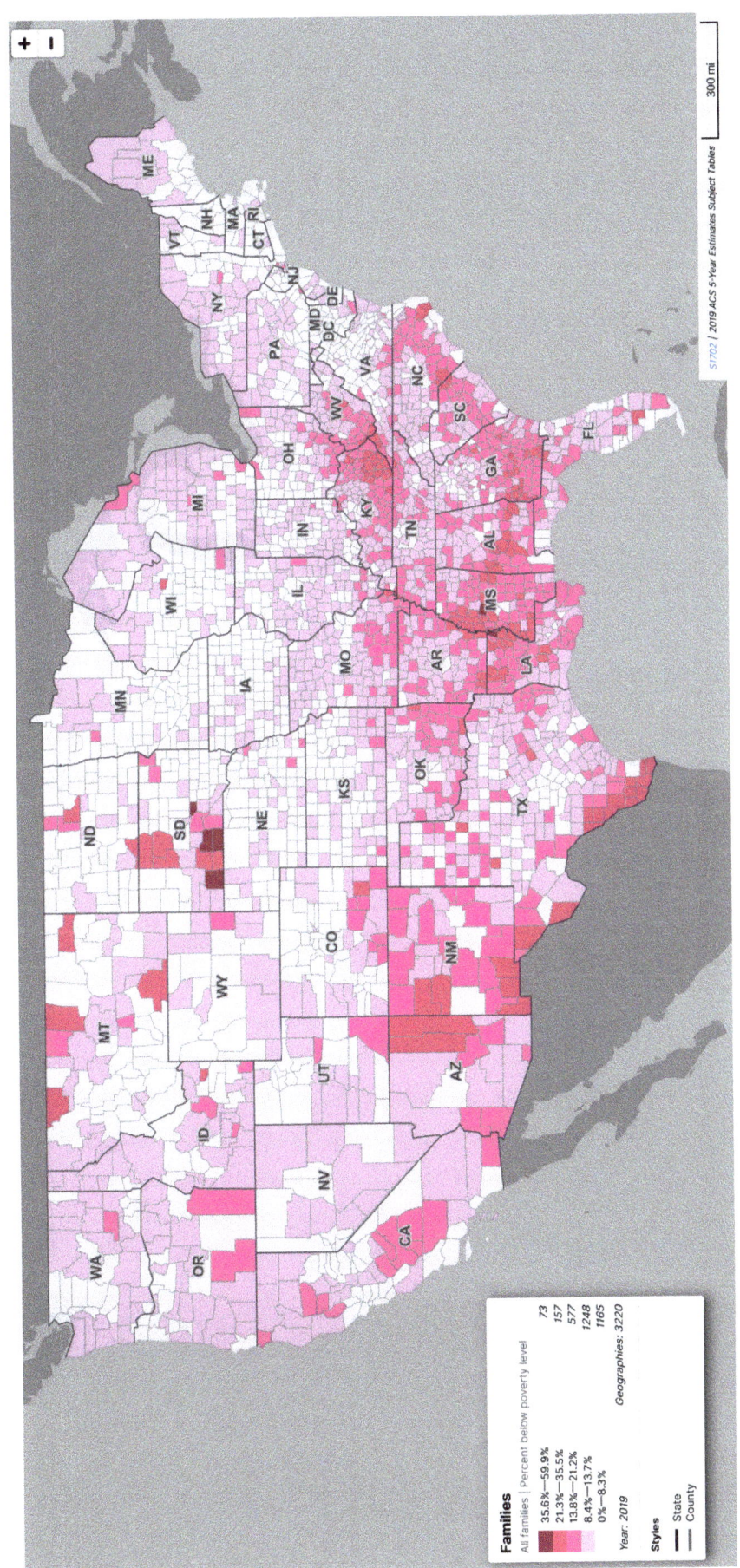

Figure 4.9

U.S. Families Below Poverty Level in 2019

Image Source: U.S. census data S1702 ACS 5-year estimates

References

1. Beck, Allen. U.S. Department of Justice (January 2021). *Race and Ethnicity of Violent Crime Offenders and Arrestees, 2018*. Retrieved from https://bjs.ojp.gov/content/pub/pdf/revcoa18.pdf

2. Adriana Rezal. U.S. News & World Report (October 2021). *The Racial Makeup of America's Prisons*. Retrieved from https://www.usnews.com/news/best-states/articles/2021-10-13/report-highlights-staggering-racial-disparities-in-us-incarceration-rates

3. FBI. *Table 43, Arrests by Race and Ethnicity, 2019*. Retrieved from https://ucr.fbi.gov/crime-in-the-u.s/2019/crime-in-the-u.s.-2019/tables/table-43

4. U.S. Census Bureau. *QuickFacts: United States*. Retrieved from https://www.census.gov/quickfacts/fact/table/US/RHI825222

5. Ibid.

6. U.S. Census Bureau. *STATE PROFILES: 2020 Census*. Retrieved from https://www.census.gov/library/stories/state-by-state.html

7. Pew Research Center (2018). *Demographic and economic trends in urban, suburban and rural communities*. Retrieved from https://www.pewresearch.org/social-trends/2018/05/22/demographic-and-economic-trends-in-urban-suburban-and-rural-communities/

CHAPTER 5

Economic and Crime Risk Map Summary

This chapter includes all the maps needed to examine the riskiness of the counties and areas in terms of economic and crime risks. Six maps summarize our findings (see Figures 5.1 to 5.6). Figure 5-7 is a safety map that created based on Figures 5.1 to 5.6 and illustrates the relatively safest regions of the United States based on the economic and crime risks. The next chapter will show all six maps on a state basis and explain the dangers and safety of every state and its counties. Not every county I chose is objectively safer than others, however, I believe that most of the ones selected are safer, and most of the ones I did not select are not. Again, the following maps illustrate the economic and crime risks that will persist throughout a depression. Figure 5.7 outlines the states and counties I believe to be relatively safe. It does not mean every single area not selected is not appropriate to live in through the coming economic depression. Though rare, there will be exceptions. Chapters 7 and 8 will explore the reasons for moving and living through a depression after the crash phase. Those chapters will consider additional reasons to move to or from a particular location to survive a depression. Chapter 9 will conclude with the safest counties to live in during a depression.

Figure 5.1 is important because it illustrates the racial demographics of the United States. Chapter 4 discussed why to avoid areas populated by non-White Americans. This is the most important thing to know. Figure 5.2 is almost as important as the Figure 5.1 because it explores industry overconcentration. Previous discussion addressed why to avoid areas that have overconcentration of certain industries, as well as metropolitan areas. Mainly avoid durable goods industry, construction, mining, and large metropolitan areas. Figure 5.3 is a real estate map. Again, we discussed why to avoid regions that are highly exposed to real estate. Figure 5.4 is a U.S. poverty map; and Figure 5.5 is a U.S. unemployment map. Avoid the areas with very high poverty and unemployment as discussed. Figure 5.6 is a U.S. density map. Avoid areas of extremely high density. At the same time, you must also be careful of the least populated areas because very low density implies uncertainty about the future. In case your small town, located in a very low-populated agricultural county surrounded by endless fields, experiences complete economic devastation, relocation could be a big trouble.

Besides those six maps, I considered other factors. Exports. Exports revenue is highly susceptible to an economic downturn. States with very high export revenue as a percentage of state gross domestic product stand to lose a very high portion of the revenue. Louisiana has notably very high export revenue, with exports making up 32.4% of Louisiana's GDP in 2023.[1] This creates an additional risk for Louisiana.

Second, there are government-owned lands and areas that are mostly in the Mountain census division. In my opinion, those areas are not very livable. We have concluded that the federal government is in a dire financial situation, which poses a huge economic danger to areas overly dependent on it. Figure 5.8 shows federal public land surface and subsurface area according to the Bureau of Land Management. I will only consider risky the large cluster of federal lands in the mountainous area that encapsulates states on the Western side of the United States (see Figure 6.6 for the elevation map of United States). Relatively small clusters in other regions will not be considered. Also, the dependency of each state on the federal government could be measured financially. I reviewed "States Most Dependent on the Federal Government—2021 Edition" and "Most & Least Federally Dependent States," published in 2023[2,3] to compile the top 10 states most dependent on the federal government (see Figures 5.9 and 5.10) Both sources share eight states. To conclude, high federal dependency is not one of the worst risks but it is a negative point to consider for the states on Figures 5.9 and 5.10.

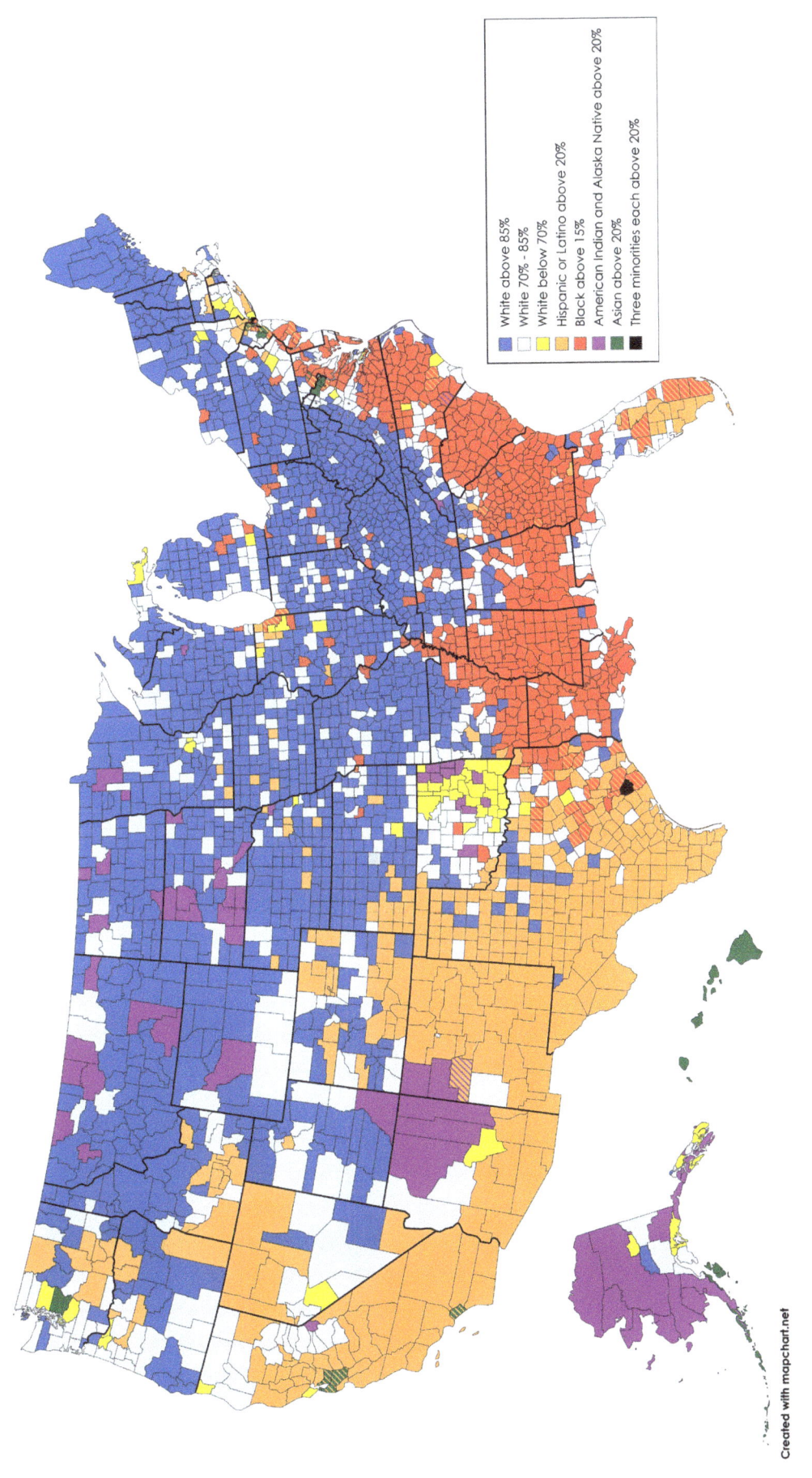

Created with mapchart.net

Legend:
- White above 85%
- White 70% - 85%
- White below 70%
- Hispanic or Latino above 20%
- Black above 15%
- American Indian and Alaska Native above 20%
- Asian above 20%
- Three minorities each above 20%

Figure 5.1

Racial Map of the United States

Data Source: U.S. Census, 2020 census state profiles. Note: The idea for the map was derived from Vivid Maps.

Visit vividmaps.com at https://vividmaps.com/

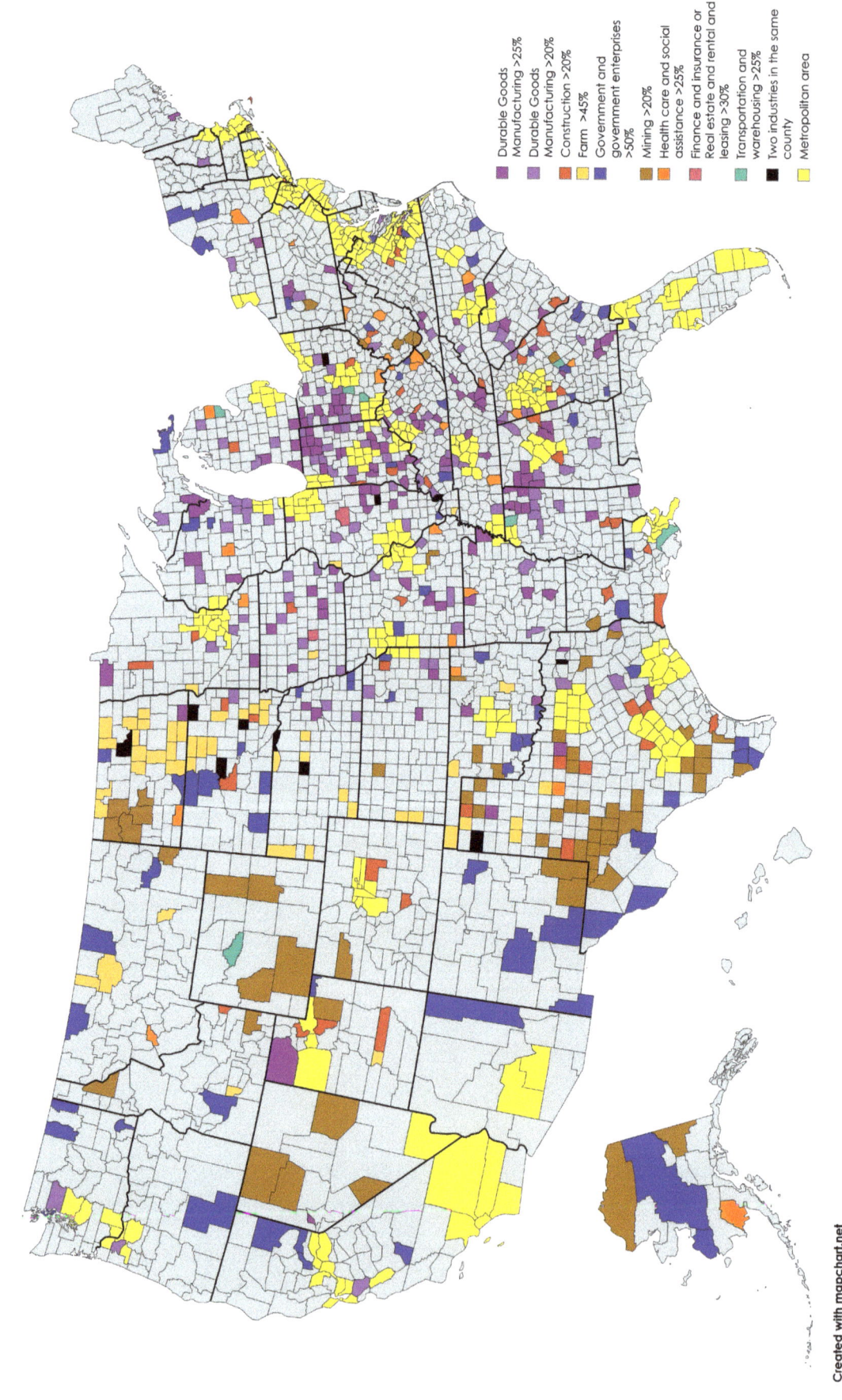

Durable Goods
Manufacturing >25%

Durable Goods
Manufacturing >20%

Construction >20%

Farm >45%

Government and
government enterprises
>50%

Mining >20%

Health care and social
assistance >25%

Finance and insurance or
Real estate and rental and
leasing >30%

Transportation and
warehousing >25%

Two industries in the same
county

Metropolitan area

Created with mapchart.net

Figure 5.2

Economic Risk by County

Note. Includes risk by industry and metro area

County Ranking

- 1-99 Highest Risk
- 100-199 High Risk
- 200-349 Mod. Risk
- 350+ Lower Risk

Figure 5.3

Housing Market Risk Measured by Local Affordability, Local Foreclosure Rates Pre-coronavirus, and the Local Percentage of Homes Underwater on their Mortgages

Image Source: G. Brian Davis, SparkRental, ATTOM Data Solutions; created with Datawrapper

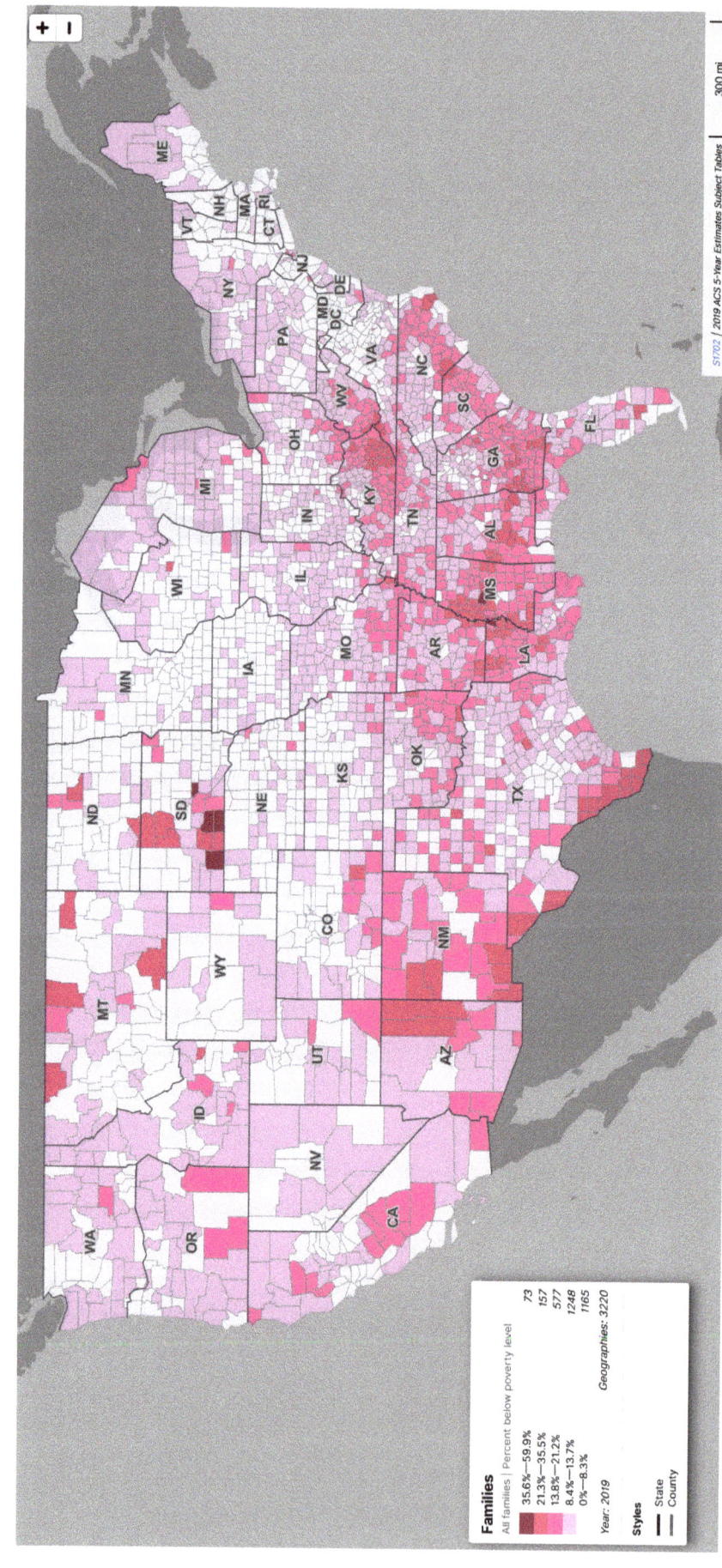

Families | Percent below poverty level

35.6%—59.9%	73
21.3%—35.5%	157
13.8%—21.2%	577
8.4%—13.7%	1248
0%—8.3%	1165

Year: 2019   *Geographies: 3220*

Styles
State
County

Figure 5.4

U.S. Families Below Poverty Level in 2019

Image Source: U.S. census data S1702 ACS 5-year estimates

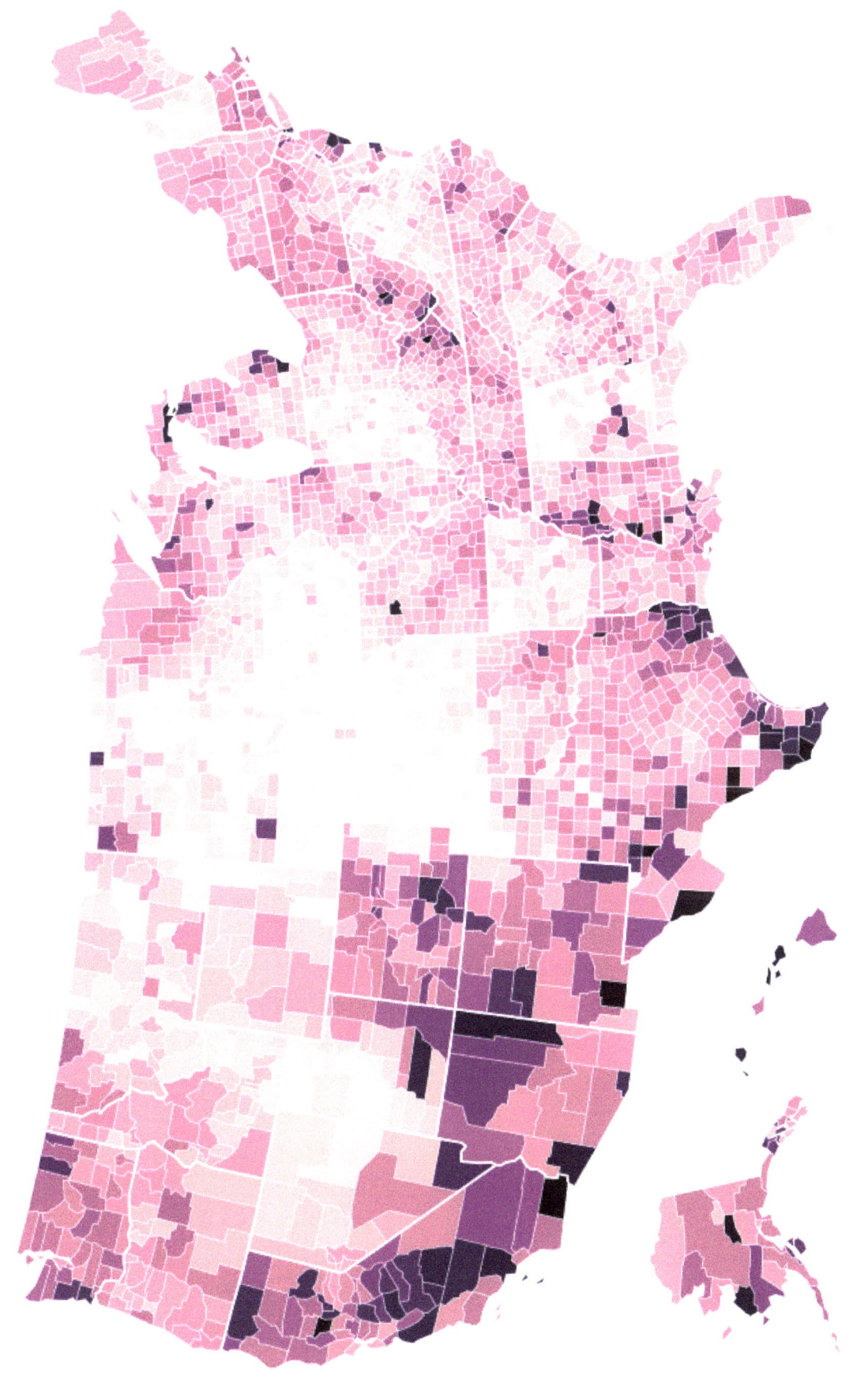

Figure 5.5

U.S. Unemployment Rate by County (December 2020 to February 2021)

Image source: G. Brian Davis, SparkRental. Data source: U.S. Bureau of Labor Statistics. Created with Datawrapper

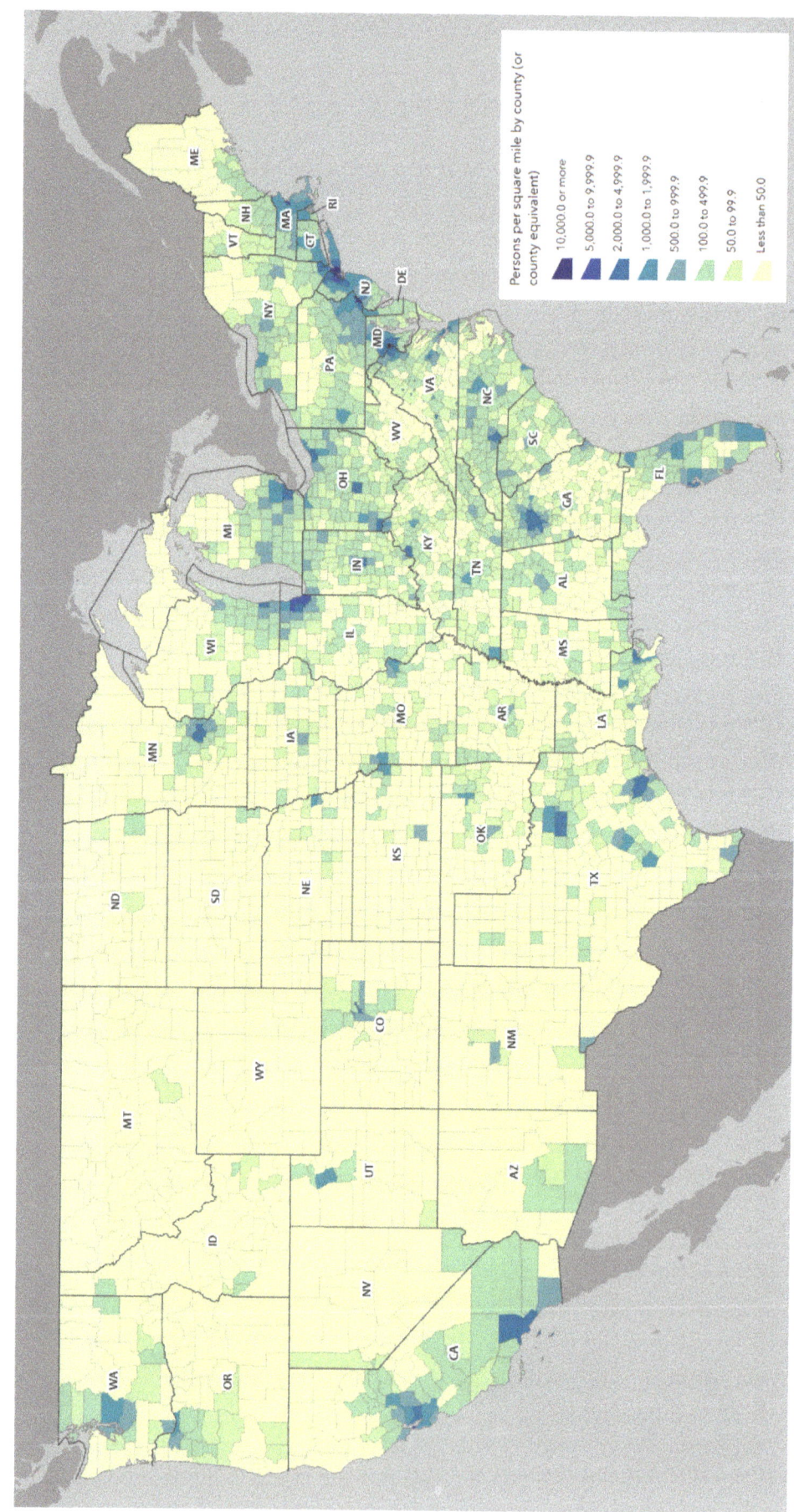

Figure 5.6

U.S. Density Map by County, 2020

Image Source: U.S. Census Bureau 2020 census demographic data map viewer

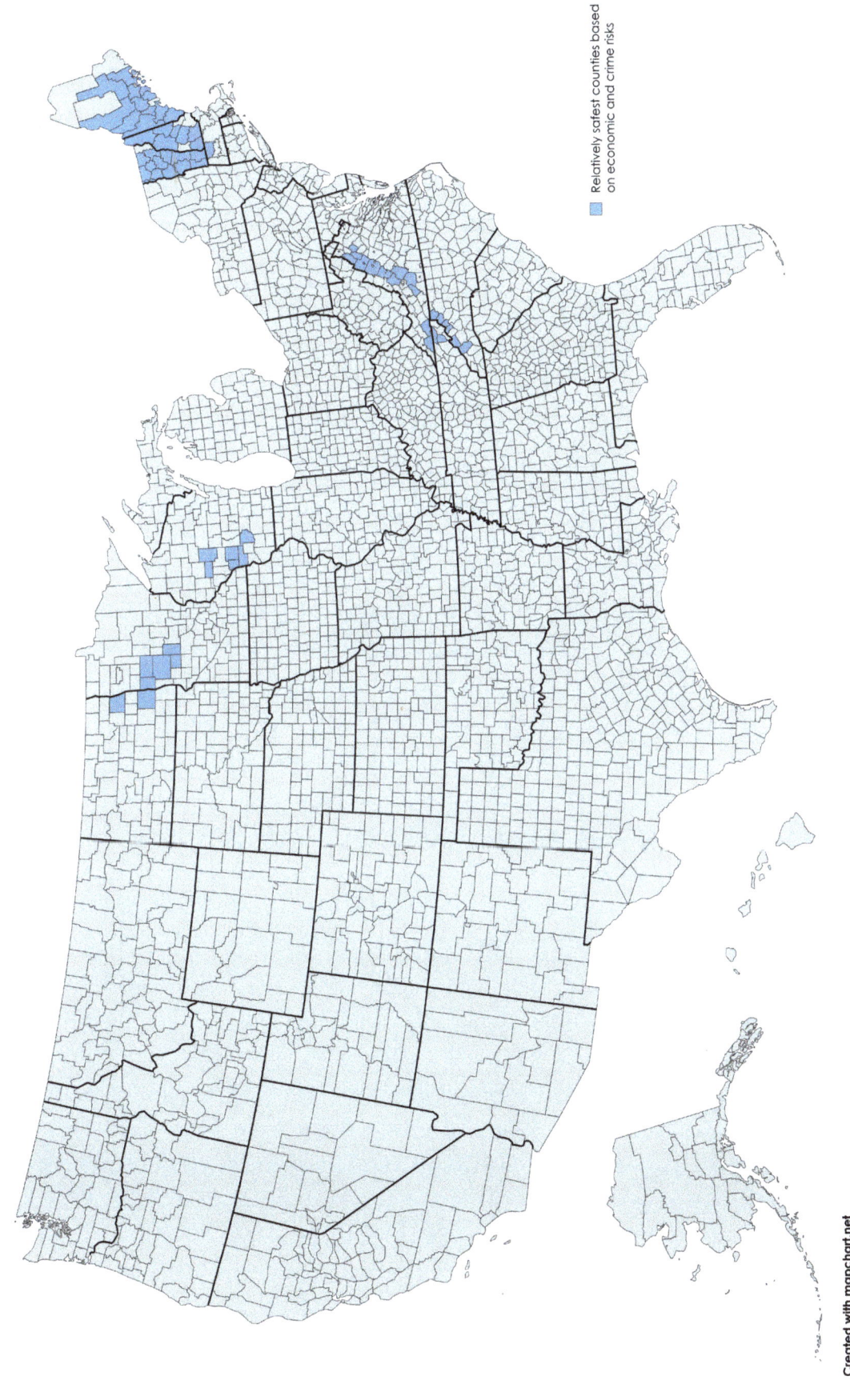

Relatively safest counties based
on economic and crime risks

Figure 5.7
U.S. Safety Map
Note. Blue-colored counties are relatively safer than others based on economic and crime risk

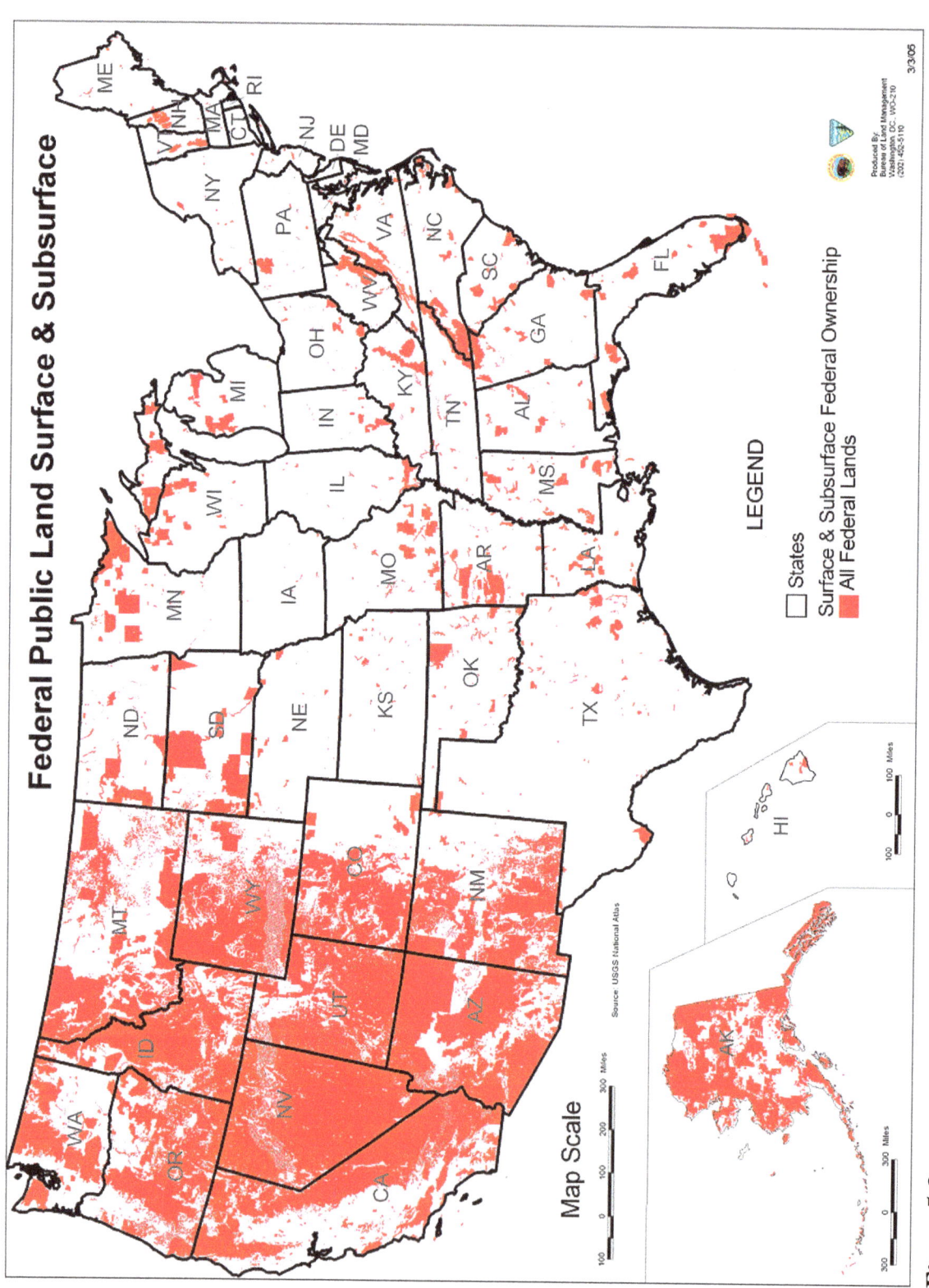

Figure 5.8

Federal Public Land Surface and Subsurface Map

Image Source: Bureau of Land Management, published on wikipedia.org. Created: March 3, 2005. Uploaded: June 24, 2013

Additional map source mentioned—USGS National Atlas

Figure 5.9

States Most Dependent on the Federal Government—2021 Edition

Data Source: Ben Geier, CEPF®, smartasset.com

Rank	State
1	New Mexico
2	West Virginia
3	Alabama
4	Mississippi
5	Louisiana
6	Alaska
7	Arizona
8	Montana
9	Maine
10	Wyoming

Figure 5.10

Most and Least Federally Dependent States—2023 Edition

Data Source: John S Kiernan, wallethub.com

Rank	State
1	Alaska
2	West Virginia
3	Mississippi
4	Kentucky
5	New Mexico
6	Wyoming
7	South Carolina
8	Arizona
9	Montana
10	Louisiana

References

1. Office of the United States Trade Representative. Louisiana. Retrieved from https://ustr.gov/map/state-benefits/la

2. John S Kiernan. WalletHub (2023). *Most & Least Federally Dependent States*. Retrieved from https://wallethub.com/edu/states-most-least-dependent-on-the-federal-government/2700

3. Ben Geier. Smartasset.com (2022). *States Most Dependent on the Federal Government*—2021 Edition. Retrieved from https://smartasset.com/taxes/states-most-dependent-on-the-federal-government-2021-edition

CHAPTER 6

State Analysis of Economic & Crime Risk Maps

The following state analysis pages include a map of each state within its census divisional distribution. A shaded relief image shows each state's elevation (see also Figure 6.6 for a shaded relief map of entire United States).

Each analysis contains the state population, land area, density, percentage of White people (not Hispanic or Latino), poverty rate, and unemployment rate. State population, land area, density, and the percentage of White people (not Hispanic or Latino) are all based on the US 2020 Census, published by the U.S. Census Bureau.[1,2] The poverty rate of individuals (not families) is based on the Census Data service website, data.census.gov, table ID: S1701, Poverty Status in the Past 12 Months for 2022, using ACS 5-year estimates. The unemployment rate for 2022 was accessed from the U.S. Bureau of Labor Statistics.

The data used for the six maps below are from slightly different years and sources. All the maps are not to scale. However, included is the Census State Regional map in this chapter, Figure 6.7.

The Racial Risk Map is based on 2020 census state profiles data. Any counties that do not have a population of White people (including Hispanic or Latino) above 85% are risky. The ones that include any minority or White population of less than 70% are very risky. Besides this legend, there are two minorities present in counties that have striped colors. The black color indicates 3 minority groups.

Figure 6.1

Legend for the Racial Risk Map
Note. Created with Mapchart.net

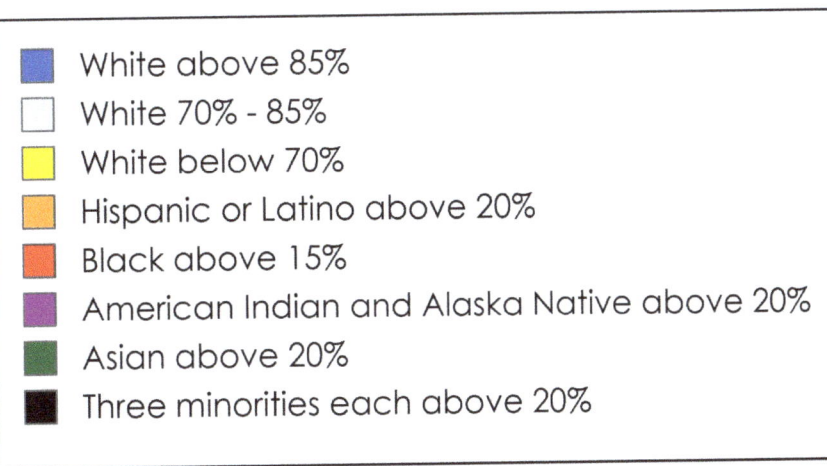

Figure 6.2

Legend for the Industry Overconcentration Risk Map

Data Source: U.S. Bureau of Economic Analysis (BEA) data.

Note. Private nonfarm earnings as a percent of total nonfarm earnings (county based). For farm industry, private nonfarm earnings as a percent of total private nonfarm and farm earnings combined.

Created with Mapchart.net

Figure 6.3

Legend for the Real Estate Risk Map

Data & Image Source: SparkRental, https://sparkrental.com/unemployment-rates-by-county-interactive-map/

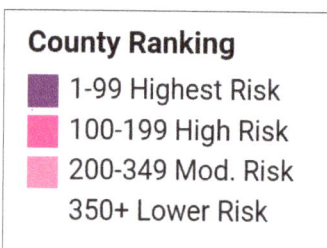

Figure 6.4

Legend for the Density Risk Map

Data & Image Source: 2020 census demographic data map viewer

Figure 6.5

Legend for the Poverty Risk Map

Data & Image Source: Census data 2019 census ACS 5-year estimates

Note. The poverty risk map data may be accessed on the Census Data service website, data.census.gov. The data ID is S1702 and refers to "Poverty Status in the Past 12 Months of Families." It does not refer to the poverty status of individuals but to families.

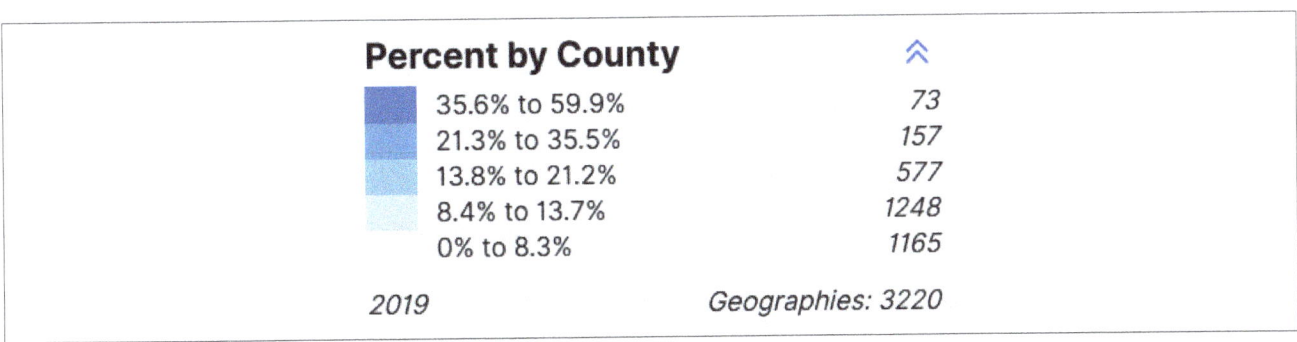

The Unemployment Risk Maps:

The Unemployment Map data is for "Dec. 2020—Released Feb. '21" period.

Figure 6.6

The National Elevation Data Set Shaded Relief of the United States

Image Source: The National Elevation Dataset of United States Geological Survey, https://usgs.gov

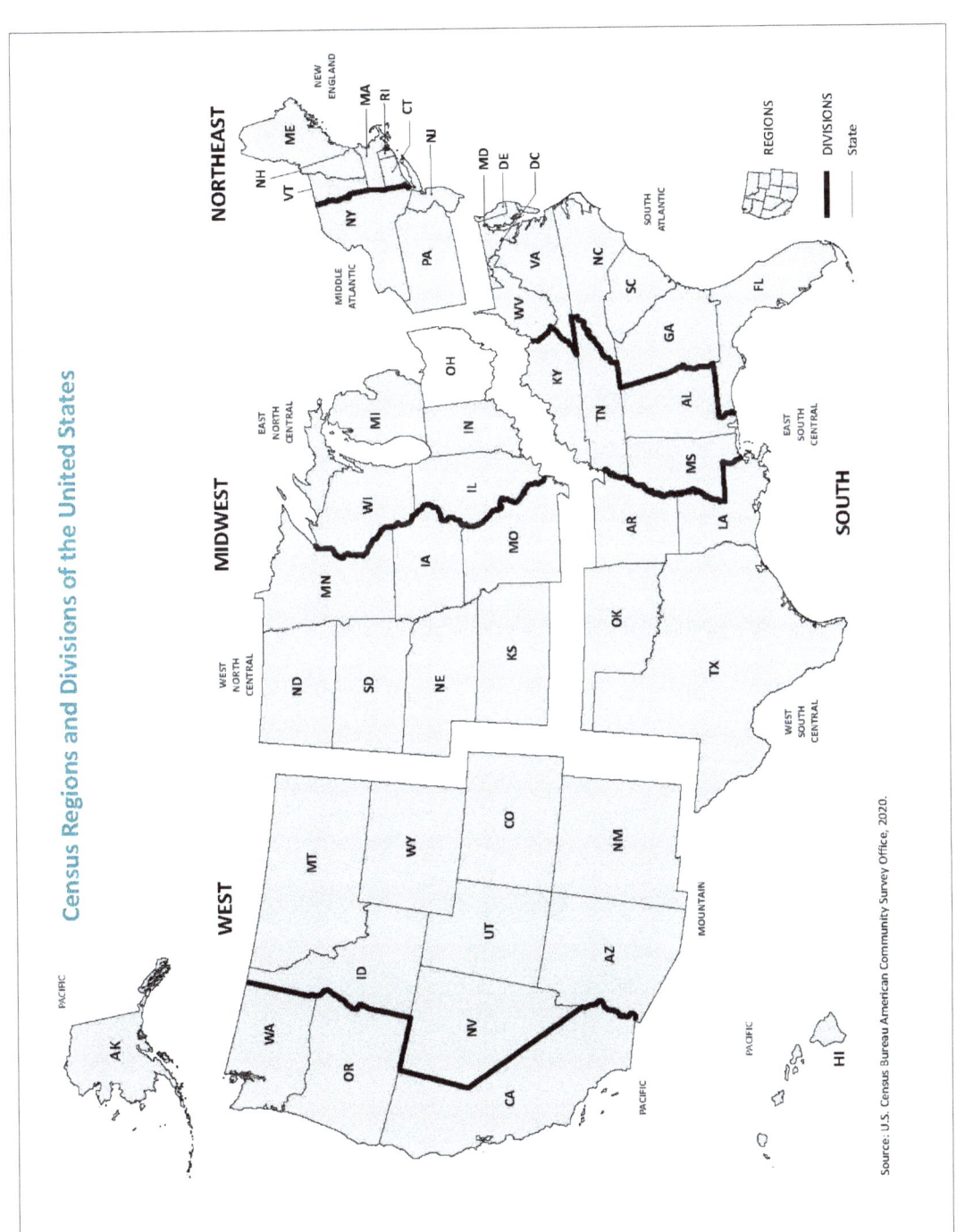

Census Regions and Divisions of the United States

Figure 6.7

Census Regions and Divisions of the United States

Image Source: U.S. Census Bureau and U.S. Census Bureau American Community Survey Office, 2020

References

1. U.S. Census Bureau. *2020 Census Demographic Data Map Viewer*. Retrieved from https://maps.geo.census.gov/ddmv/map.html

2. U.S. Census Bureau (2010). *State Area Measurements and Internal Point Coordinates*. Retrieved from https://www.census.gov/geographies/reference-files/2010/geo/state-area.html

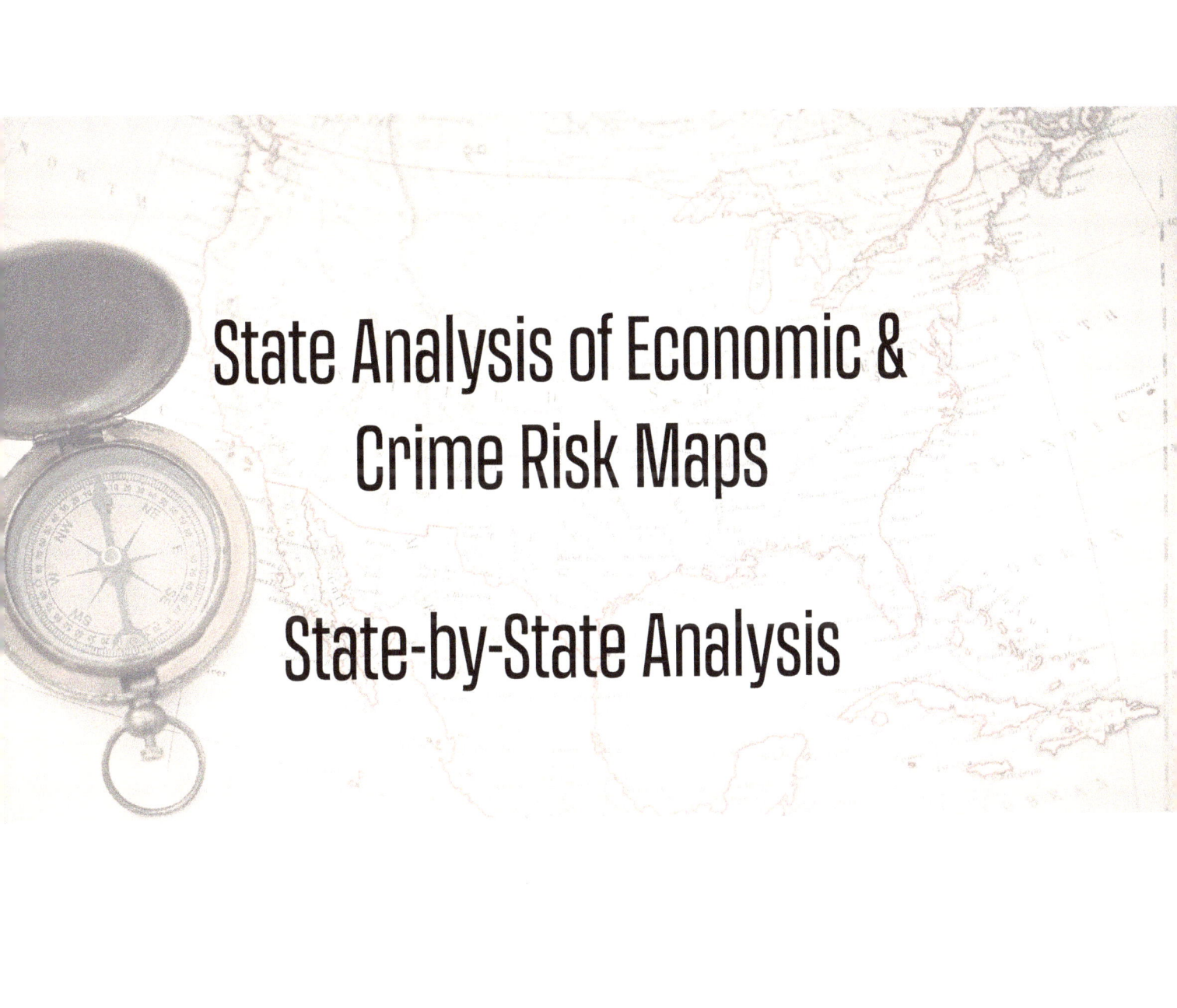

State Analysis of Economic & Crime Risk Maps

State-by-State Analysis

State	Maine
Population	1,362 thous.
Land Area	30,843 sq mile
Density/mi2	44.2 people
Percent White	90.2%
Poverty Rate	10.9%
Unempl. Rate	3.0%

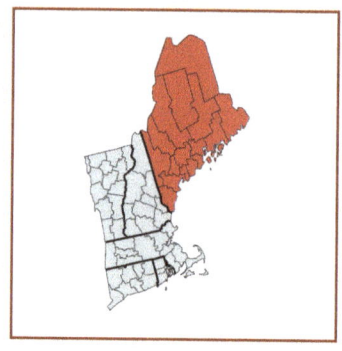

State Location Map
Created with Mapchart.net

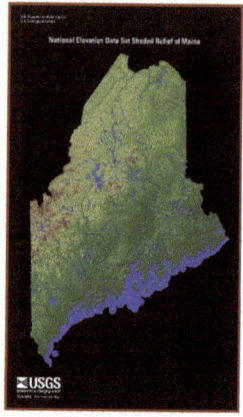

Maine—Shaded Relief Image
Credit: National Elevation Dataset, compiled
by the U.S. Geological Survey
Visit the USGS at https://usgs.gov.

Racial Risk Map
Created with Mapchart.net, data—US Census

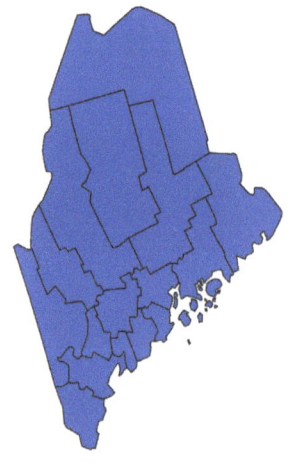
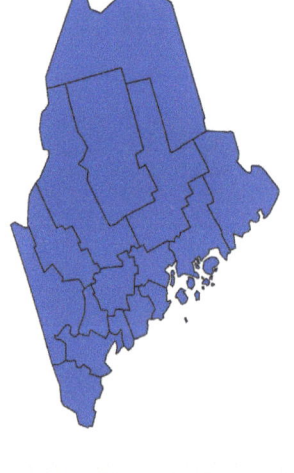

Industry Overconcentration Risk Map
Created with Mapchart.net, data—US Census

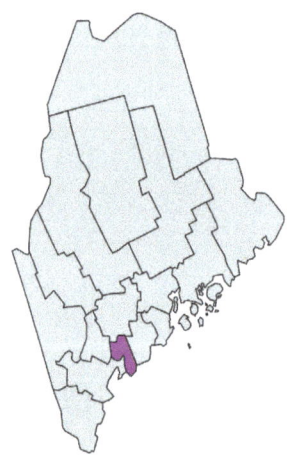

Real Estate Risk Map; G. Brian Davis, SparkRental,
ATTOM Data Solutions, Created with Datawrapper

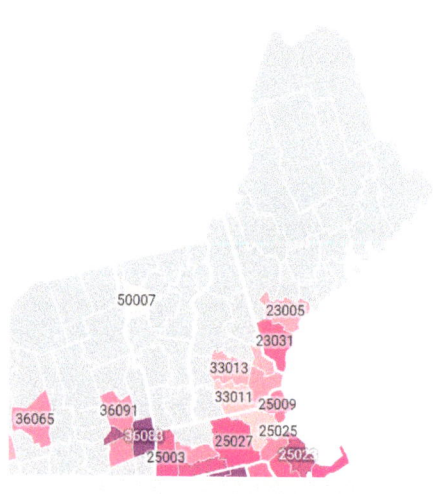

Density Risk Map
Source: US Census

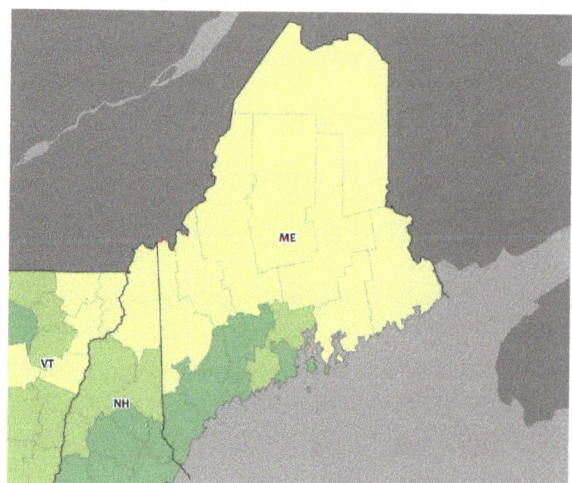

Poverty Risk Map
Source: US Census

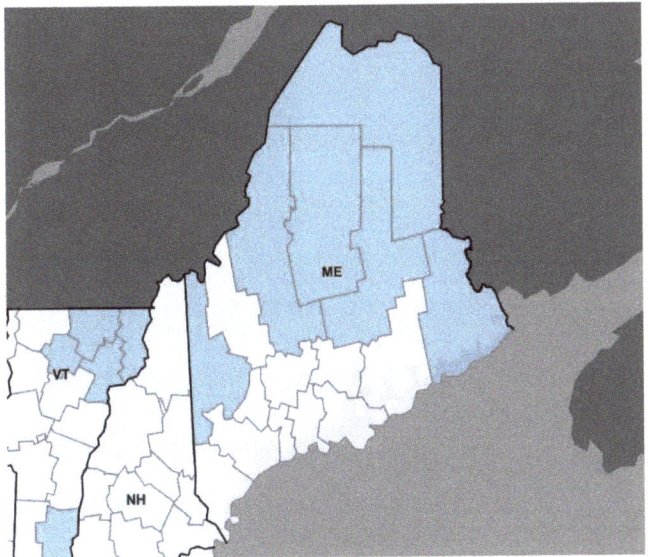

Unemployment Risk Map
Source: SparkRental & BLS

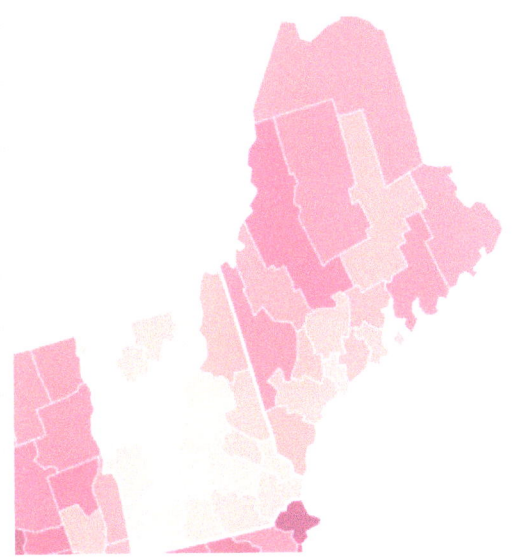

Economic & Crime Risk Map

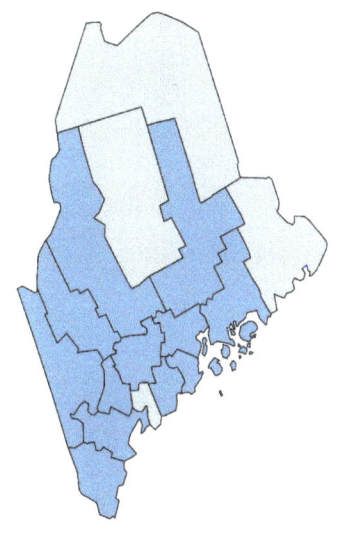

Main Summaries of Risk Maps

- The percentage of the White population is very high, which is amazing in terms of safety.
- No substantial industry overconcentration.
- No metro area risk.
- Low population density in northern regions.
- Moderate poverty and unemployment rates.

Conclusions

Maine consistently ranks in the top 3 in terms of safety from violent crime. It is often considered the safest state in that regard. The high percentage of White people and extremely low violent crime rate make this state an exceptionally good state. Also, it is not subject to significant industry overconcentration risk. Maine will suffer much less than other states in terms of violent crime.

State	New Hampshire
Population	1,378 thous.
Land Area	8,953 sq mile
Density/mi2	153.8 people
Percent White	87.2%
Poverty Rate	7.3%
Unempl. Rate	2.5%

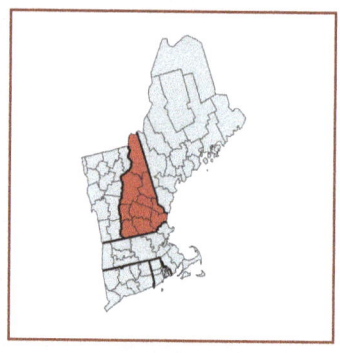

State Location Map
Created with Mapchart.net

New Hampshire—Shaded Relief Image
Credit: National Elevation Dataset, compiled
by the U.S. Geological Survey
Visit the USGS at https://usgs.gov.

Racial Risk Map
Created with Mapchart.net, data—US Census

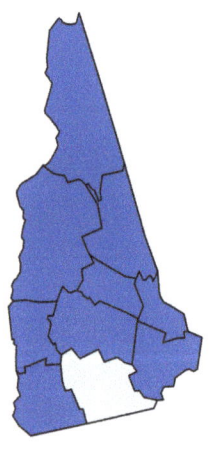

Industry Overconcentration Risk Map
Created with Mapchart.net, data—US Census

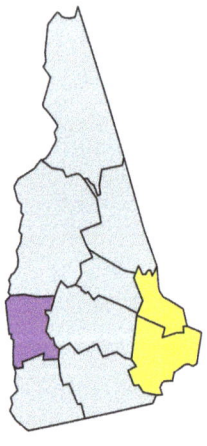

Real Estate Risk Map; G. Brian Davis, SparkRental,
ATTOM Data Solutions, Created with Datawrapper

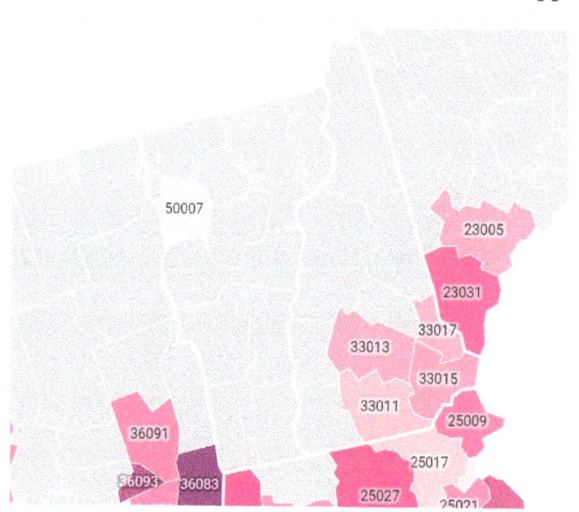

Density Risk Map
Source: US Census

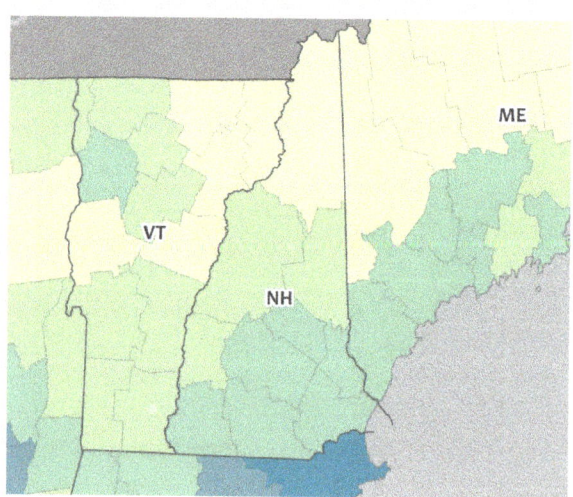

Poverty Risk Map
Source: US Census

Unemployment Risk Map
Source: SparkRental & BLS

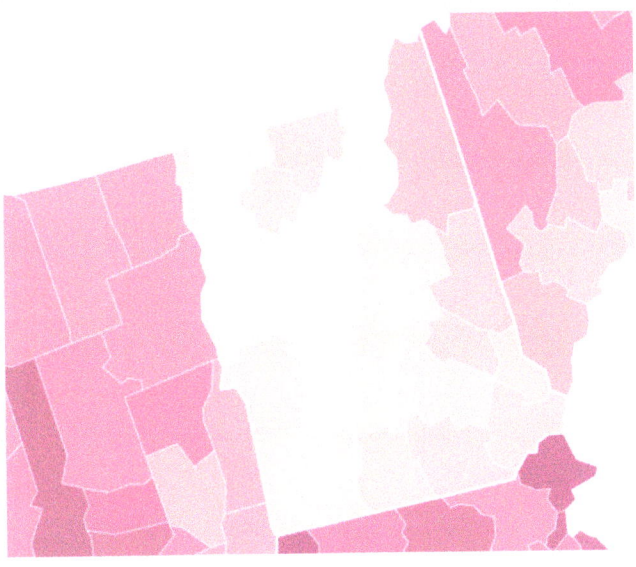

Economic & Crime Risk Map

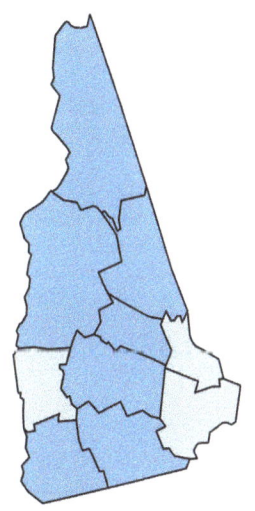

Main Summaries of Risk Maps

- The percentage of the White population is very high, which is amazing in terms of safety.
- No substantial industry overconcentration.
- Southern New Hampshire is subject to some metro-area risk.
- Southern New Hampshire is subject to real estate risk.
- Medium population density.
- Lowest poverty rate in the country.

Conclusions

Please see the previous conclusions for the state of Maine. They are very similar to New Hampshire's. New Hampshire consistently ranks in the top 3 safest states from violent crime risk. New Hampshire is a predominantly White state with the lowest poverty in the country. Also, the population density is very reasonable.

However, southern New Hampshire includes the metro area and is exposed to real estate risk. During the Great Depression, southern New Hampshire was exposed to textile manufacturing, which suffered severe bust. Thus, avoid small industrial or mill towns, where employment comes from few factories or companies.

Overall, New Hampshire will be much safer than most states in terms of violent crime but not so much in terms of economic performance, though, it will still be better than many other states.

State	Vermont
Population	643 thous.
Land Area	9,217 sq mile
Density/mi2	69.8 people
Percent White	89.1%
Poverty Rate	10.4%
Unempl. Rate	2.6%

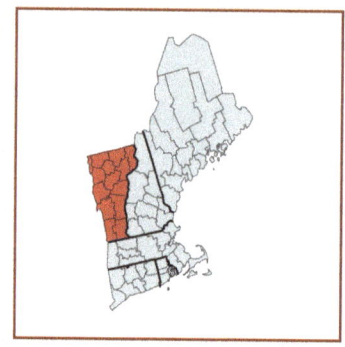

State Location Map
Created with Mapchart.net

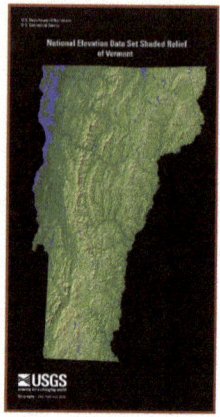

Vermont - Shaded Relief Image
Credit: National Elevation Dataset, compiled
by the U.S. Geological Survey
Visit the USGS at https://usgs.gov.

Racial Risk Map
Created with Mapchart.net, data—US Census

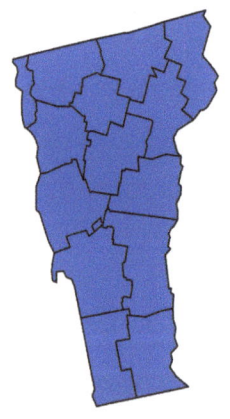

Industry Overconcentration Risk Map
Created with Mapchart.net, data—US Census

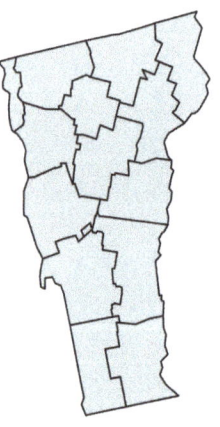

Real Estate Risk Map; G. Brian Davis, SparkRental,
ATTOM Data Solutions, Created with Datawrapper

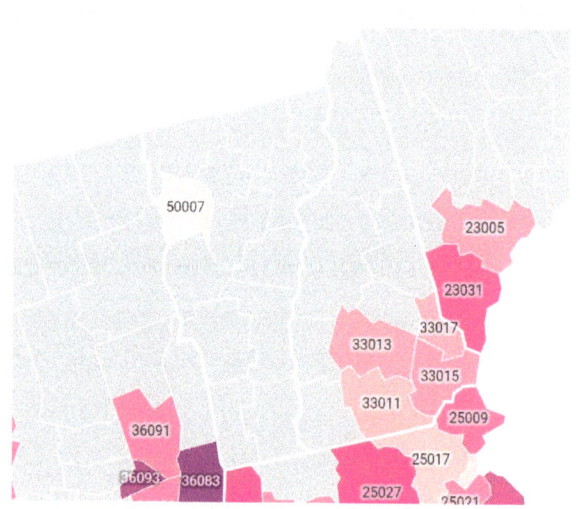

Density Risk Map
Source: US Census

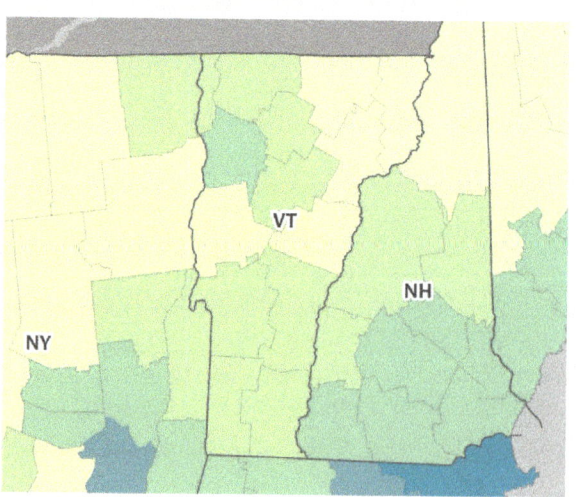

Poverty Risk Map
Source: US Census

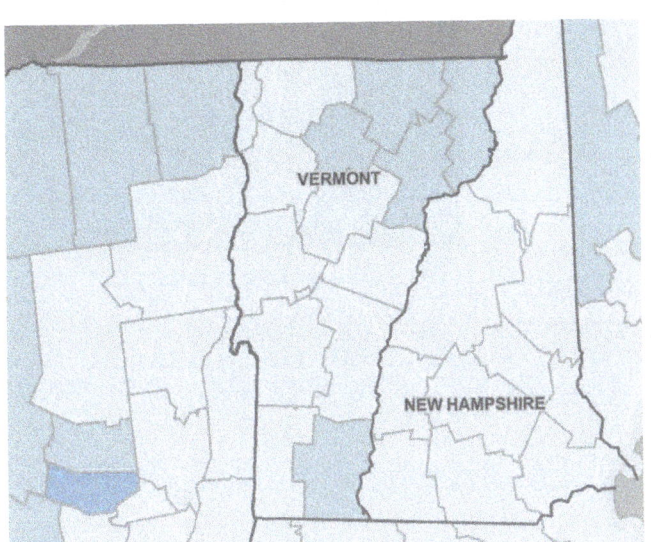

Unemployment Risk Map
Source: SparkRental & BLS

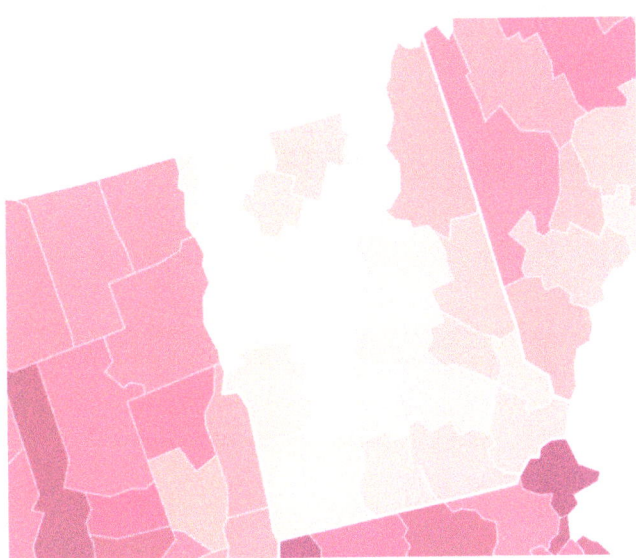

Economic & Crime Risk Map

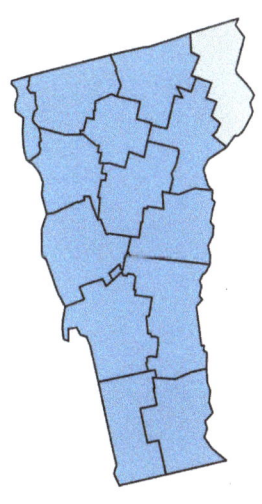

Main Summaries of Risk Maps

- The percentage of the White population is very high, which is amazing in terms of safety.
- No substantial industry overconcentration.
- Below-average population density.
- Moderate poverty and unemployment rates.

Conclusions

The state has conclusions similar to those of Maine and New Hampshire. Vermont consistently ranks in the top 3 in terms of safety from violent crime. It is a predominantly White state. Additionally, there are no extreme real estate risks or metro area risks, and there is no industry overconcentration risk. Vermont will be much safer than most states in terms of violent crime. It is also comparably safer than most states in terms of economic downturn.

State	Massachusetts
Population	7,030 thous.
Land Area	7,800 sq mile
Density/mi2	901.2 people
Percent White	67.6%
Poverty Rate	9.9%
Unempl. Rate	3.8%

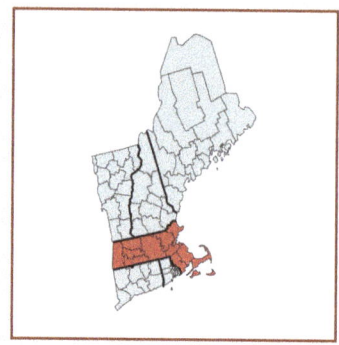

State Location Map
Created with Mapchart.net

Massachusetts - Shaded Relief Image
Credit: National Elevation Dataset, compiled
by the U.S. Geological Survey
Visit the USGS at https://usgs.gov.

Racial Risk Map
Created with Mapchart.net, data—US Census

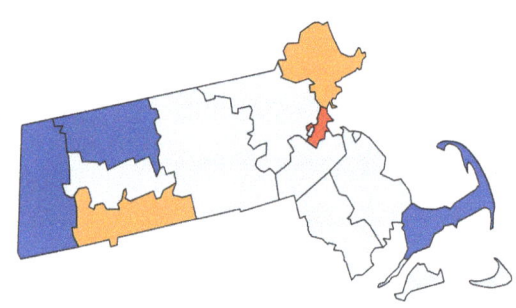

Industry Overconcentration Risk Map
Created with Mapchart.net, data—US Census

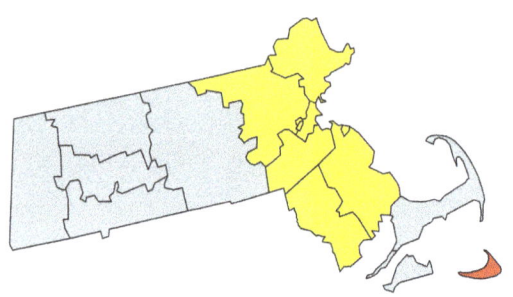

Real Estate Risk Map; G. Brian Davis, SparkRental,
ATTOM Data Solutions, Created with Datawrapper

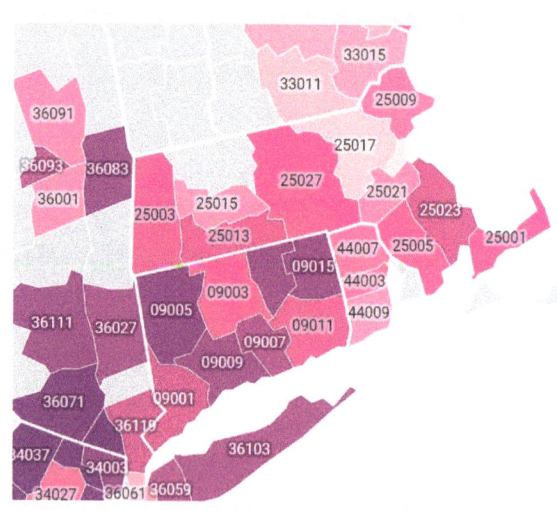

Density Risk Map
Source: US Census

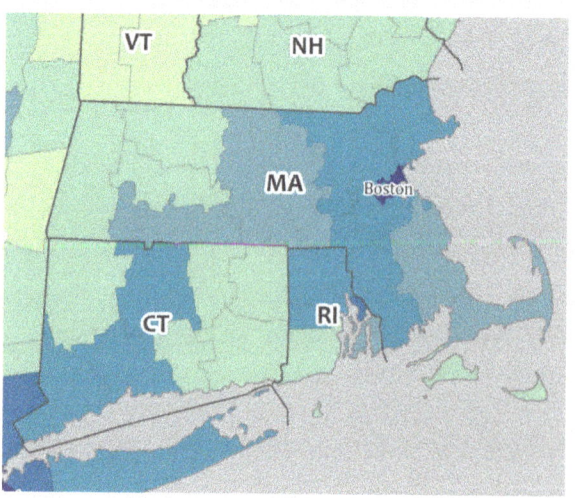

Poverty Risk Map
Source: US Census

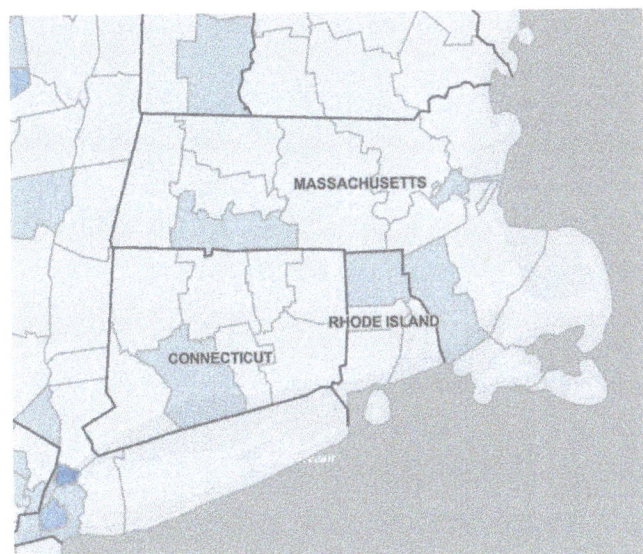

Unemployment Risk Map
Source: SparkRental & BLS

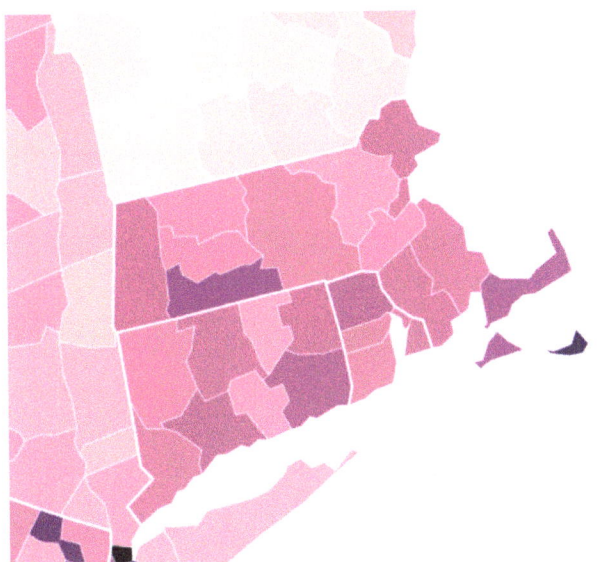

Economic & Crime Risk Map

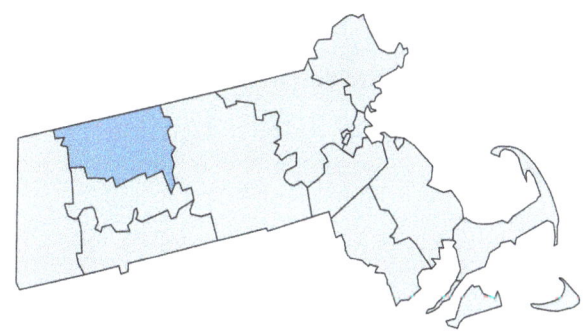

Main Summaries of Risk Maps

- The percentage of the White population is not enough to be considered safe. In the Boston area safety is not high because the percentage of Whites is lower there.
- The eastern half of Massachusetts is subject to metro-area risk.
- Massachusetts is subject to high real estate risk.
- Very high population density.
- Moderate poverty and unemployment rates.

Conclusions

Very high density, real estate risk, and not very good racial demographics will lead to severe economic downturn and relatively high crime risk.

There are regions and small towns that have a high percentage of White population, so they will be subject to less crime risk. However, because the region will suffer overall, the spillover effects will affect some of those small metaphorical islands of safety, perhaps not all of them. Boston, as one of the largest cities, will witness less trouble than similarly large metropolitan areas. There will be a tremendous economic downturn, but comparatively, it will be better than New York City, Los Angeles, or San Francisco, especially regarding crime safety. Overall, Massachusetts is not a safe state from economic and crime risks. And it is more exposed to economic risk than crime risk. However, there is one county that is relatively less dangerous.

State	Connecticut
Population	3,606 thous.
Land Area	4,842 sq mile
Density/mi2	744.7 people
Percent White	63.2%
Poverty Rate	10.1%
Unempl. Rate	4.2%

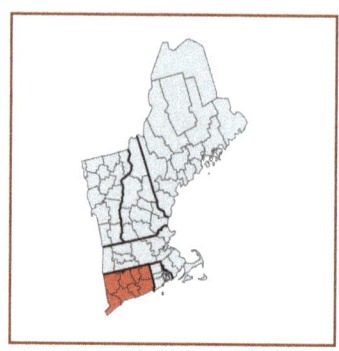

State Location Map
Created with Mapchart.net

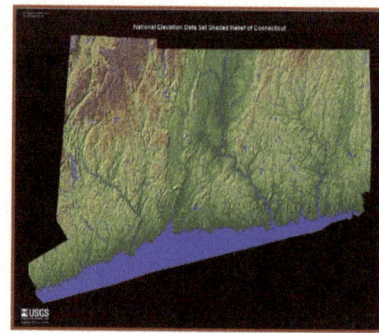

Connecticut - Shaded Relief Image
Credit: National Elevation Dataset, compiled
by the U.S. Geological Survey
Visit the USGS at https://usgs.gov.

Racial Risk Map
Created with Mapchart.net, data—US Census

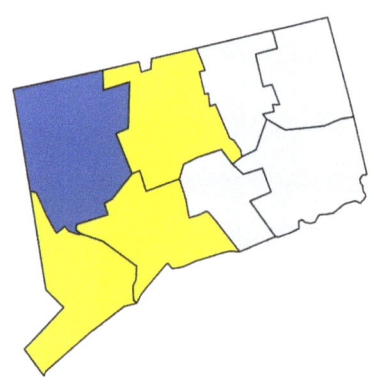

Industry Overconcentration Risk Map
Created with Mapchart.net, data—US Census

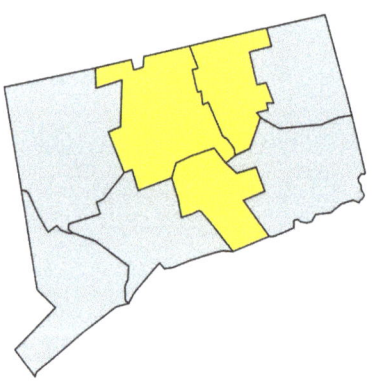

Real Estate Risk Map; G. Brian Davis, SparkRental,
ATTOM Data Solutions, Created with Datawrapper

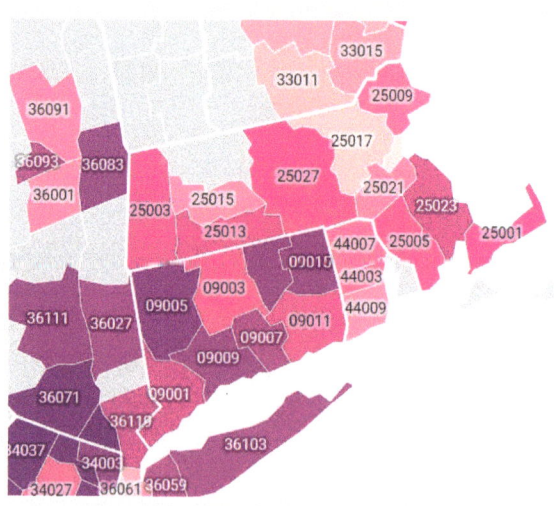

Density Risk Map
Source: US Census

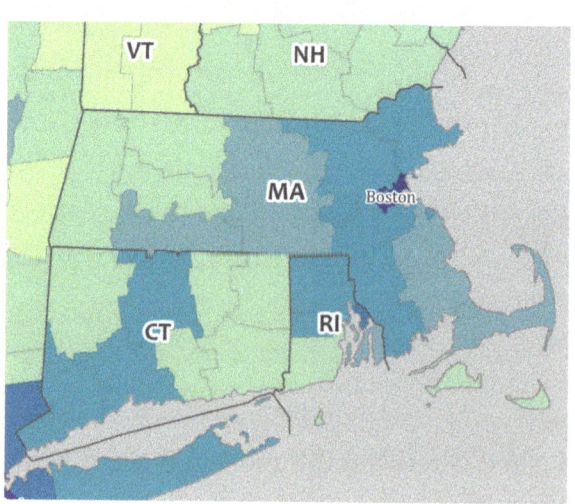

Poverty Risk Map
Source: US Census

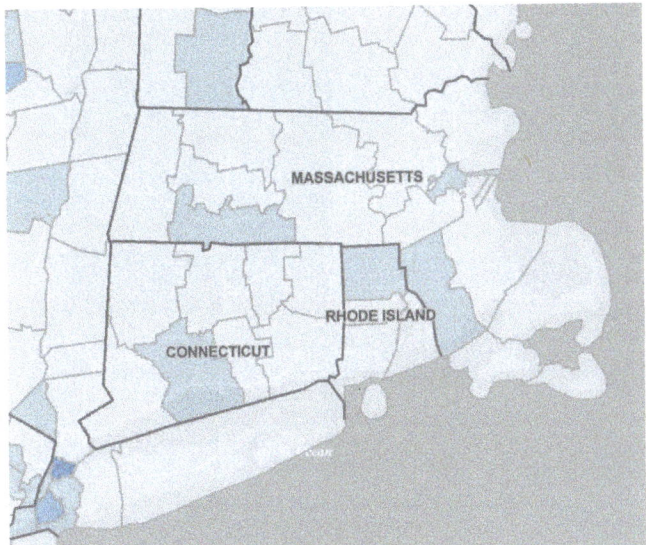

Unemployment Risk Map
Source: SparkRental & BLS

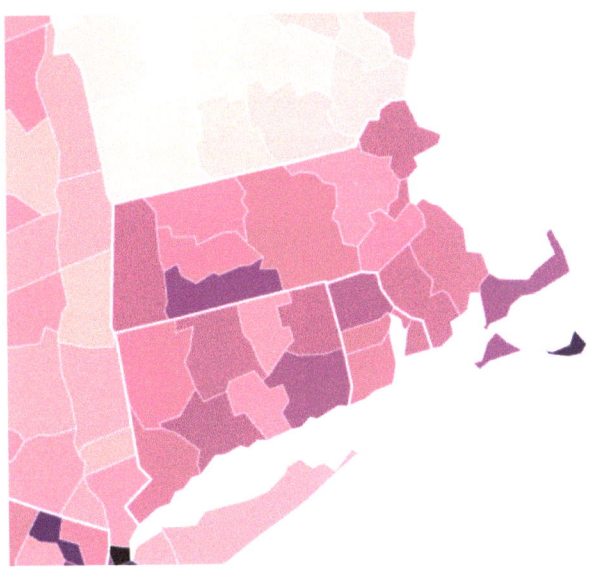

Economic & Crime Risk Map

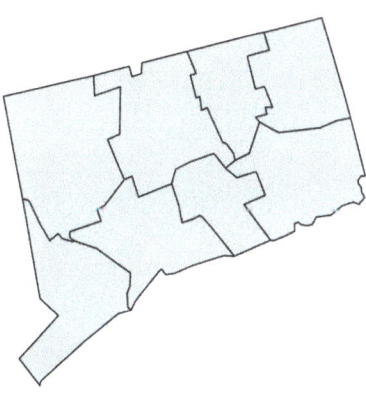

Main Summaries of Risk Maps

- The percentage of the White population is not enough to be considered safe.
- Connecticut is subject to metro-area risk.
- Connecticut is subject to very high real estate risk.
- Very high population density.
- Moderate poverty and unemployment rates.

Conclusions

Very high density, real estate risk, and not very good racial demographics will lead to a severe economic downturn and relatively high crime risk. See the conclusions for Massachusetts. Overall, I think Massachusetts will be slightly safer than Connecticut, perhaps from the crime risk perspective. Connecticut is also closer to the New York metro area, which is one of the riskiest metros in terms of economic and crime risk.

State	Rhode Island
Population	1,097 thous.
Land Area	1,034 sq mile
Density/mi2	1,061.4 people
Percent White	68.7%
Poverty Rate	11.2%
Unempl. Rate	3.2%

State Location Map
Created with Mapchart.net

Rhode Island - Shaded Relief Image
Credit: National Elevation Dataset, compiled
by the U.S. Geological Survey
Visit the USGS at https://usgs.gov.

Racial Risk Map
Created with Mapchart.net, data—US Census

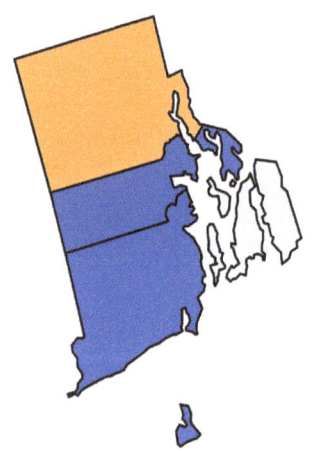

Industry Overconcentration Risk Map
Created with Mapchart.net, data—US Census

Real Estate Risk Map; G. Brian Davis, SparkRental,
ATTOM Data Solutions, Created with Datawrapper

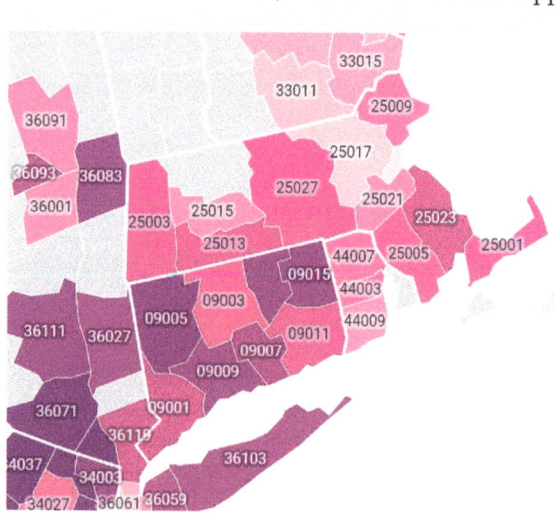

Density Risk Map
Source: US Census

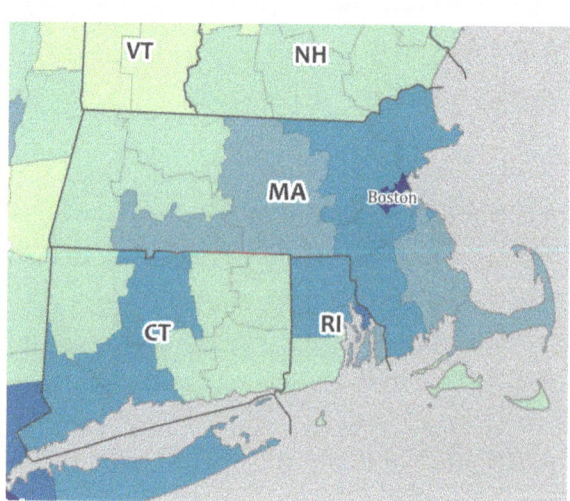

Poverty Risk Map
Source: US Census

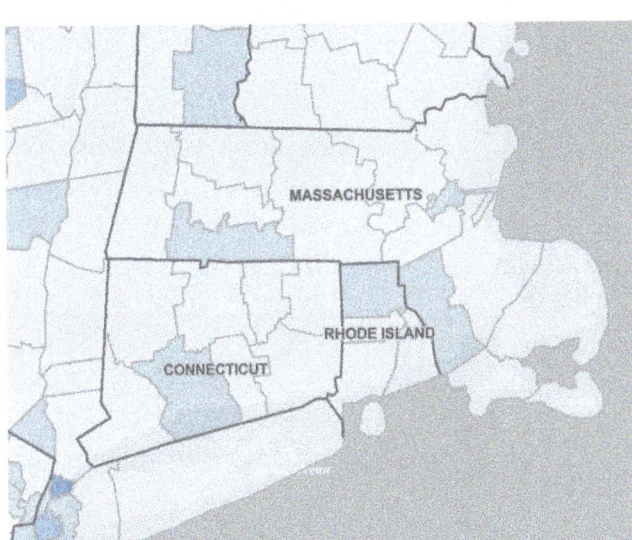

Unemployment Risk Map
Source: SparkRental & BLS

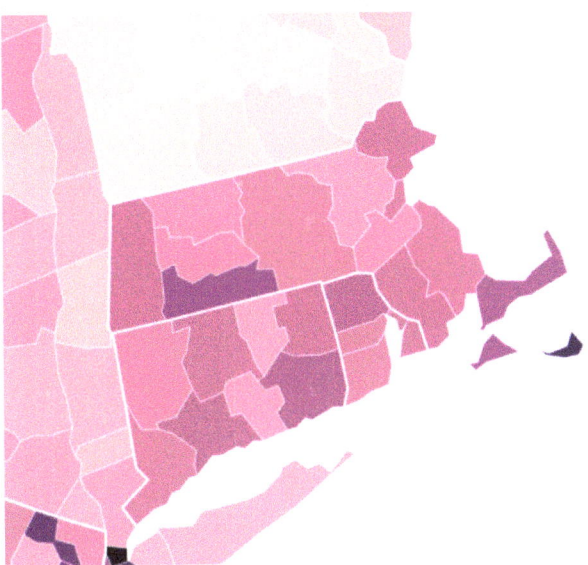

Economic & Crime Risk Map

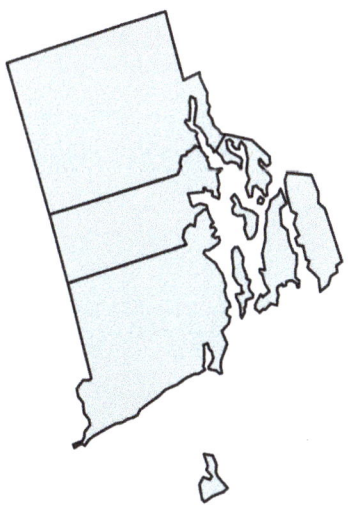

Main Summaries of Risk Maps

- The percentage of the White population is not enough to be considered safe.
- Rhode Island is subject to metro-area risk.
- Rhode Island is subject to high real estate risk.
- Very high population density.
- Moderate poverty and unemployment rates.

Conclusions

Rhode Island is similar to Massachusetts and Connecticut. See their conclusions.

State	New York
Population	20,201 thous.
Land Area	47,126 sq mile
Density/mi2	428.7 people
Percent White	52.5%
Poverty Rate	13.6%
Unempl. Rate	4.3%

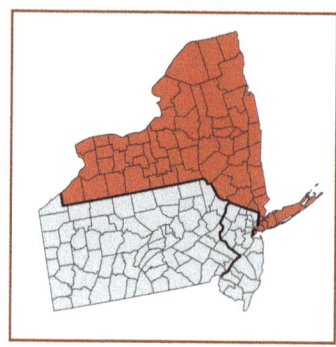

State Location Map
Created with Mapchart.net

New York - Shaded Relief Image
Credit: National Elevation Dataset, compiled
by the U.S. Geological Survey
Visit the USGS at https://usgs.gov.

Racial Risk Map
Created with Mapchart.net, data—US Census

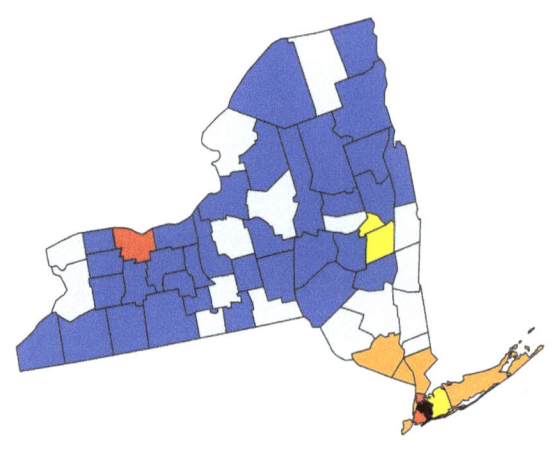

Industry Overconcentration Risk Map
Created with Mapchart.net, data—US Census

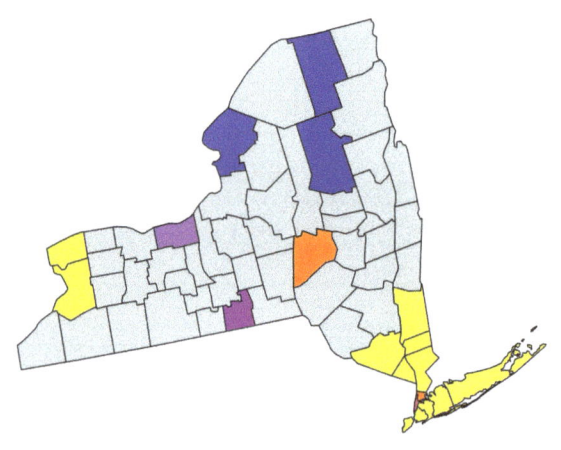

Real Estate Risk Map; G. Brian Davis, SparkRental,
ATTOM Data Solutions, Created with Datawrapper

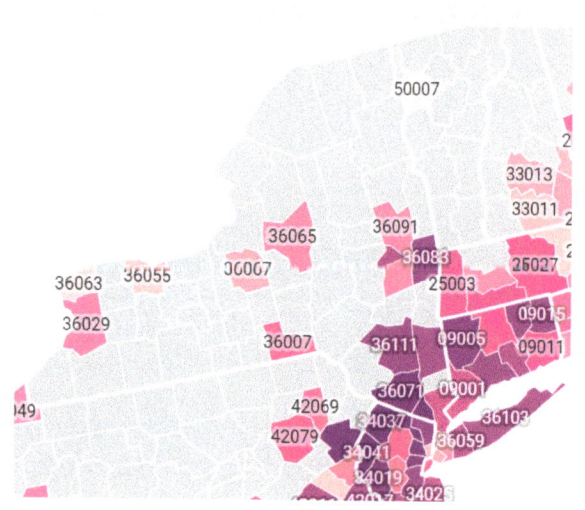

Density Risk Map
Source: US Census

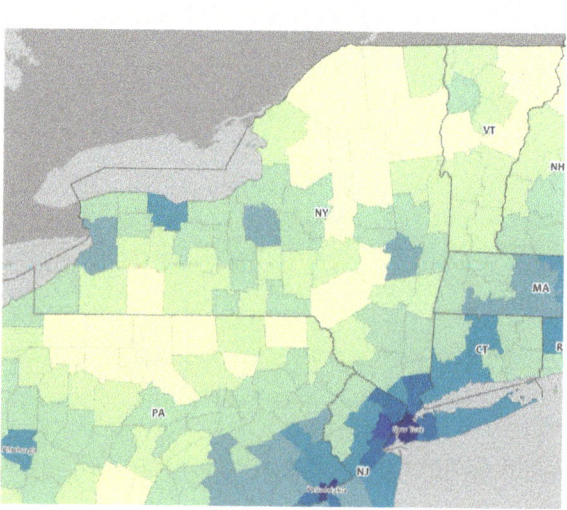

Poverty Risk Map
Source: US Census

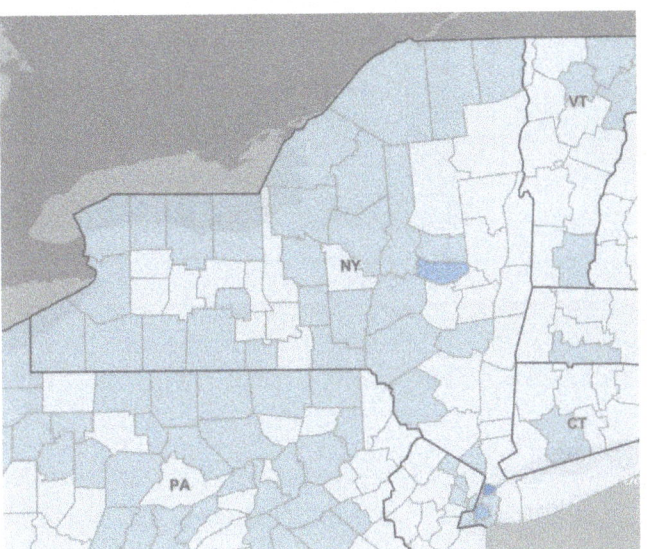

Unemployment Risk Map
Source: SparkRental & BLS

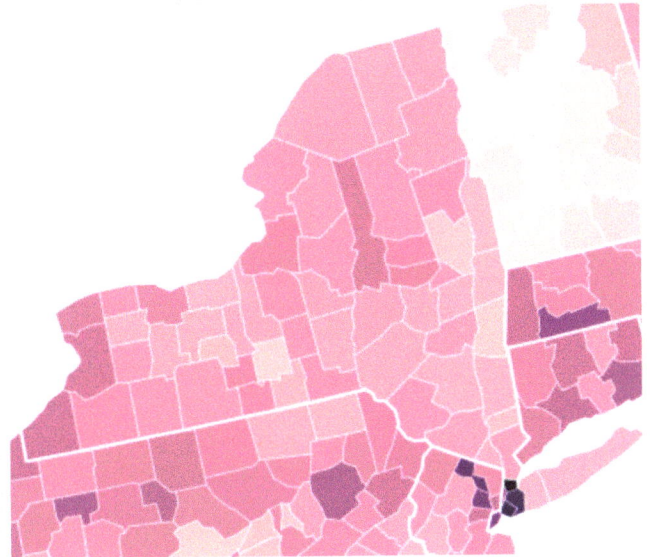

Economic & Crime Risk Map

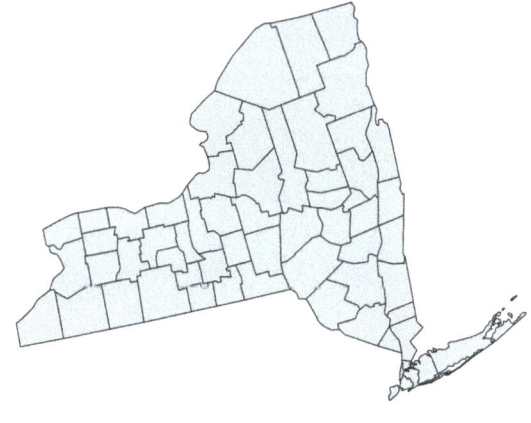

Main Summaries of Risk Maps

- The percentage of the White population is low. The New York City area included in the "New York-Newark-Jersey City" metropolitan area, the largest in the United States, has a very low percentage of White people. The rest of the state has a reasonable population of White people.

- The New York City area is subject to very high metro area risk.

- The New York City area is subject to extreme real estate risk.

- The New York City area has a very high population density, while the rest of the state is much less dense.

Conclusions

New York City will be one of the main epicenters of the depression. That area will be extremely dangerous in terms of violent crime. The rest of the state has cities and counties with reasonably high percentage of White population. However, there is an overconcentration of industries spread in several locations, so choosing a cluster of safe counties is difficult. Also, the state is not very freedom oriented. Thus, I do not want to cherry-pick counties I am not personally familiar with.

State	Pennsylvania
Population	13,003 thous.
Land Area	44,743 sq mile
Density/mi2	290.6 people
Percent White	73.5%
Poverty Rate	11.8%
Unempl. Rate	4.4%

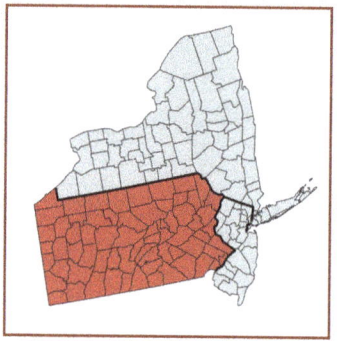

State Location Map
Created with Mapchart.net

Pennsylvania - Shaded Relief Image
Credit: National Elevation Dataset, compiled
by the U.S. Geological Survey
Visit the USGS at https://usgs.gov.

Racial Risk Map
Created with Mapchart.net, data—US Census

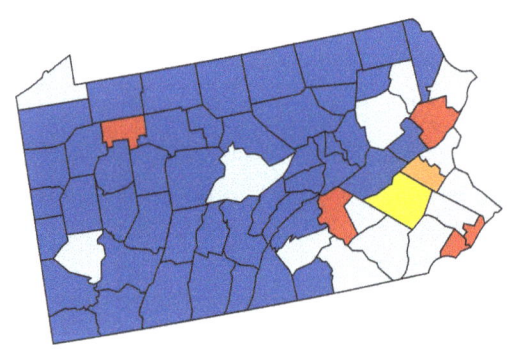

Industry Overconcentration Risk Map
Created with Mapchart.net, data—US Census

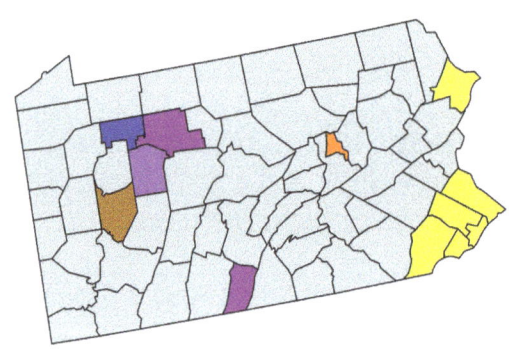

Real Estate Risk Map; G. Brian Davis, SparkRental,
ATTOM Data Solutions, Created with Datawrapper

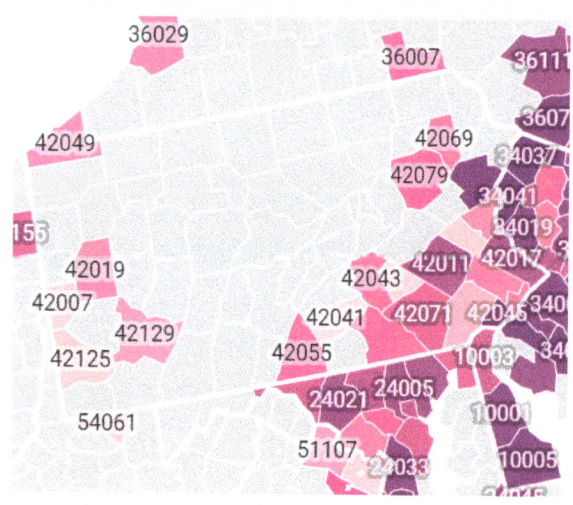

Density Risk Map
Source: US Census

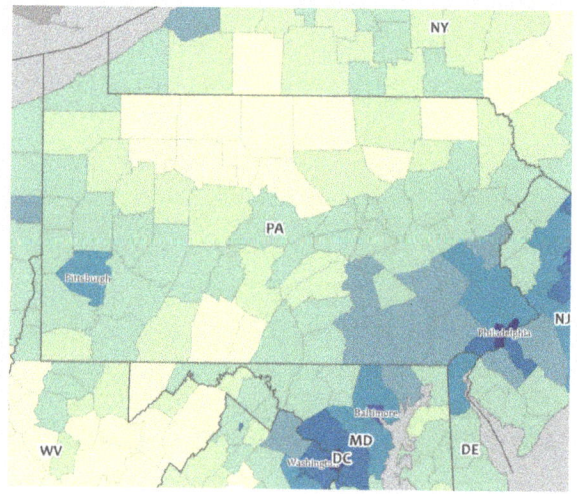

Poverty Risk Map
Source: US Census

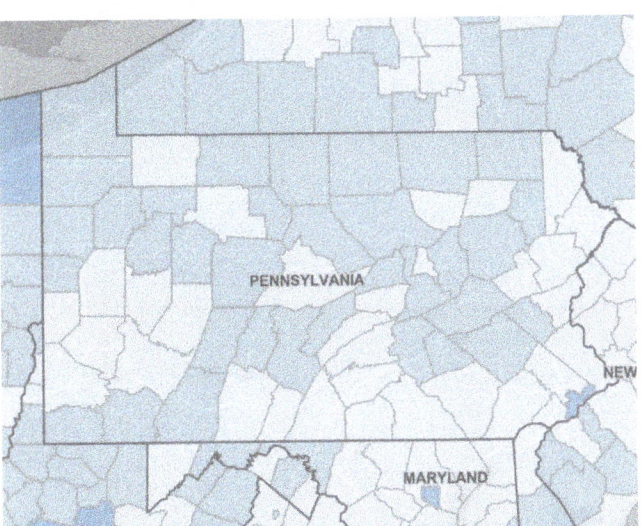

Unemployment Risk Map
Source: SparkRental & BLS

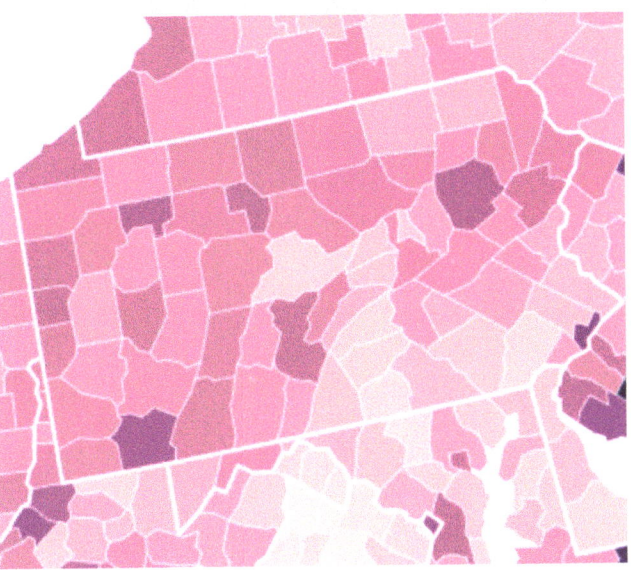

Economic & Crime Risk Map

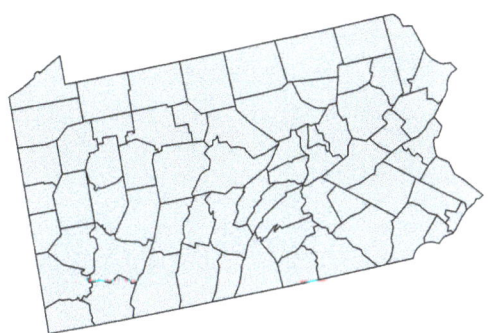

Main Summaries of Risk Maps

- The percentage of the White population is not desirable enough. Pennsylvania has a low percentage of White people in the East and near the Pittsburg area in the West. However, in the rest of the state, the percentage of White people in many counties is above 85%.
- Real estate risk is present in the West in the Pittsburg area, and it is very high in the East in the Philadelphia area. Pittsburg is not included in the top 50 largest metros in the United States. However, we know that Pittsburg is quite a large city.
- Very high real estate risk is in the Southeast and in Pittsburgh to some extent. The rest of the state does not have extreme real estate risk.
- High population density in the southeast and the Pittsburgh area.
- Unemployment rate is high in some counties.

Conclusions

Similar to New York City, the Philadelphia city area in the Southeast is subject to extremely high real estate risk. Also, that area is subject to metro risk and has a very high population density, which is terrible. The Pittsburgh city area in the West is also subject to the mentioned risks. The percentage of White people is low in Philadelphia and Pittsburgh. Nevertheless, there are many White counties. Among them, there are several that might be considered safe. However, it is tough to choose a cluster of safe counties. There might be a few safe ones but pinpointing them is difficult unless you have personally lived in the region.

State	New Jersey
Population	9,289 thous.
Land Area	7,354 sq mile
Density/mi2	1,263 people
Percent White	51.9%
Poverty Rate	9.7%
Unempl. Rate	3.7%

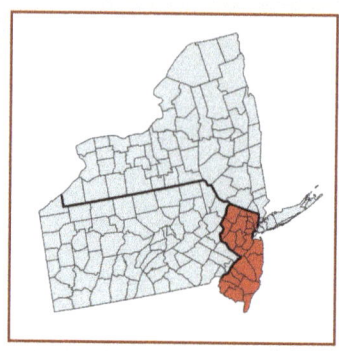

State Location Map
Created with Mapchart.net

New Jersey - Shaded Relief Image
Credit: National Elevation Dataset, compiled
by the U.S. Geological Survey
Visit the USGS at https://usgs.gov.

Racial Risk Map
Created with Mapchart.net, data—US Census

Industry Overconcentration Risk Map
Created with Mapchart.net, data—US Census

Real Estate Risk Map; G. Brian Davis, SparkRental,
ATTOM Data Solutions, Created with Datawrapper

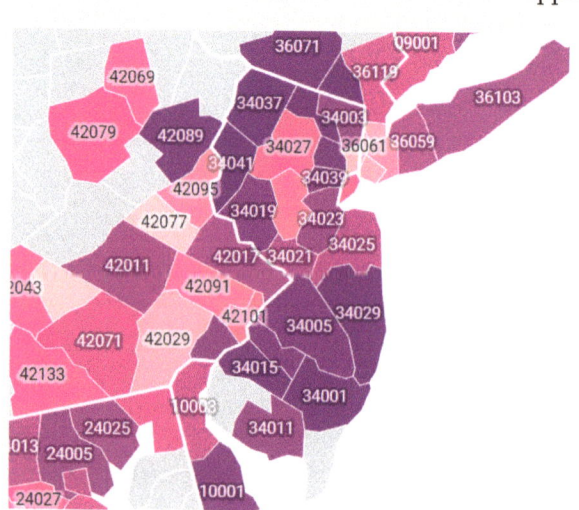

Density Risk Map
Source: US Census

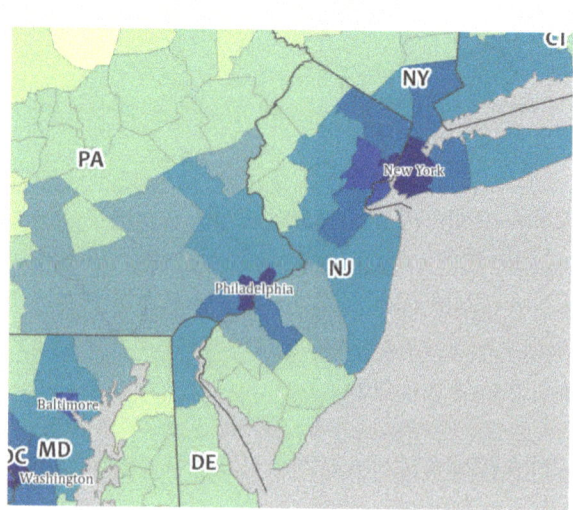

Poverty Risk Map
Source: US Census

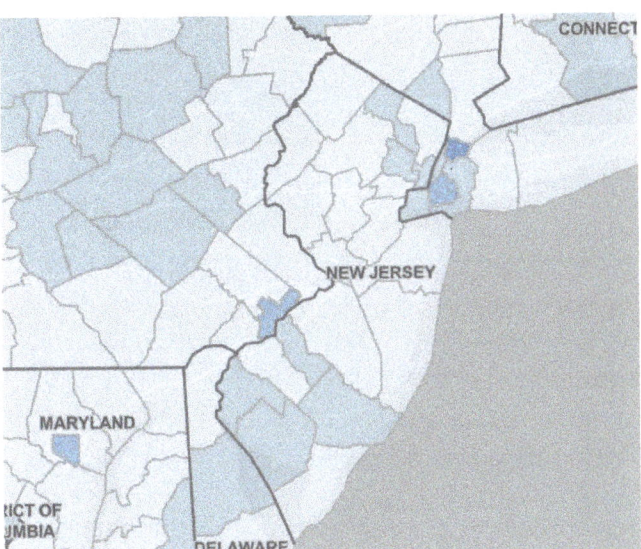

Unemployment Risk Map
Source: SparkRental & BLS

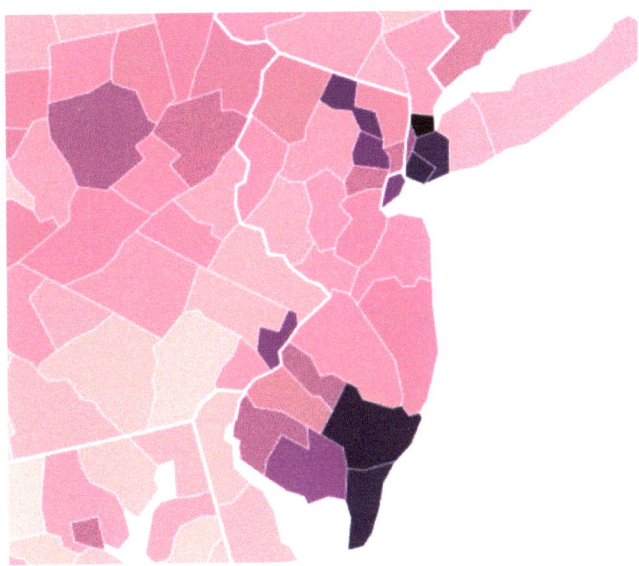

Economic & Crime Risk Map

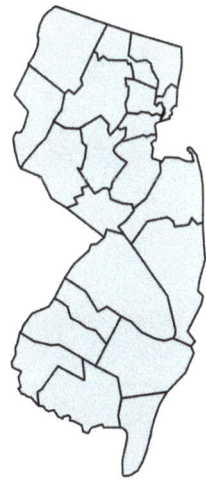

Main Summaries of Risk Maps

- The percentage of the White population is low.
- New Jersey is subject to very high metro-area risk.
- New Jersey is subject to extreme real estate risk.
- Very high population density.

Conclusions

There is no need for many words. The above facts indicate that New Jersey will be a terrible place in the coming depression regarding economic downturn and crime rate.

State	Michigan
Population	10,077 thous.
Land Area	56,539 sq mile
Density/mi2	178 people
Percent White	72.4%
Poverty Rate	13.1%
Unempl. Rate	4.2%

State Location Map
Created with Mapchart.net

Michigan - Shaded Relief Image
Credit: National Elevation Dataset, compiled
by the U.S. Geological Survey
Visit the USGS at https://usgs.gov.

Racial Risk Map
Created with Mapchart.net, data—US Census

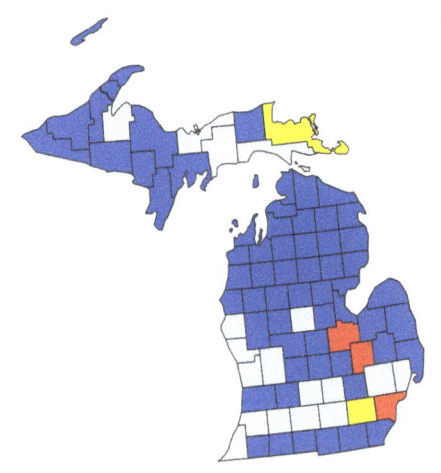

Industry Overconcentration Risk Map
Created with Mapchart.net, data—US Census

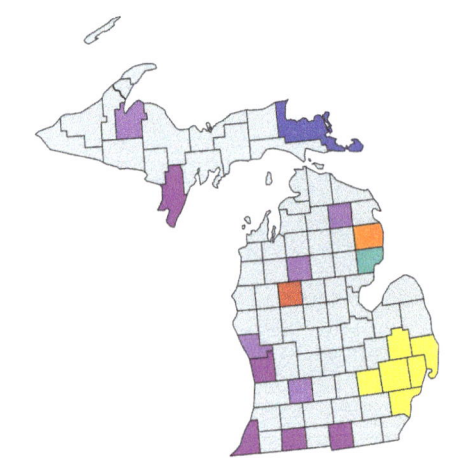

Real Estate Risk Map; G. Brian Davis, SparkRental,
ATTOM Data Solutions, Created with Datawrapper

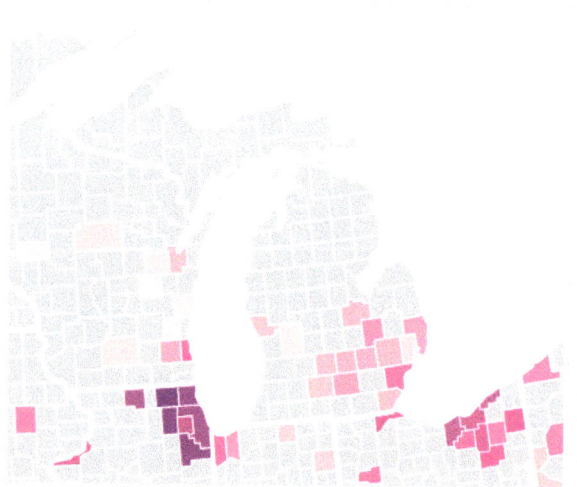

Density Risk Map
Source: US Census

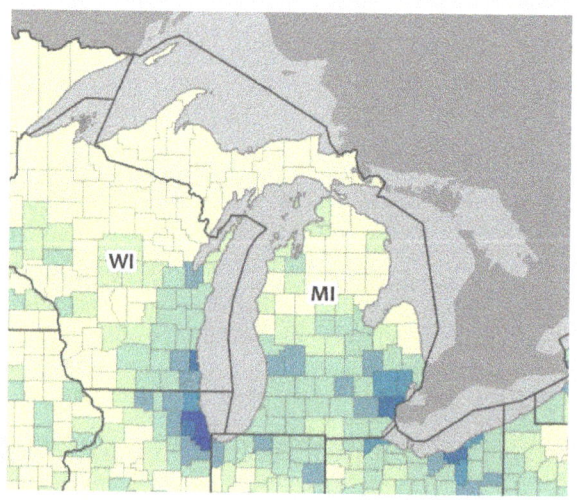

Poverty Risk Map
Source: US Census

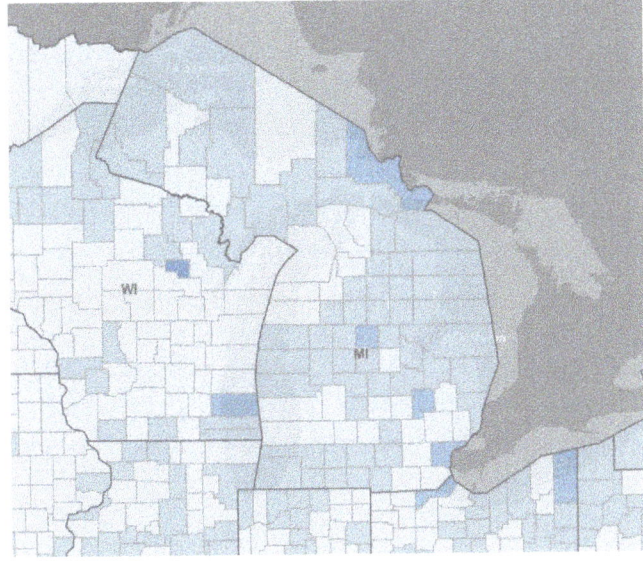

Unemployment Risk Map
Source: SparkRental & BLS

Economic & Crime Risk Map

Main Summaries of Risk Maps

- The percentage of the White population is not enough. It is very low in the Detroit area—the metro area marked as yellow on the industry overconcentration map.
- Michigan is subject to durable goods industry overconcentration.
- Metro area risk is present in the Detroit area.
- Southern regions in Michigan are subject to real estate risk.
- High population density in the Detroit area.
- Unemployment rate is high in the Detroit area and some northern counties.

Conclusions

Michigan has a high concentration of durable goods manufacturing, which is a very risky industry. The spillover effect will negatively affect cities and towns near those manufacturing centers. The Detroit area has a high metro density and a high unemployment rate. There is no need to remind one about Detroit after the 2008 crash. Because Michigan is an industrial manufacturing powerhouse, I am not willing to consider certain northern areas economically safe. Though these northern areas have a White population above 85%, there is still some overconcentration of various industries in the north. Poverty is not high in the north, but unemployment is high in several northern counties. Southern Michigan is risky both economically and in terms of crime. Overall, I consider Michigan a very risky state.

State	Ohio
Population	11,799 thous.
Land Area	40,861 sq mile
Density/mi2	288.8 people
Percent White	75.9%
Poverty Rate	13.3%
Unempl. Rate	4.0%

State Location Map
Created with Mapchart.net

Ohio - Shaded Relief Image
Credit: National Elevation Dataset, compiled
by the U.S. Geological Survey
Visit the USGS at https://usgs.gov.

Racial Risk Map
Created with Mapchart.net, data—US Census

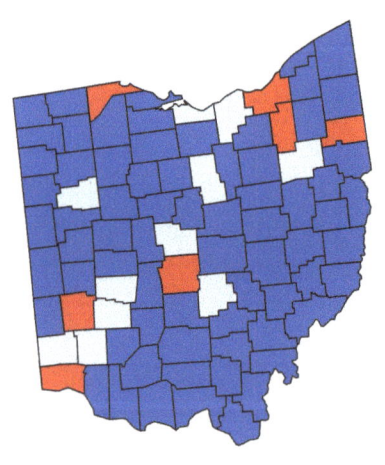

Industry Overconcentration Risk Map
Created with Mapchart.net, data—US Census

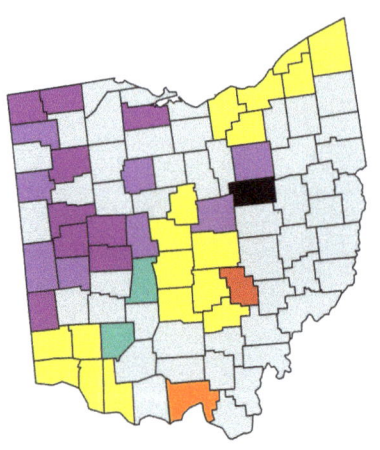

Real Estate Risk Map; G. Brian Davis, SparkRental,
ATTOM Data Solutions, Created with Datawrapper

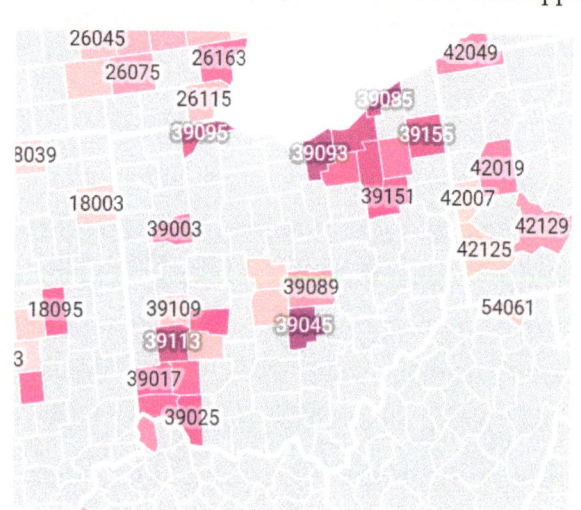

Density Risk Map
Source: US Census

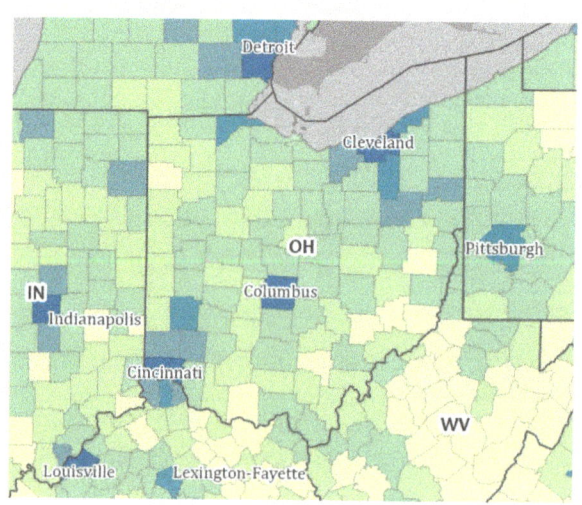

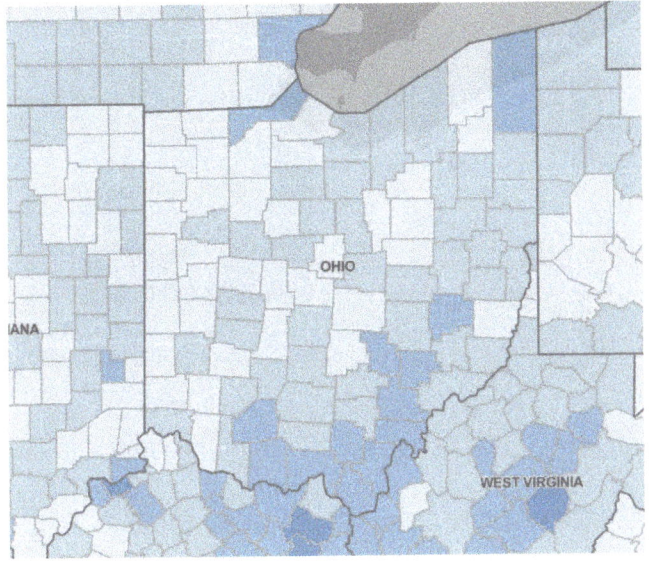

Poverty Risk Map
Source: US Census

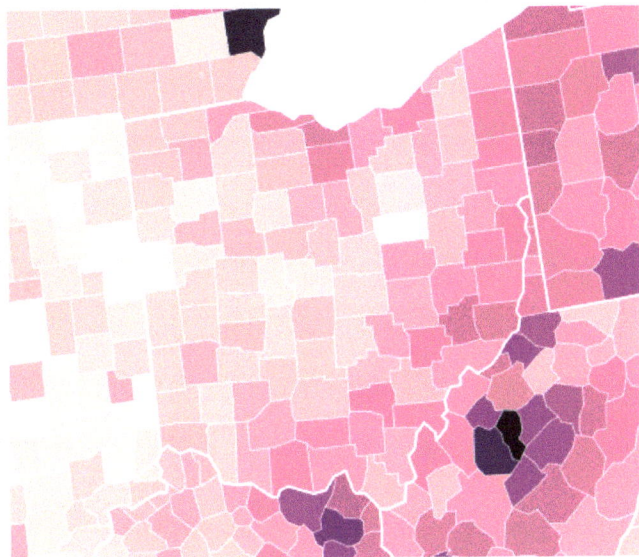

Unemployment Risk Map
Source: SparkRental & BLS

Economic & Crime Risk Map

Main Summaries of Risk Maps

- The percentage of the White population is not desirable enough.
- High durable goods industry overconcentration.
- Metro-area risk is present.
- Metro areas of Ohio are subject to real estate risk.

Conclusions

Ohio, like Michigan, is one of the powerhouses of durable goods manufacturing in the Rust Belt region. The downturn in the durable goods industry will be massive and affect most of the state. This risk overrides other issues and is the primary reason why this state is very risky. Ohio is economically a very risky state.

State	Indiana
Population	6,786 thous.
Land Area	35,826 sq mile
Density/mi2	189.4 people
Percent White	75.5%
Poverty Rate	12.3%
Unempl. Rate	3.0%

State Location Map
Created with Mapchart.net

Indiana - Shaded Relief Image
Credit: National Elevation Dataset, compiled
by the U.S. Geological Survey
Visit the USGS at https://usgs.gov.

Racial Risk Map
Created with Mapchart.net, data—US Census

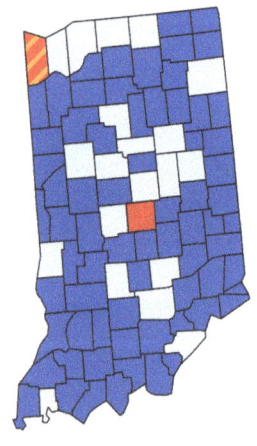

Industry Overconcentration Risk Map
Created with Mapchart.net, data—US Census

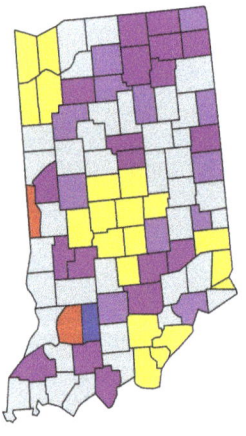

Real Estate Risk Map; G. Brian Davis, SparkRental,
ATTOM Data Solutions, Created with Datawrapper

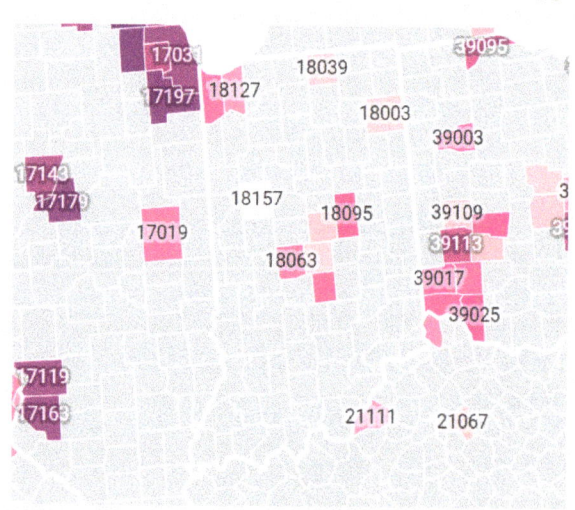

Density Risk Map
Source: US Census

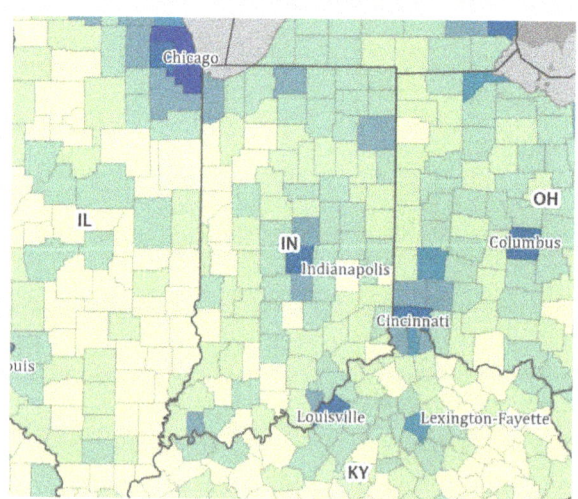

Poverty Risk Map
Source: US Census

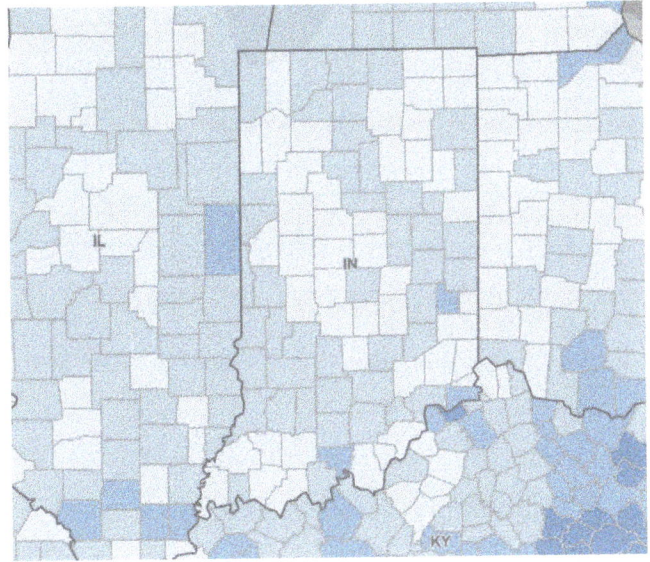

Unemployment Risk Map
Source: SparkRental & BLS

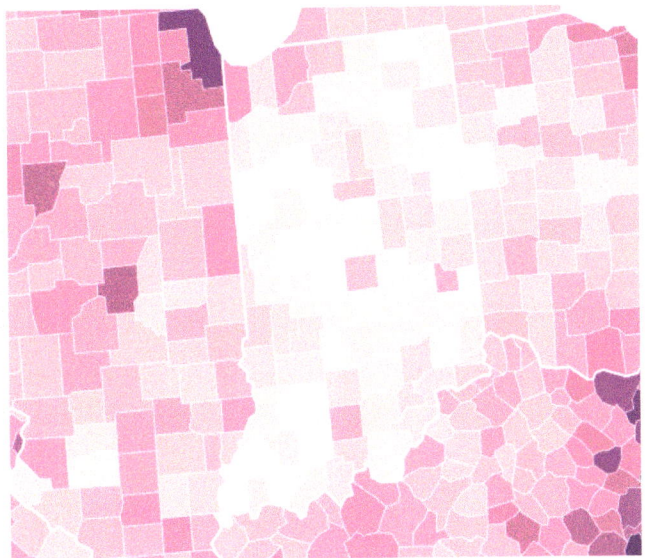

Economic & Crime Risk Map

Main Summaries of Risk Maps

- The percentage of the White population is not desirable enough.
- High durable goods industry overconcentration.
- Metro-area risk is present.

Conclusions

Indiana is a durable goods manufacturing powerhouse. The consequences of the decline of the durable goods industry will be very severe. This is an extremely serious issue, which means this state will be an epicenter of a manufacturing downturn. In general, Southern Michigan, Ohio, and Indiana share similar problems and are very economically risky states.

State	Wisconsin
Population	5,894 thous.
Land Area	54,158 sq mile
Density/mi2	108.8 people
Percent White	78.6%
Poverty Rate	10.7%
Unempl. Rate	2.9%

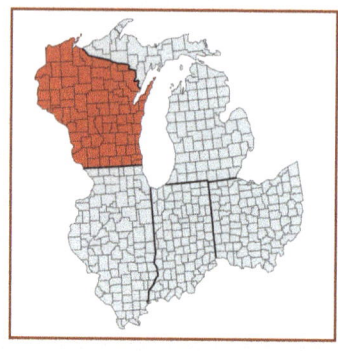

State Location Map
Created with Mapchart.net

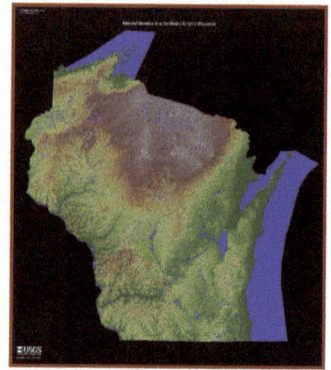

Wisconsin - Shaded Relief Image
Credit: National Elevation Dataset, compiled
by the U.S. Geological Survey
Visit the USGS at https://usgs.gov.

Racial Risk Map
Created with Mapchart.net, data—US Census

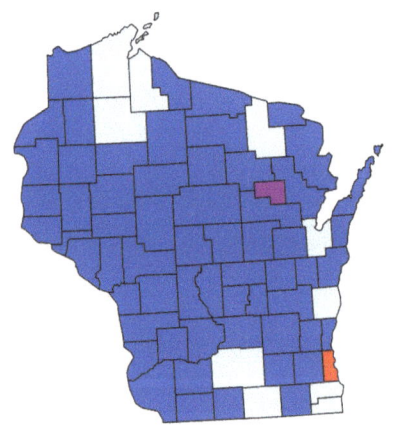

Industry Overconcentration Risk Map
Created with Mapchart.net, data—US Census

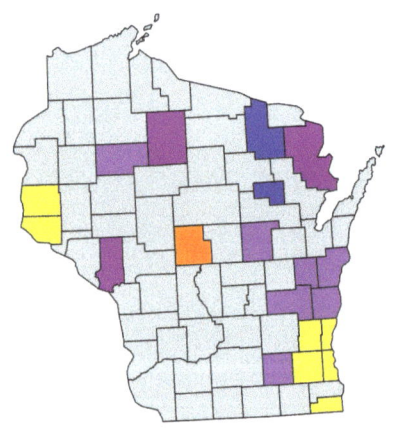

Real Estate Risk Map; G. Brian Davis, SparkRental,
ATTOM Data Solutions, Created with Datawrapper

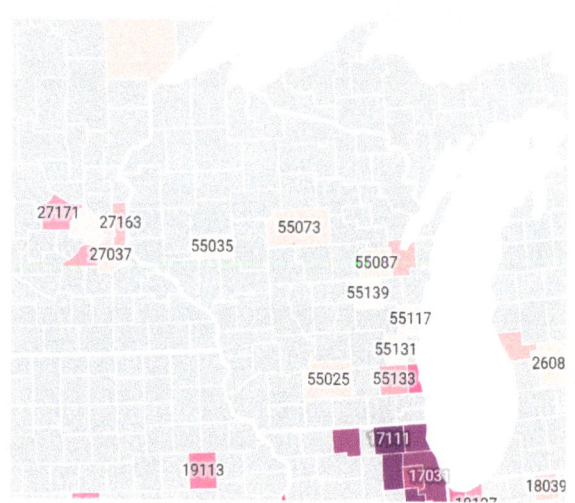

Density Risk Map
Source: US Census

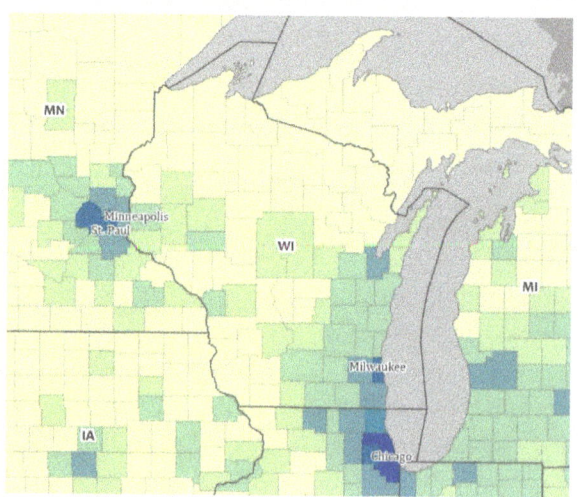

Poverty Risk Map
Source: US Census

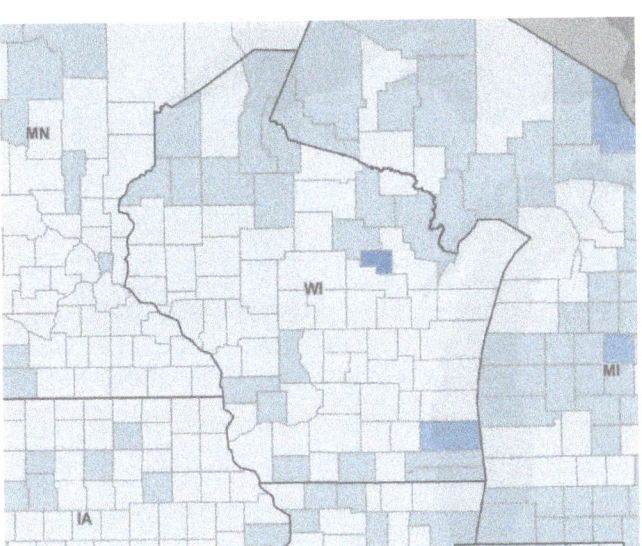

Unemployment Risk Map
Source: SparkRental & BLS

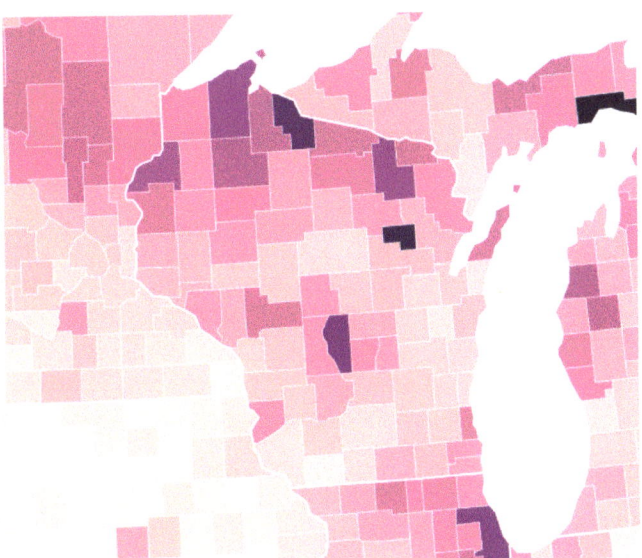

Economic & Crime Risk Map

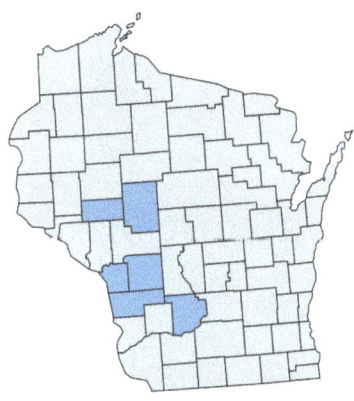

Main Summaries of Risk Maps

- The percentage of the White population is reasonable.
- Wisconsin is subject to durable goods overconcentration.
- Real estate risk is present in the Milwaukee area–Southeast.
- Unemployment rate is high in the north.

Conclusions

Wisconsin shares similar risks as Indiana, Ohio, and Michigan. They are all exposed to the durable goods industry. Counties with a high concentration of durable goods manufacturing are risky. However, the areas further away in Wisconsin are not highly exposed to the durable goods industry. They have a high percentage of the White population, good density and poverty rates. Also, there is no extreme exposure to real estate risk in those Western areas. Thus, certain Western counties and cities in Wisconsin will be less risky in an economic downturn. Perhaps, less risky in terms of crime.

State	Illinois
Population	12,813 thous.
Land Area	55,519 sq mile
Density/mi2	230.8 people
Percent White	58.3%
Poverty Rate	11.8%
Unempl. Rate	4.6%

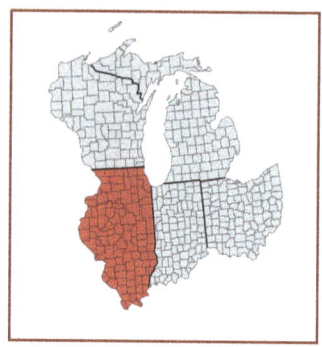

State Location Map
Created with Mapchart.net

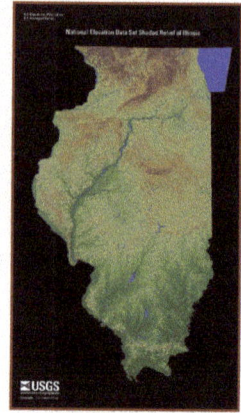

Illinois - Shaded Relief Image
Credit: National Elevation Dataset, compiled
by the U.S. Geological Survey
Visit the USGS at https://usgs.gov.

Racial Risk Map
Created with Mapchart.net, data—US Census

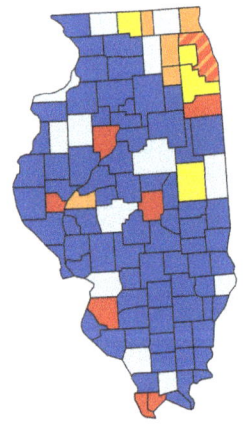

Industry Overconcentration Risk Map
Created with Mapchart.net, data—US Census

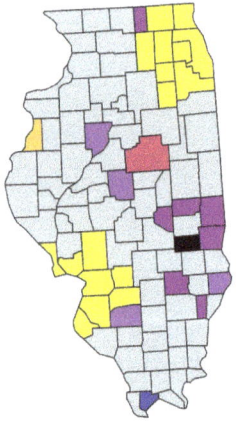

Real Estate Risk Map; G. Brian Davis, SparkRental,
ATTOM Data Solutions, Created with Datawrapper

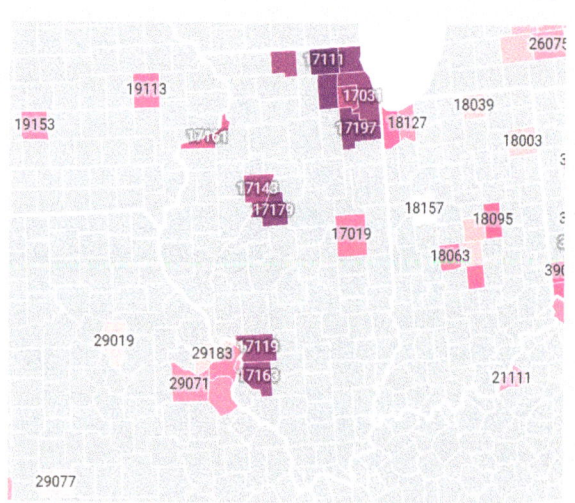

Density Risk Map
Source: US Census

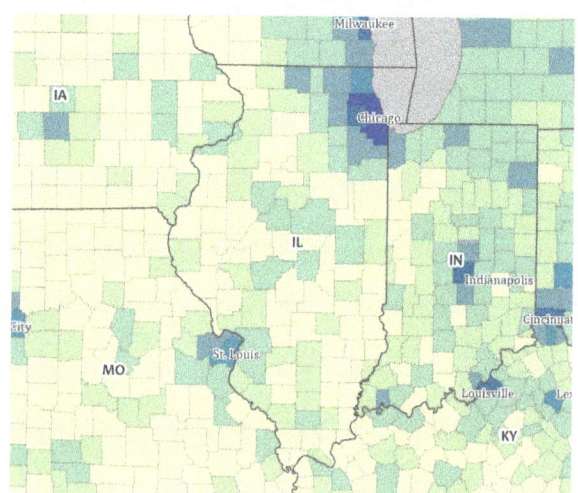

Poverty Risk Map
Source: US Census

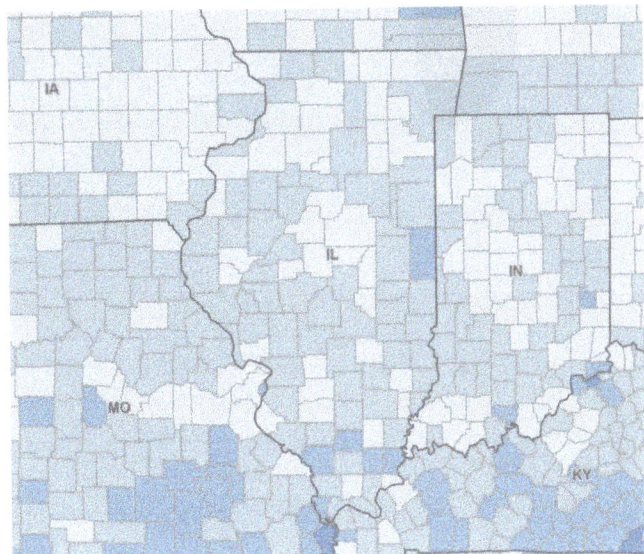

Unemployment Risk Map
Source: SparkRental & BLS

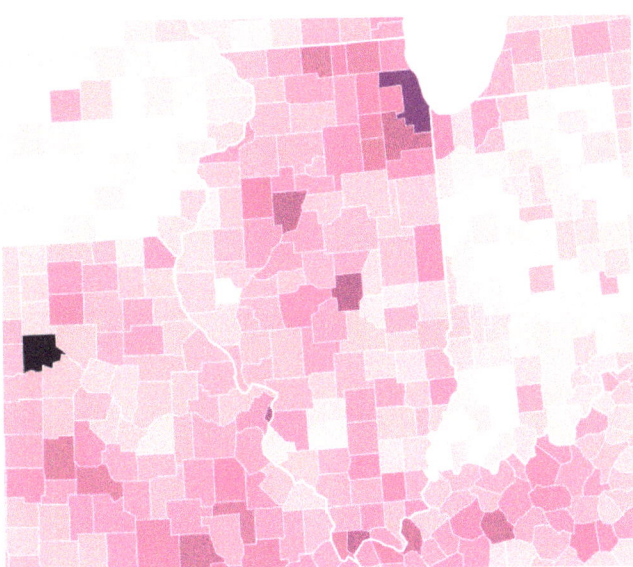

Economic & Crime Risk Map

Main Summaries of Risk Maps

- The percentage of the White population is low.
- Eastern Illinois has durable goods industry overconcentration
- St. Louis and Chicago areas are subject to metro area risk.
- Extreme real estate risk is present in Chicago, and it is high in the St. Louis area.

Conclusions

The Chicago area in the north and the St. Louis area in the southwest have a very high percentage of Black population and very high crime rates. What will happen in the depression if high crime rates are already unbearable in some Chicago and St. Louis regions? Finding safe places in this state is challenging because areas adjacent to Chicago and St. Louis are also subject to metro risk. There might be a few individual counties, but regionally speaking, North and South are to be avoided, the East side has durable goods manufacturing overconcentration, and the West side does not seem riskless either.

State	Maryland
Population	6,177 thous.
Land Area	9,707 sq mile
Density/mi2	636.1 people
Percent White	47.2%
Poverty Rate	9.3%
Unempl. Rate	3.2%

State Location Map
Created with Mapchart.net

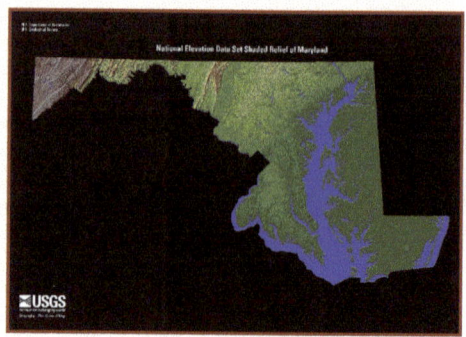

Maryland - Shaded Relief Image
Credit: National Elevation Dataset, compiled
by the U.S. Geological Survey
Visit the USGS at https://usgs.gov.

Racial Risk Map
Created with Mapchart.net, data—US Census

Industry Overconcentration Risk Map
Created with Mapchart.net, data—US Census

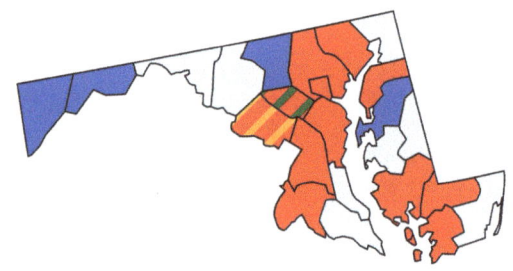

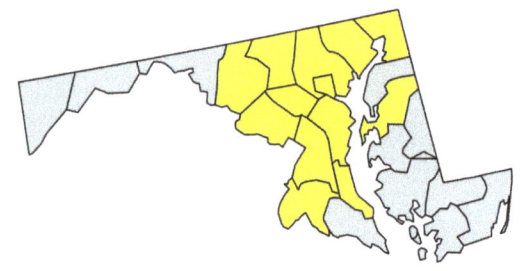

Real Estate Risk Map; G. Brian Davis, SparkRental,
ATTOM Data Solutions, Created with Datawrapper

Density Risk Map
Source: US Census

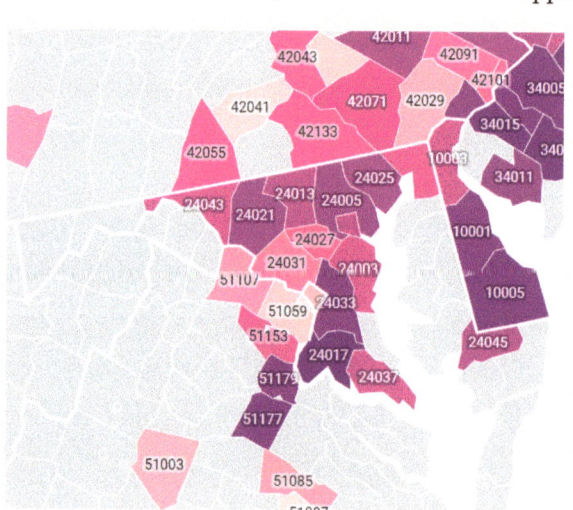

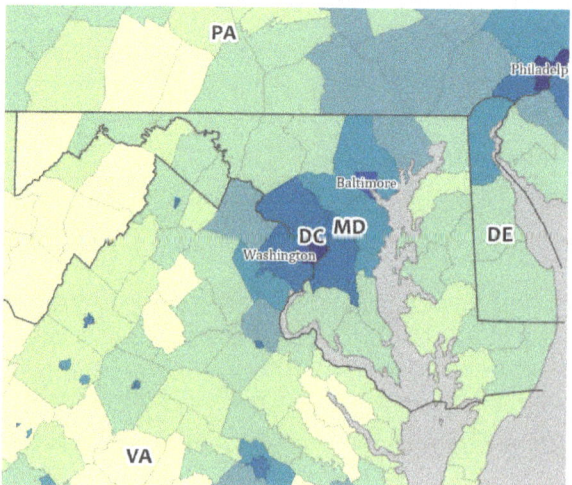

Poverty Risk Map
Source: US Census

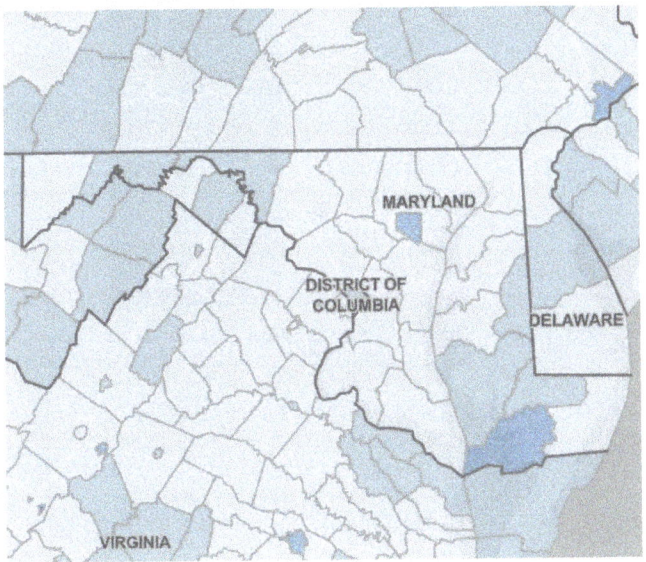

Unemployment Risk Map
Source: SparkRental & BLS

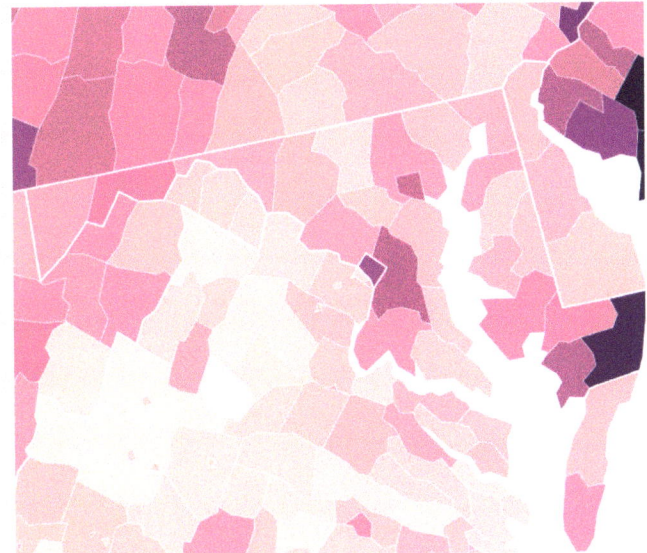

Economic & Crime Risk Map

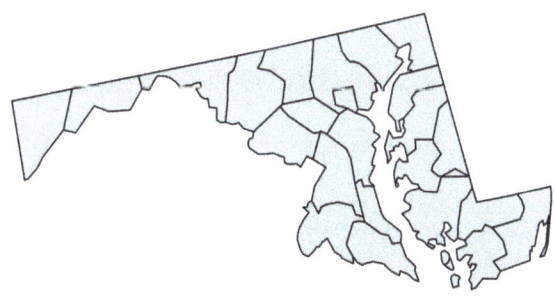

Main Summaries of Risk Maps

- The percentage of the White population is very low.
- Maryland is subject to very high metro-area risk.
- Maryland is subject to extreme real estate risk.
- Very high population density.

Conclusions

Maryland is very similar to New Jersey in terms of risks. Not many words are needed. Maryland will be very hard hit in the coming depression both in terms of economy and rise in violent crime.

State	Delaware
Population	990 thous.
Land Area	1,949 sq mile
Density/mi2	508 people
Percent White	58.6%
Poverty Rate	11.1%
Unempl. Rate	4.5%

State Location Map
Created with Mapchart.net

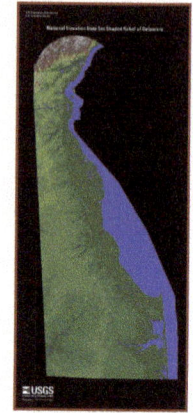

Delaware - Shaded Relief Image
Credit: National Elevation Dataset, compiled
by the U.S. Geological Survey
Visit the USGS at https://usgs.gov.

Racial Risk Map
Created with Mapchart.net, data—US Census

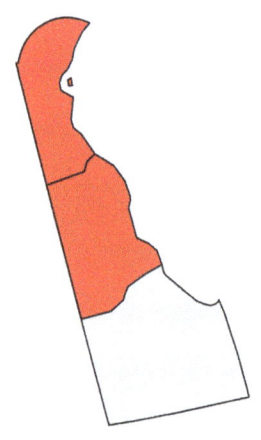

Industry Overconcentration Risk Map
Created with Mapchart.net, data—US Census

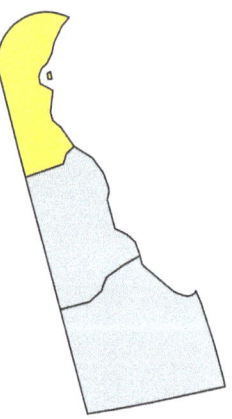

Real Estate Risk Map; G. Brian Davis, SparkRental,
ATTOM Data Solutions, Created with Datawrapper

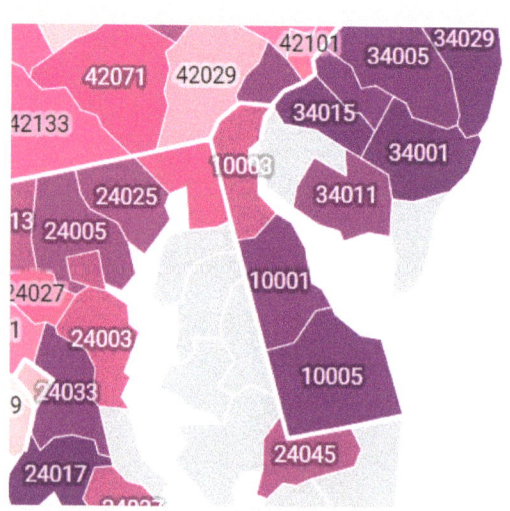

Density Risk Map
Source: US Census

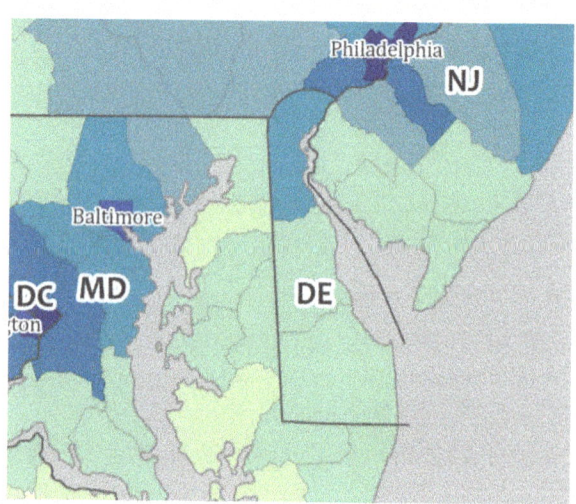

Poverty Risk Map
Source: US Census

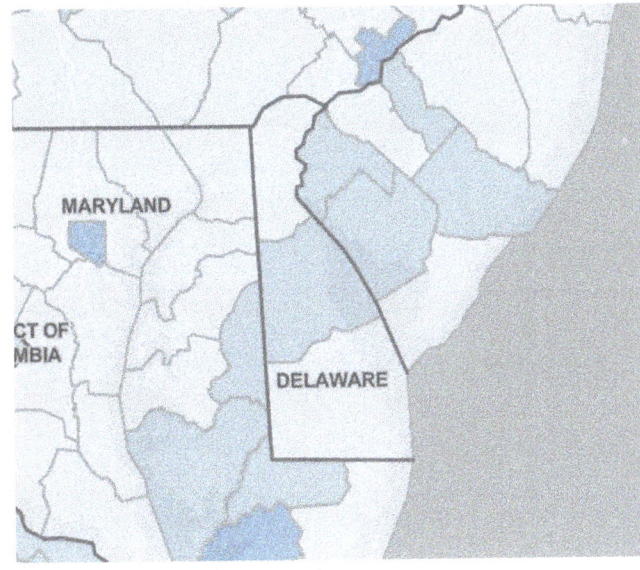

Unemployment Risk Map
Source: SparkRental & BLS

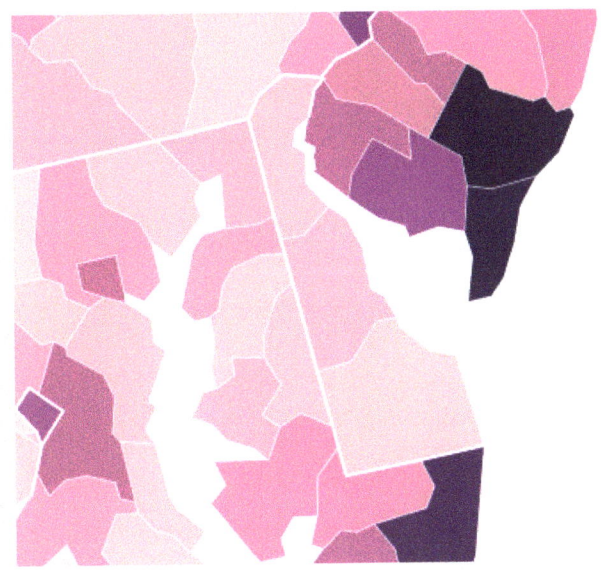

Economic & Crime Risk Map

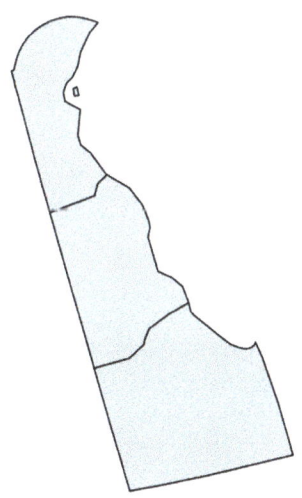

Main Summaries of Risk Maps

- The percentage of the White population is low.
- Delaware is subject to extreme real estate risk.
- High population density.

Conclusions

Delaware's conclusions are similar to Maryland's and New Jersey's. Please see their descriptions for comparison. This is not surprising because Delaware is located nearby. Delaware is a very risky state in the coming depression in terms of economy and rise in violent crime.

State	Virginia
Population	8,631 thous.
Land Area	39,490 sq mile
Density/mi2	218.6 people
Percent White	58.6%
Poverty Rate	10.0%
Unempl. Rate	2.9%

State Location Map
Created with Mapchart.net

Virginia - Shaded Relief Image
Credit: National Elevation Dataset, compiled
by the U.S. Geological Survey
Visit the USGS at https://usgs.gov.

Racial Risk Map
Created with Mapchart.net, data—US Census

Industry Overconcentration Risk Map
Created with Mapchart.net, data—US Census

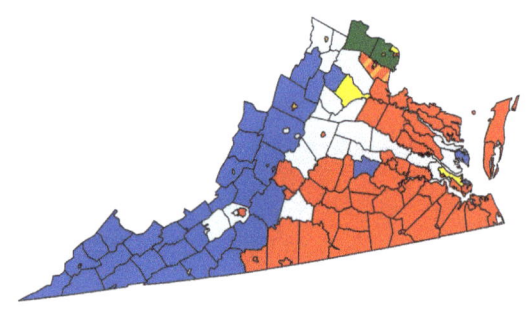

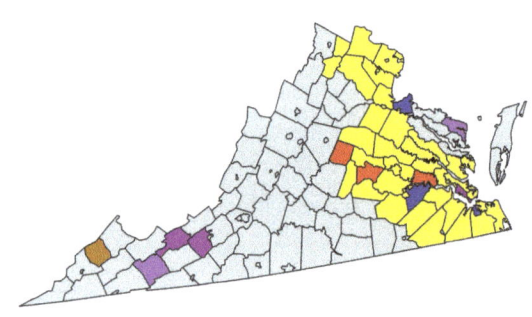

Real Estate Risk Map; G. Brian Davis, SparkRental,
ATTOM Data Solutions, Created with Datawrapper

Density Risk Map
Source: US Census

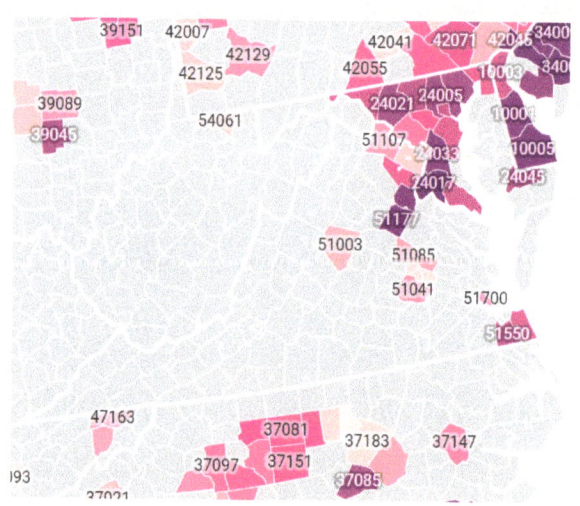

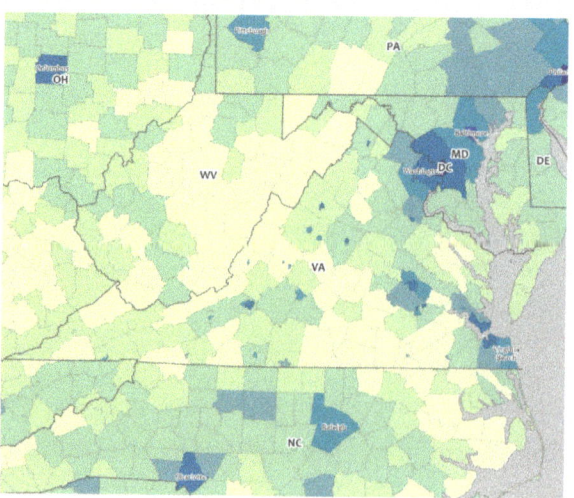

Poverty Risk Map
Source: US Census

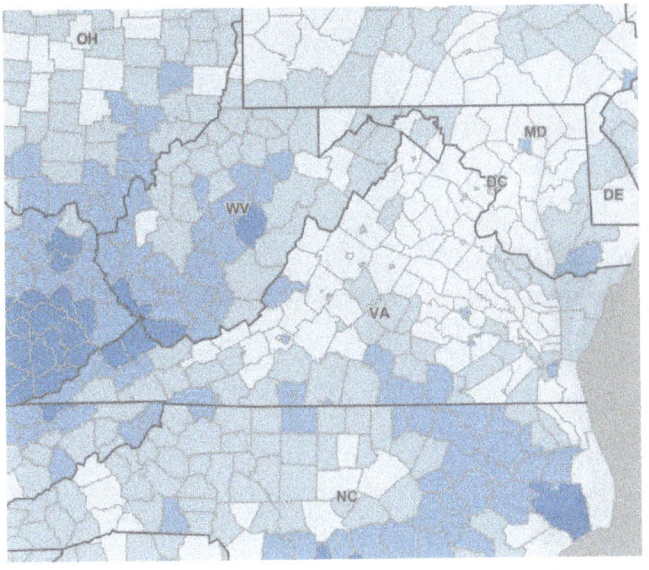

Unemployment Risk Map
Source: SparkRental & BLS

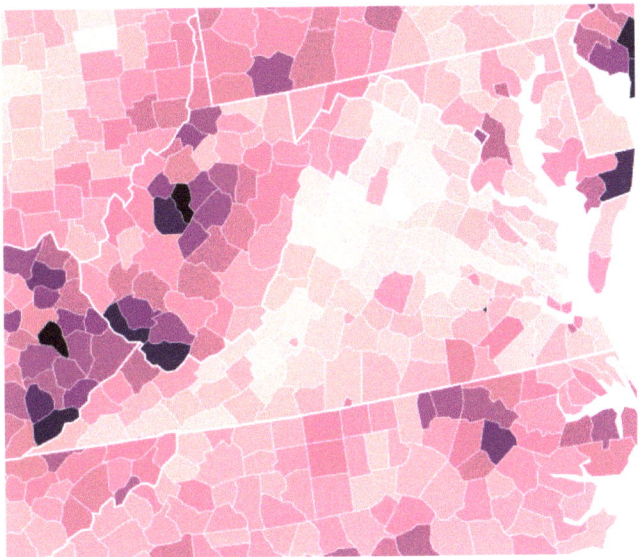

Economic & Crime Risk Map

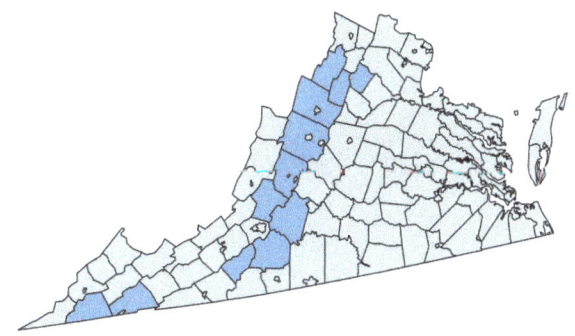

Main Summaries of Risk Maps

- On the East side, the percentage of the White population is very low. On the West side, it is good.
- Metro-area risk is present on the East side.
- Real estate risk is present in the East.
- Not very high poverty and unemployment rates.

Conclusions

Eastern Virginia must be avoided as the percentage of Blacks is high there, and therefore, the predicted crime rate will be high, too. The West is predominantly White and more rural. No extreme real estate risk or industry overconcentration. Unemployment and poverty are not high, so certain counties in the West are safer than East ones in terms of economic downturn and rise in crime. Make sure to avoid mill towns and small factory towns.

State	West Virginia
Population	1,794 thous.
Land Area	24,038 sq mile
Density/mi2	74.6 people
Percent White	89.1%
Poverty Rate	16.8%
Unempl. Rate	3.9%

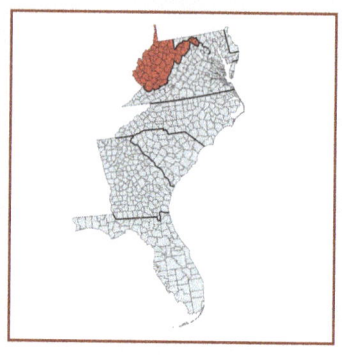

State Location Map
Created with Mapchart.net

West Virginia - Shaded Relief Image
Credit: National Elevation Dataset, compiled
by the U.S. Geological Survey
Visit the USGS at https://usgs.gov.

Racial Risk Map
Created with Mapchart.net, data—US Census

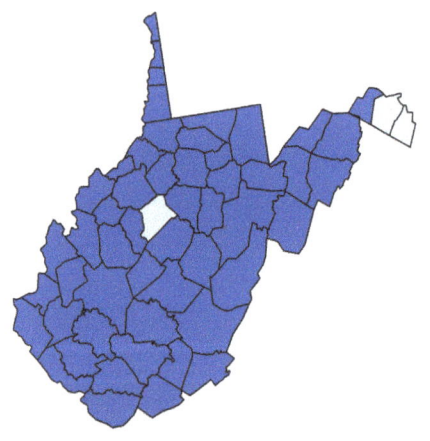

Industry Overconcentration Risk Map
Created with Mapchart.net, data—US Census

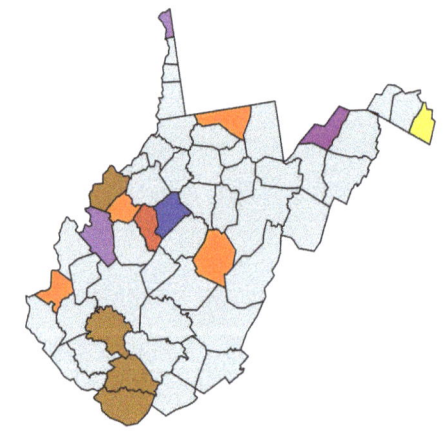

Real Estate Risk Map; G. Brian Davis, SparkRental,
ATTOM Data Solutions, Created with Datawrapper

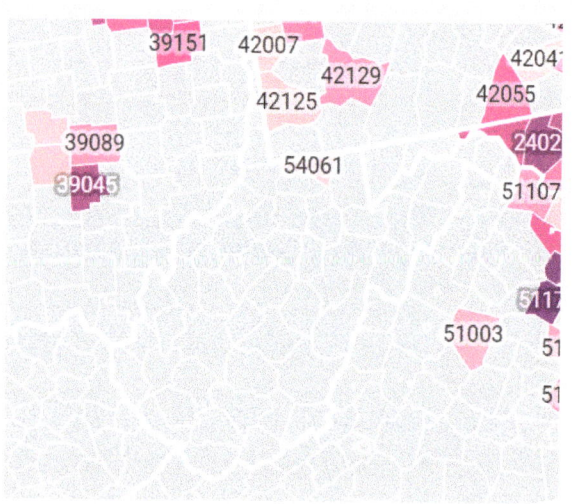

Density Risk Map
Source: US Census

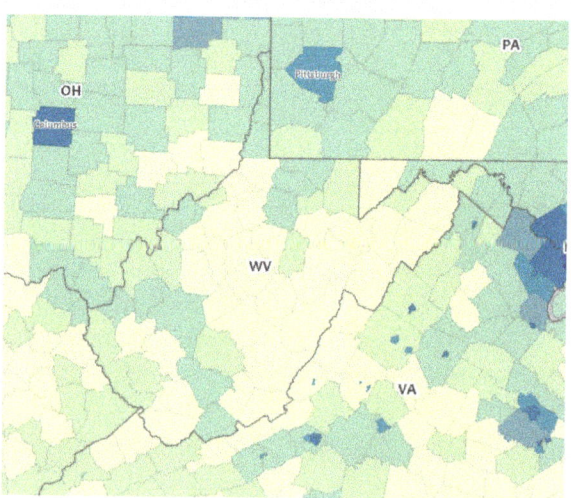

Poverty Risk Map
Source: US Census

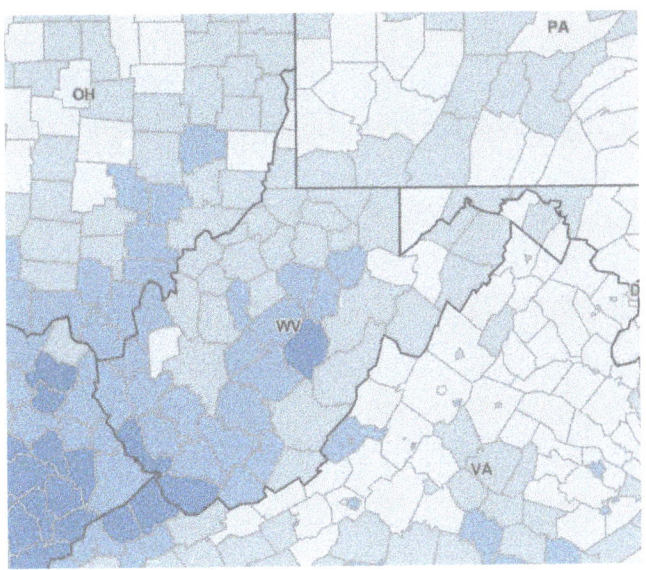

Unemployment Risk Map
Source: SparkRental & BLS

Economic & Crime Risk Map

Main Summaries of Risk Maps

- The percentage of the White population is very high.
- Industry overconcentration is present.
- High poverty rate.

Conclusions

The Appalachian region, which includes West Virginia and a few other states, has a high percentage of White people. This is a significant reason for choosing these states. However, West Virginia and the Appalachian region are quite poor, and some locations have a high unemployment rate. Some counties are also exposed to the mining industry, which will suffer severely during the depression. One could say that the state is already poor, so it has relatively less risk from the downturn, as there is no room to fall. I suspect there is, and if unemployment grows even further in some of its highly unemployed counties, it will be highly undesirable for life. Of course, there are a few reasonable locations, but I would rather avoid pinpointing them.

State	North Carolina
Population	10,439 thous.
Land Area	48,618 sq mile
Density/mi2	214.7 people
Percent White	60.5%
Poverty Rate	13.3%
Unempl. Rate	3.7%

State Location Map
Created with Mapchart.net

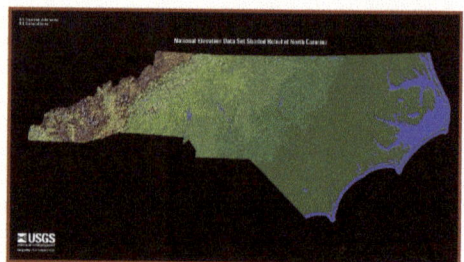

North Carolina - Shaded Relief Image
Credit: National Elevation Dataset, compiled
by the U.S. Geological Survey
Visit the USGS at https://usgs.gov.

Racial Risk Map
Created with Mapchart.net, data—US Census

Industry Overconcentration Risk Map
Created with Mapchart.net, data—US Census

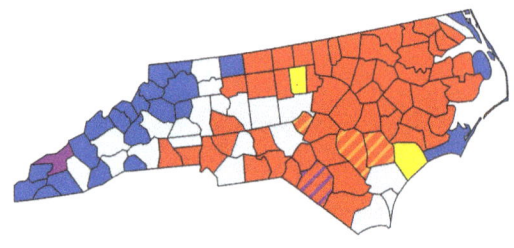

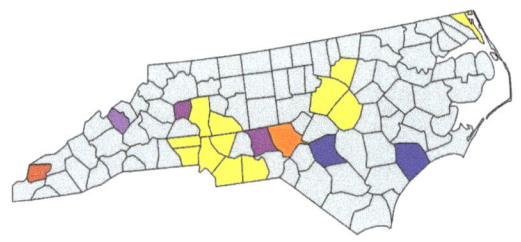

Real Estate Risk Map; G. Brian Davis, SparkRental,
ATTOM Data Solutions, Created with Datawrapper

Density Risk Map
Source: US Census

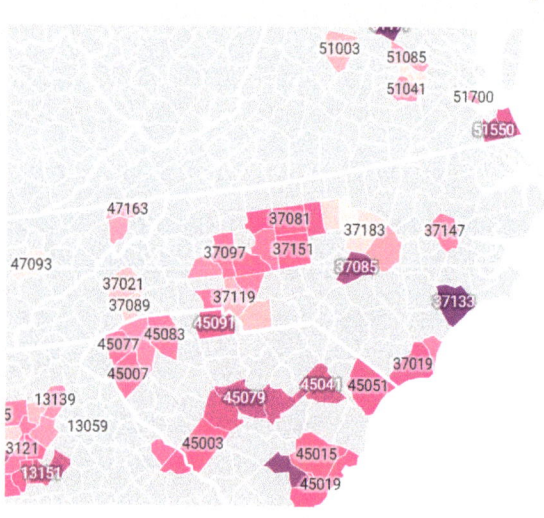

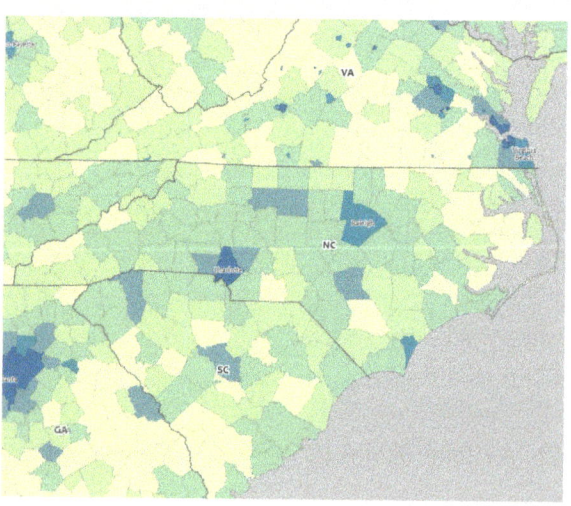

Poverty Risk Map
Source: US Census

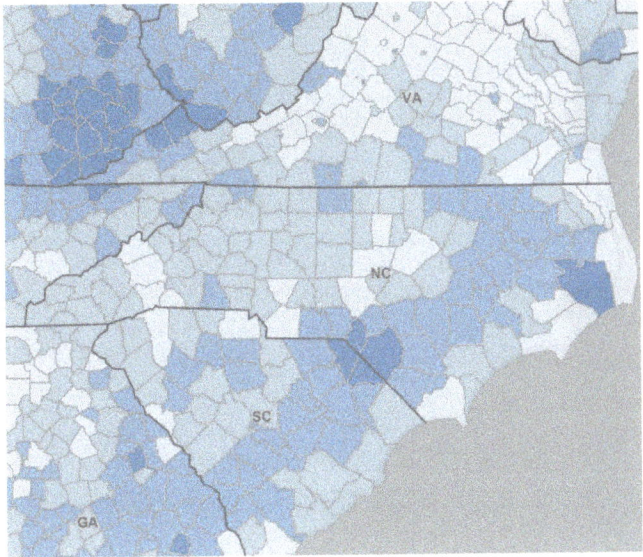

Unemployment Risk Map
Source: SparkRental & BLS

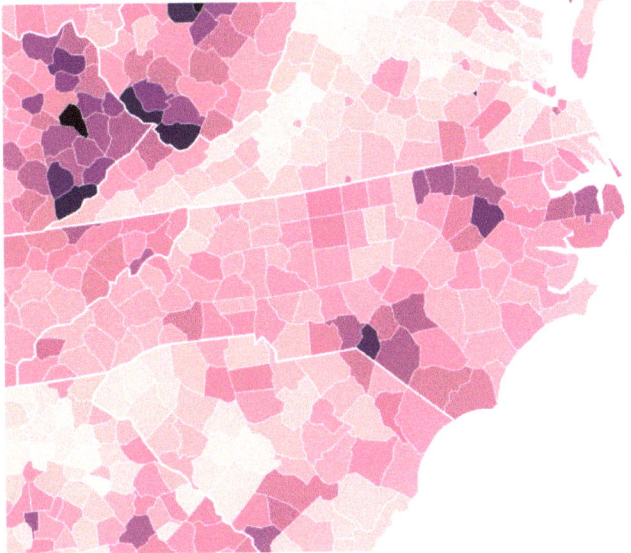

Economic & Crime Risk Map

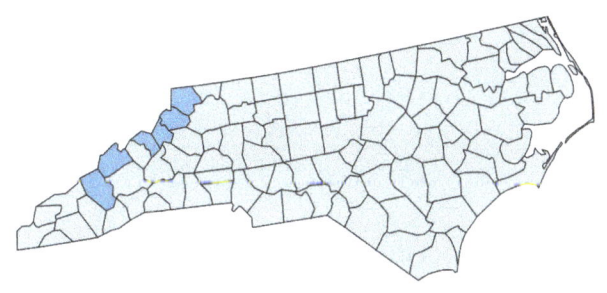

Main Summaries of Risk Maps

- Except for a small region with a predominantly White population in the West, the state overall has poor race demographics.
- The very West side of North Carolina does not have extreme real estate risk, poverty rate, or unemployment rate.

Conclusions

A large portion of North Carolina has a high Black population. Thus, most of North Carolina is risky in terms of future crime. There is no point looking further than that. There are few counties in the West that I would consider less risky, especially in terms of crime, because they are predominantly White. These are relatively rural regions without significant issues. Some of them, similar to those Western counties in Virginia, located right above North Carolina, could be safe spaces from the coming rise in crime.

State	South Carolina
Population	5,118 thous.
Land Area	30,061 sq mile
Density/mi2	170.2 people
Percent White	62.1%
Poverty Rate	14.4%
Unempl. Rate	3.2%

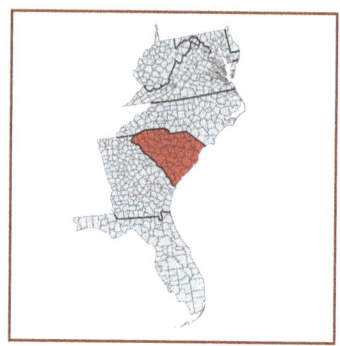

State Location Map
Created with Mapchart.net

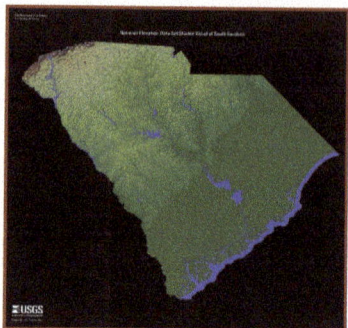

South Carolina - Shaded Relief Image
Credit: National Elevation Dataset, compiled
by the U.S. Geological Survey
Visit the USGS at https://usgs.gov.

Racial Risk Map
Created with Mapchart.net, data—US Census

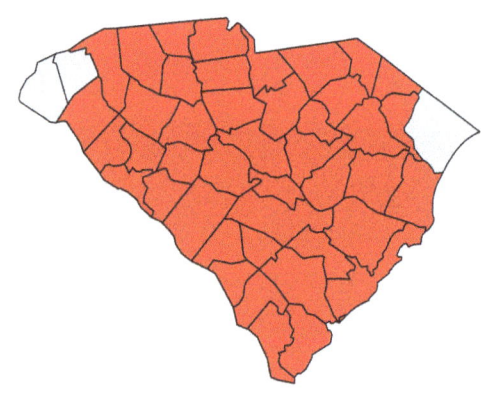

Industry Overconcentration Risk Map
Created with Mapchart.net, data—US Census

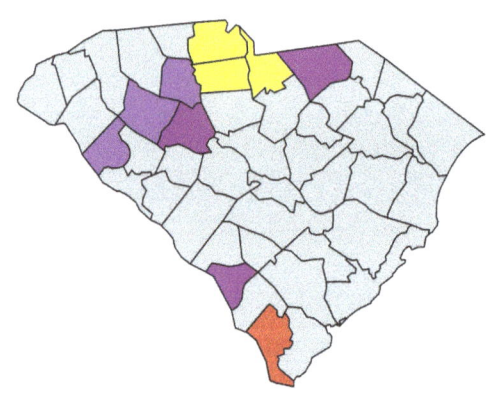

Real Estate Risk Map; G. Brian Davis, SparkRental,
ATTOM Data Solutions, Created with Datawrapper

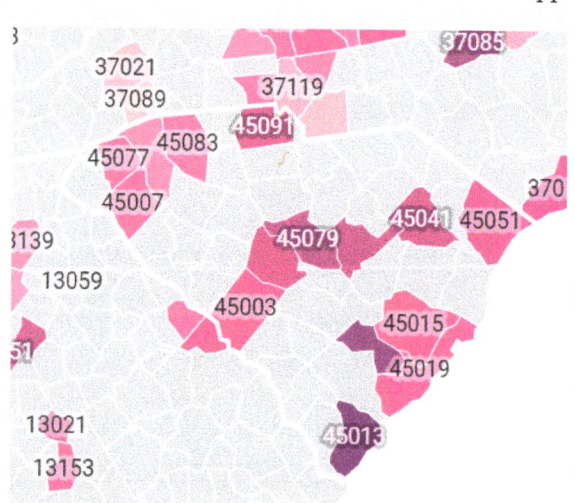

Density Risk Map
Source: US Census

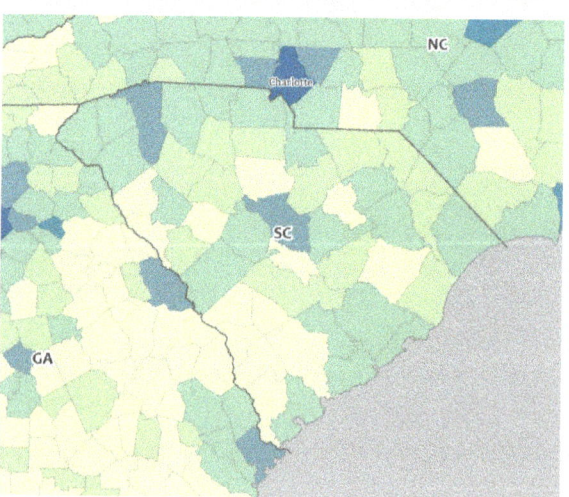

Poverty Risk Map
Source: US Census

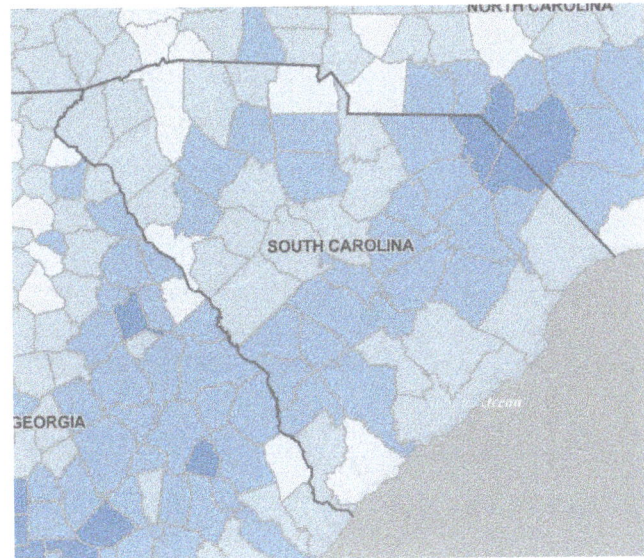

Unemployment Risk Map
Source: SparkRental & BLS

Economic & Crime Risk Map

Main Summaries of Risk Maps

- Most of the state has a high Black population, which is a must-avoid risk.

Conclusions

There is no point researching this state further than just looking at its race demographics picture. Everything is very straightforward. The state is very risky in terms of crime risk. This is a common issue in the South, which is why the South has a high crime rate.

State	Georgia
Population	10,712 thous.
Land Area	57,513 sq mile
Density/mi2	185.6 people
Percent White	50.1%
Poverty Rate	13.5%
Unempl. Rate	3.0%

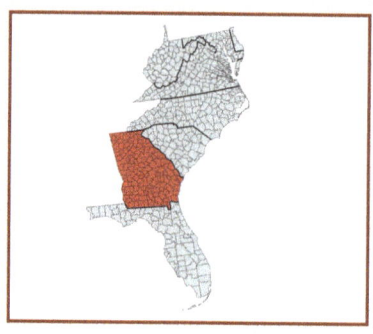

State Location Map
Created with Mapchart.net

Georgia - Shaded Relief Image
Credit: National Elevation Dataset, compiled
by the U.S. Geological Survey
Visit the USGS at https://usgs.gov.

Racial Risk Map
Created with Mapchart.net, data—US Census

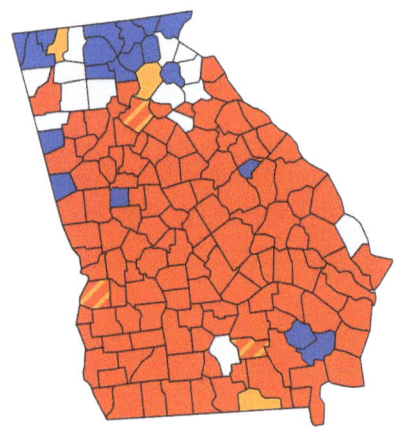

Industry Overconcentration Risk Map
Created with Mapchart.net, data—US Census

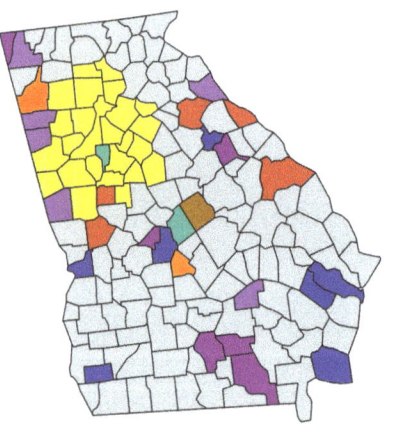

Real Estate Risk Map; G. Brian Davis, SparkRental,
ATTOM Data Solutions, Created with Datawrapper

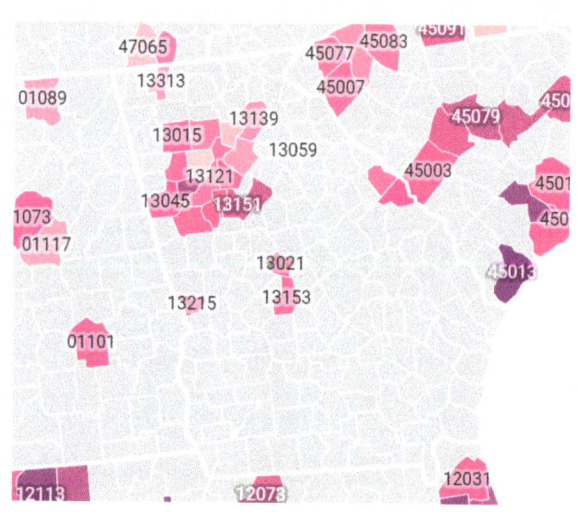

Density Risk Map
Source: US Census

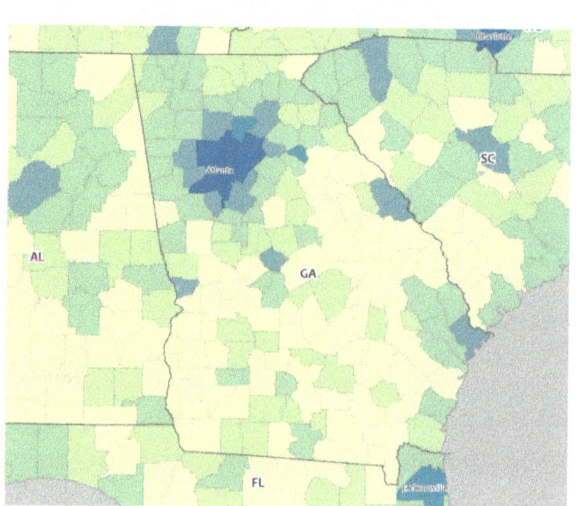

Poverty Risk Map
Source: US Census

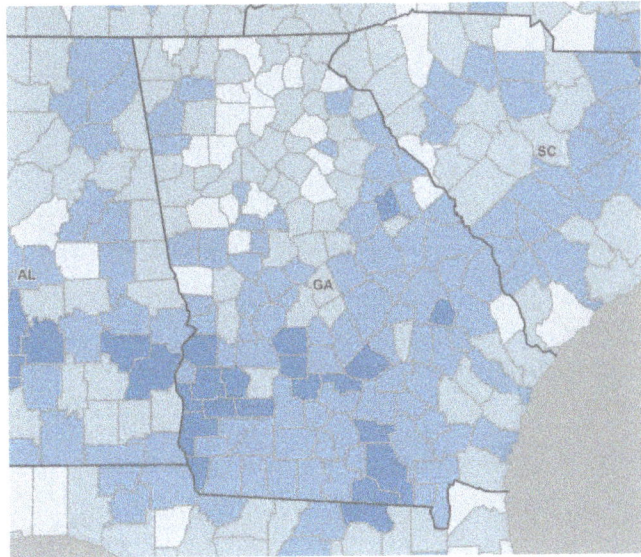

Unemployment Risk Map
Source: SparkRental & BLS

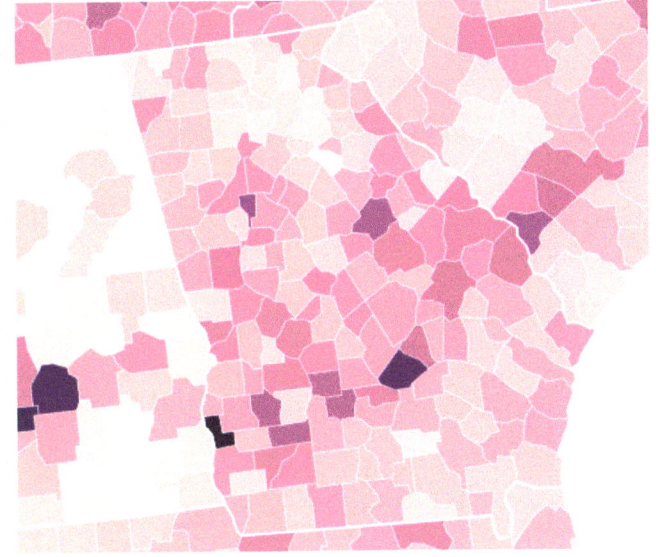

Economic & Crime Risk Map

Main Summaries of Risk Maps

- Most of the state has a high Black population, which is a must-avoid risk.

Conclusions

The conclusion is identical to the one for South Carolina: "There is no point researching this state further than just looking at its race demographics picture. Everything is very straightforward. The state is very risky in terms of crime risk. This is a common issue in the South, which is why the South has a high crime rate."

State	Florida
Population	21,538 thous.
Land Area	53,625 sq mile
Density/mi2	401.4 people
Percent White	51.5%
Poverty Rate	12.9%
Unempl. Rate	2.9%

State Location Map
Created with Mapchart.net

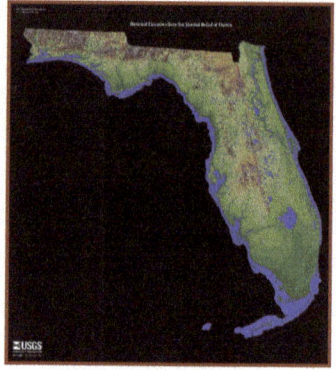

Florida - Shaded Relief Image
Credit: National Elevation Dataset, compiled
by the U.S. Geological Survey
Visit the USGS at https://usgs.gov.

Racial Risk Map
Created with Mapchart.net, data—US Census

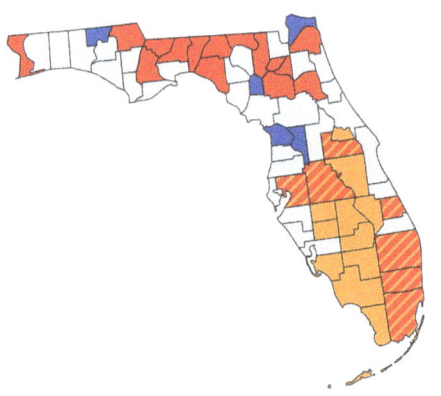

Industry Overconcentration Risk Map
Created with Mapchart.net, data—US Census

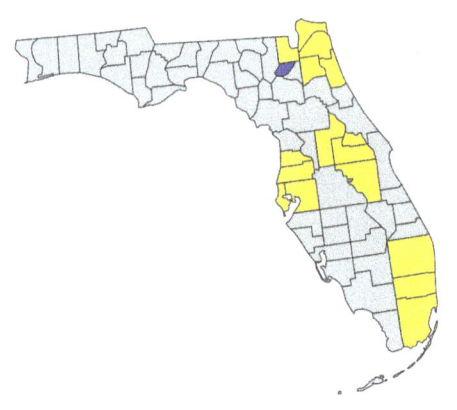

Real Estate Risk Map; G. Brian Davis, SparkRental,
ATTOM Data Solutions, Created with Datawrapper

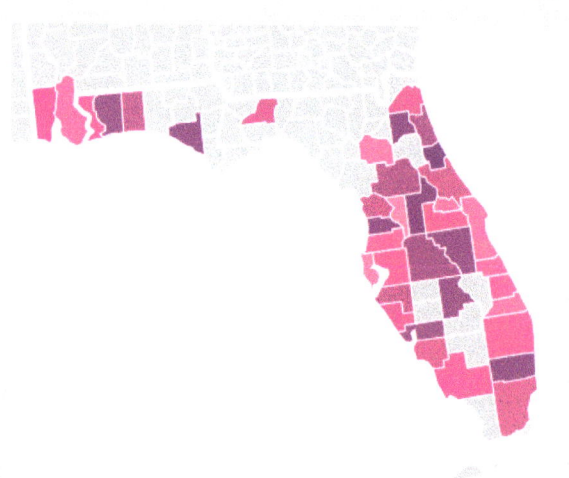

Density Risk Map
Source: US Census

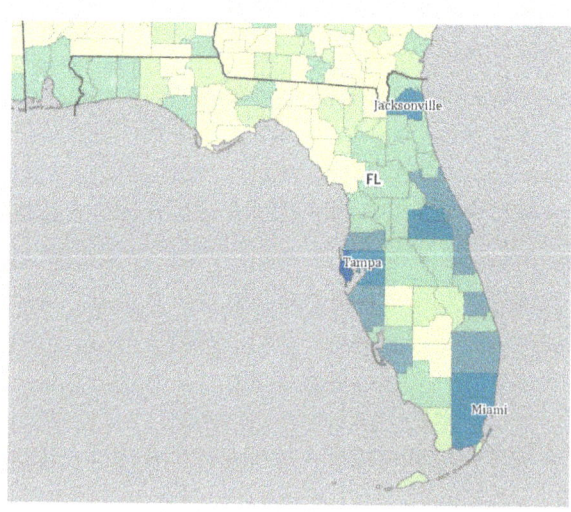

Poverty Risk Map
Source: US Census

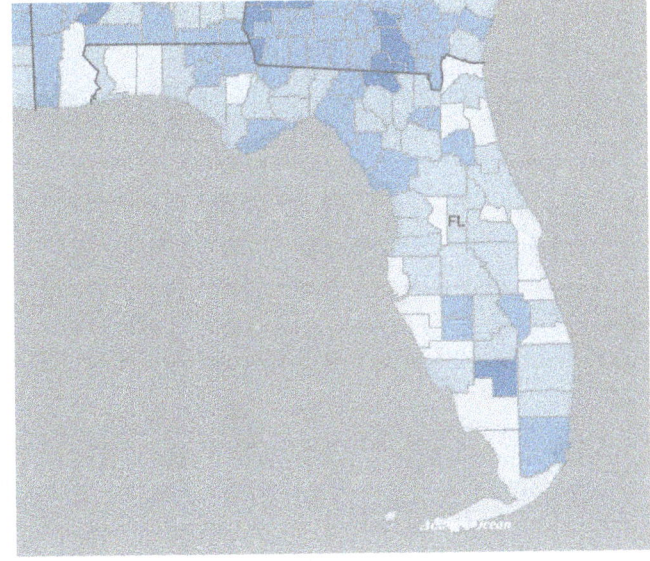

Unemployment Risk Map
Source: SparkRental & BLS

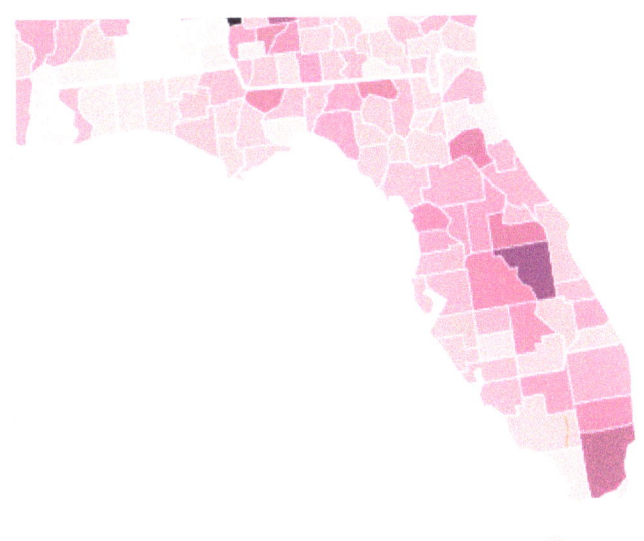

Economic & Crime Risk Map

Main Summaries of Risk Maps

- The percentage of the White population is very low.
- Metro-area risk is present.
- Florida is subject to extreme real estate risk.

Conclusions

Florida has thrived in a booming economy, but consequently, as an ultimate product of good times, it will be ruined by an economic downturn. The boom fueled Miami and its luxury, so prepare for the bust. The massive decline in property values will bring a financial debacle for the state and its people. Considering terrible race demographics, the state is very risky both economically and in terms of crime.

State	Kentucky
Population	4,506 thous.
Land Area	39,486 sq mile
Density/mi2	114.1 people
Percent White	81.3%
Poverty Rate	16.1%
Unempl. Rate	3.9%

State Location Map
Created with Mapchart.net

Kentucky - Shaded Relief Image
Credit: National Elevation Dataset, compiled
by the U.S. Geological Survey
Visit the USGS at https://usgs.gov.

Racial Risk Map
Created with Mapchart.net, data—US Census

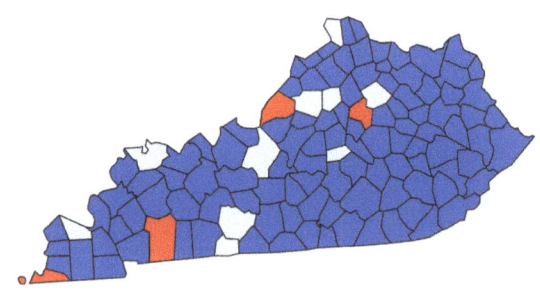

Industry Overconcentration Risk Map
Created with Mapchart.net, data—US Census

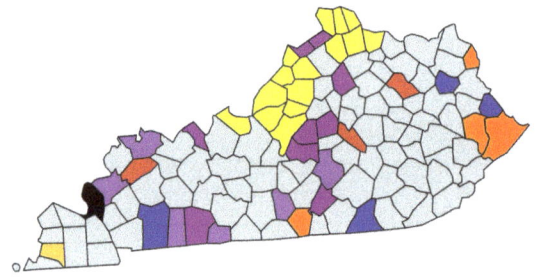

Real Estate Risk Map; G. Brian Davis, SparkRental,
ATTOM Data Solutions, Created with Datawrapper

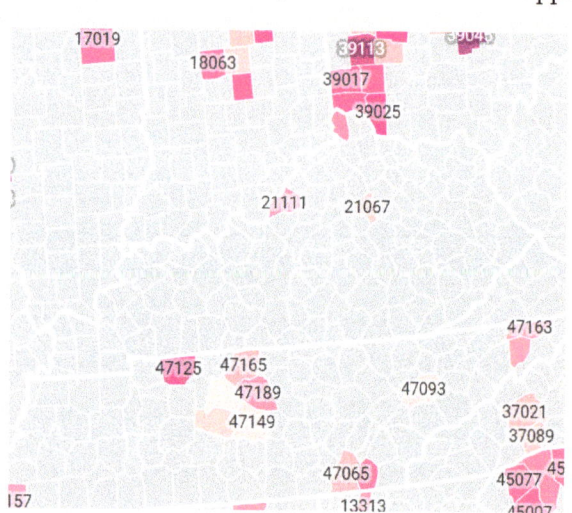

Density Risk Map
Source: US Census

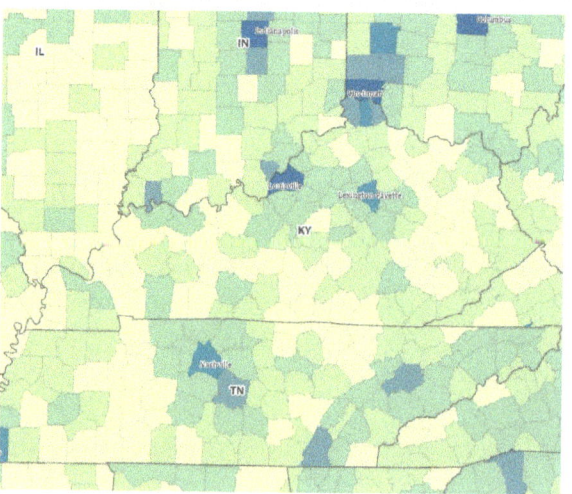

Poverty Risk Map
Source: US Census

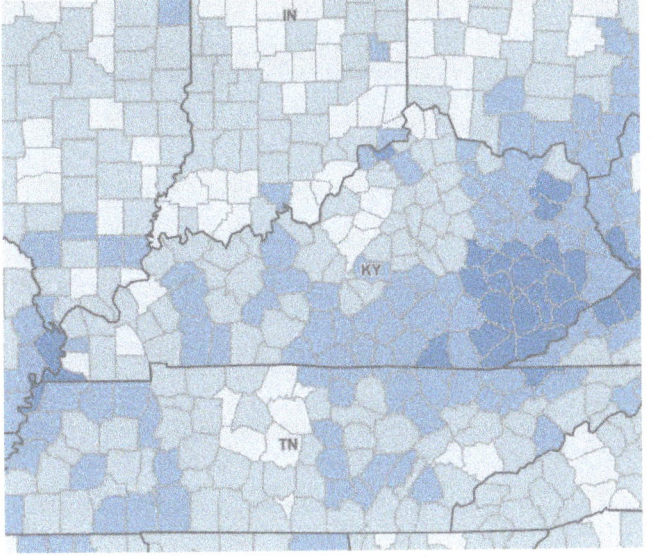

Unemployment Risk Map
Source: SparkRental & BLS

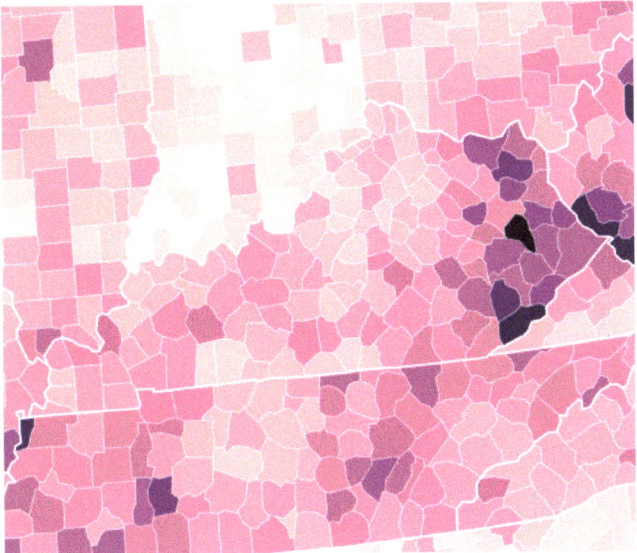

Economic & Crime Risk Map

Main Summaries of Risk Maps

- The percentage of the White population is good.
- Kentucky is subject to durable goods industry overconcentration.
- Poverty and unemployment rates are high in the East.

Conclusions

Kentucky is subject to durable goods manufacturing risk as employment in this industry is relatively high in Kentucky. Because there are many White counties, there are two areas to consider. The middle-to-west side and East Kentucky. The middle-to-west region is surrounded by an overconcentration of durable goods manufacturing counties, and there are several counties with a percentage of White people of less than 85%. In East Kentucky, which is a high-elevation region, the poverty and unemployment rates are high. This state has a good percentage of White people, so in terms of crime, this state will not be one of the worst states, but in terms of economy, it is quite risky.

State	Tennessee
Population	6,911 thous.
Land Area	41,235 sq mile
Density/mi2	167.6 people
Percent White	70.9%
Poverty Rate	14.0%
Unempl. Rate	3.4%

State Location Map
Created with Mapchart.net

Tennessee - Shaded Relief Image
Credit: National Elevation Dataset, compiled
by the U.S. Geological Survey
Visit the USGS at https://usgs.gov.

Racial Risk Map
Created with Mapchart.net, data—US Census

Industry Overconcentration Risk Map
Created with Mapchart.net, data—US Census

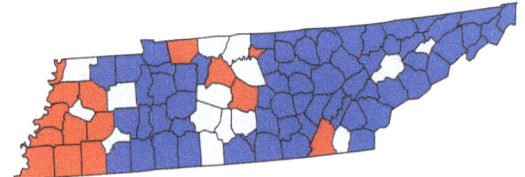

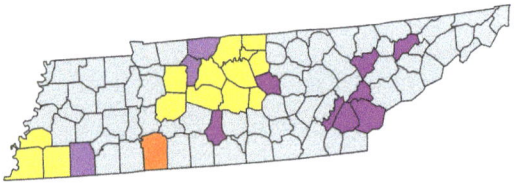

Real Estate Risk Map; G. Brian Davis, SparkRental,
ATTOM Data Solutions, Created with Datawrapper

Density Risk Map
Source: US Census

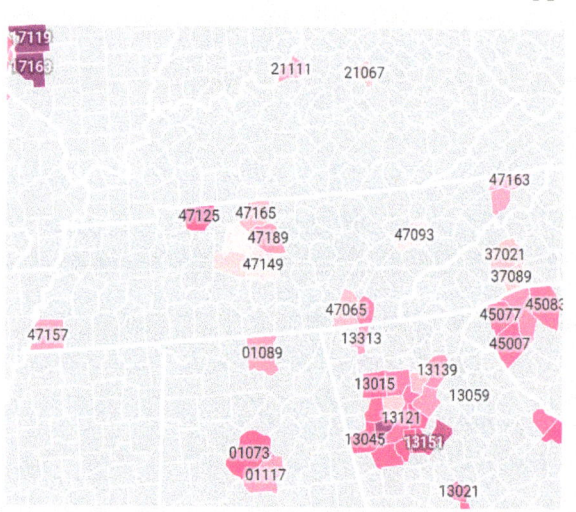

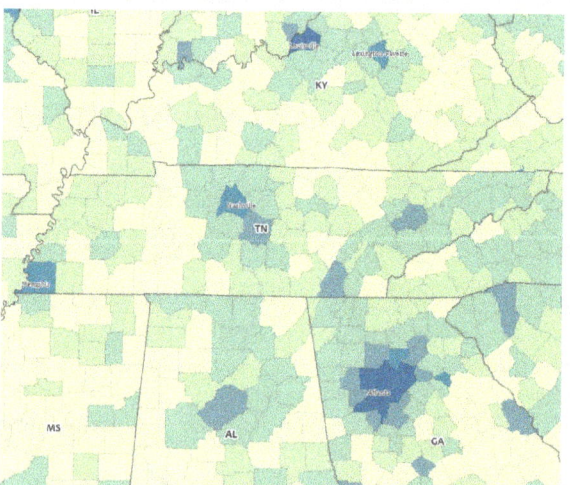

Poverty Risk Map
Source: US Census

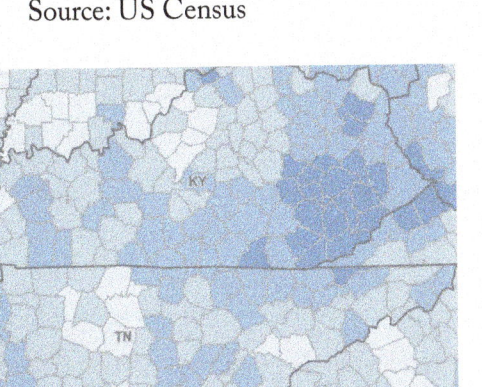

Unemployment Risk Map
Source: SparkRental & BLS

Economic & Crime Risk Map

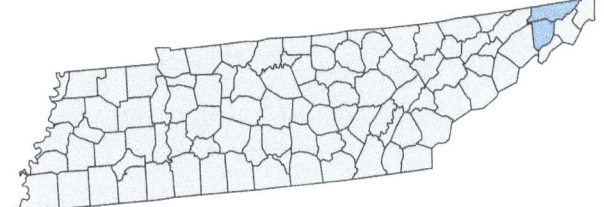

Main Summaries of Risk Maps

- The percentage of the White population is not enough. Memphis, located in the Southwest portion of the state, is one of the worst cities in the United States in terms of race demographics. Nashville, located in the middle, also has bad race demographics. Therefore, in terms of crime, these two largest cities of Tennessee are very risky, especially Memphis.
- Tennessee has some durable goods industry overconcentration.
- Memphis and Nashville areas are subject to metro area risk.
- Poverty and unemployment rates are high in some counties.

Conclusions

When it comes to Memphis, located in the Southwest, it must be avoided at least in the 200-mile radius. Only the East part of Tennessee can be considered. However, there is a cluster of durable goods industry, the downturn of which will influence that region to some extent. Memphis area already has a very high crime rate. After the crash, it will be even worse. Sadly, the counties where White people are above 85% of the population are subject to durable goods industry overconcentration. However, there are two counties on the East side, which are relatively less dangerous.

State	Alabama
Population	5,024 thous.
Land Area	50,645 sq mile
Density/mi2	99.2 people
Percent White	63.1%
Poverty Rate	15.7%
Unempl. Rate	2.6%

State Location Map
Created with Mapchart.net

Alabama - Shaded Relief Image
Credit: National Elevation Dataset, compiled
by the U.S. Geological Survey
Visit the USGS at https://usgs.gov.

Racial Risk Map
Created with Mapchart.net, data—US Census

Industry Overconcentration Risk Map
Created with Mapchart.net, data—US Census

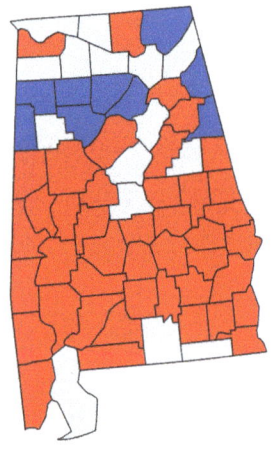

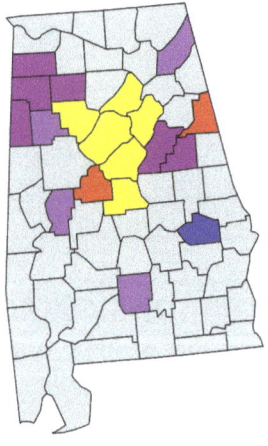

Real Estate Risk Map; G. Brian Davis, SparkRental,
ATTOM Data Solutions, Created with Datawrapper

Density Risk Map
Source: US Census

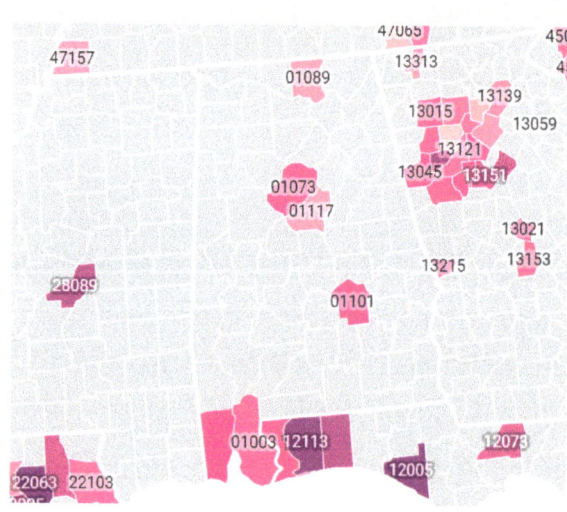

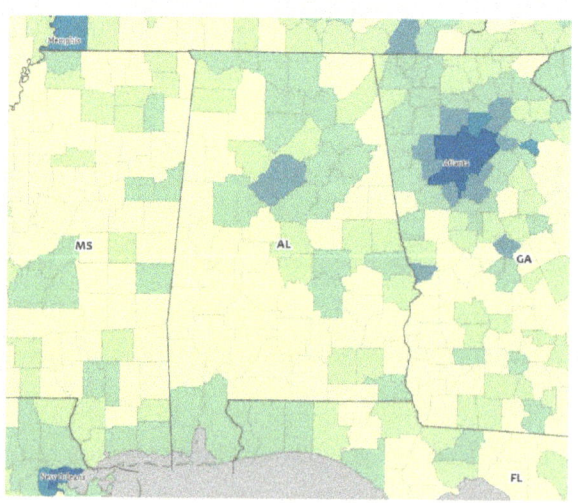

Poverty Risk Map
Source: US Census

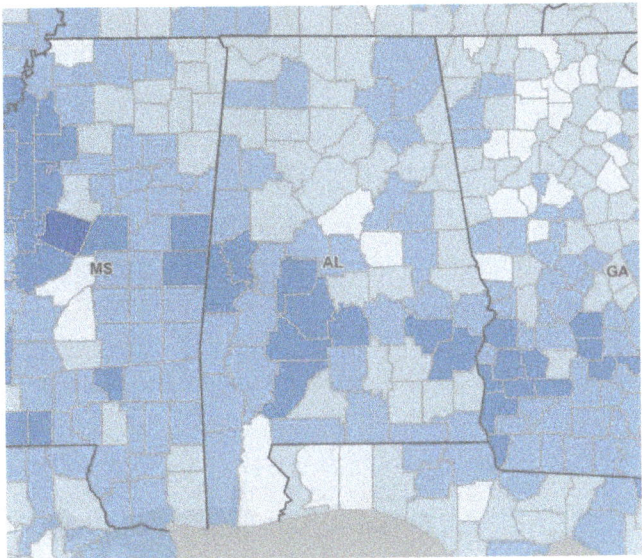

Unemployment Risk Map
Source: SparkRental & BLS

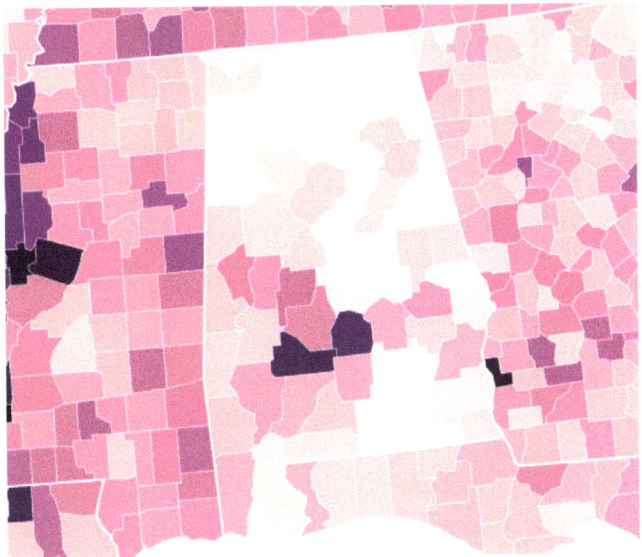

Economic & Crime Risk Map

Main Summaries of Risk Maps

- Most of the state has a high Black population, which is a must-avoid risk.

Conclusions

There is not a lot to say. Alabama is a classic southern state: high poverty and a high percentage of the Black population. Alabama is an extremely risky state.

State	Mississippi
Population	2,961 thous.
Land Area	46,923 sq mile
Density/mi2	63.1 people
Percent White	55.4%
Poverty Rate	19.2%
Unempl. Rate	3.9%

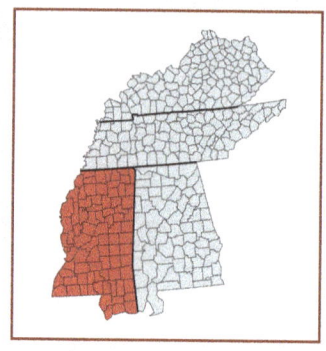

State Location Map
Created with Mapchart.net

Mississippi - Shaded Relief Image
Credit: National Elevation Dataset, compiled
by the U.S. Geological Survey
Visit the USGS at https://usgs.gov.

Racial Risk Map
Created with Mapchart.net, data—US Census

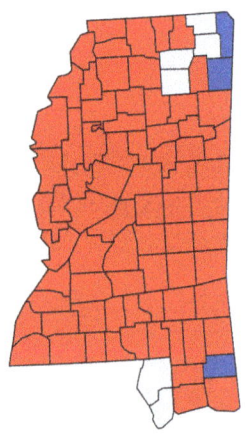

Industry Overconcentration Risk Map
Created with Mapchart.net, data—US Census

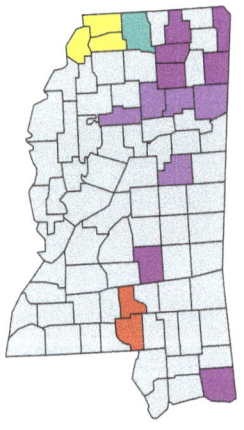

Real Estate Risk Map; G. Brian Davis, SparkRental,
ATTOM Data Solutions, Created with Datawrapper

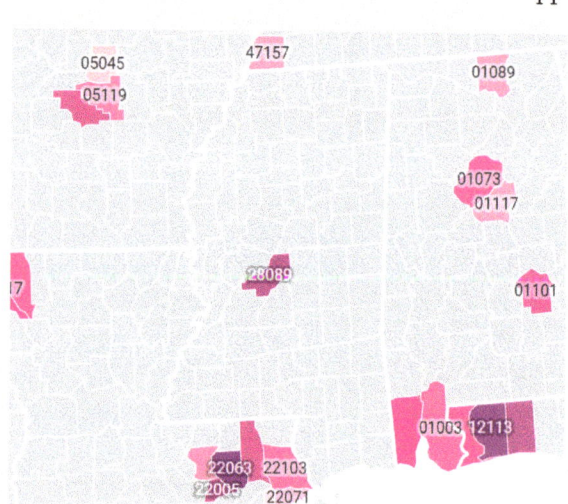

Density Risk Map
Source: US Census

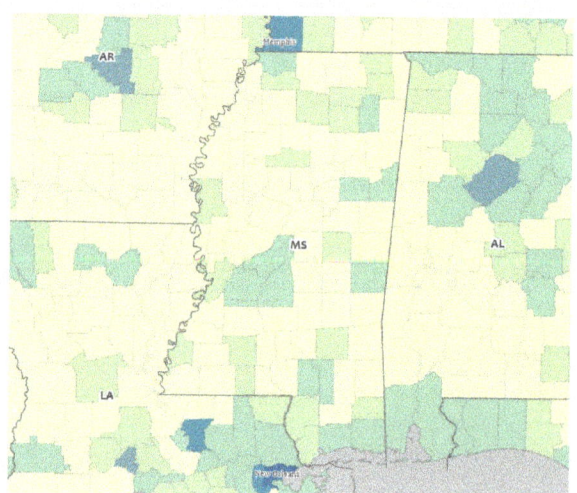

Poverty Risk Map
Source: US Census

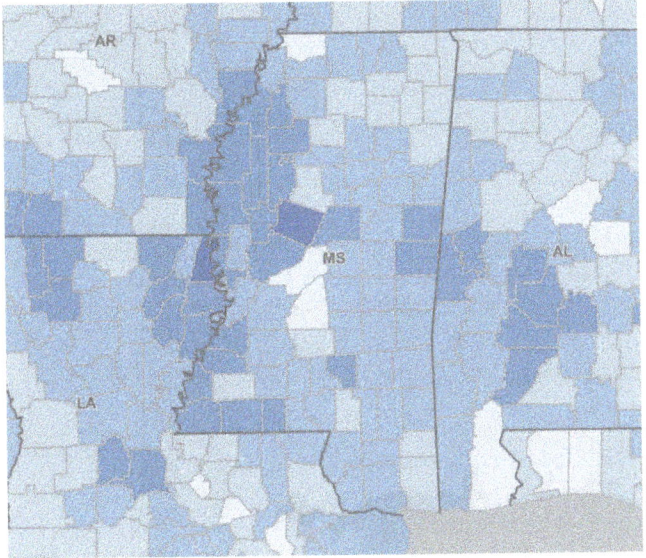

Unemployment Risk Map
Source: SparkRental & BLS

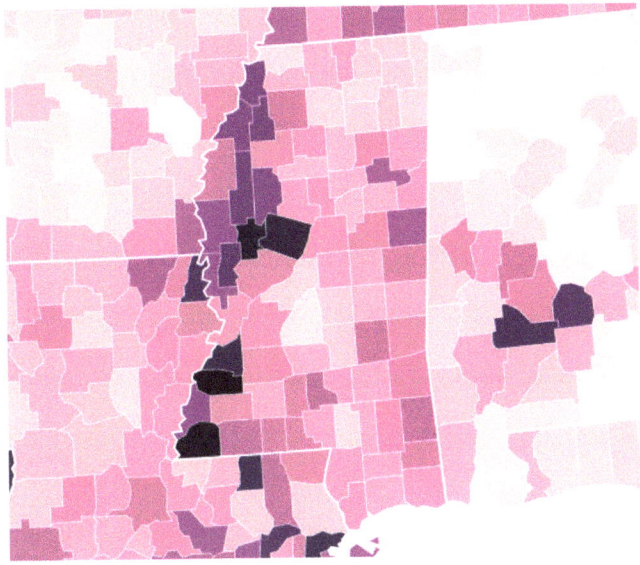

Economic & Crime Risk Map

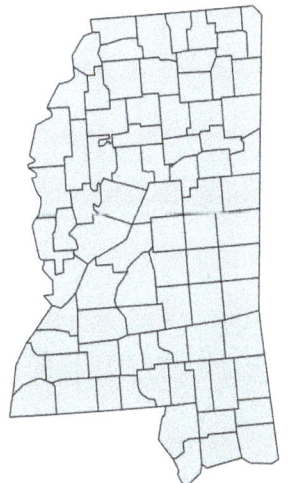

Main Summaries of Risk Maps

- Most of the state has a high black population, which is a must-avoid risk.

Conclusions

Mississippi is another classic southern state. Similar to Alabama, there is a very high percentage of the Black population. Therefore, the crime risk will be very high. There is no need to think any further. Mississippi is an extremely risky state.

State	Minnesota
Population	5,706 thous.
Land Area	79,627 sq mile
Density/mi2	71.7 people
Percent White	76.3%
Poverty Rate	9.3%
Unempl. Rate	2.7%

State Location Map
Created with Mapchart.net

Minnesota - Shaded Relief Image
Credit: National Elevation Dataset, compiled
by the U.S. Geological Survey
Visit the USGS at https://usgs.gov.

Racial Risk Map
Created with Mapchart.net, data—US Census

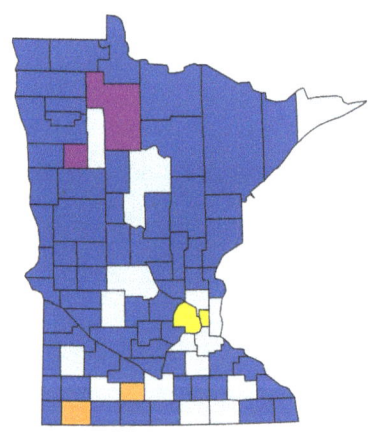

Industry Overconcentration Risk Map
Created with Mapchart.net, data—US Census

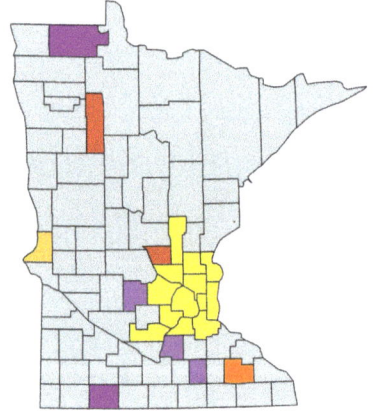

Real Estate Risk Map; G. Brian Davis, SparkRental,
ATTOM Data Solutions, Created with Datawrapper

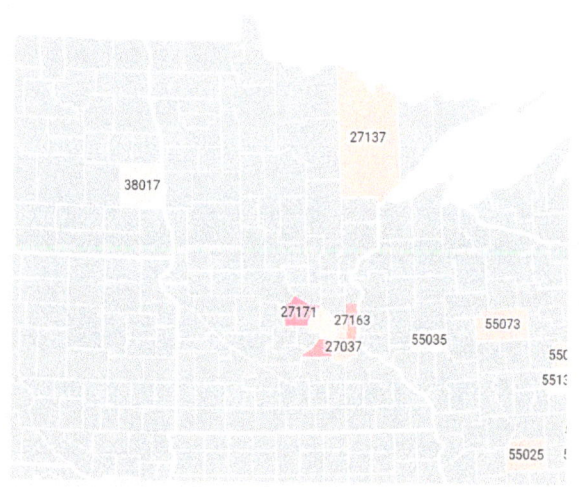

Density Risk Map
Source: US Census

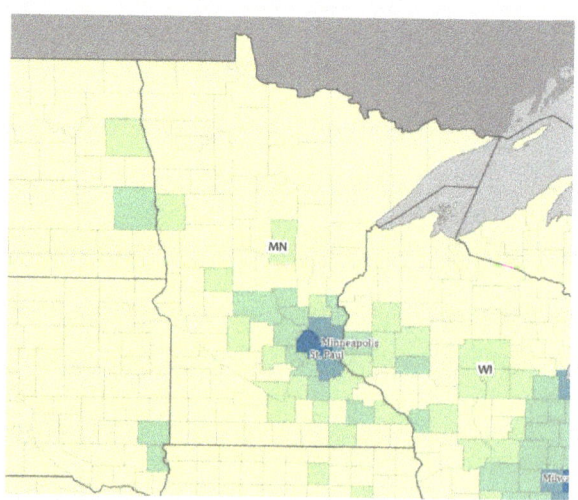

Poverty Risk Map
Source: US Census

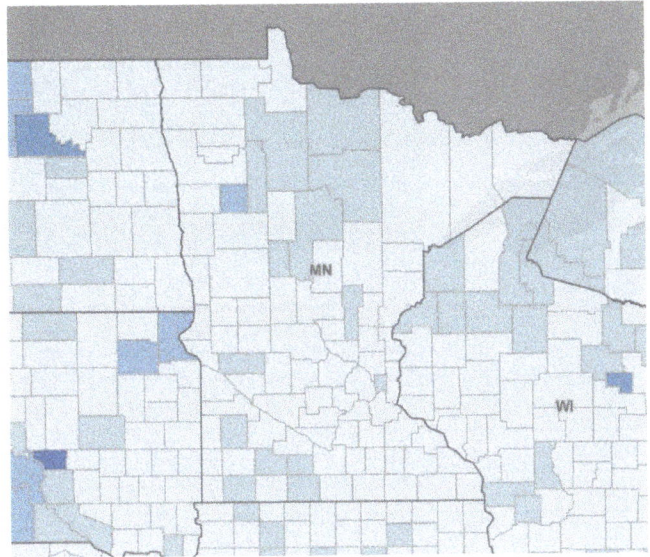

Unemployment Risk Map
Source: SparkRental & BLS

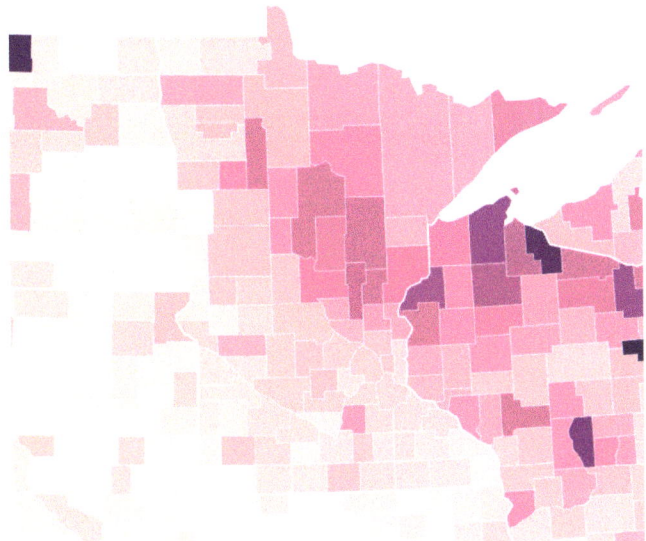

Economic & Crime Risk Map

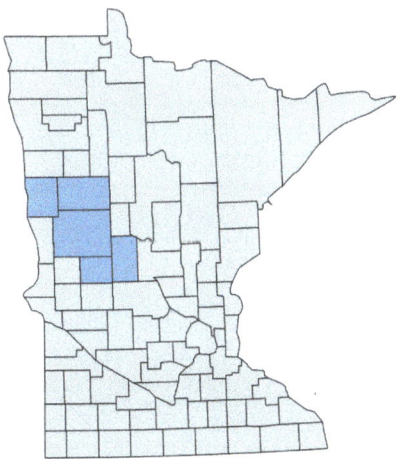

Main Summaries of Risk Maps

- The percentage of the White population is not enough. It is not reasonable in the Minneapolis metropolitan area, the largest city in the state, but it is above 85% in several other counties.
- No substantial industry overconcentration.
- Metro-area risk is present in the Minneapolis area.
- Real estate risk is present in the Minneapolis area but lower in the rest of the state.

Conclusions

Besides Minneapolis, the predominantly White areas on the West side are relatively devoid of extreme real estate risk, metro area risk, and industry overconcentration risk. Also, they are not very poor, and unemployment is not high. I think several counties on the Western side are relatively safe from economic and crime risks. Perhaps more in terms of crime.

State	Iowa
Population	3,190 thous.
Land Area	55,857 sq mile
Density/mi2	57.1 people
Percent White	82.7%
Poverty Rate	11.1%
Unempl. Rate	2.7%

State Location Map
Created with Mapchart.net

Iowa - Shaded Relief Image
Credit: National Elevation Dataset, compiled
by the U.S. Geological Survey
Visit the USGS at https://usgs.gov.

Racial Risk Map
Created with Mapchart.net, data—US Census

Industry Overconcentration Risk Map
Created with Mapchart.net, data—US Census

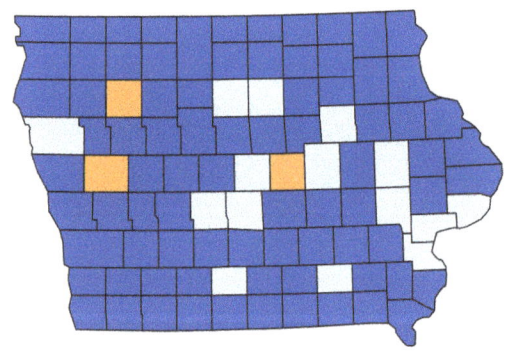

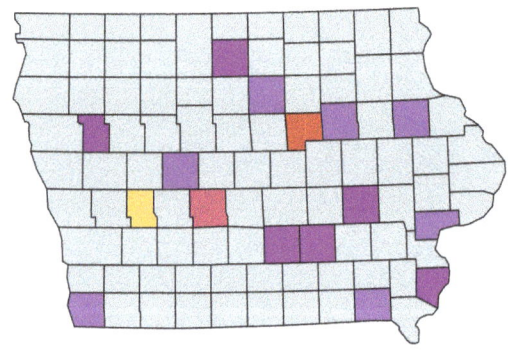

Real Estate Risk Map; G. Brian Davis, SparkRental,
ATTOM Data Solutions, Created with Datawrapper

Density Risk Map
Source: US Census

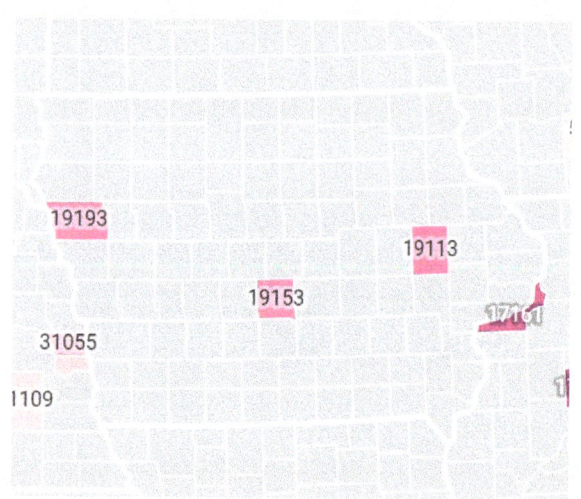

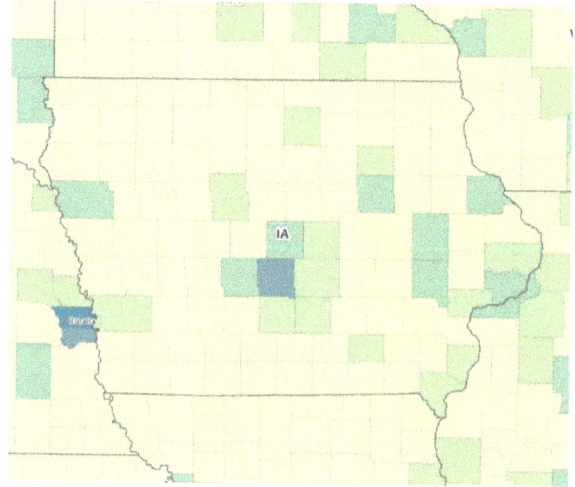

Poverty Risk Map
Source: US Census

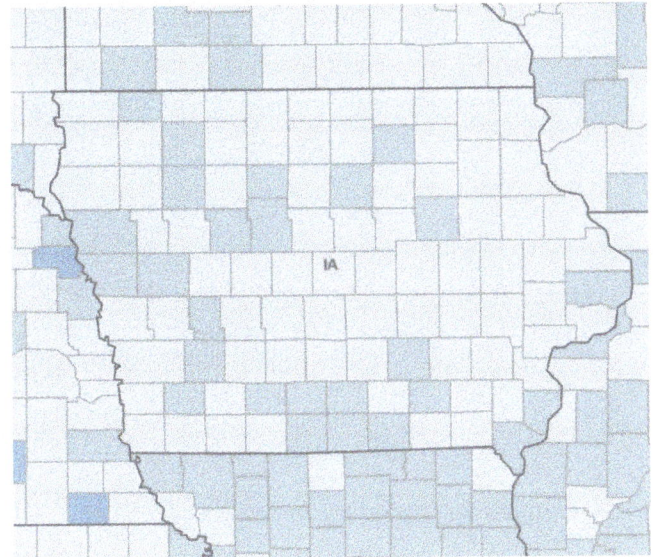

Unemployment Risk Map
Source: SparkRental & BLS

Economic & Crime Risk Map

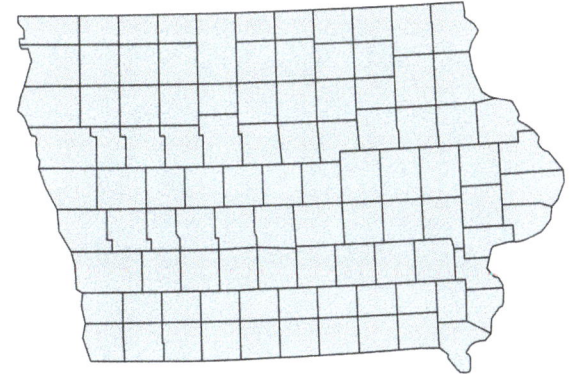

Main Summaries of Risk Maps

- The percentage of the White population is good.
- Durable goods industry overconcentration is present.
- No metro-area risk.
- Low population density in some counties.

Conclusions

Durable goods manufacturing is present but is not clustered significantly. The state has counties that correspond to my requirements, and there is hardly any reason not to choose those counties as safe ones. Iowa is quite an agricultural state located in the heart of the Corn Belt of the United States. You can find endless corn fields, then a very small town, then endless corn fields again, then a very small town again, and so on. The well-being of these cities is highly dependent on the agricultural industry, though there is no statistical overconcentration according to the industry overconcentration map, which is strange. Population density is very low in these agricultural counties. The combination of these reasons makes me abstain from considering the heart of the corn belt economically safe. However, Iowa is less risky from a violent crime perspective.

State	Missouri
Population	6,155 thous.
Land Area	68,742 sq mile
Density/mi2	89.5 people
Percent White	75.8%
Poverty Rate	12.8%
Unempl. Rate	2.5%

State Location Map
Created with Mapchart.net

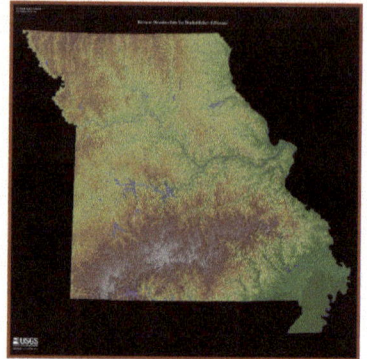

Missouri - Shaded Relief Image
Credit: National Elevation Dataset, compiled
by the U.S. Geological Survey
Visit the USGS at https://usgs.gov.

Racial Risk Map
Created with Mapchart.net, data—US Census

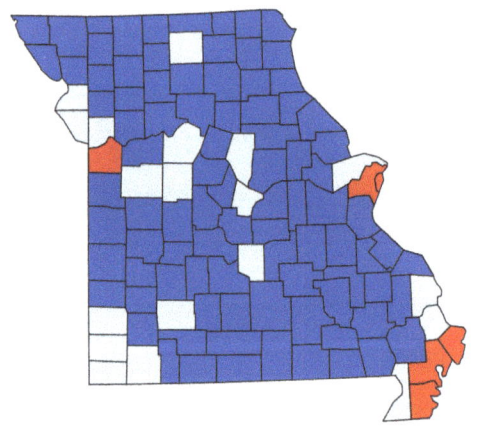

Industry Overconcentration Risk Map
Created with Mapchart.net, data—US Census

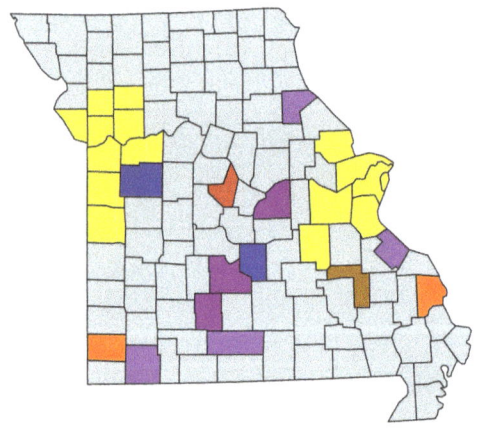

Real Estate Risk Map; G. Brian Davis, SparkRental,
ATTOM Data Solutions, Created with Datawrapper

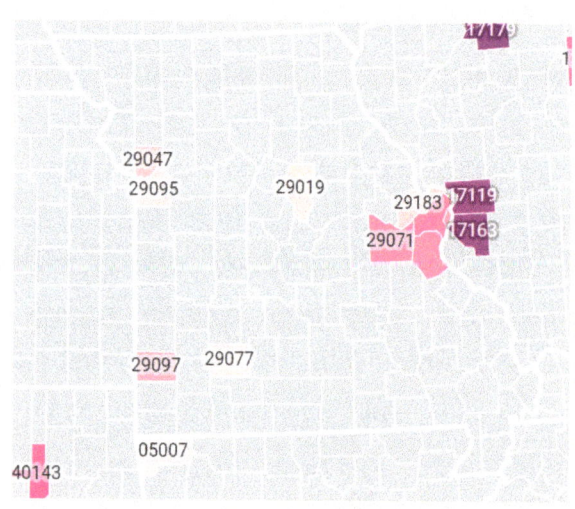

Density Risk Map
Source: US Census

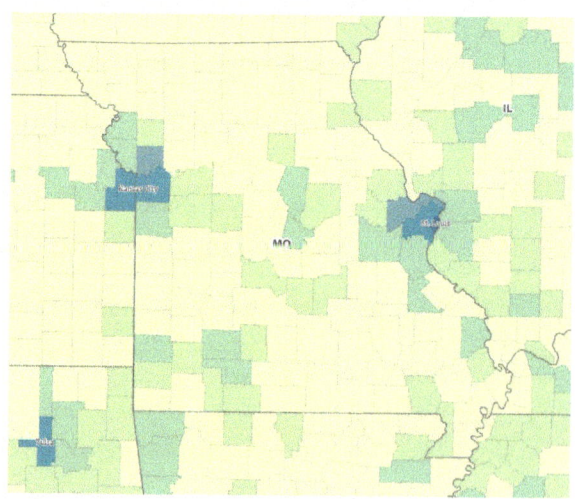

Poverty Risk Map
Source: US Census

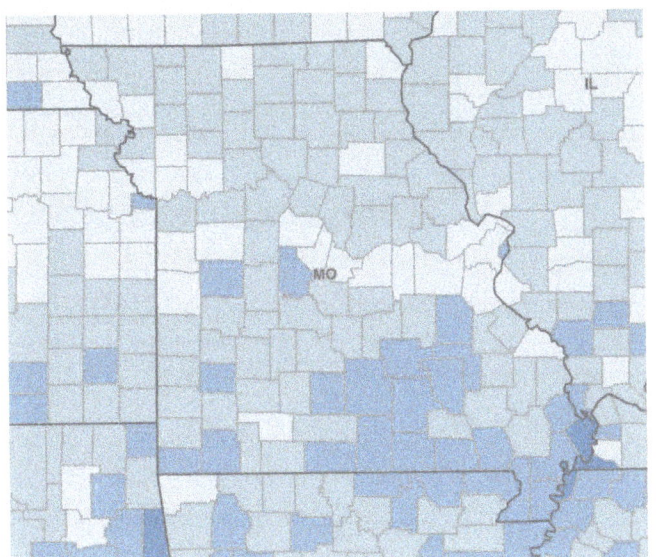

Unemployment Risk Map
Source: SparkRental & BLS

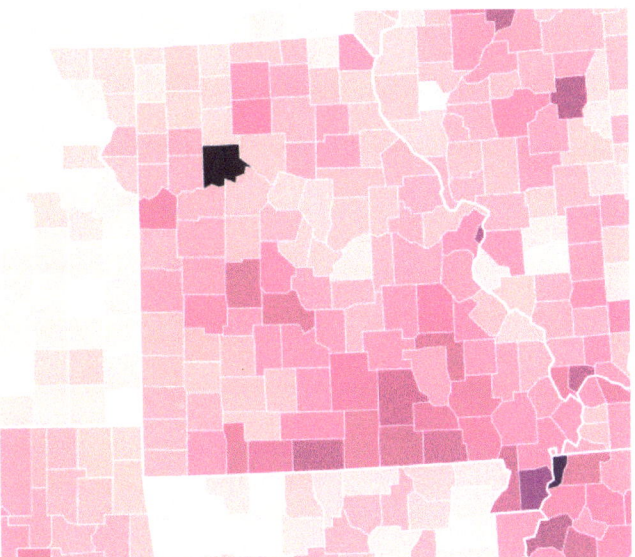

Economic & Crime Risk Map

Main Summaries of Risk Maps

- The percentage of the White population is not desirable enough.
- Several counties are subject to durable goods industry overconcentration.
- Metro-area risk is present in the West (Kansas City metro) and in the East (St. Louis metro).
- Population density is high in metro areas and low in the rest of the state.
- Poverty and unemployment rates are high in the south of Missouri.

Conclusions

Kansas City on the west side is quite risky as a metro area. St. Louis on the East must be avoided, as discussed in the Illinois state conclusions. The rest of the state is very different from these metro areas. The South is quite poor, and unemployment is high. Also, the Southeast is close to the Mississippi River area, where the percentage of Blacks is high, as we saw in Western Tennessee and Mississippi. Obviously, it is within a 200-mile radius of Memphis. The north of Missouri resembles Iowa in terms of the geography of cities, miles of fields and then a very small town, then the same. This pattern repeats in the "West North Central" Census division states. The density is very low in the north. I am not willing to consider any large area of this state safe. There might be a few individual counties, but not a cluster of safe counties.

State	North Dakota
Population	779 thous.
Land Area	69,001 sq mile
Density/mi2	11.3 people
Percent White	81.7%
Poverty Rate	10.8%
Unempl. Rate	2.1%

State Location Map
Created with Mapchart.net

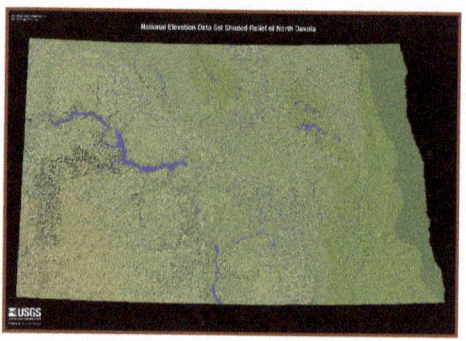

North Dakota - Shaded Relief Image
Credit: National Elevation Dataset, compiled
by the U.S. Geological Survey
Visit the USGS at https://usgs.gov.

Racial Risk Map
Created with Mapchart.net, data—US Census

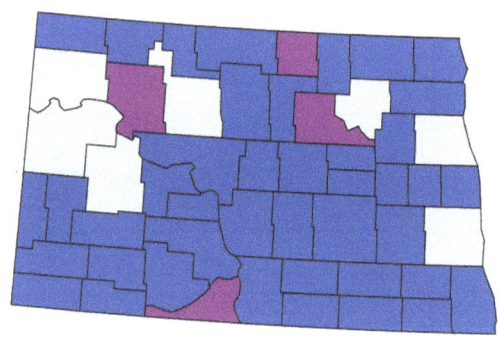

Industry Overconcentration Risk Map
Created with Mapchart.net, data—US Census

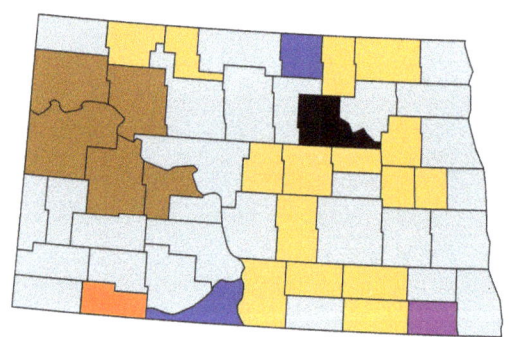

Real Estate Risk Map; G. Brian Davis, SparkRental,
ATTOM Data Solutions, Created with Datawrapper

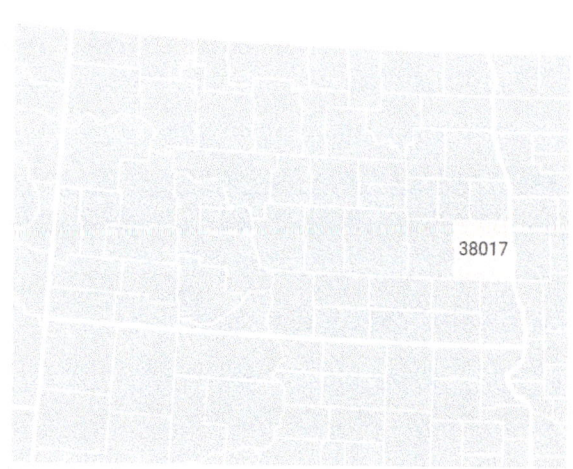

Density Risk Map
Source: US Census

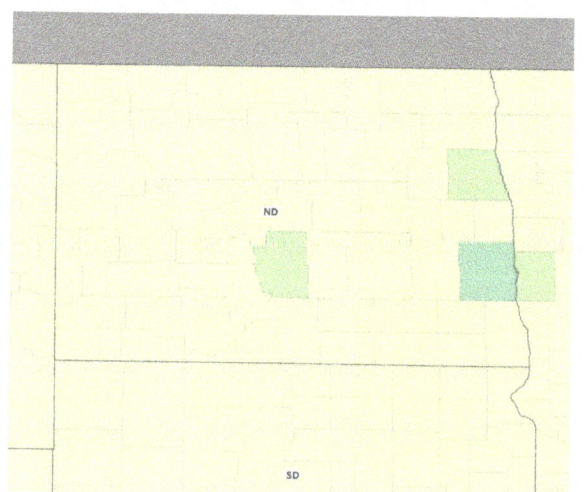

Poverty Risk Map
Source: US Census

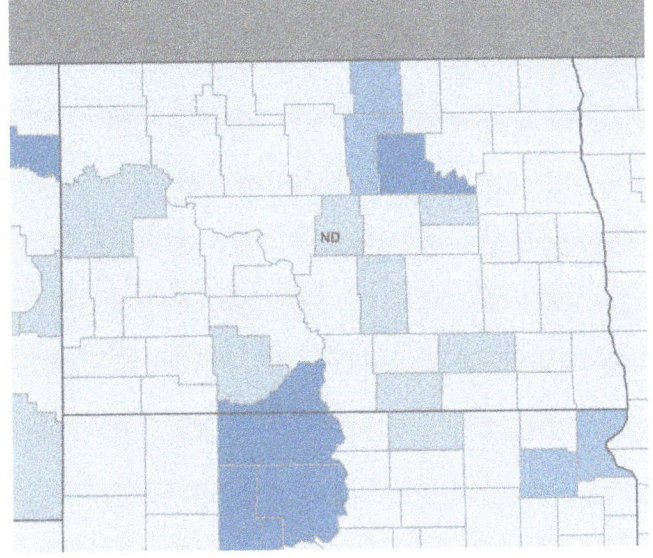

Unemployment Risk Map
Source: SparkRental & BLS

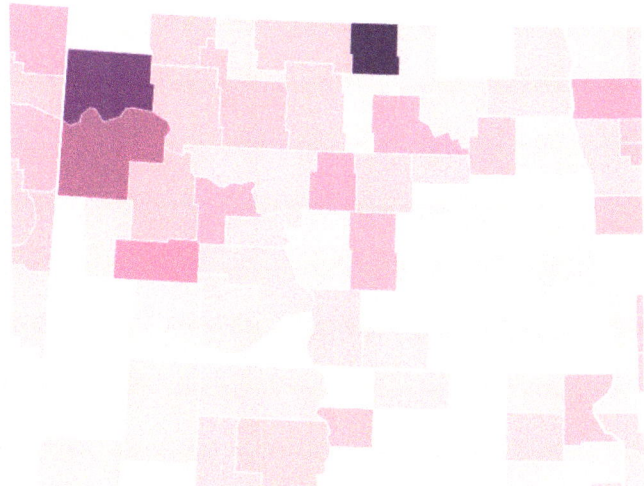

Economic & Crime Risk Map

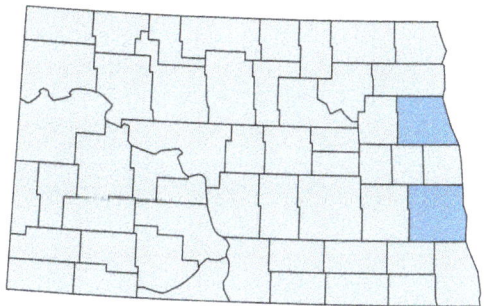

Main Summaries of Risk Maps

- The percentage of the White population is good.
- High industry overconcentration.
- No metro-area risk.
- Low population density.

Conclusions

North Dakota would have been relatively safe if not for two issues. The state has a high industry over-concentration risk, primarily agricultural overconcentration. Secondly, the density is very low in some counties. The low-density counties similarly resemble the pattern found in Iowa. I already reflected on my opinion that I consider it quite risky because of the overemphasis on agriculture. I do not know and think it is difficult to predict which small towns within miles of fields can be considered safe. However, I chose two counties next to the Minnesota border. Nevertheless, the state will be among the safe ones in terms of violent crime safety.

State	South Dakota
Population	887 thous.
Land Area	75,811 sq mile
Density/mi2	11.7 people
Percent White	79.6%
Poverty Rate	12.3%
Unempl. Rate	2.1%

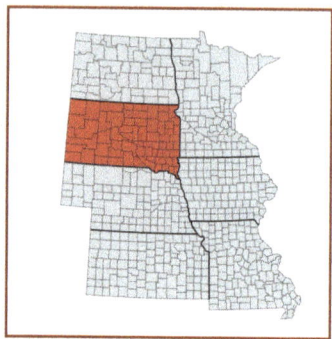

State Location Map
Created with Mapchart.net

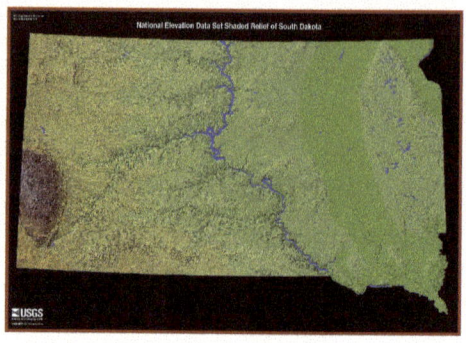

South Dakota - Shaded Relief Image
Credit: National Elevation Dataset, compiled
by the U.S. Geological Survey
Visit the USGS at https://usgs.gov.

Racial Risk Map
Created with Mapchart.net, data—US Census

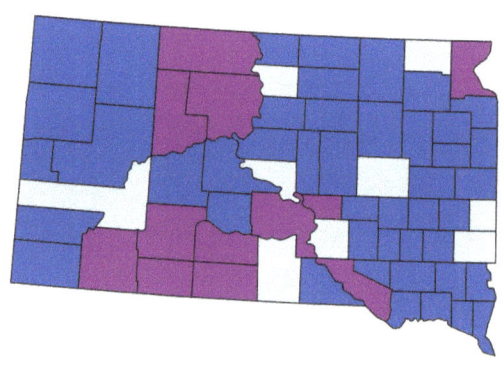

Industry Overconcentration Risk Map
Created with Mapchart.net, data—US Census

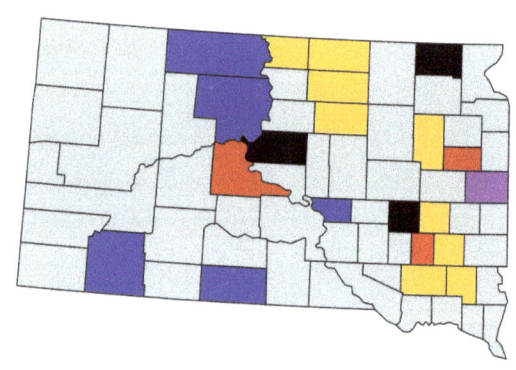

Real Estate Risk Map; G. Brian Davis, SparkRental,
ATTOM Data Solutions, Created with Datawrapper

Density Risk Map
Source: US Census

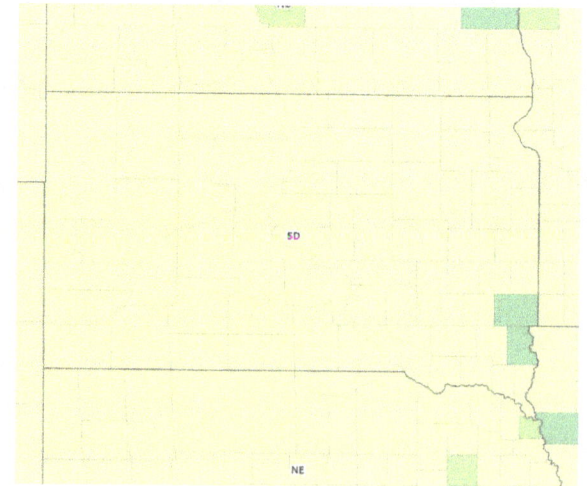

Poverty Risk Map
Source: US Census

Unemployment Risk Map
Source: SparkRental & BLS

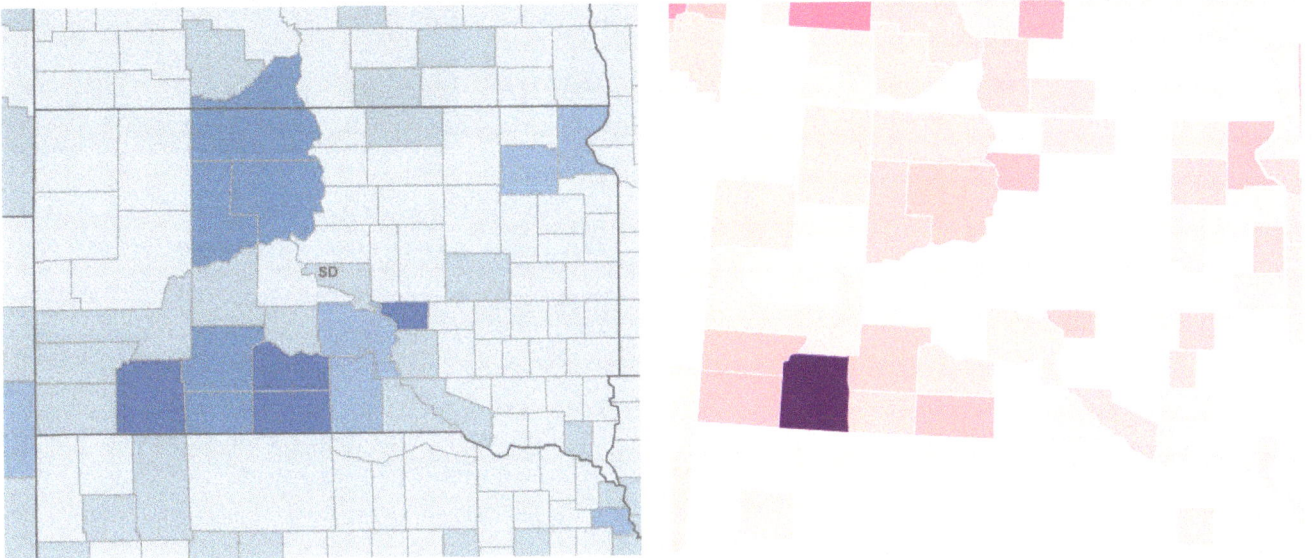

Economic & Crime Risk Map

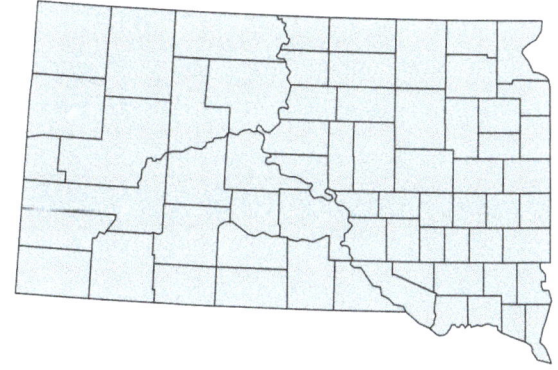

Main Summaries of Risk Maps

- The percentage of the White population is reasonable.
- High industry overconcentration.
- No metro-area risk.
- Low population density.

Conclusions

It is very similar to North Dakota in many ways. Both North Dakota and South Dakota are very calm and peaceful states in many ways. See North Dakota and Iowa for similar conclusions. I wish I could consider this state safe because race demographics are reasonable, and there is no significant metro area risk and no extreme real estate risk. However, density is very low in many counties, and economic risk is high due to high industry overconcentration. Nevertheless, the state will be among the safe ones in terms of violent crime safety.

State	Nebraska
Population	1,962 thous.
Land Area	76,824 sq mile
Density/mi2	25.5 people
Percent White	75.7%
Poverty Rate	10.4%
Unempl. Rate	2.3%

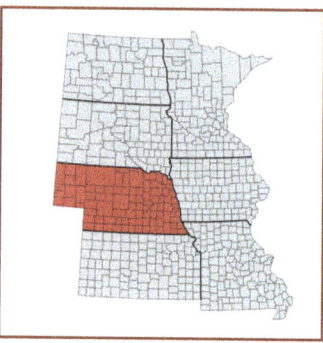

State Location Map
Created with Mapchart.net

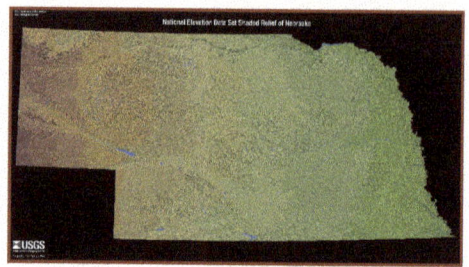

Nebraska - Shaded Relief Image
Credit: National Elevation Dataset, compiled
by the U.S. Geological Survey
Visit the USGS at https://usgs.gov.

Racial Risk Map
Created with Mapchart.net, data—US Census

Industry Overconcentration Risk Map
Created with Mapchart.net, data—US Census

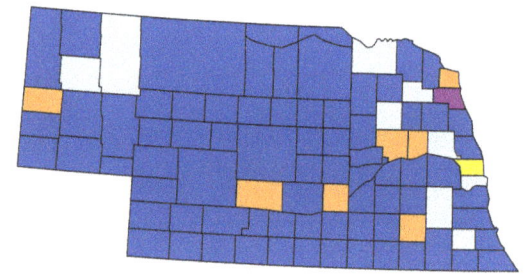

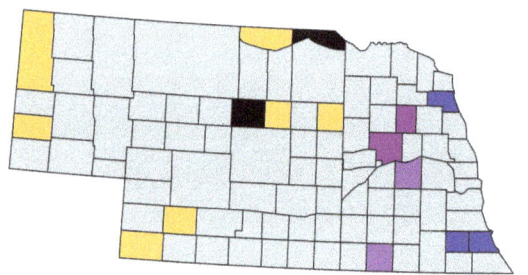

Real Estate Risk Map; G. Brian Davis, SparkRental,
ATTOM Data Solutions, Created with Datawrapper

Density Risk Map
Source: US Census

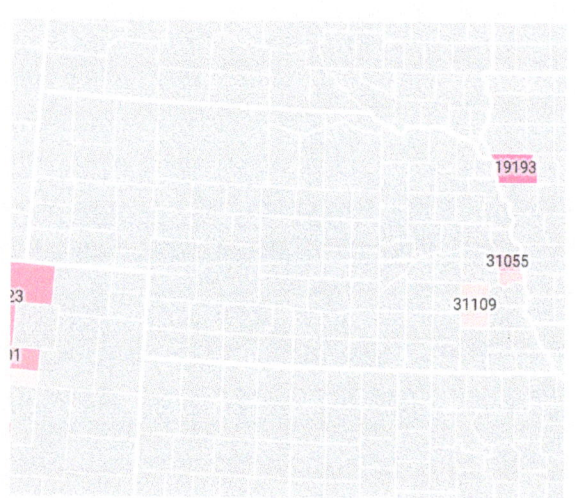

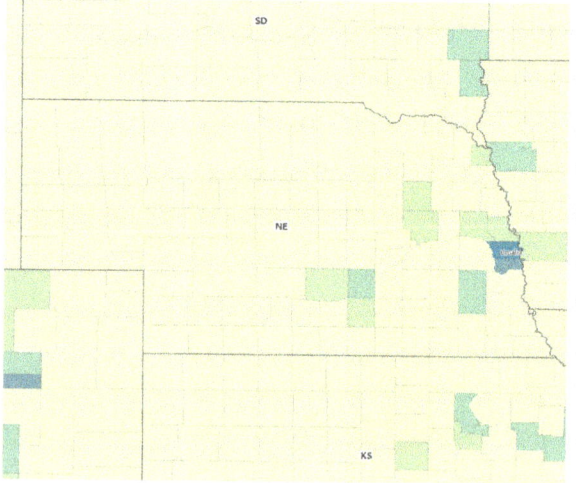

Poverty Risk Map
Source: US Census

Unemployment Risk Map
Source: SparkRental & BLS

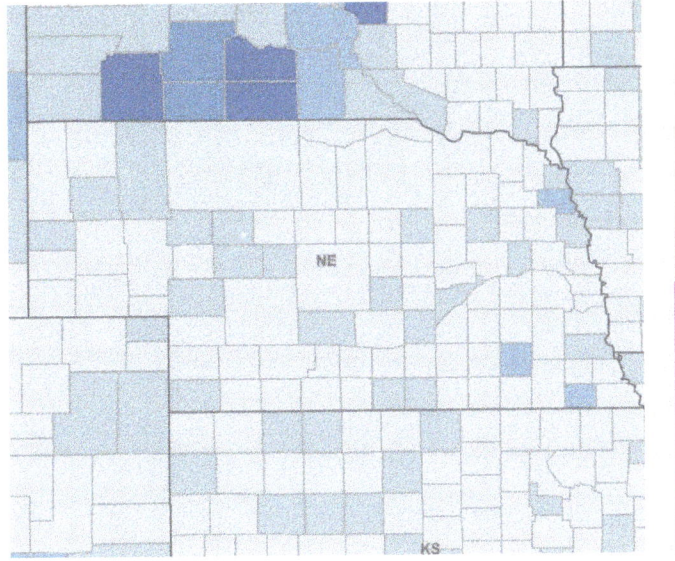

Economic & Crime Risk Map

Main Summaries of Risk Maps

- The percentage of the White population is not desirable enough.
- Some industry overconcentration.
- No metro-area risk, except in the Omaha area. However, Omaha is not considered one of the largest 50 metro areas.
- Low population density.

Conclusions

Once again, the same issue of endless fields and very small towns, as in Iowa, North Dakota, and South Dakota. The percentage of White people is not desirable enough, but not awful. Omaha in the East and its nearby areas seem quite attractive to me in terms of race demographics, considering that it is a city with half a million population. This medium metro area, not included in the top 50 largest metros, will be relatively safer than most metro areas in terms of violent crime and economic downturn. It is one of the only relatively medium-sized cities that can be considered quite safe, besides those included in the New Hampshire counties, namely Manchester, NH. Thus, if you only want to live in metro areas, then you may consider Omaha, though the crime safety is only relative to other metro areas and overall, it is still risky, which is why I did not consider it safe in my Risk Map.

State	Kansas
Population	2,938 thous.
Land Area	81,759 sq mile
Density/mi2	35.9 people
Percent White	72.2%
Poverty Rate	11.6%
Unempl. Rate	2.7%

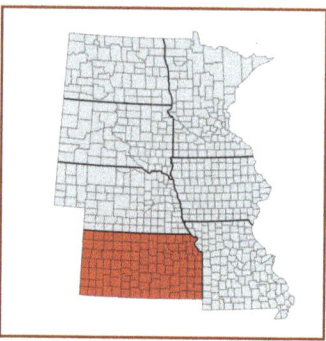

State Location Map
Created with Mapchart.net

Kansas - Shaded Relief Image
Credit: National Elevation Dataset, compiled
by the U.S. Geological Survey
Visit the USGS at https://usgs.gov.

Racial Risk Map
Created with Mapchart.net, data—US Census

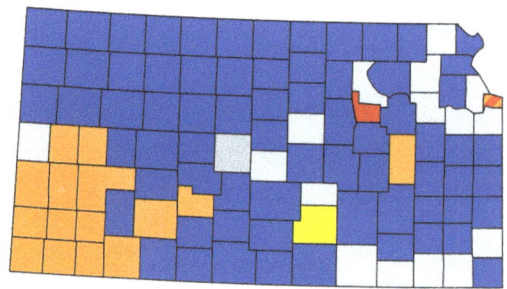

Industry Overconcentration Risk Map
Created with Mapchart.net, data—US Census

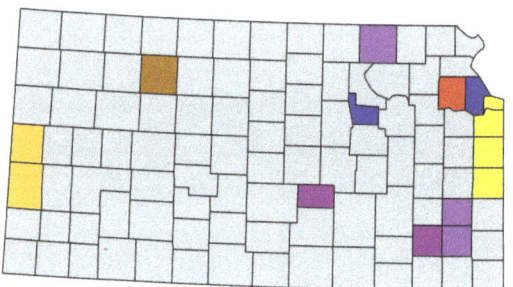

Real Estate Risk Map; G. Brian Davis, SparkRental,
ATTOM Data Solutions, Created with Datawrapper

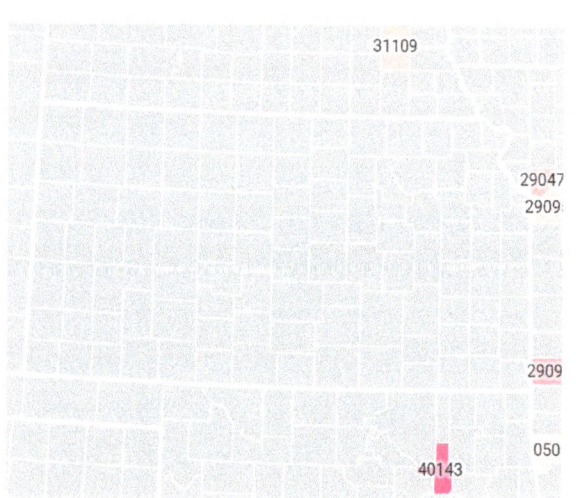

Density Risk Map
Source: US Census

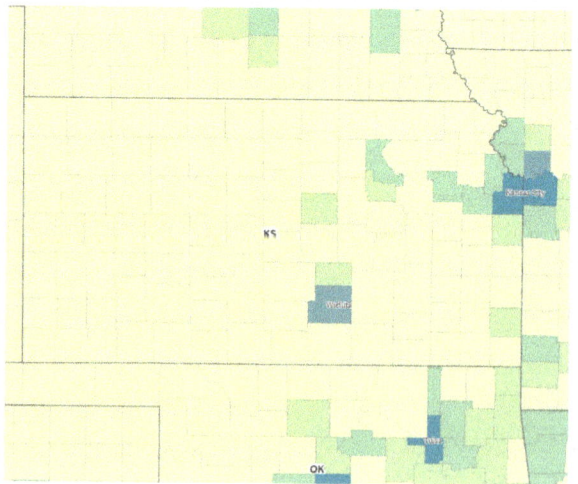

Poverty Risk Map
Source: US Census

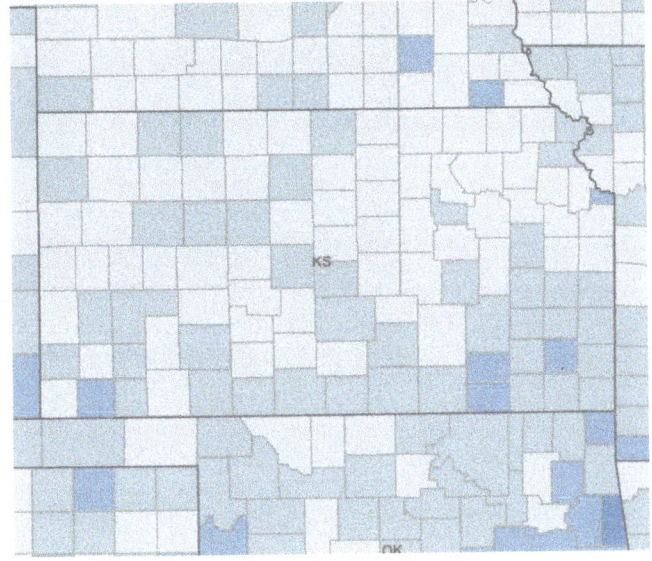

Unemployment Risk Map
Source: SparkRental & BLS

Economic & Crime Risk Map

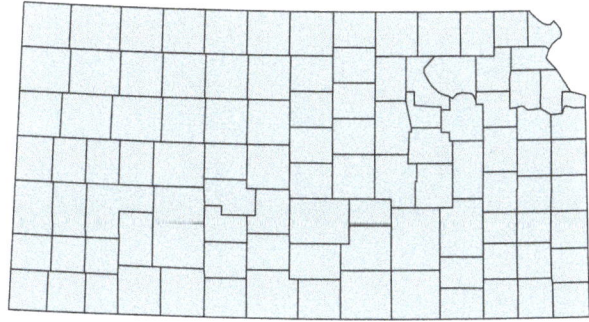

Main Summaries of Risk Maps

- The percentage of the White population is not enough.
- No metro-area risk besides the Kansas City metro on the East.
- Low population density.

Conclusions

The state has the same issue as Nebraska, Iowa, North Dakota, and South Dakota. However, Kansas is located more to the south, and many counties have lower percentage of the White population. The Kansas City area, which covers part of Missouri, has adverse race demographics. Northern Kansas has the same uncertainty issue as other highly agricultural states such as Iowa, Nebraska and Dakotas. Also, if you look at the rest of Kansas, it is hard to choose any other cluster of counties that have satisfactory race demographics, no industry overconcentration risk, and no poverty issues. The poverty issue is quite known in southeastern Kansas. I do not consider this state safe either economically or in terms of crime.

State	Arkansas
Population	3,012 thous.
Land Area	52,035 sq mile
Density/mi2	57.9 people
Percent White	68.5%
Poverty Rate	16.2%
Unempl. Rate	3.3%

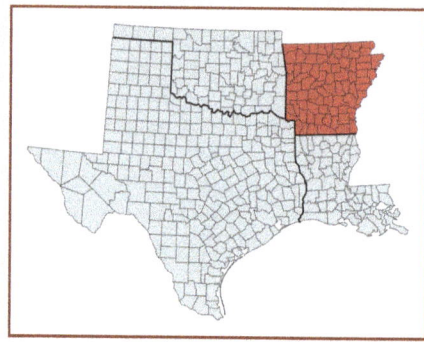

State Location Map
Created with Mapchart.net

Arkansas - Shaded Relief Image
Credit: National Elevation Dataset, compiled
by the U.S. Geological Survey
Visit the USGS at https://usgs.gov.

Racial Risk Map
Created with Mapchart.net, data—US Census

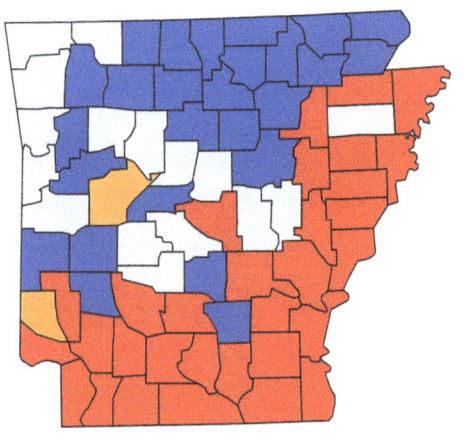

Industry Overconcentration Risk Map
Created with Mapchart.net, data—US Census

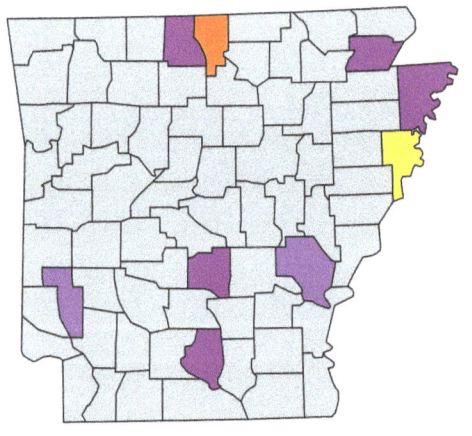

Real Estate Risk Map; G. Brian Davis, SparkRental,
ATTOM Data Solutions, Created with Datawrapper

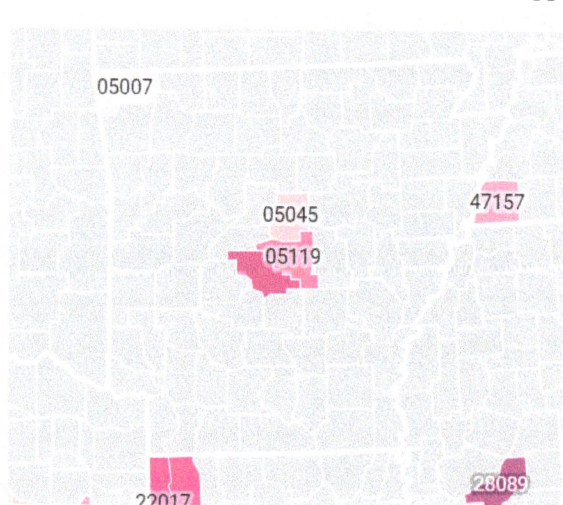

Density Risk Map
Source: US Census

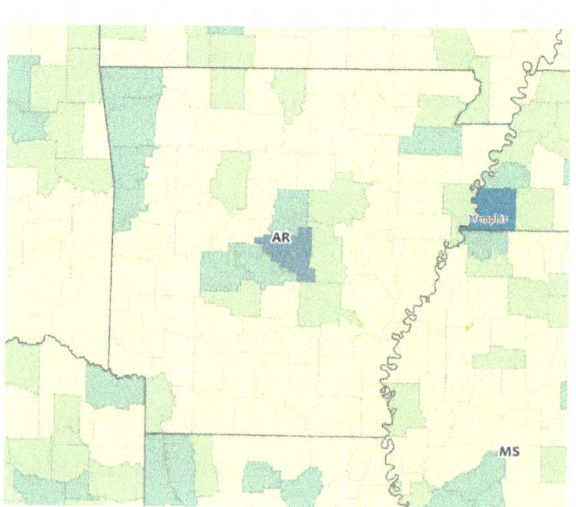

Poverty Risk Map
Source: US Census

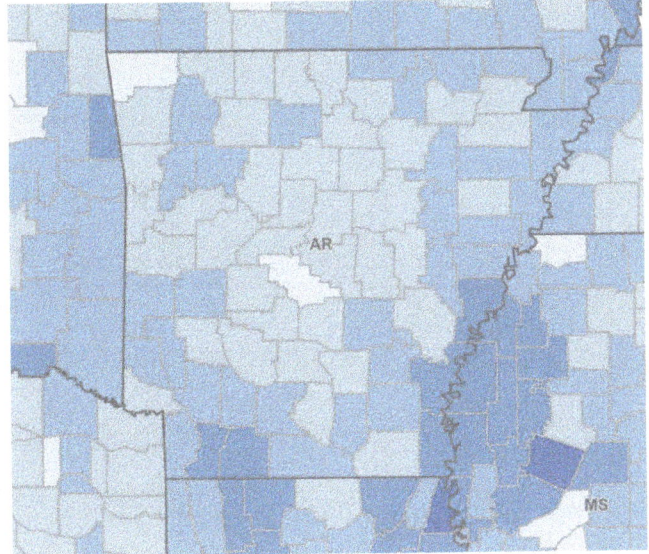

Unemployment Risk Map
Source: SparkRental & BLS

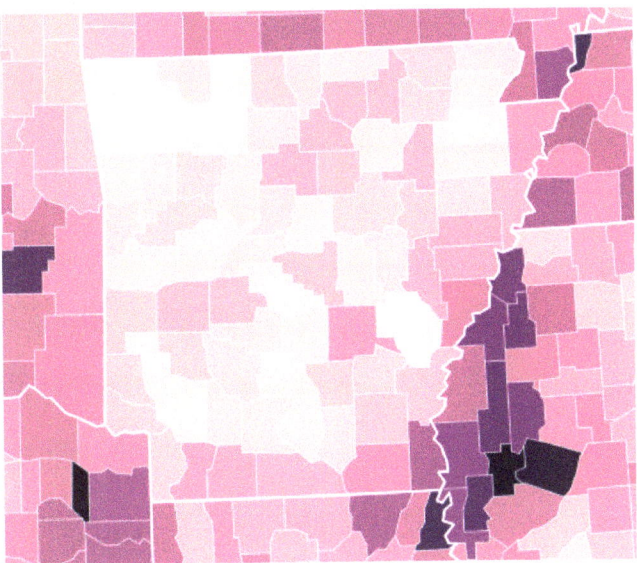

Economic & Crime Risk Map

Main Summaries of Risk Maps

- The percentage of the White population is not enough. Many counties have a Black population above 15%. Both facts are negative.

- Below average population density.

- High poverty rate.

Conclusions

This state has the South's common issue—terrible race demographics—which will lead to the crime issue. High crime is already present in the southern states, but it will be a massive issue in tough times. Some counties with predominantly White population are quite poor. This state is quite risky in terms of crime, especially in its not predominantly White areas.

State	Louisiana
Population	4,658 thous.
Land Area	43,204 sq mile
Density/mi2	107.8 people
Percent White	55.8%
Poverty Rate	18.7%
Unempl. Rate	3.7%

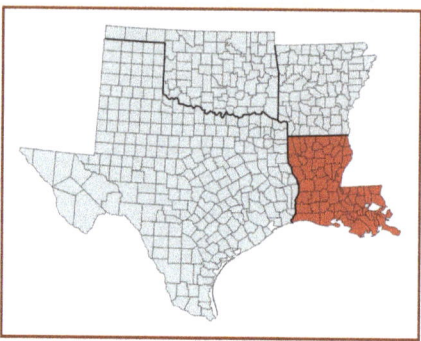

State Location Map
Created with Mapchart.net

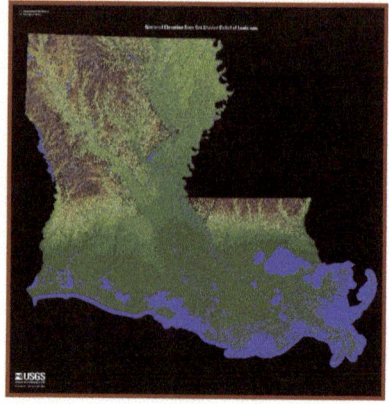

Louisiana - Shaded Relief Image
Credit: National Elevation Dataset, compiled
by the U.S. Geological Survey
Visit the USGS at https://usgs.gov.

Racial Risk Map
Created with Mapchart.net, data—US Census

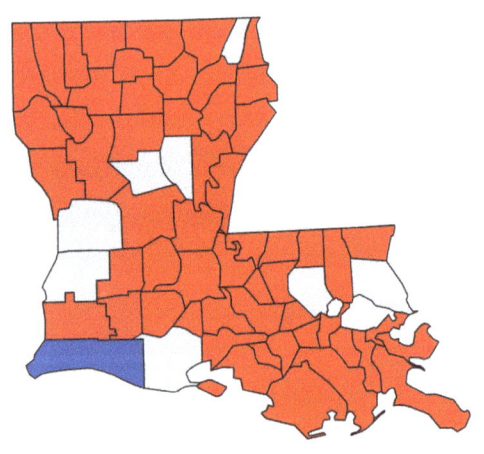

Industry Overconcentration Risk Map
Created with Mapchart.net, data—US Census

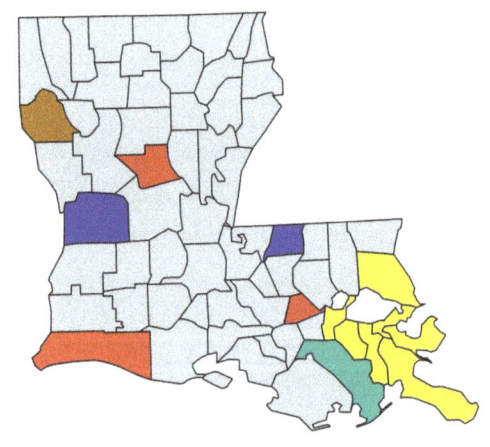

Real Estate Risk Map; G. Brian Davis, SparkRental,
ATTOM Data Solutions, Created with Datawrapper

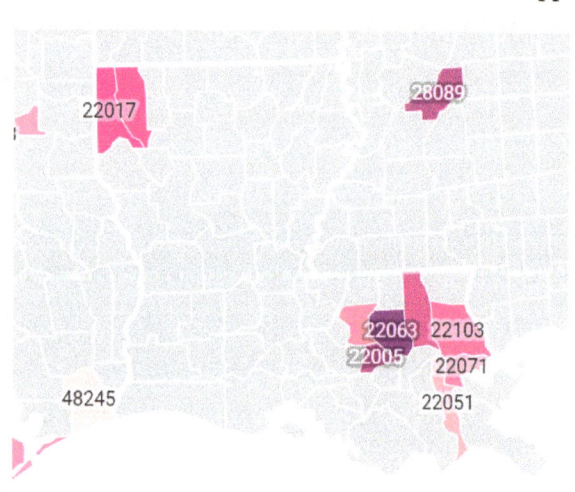

Density Risk Map
Source: US Census

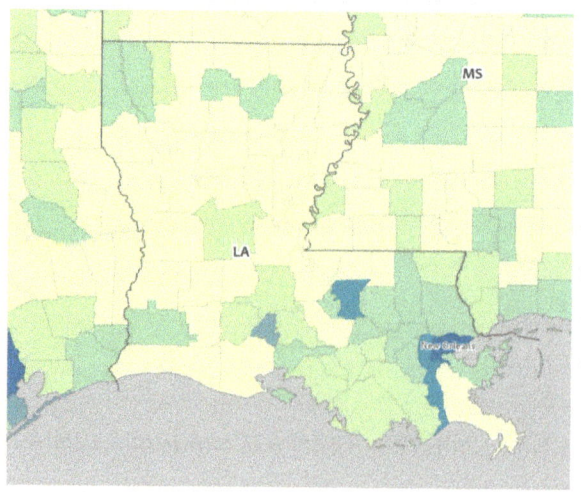

Poverty Risk Map
Source: US Census

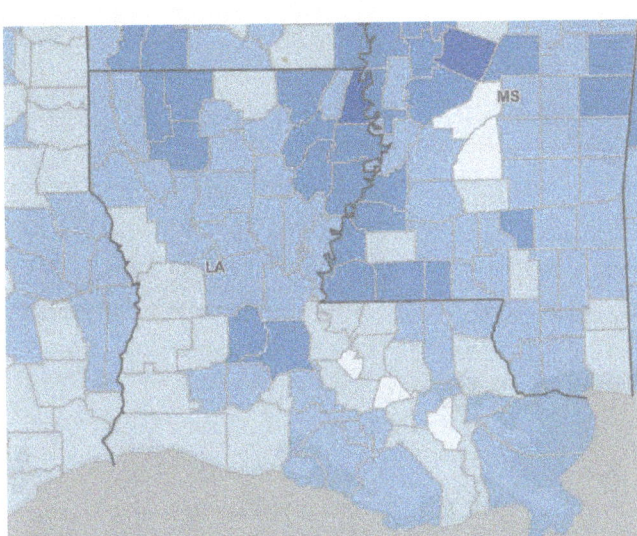

Unemployment Risk Map
Source: SparkRental & BLS

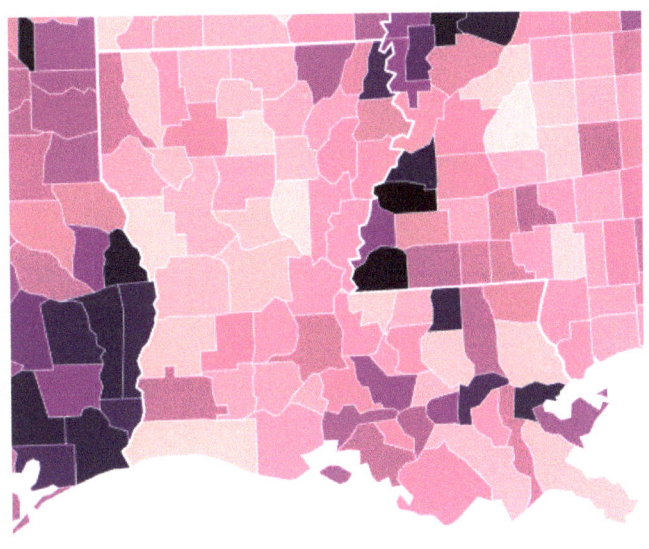

Economic & Crime Risk Map

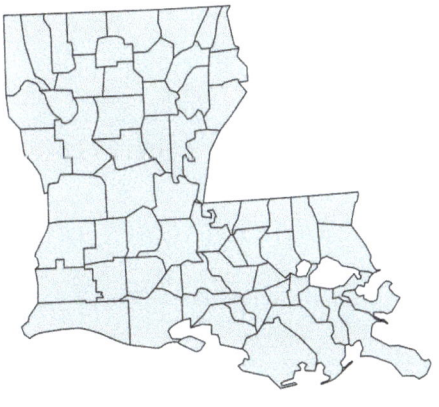

Main Summaries of Risk Maps

- Most of the state has a high Black population, which is a must-avoid risk.
- Some counties are subject to industry overconcentration.
- Metro-area risk is present in the New Orleans area in the Southeast of the state.
- Very high real estate risk in the New Orleans metro area.
- High poverty rate overall and high unemployment rate in some counties.

Conclusions

Awful race demographics. The crime rate issue will be terrible. Parts of New Orleans are already unlivable for civilized people. Also, this state is highly dependent on exports, which decline a lot in depressions. Thus, this state has high economic risk and extremely high crime risk.

State	Texas
Population	29,146 thous.
Land Area	261,232 sq mile
Density/mi2	111.6 people
Percent White	39.7%
Poverty Rate	13.9%
Unempl. Rate	3.9%

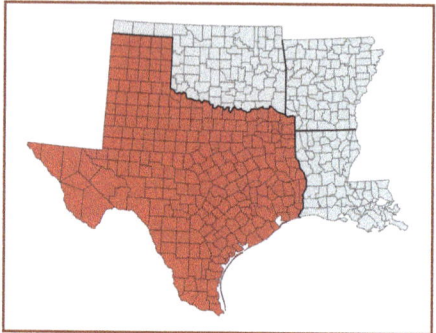

State Location Map
Created with Mapchart.net

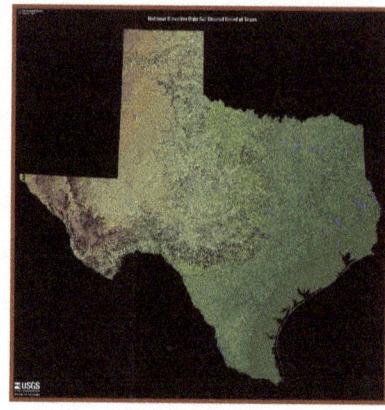

Texas - Shaded Relief Image
Credit: National Elevation Dataset, compiled
by the U.S. Geological Survey
Visit the USGS at https://usgs.gov.

Racial Risk Map
Created with Mapchart.net, data—US Census

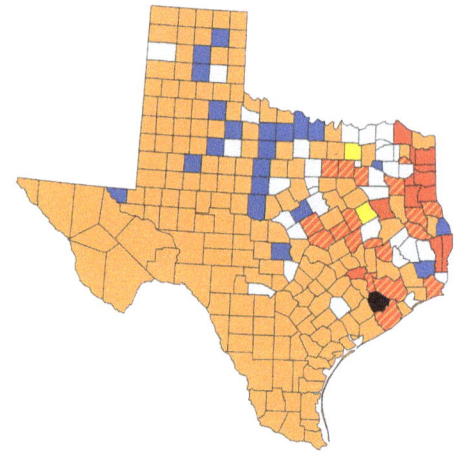

Industry Overconcentration Risk Map
Created with Mapchart.net, data—US Census

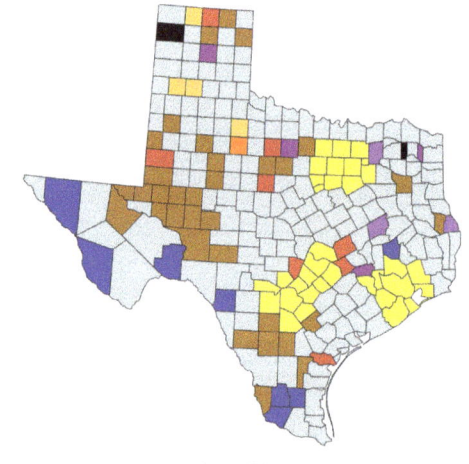

Real Estate Risk Map; G. Brian Davis, SparkRental,
ATTOM Data Solutions, Created with Datawrapper

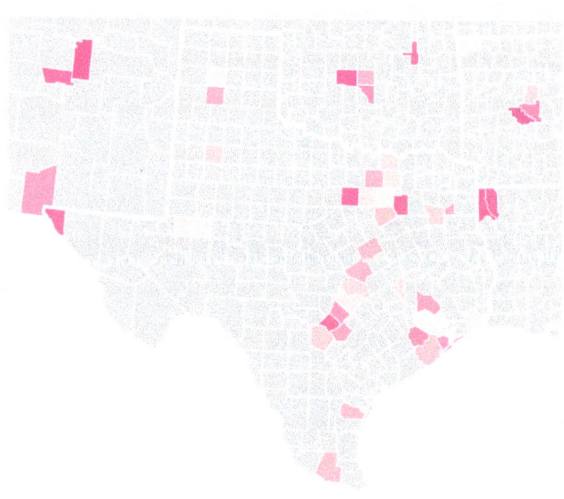

Density Risk Map
Source: US Census

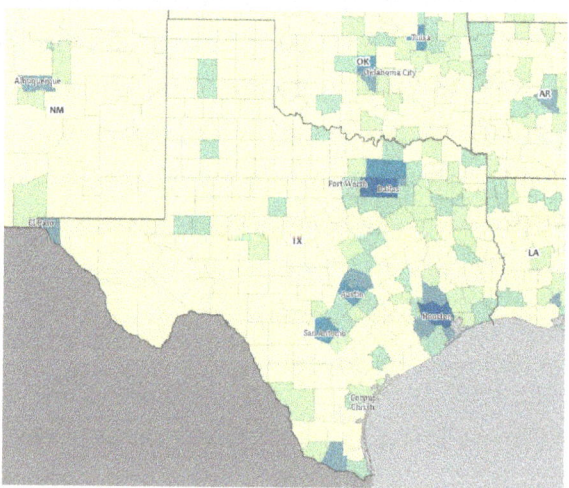

Poverty Risk Map
Source: US Census

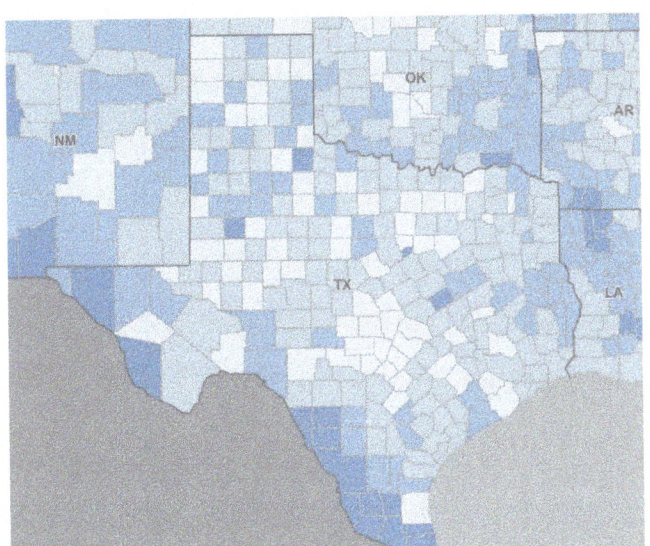

Unemployment Risk Map
Source: SparkRental & BLS

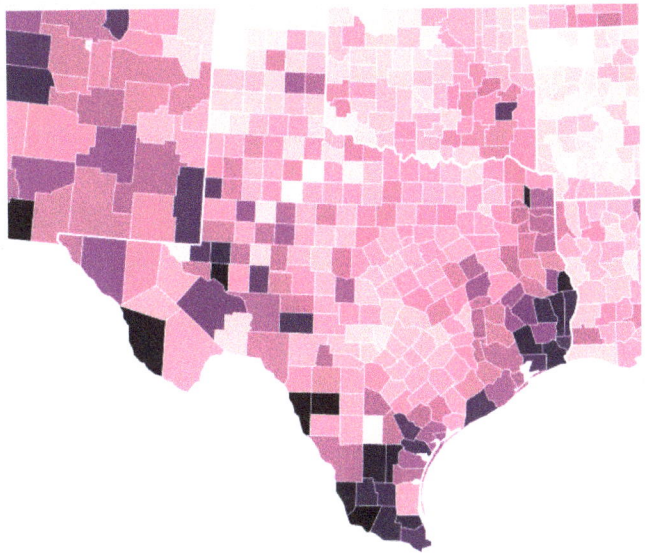

Economic & Crime Risk Map

Main Summaries of Risk Maps

- The percentage of the White population is very low.
- High mining industry overconcentration.
- Metro-area risk is present.
- High real estate risk is present in Texas's metro areas.
- High poverty and unemployment rates in many counties.

Conclusions

I wish Texas could have been a state that you could always rely on in times of trouble. However, modern Texas was fueled by the booming economy. There are so many reasons why this state is risky. Many of you would say, "No, you are wrong. Texas is one of the most recession-proof states." I wish so, but how? Less than 40% of the White (non-Hispanic or Latino) population and several counties have high exposure to the mining industry, which is extremely risky and will experience a deep decline, similar to the oil industry, which Texas relies on. Metro areas do not offer any safety. Texas metro areas such as Dallas, Austin, and Houston will experience severe real estate price declines. There are a few individual safe counties, but I am unwilling to pinpoint them. I prefer choosing a cluster of counties, which I cannot accomplish. Texas is risky in terms of both economic downturn and crime risk.

State	Oklahoma
Population	3,959 thous.
Land Area	68,595 sq mile
Density/mi2	57.7 people
Percent White	60.8%
Poverty Rate	15.2%
Unempl. Rate	3.0%

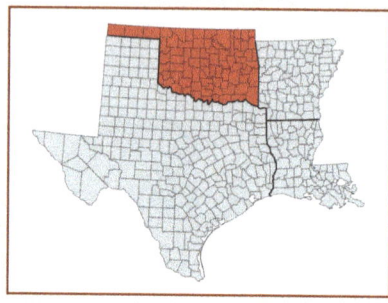

State Location Map
Created with Mapchart.net

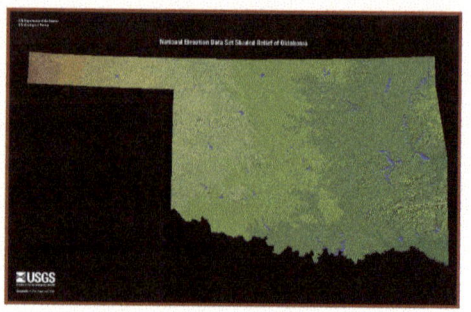

Oklahoma - Shaded Relief Image
Credit: National Elevation Dataset, compiled
by the U.S. Geological Survey
Visit the USGS at https://usgs.gov.

Racial Risk Map
Created with Mapchart.net, data—US Census

Industry Overconcentration Risk Map
Created with Mapchart.net, data—US Census

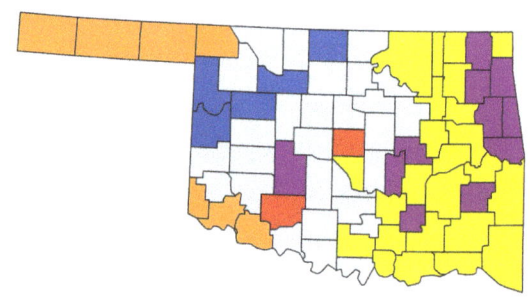

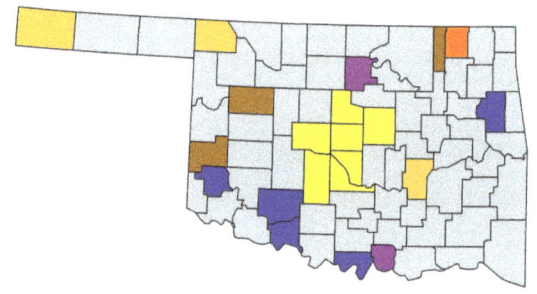

Real Estate Risk Map; G. Brian Davis, SparkRental,
ATTOM Data Solutions, Created with Datawrapper

Density Risk Map
Source: US Census

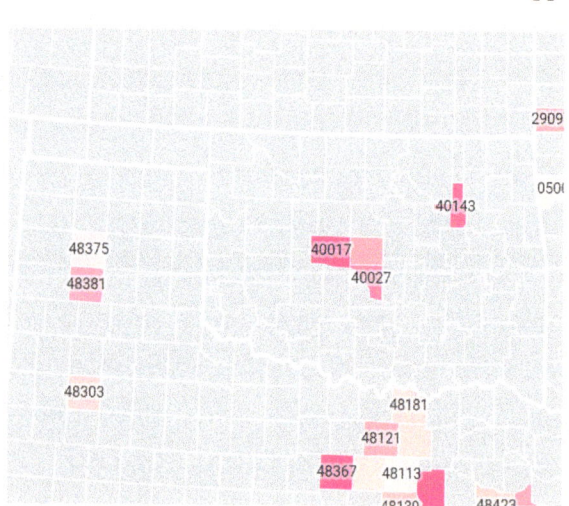

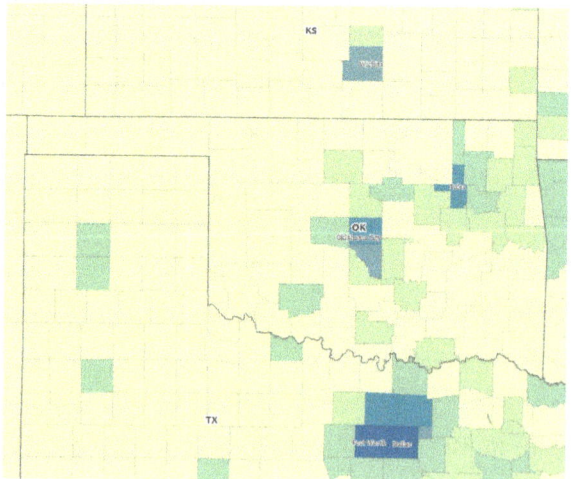

Poverty Risk Map
Source: US Census

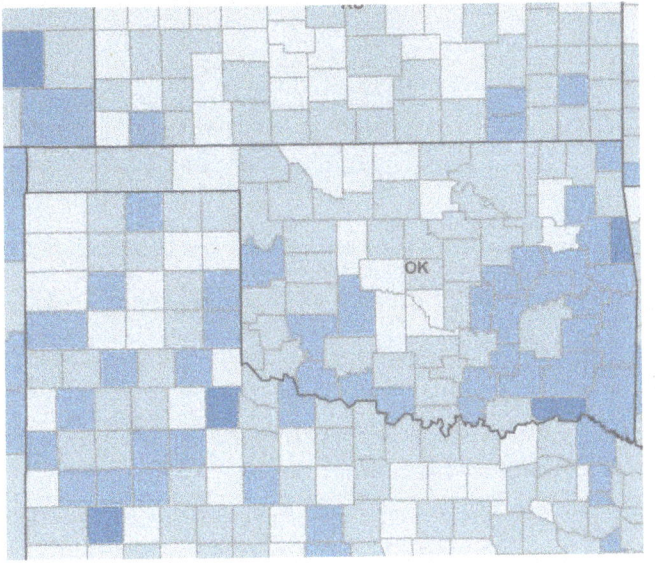

Unemployment Risk Map
Source: SparkRental & BLS

Economic & Crime Risk Map

Main Summaries of Risk Maps

- The percentage of the White population is low.
- Some industry overconcentration is present.
- Some metro-area risk is present.
- High poverty rate in some counties.

Conclusions

There is a race demographics issue. Also, the poverty rate is high in many counties. Oklahoma City metro area, located in the state's center, is highly susceptible to economic downturn and crime risk. The rest of the state does not have a high percentage of the White population, so it is unsafe.

State	Montana
Population	1,084 thous.
Land Area	145,546 sq mile
Density/mi2	7.4 people
Percent White	83.1%
Poverty Rate	12.4%
Unempl. Rate	2.6%

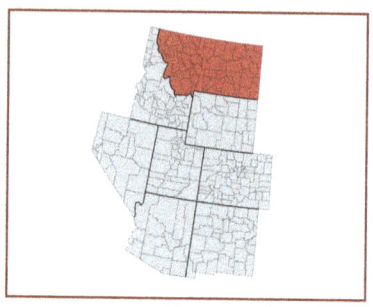

State Location Map
Created with Mapchart.net

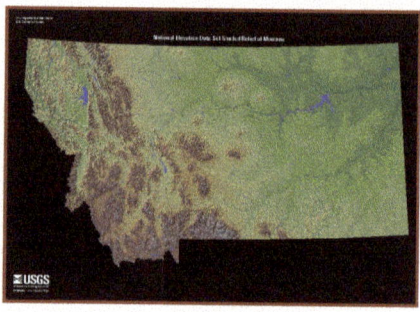

Montana - Shaded Relief Image
Credit: National Elevation Dataset, compiled
by the U.S. Geological Survey
Visit the USGS at https://usgs.gov.

Racial Risk Map
Created with Mapchart.net, data—US Census

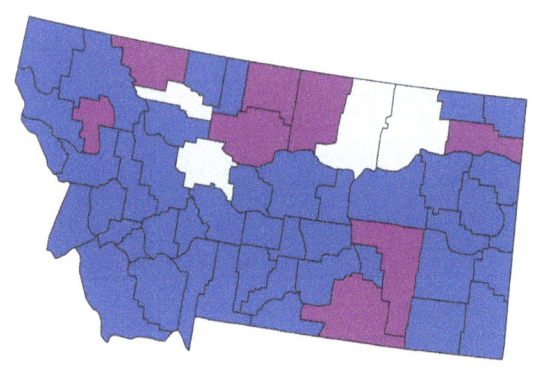

Industry Overconcentration Risk Map
Created with Mapchart.net, data—US Census

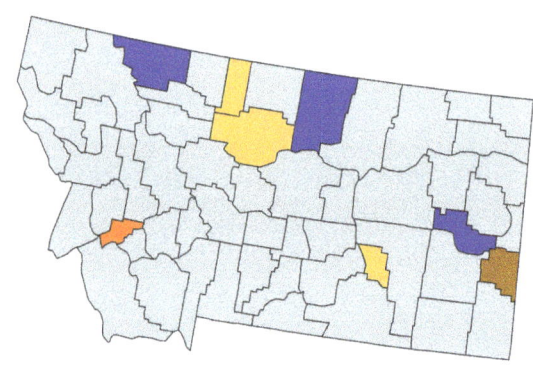

Real Estate Risk Map; G. Brian Davis, SparkRental,
ATTOM Data Solutions, Created with Datawrapper

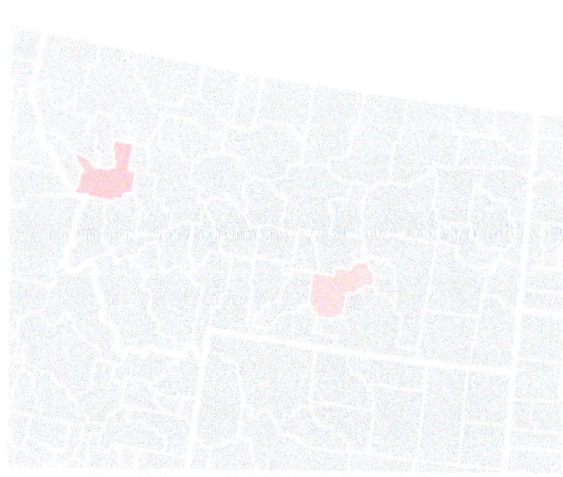

Density Risk Map
Source: US Census

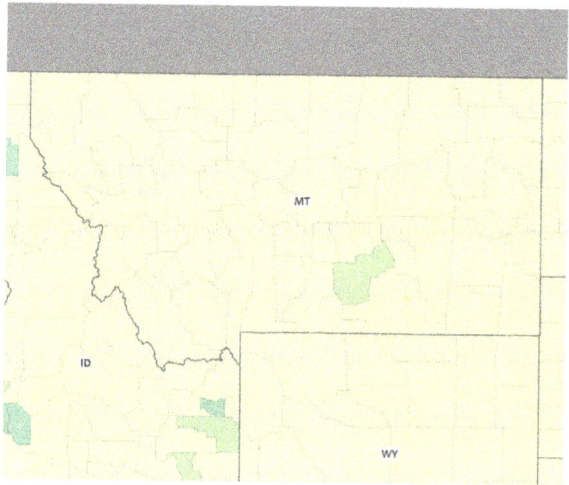

Poverty Risk Map
Source: US Census

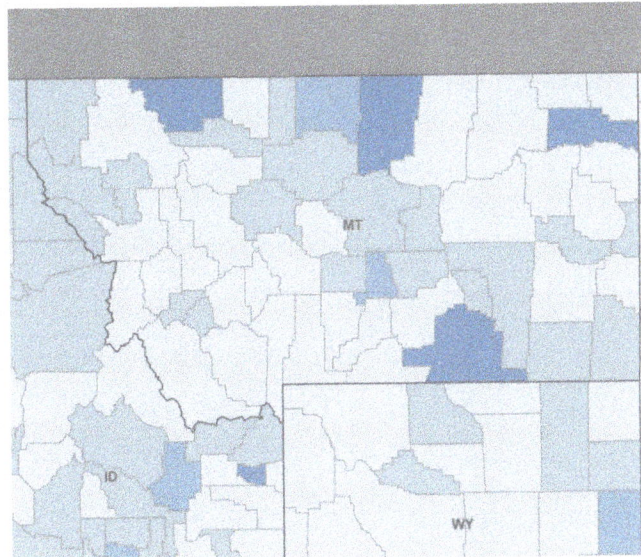

Unemployment Risk Map
Source: SparkRental & BLS

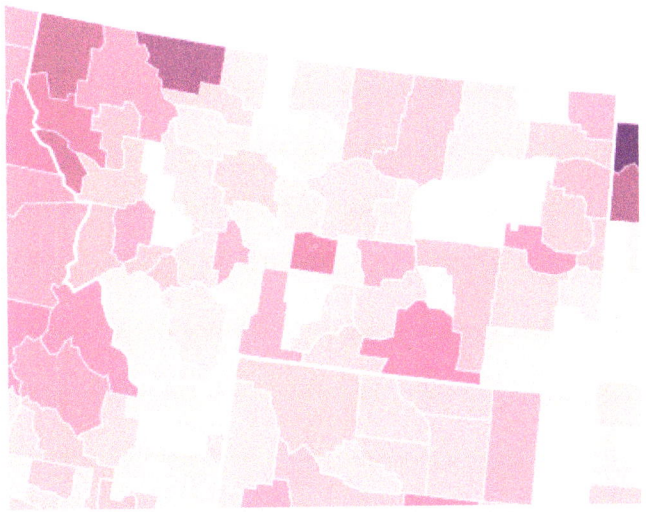

Economic & Crime Risk Map

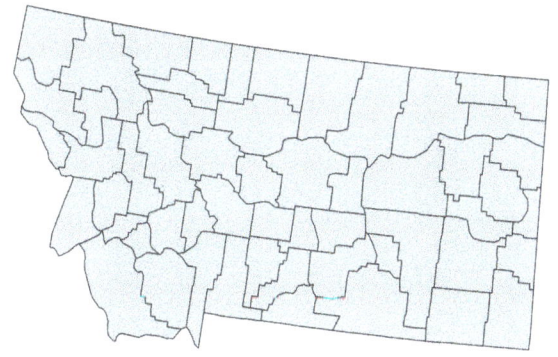

Main Summaries of Risk Maps

- The percentage of the White population is good.
- No metro-area risk.
- Very low population density.

Conclusions

There are few counties with Native American population above 20% and few counties with Whites less than 85% but higher than 70%. Because the state is somewhat detached from the world, I think there is a degree of relative safety. In terms of crime, the areas populated by White people will have less violent crime than other states. However, the state density is extremely low. Montana is the third least dense state after Alaska and Wyoming. The region is elevated on the West side, covered in mountains. Most counties have several small towns, which are very small. The uncertainty of the depression is that some of these towns could easily disappear because of the depression. I have no objective gauge to research every town with a population of a few thousand people. I would leave this research to someone else. Very low density, which carries certain risks, combined with the uncertainty of the mountainous region, urges me to abstain from predicting the risks of each county. In general, I think that in some of the predominantly White counties violent crime will be less severe than in most other states. However, I can't say which part of Montana will offer that safety.

State	Wyoming
Population	577 thous.
Land Area	97,093 sq mile
Density/mi2	5.9 people
Percent White	81.4%
Poverty Rate	10.7%
Unempl. Rate	3.6%

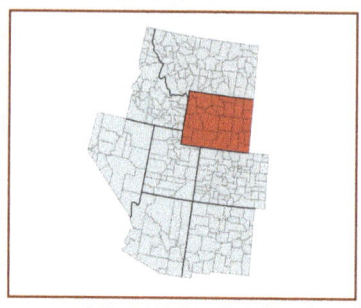

State Location Map
Created with Mapchart.net

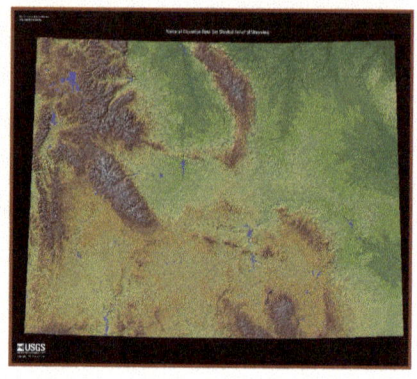

Wyoming - Shaded Relief Image
Credit: National Elevation Dataset, compiled
by the U.S. Geological Survey
Visit the USGS at https://usgs.gov.

Racial Risk Map
Created with Mapchart.net, data—US Census

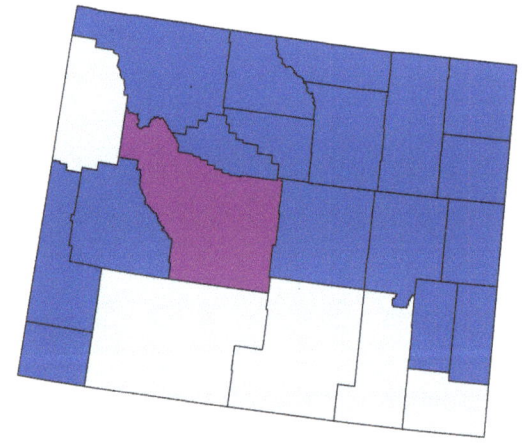

Industry Overconcentration Risk Map
Created with Mapchart.net, data—US Census

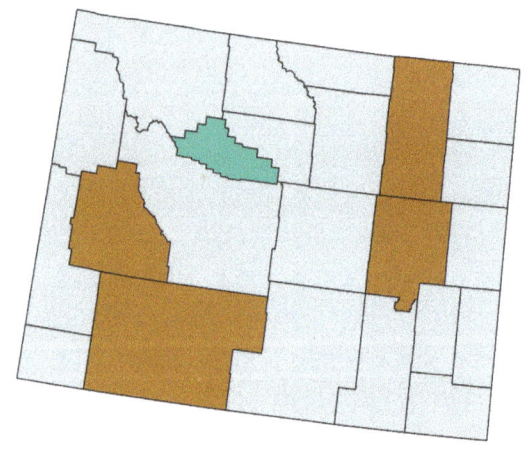

Real Estate Risk Map; G. Brian Davis, SparkRental,
ATTOM Data Solutions, Created with Datawrapper

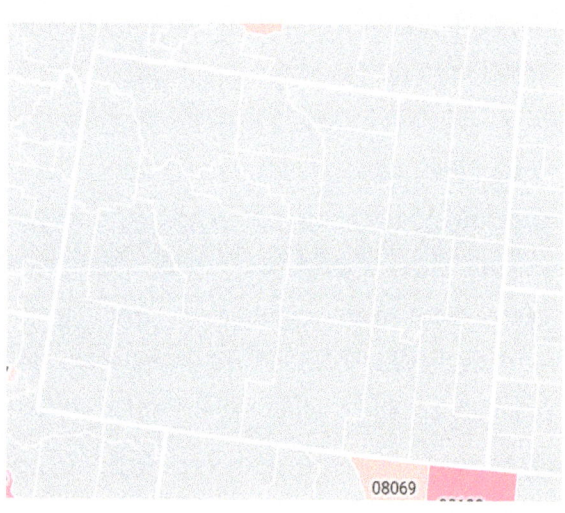

Density Risk Map
Source: US Census

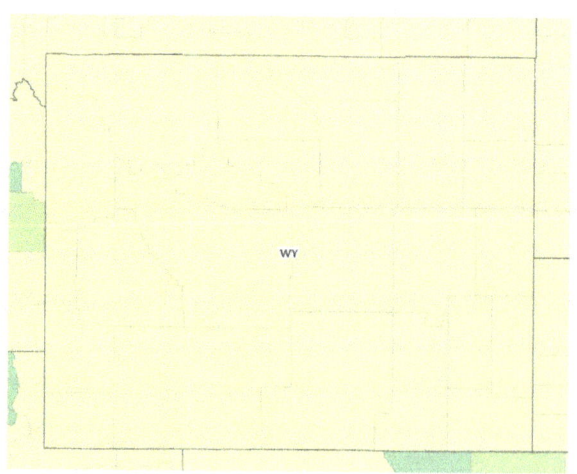

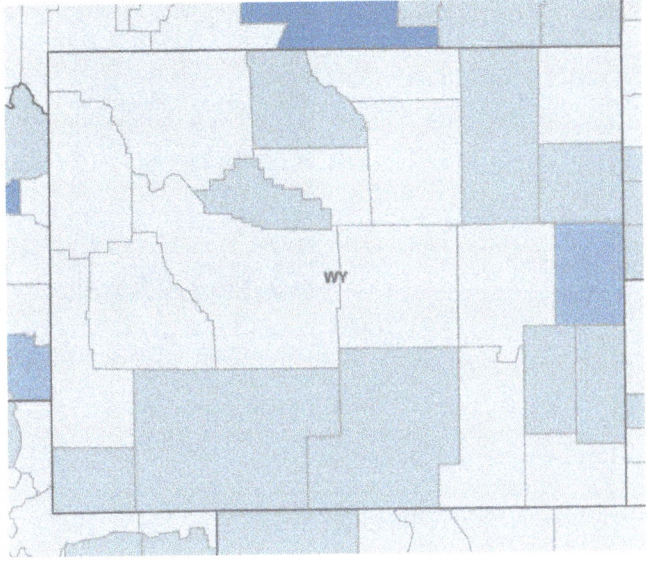

Poverty Risk Map
Source: US Census

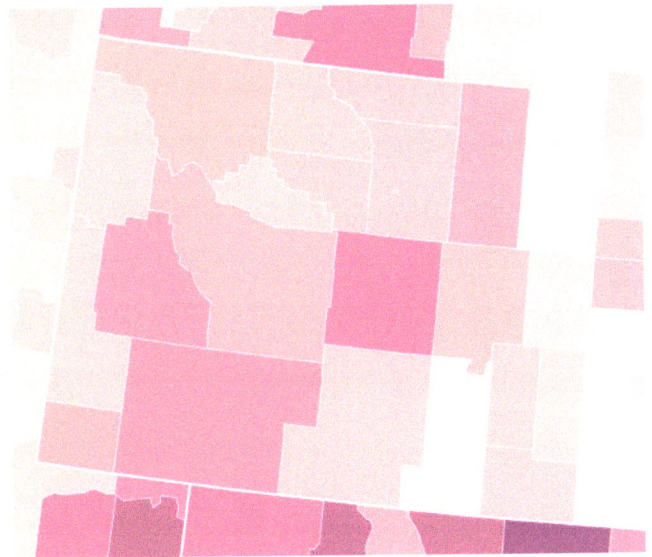

Unemployment Risk Map
Source: SparkRental & BLS

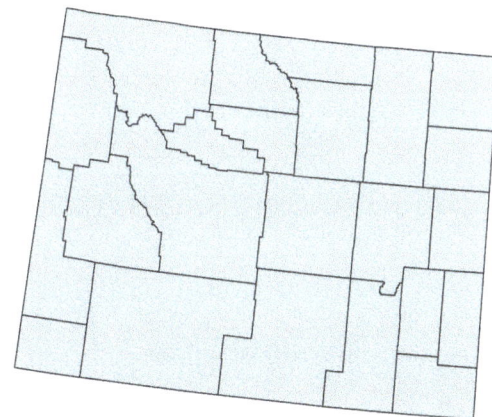

Economic & Crime Risk Map

Main Summaries of Risk Maps

- The percentage of the White population is good.
- Mining industry overconcentration is present.
- No metro-area risk.
- Very low population density.

Conclusions

Several counties have an overconcentration of the mining industry, which is very risky. The effects of the mining downturn could affect its nearby counties. Also, the same issue as in Montana is uncertainty in very low-populated areas. Similarly, Wyoming has highly elevated, mountainous, very low populated areas. Thus, it is very difficult to pinpoint counties that will be economically relatively safe. Regarding crime risk, perhaps predominantly White counties will likely be safer than most other states.

State	Idaho
Population	1,839 thous.
Land Area	82,643 sq mile
Density/mi2	22.3 people
Percent White	78.9%
Poverty Rate	11.0%
Unempl. Rate	2.7%

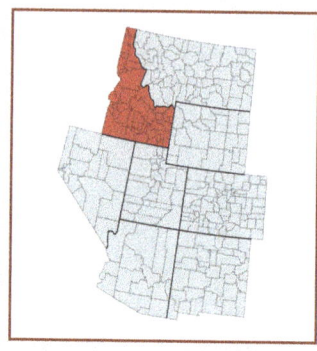

State Location Map
Created with Mapchart.net

Idaho - Shaded Relief Image
Credit: National Elevation Dataset, compiled
by the U.S. Geological Survey
Visit the USGS at https://usgs.gov.

Racial Risk Map
Created with Mapchart.net, data—US Census

Industry Overconcentration Risk Map
Created with Mapchart.net, data—US Census

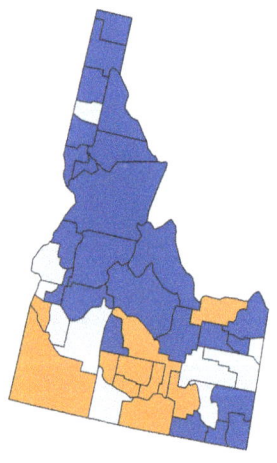

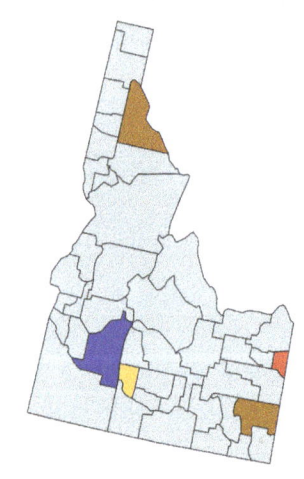

Real Estate Risk Map; G. Brian Davis, SparkRental,
ATTOM Data Solutions, Created with Datawrapper

Density Risk Map
Source: US Census

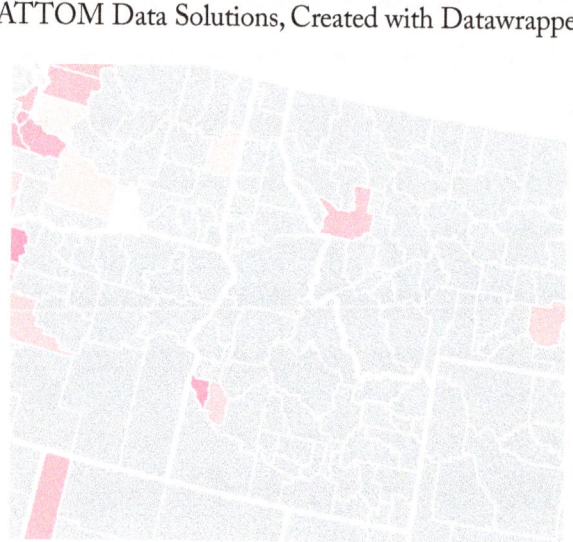

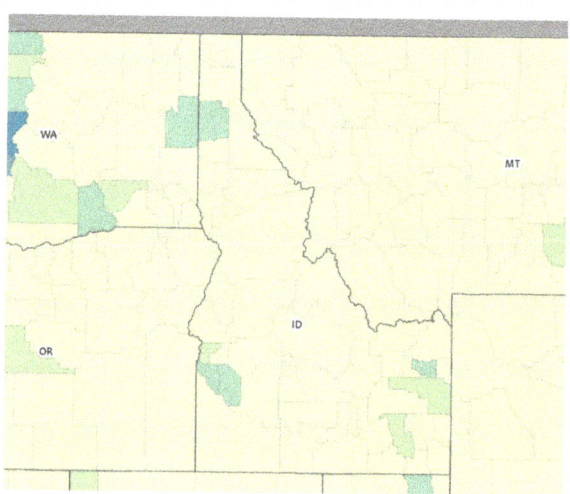

Poverty Risk Map
Source: US Census

Unemployment Risk Map
Source: SparkRental & BLS

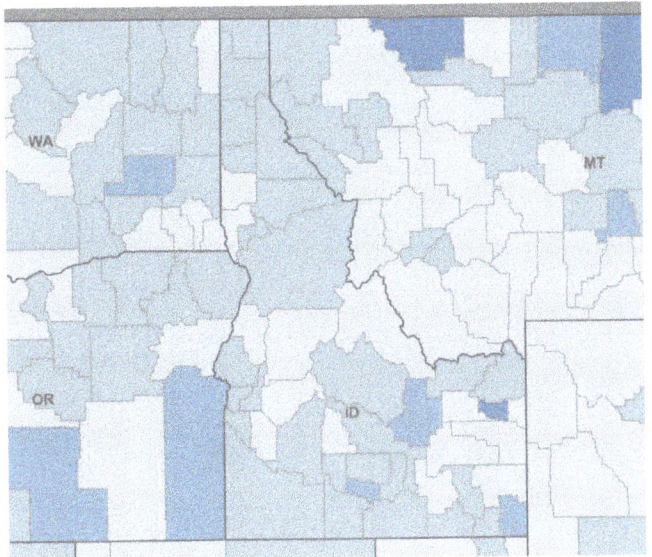

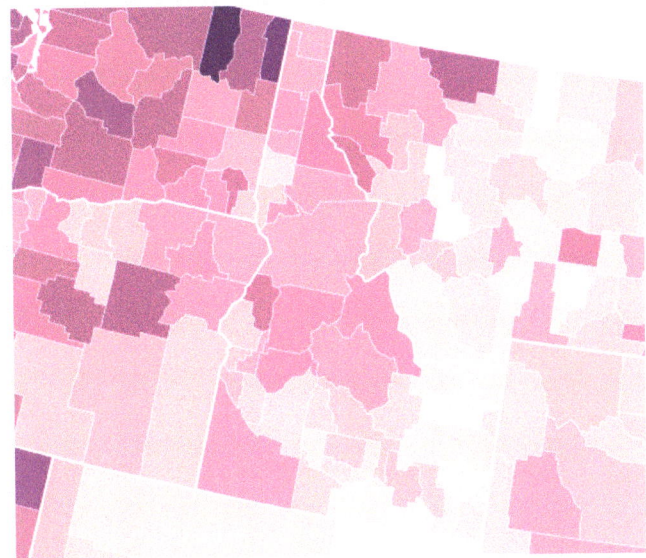

Economic & Crime Risk Map

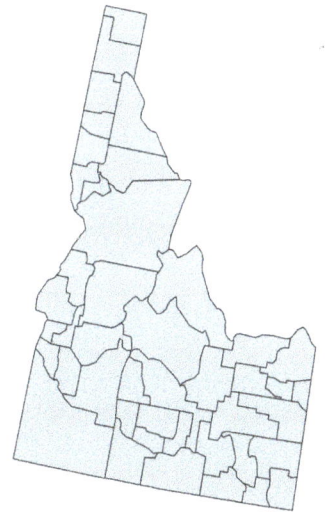

Main Summaries of Risk Maps

- The percentage of the White population is reasonable.
- No metro-area risk.
- Low population density.

Conclusions

Sadly, non-mountainous areas of Idaho are not predominantly White, otherwise, I would have considered those areas relatively safe. In the mountainous regions, there is the same uncertainty as with Montana and Wyoming. Predominantly White areas of Idaho would probably suffer less than many states in terms of violent crime.

State	Colorado
Population	5,774 thous.
Land Area	103,642 sq mile
Density/mi2	55.7 people
Percent White	65.1%
Poverty Rate	9.6%
Unempl. Rate	3.0%

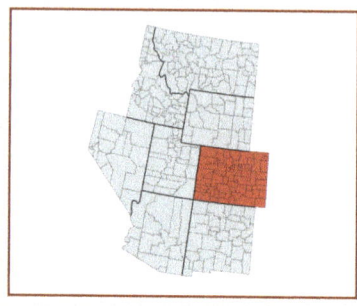

State Location Map
Created with Mapchart.net

Colorado - Shaded Relief Image
Credit: National Elevation Dataset, compiled
by the U.S. Geological Survey
Visit the USGS at https://usgs.gov.

Racial Risk Map
Created with Mapchart.net, data—US Census

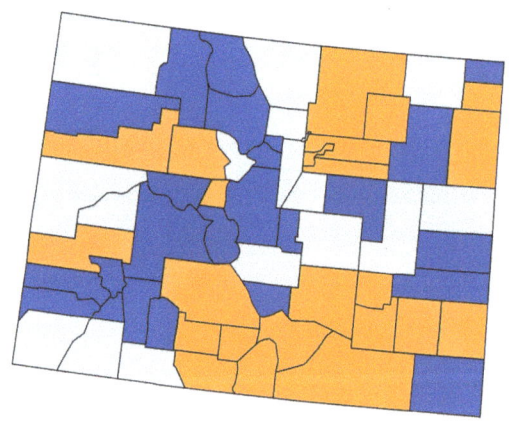

Industry Overconcentration Risk Map
Created with Mapchart.net, data—US Census

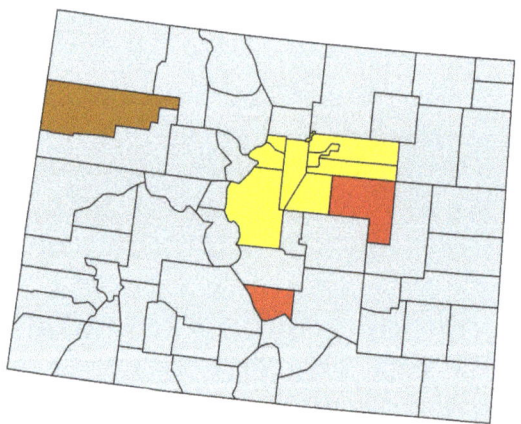

Real Estate Risk Map; G. Brian Davis, SparkRental,
ATTOM Data Solutions, Created with Datawrapper

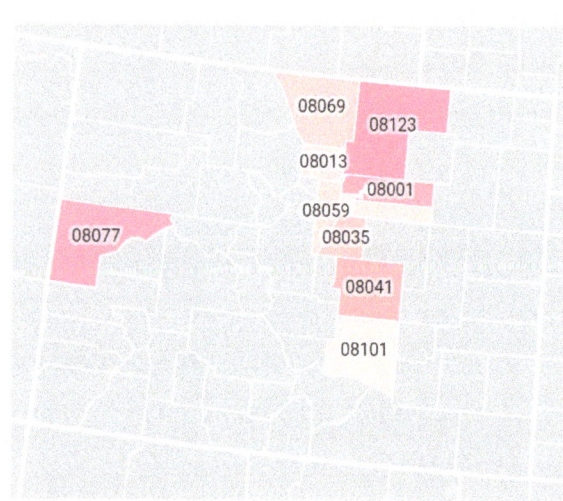

Density Risk Map
Source: US Census

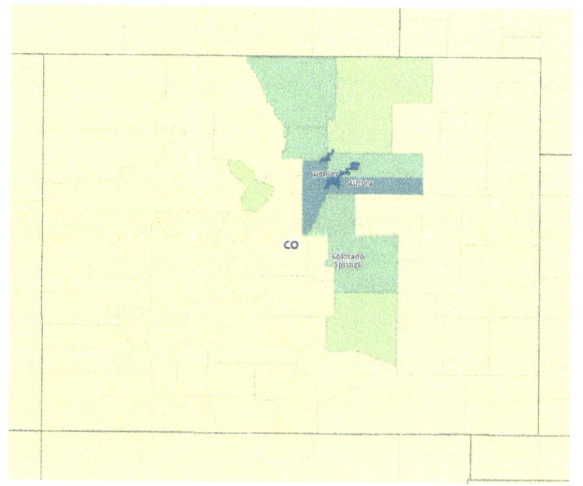

Poverty Risk Map
Source: US Census

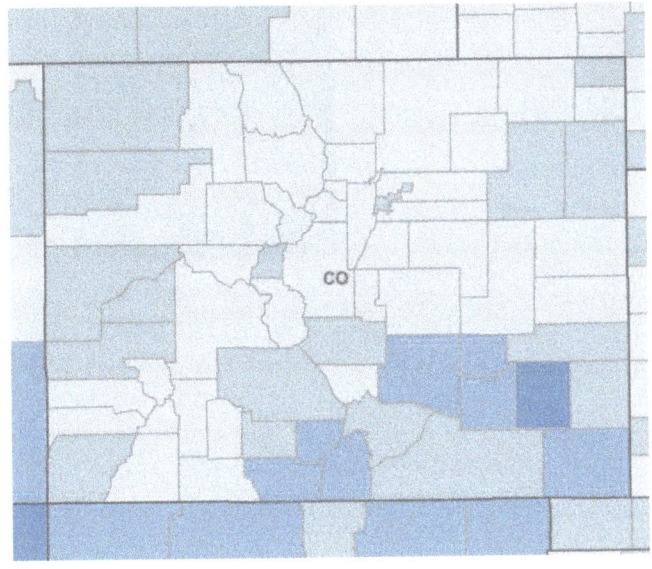

Unemployment Risk Map
Source: SparkRental & BLS

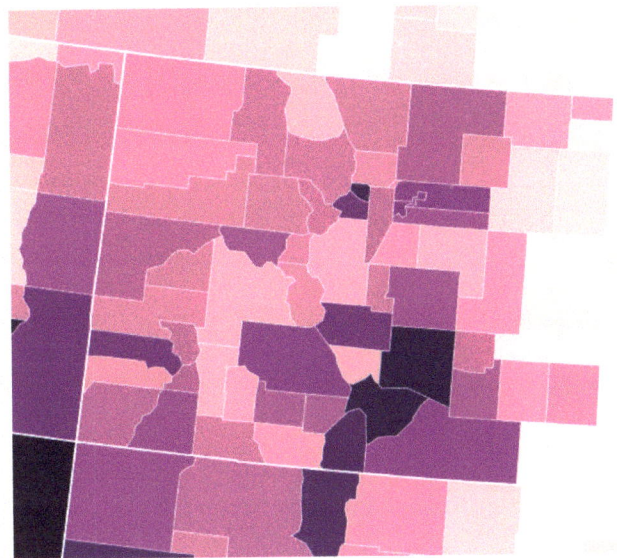

Economic & Crime Risk Map

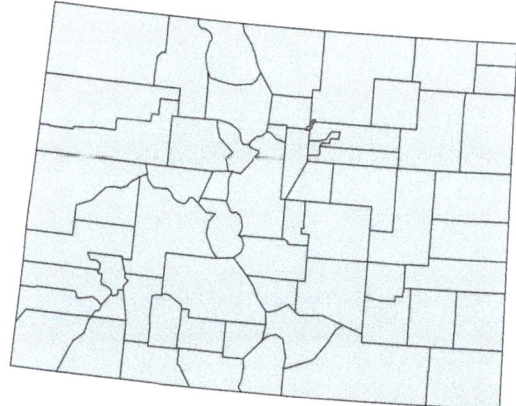

Main Summaries of Risk Maps

- The percentage of the White population is not enough.
- Metro-area risk is present in the Denver area.
- High real estate risk is present in the Denver area.

Conclusions

Colorado does not have a high percentage of White (non-Hispanic or Latino) population. There are mountains in Western Colorado. See the state of Montana on this issue. Many counties have a high unemployment rate. Overall, I do not think this state is not unsafe from economic or crime perspectives.

State	Utah
Population	3,272 thous.
Land Area	82,170 sq mile
Density/mi2	39.7 people
Percent White	75.4%
Poverty Rate	8.5%
Unempl. Rate	2.3%

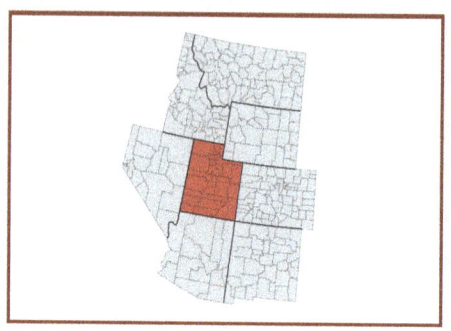

State Location Map
Created with Mapchart.net

Utah - Shaded Relief Image
Credit: National Elevation Dataset, compiled
by the U.S. Geological Survey
Visit the USGS at https://usgs.gov.

Racial Risk Map
Created with Mapchart.net, data—US Census

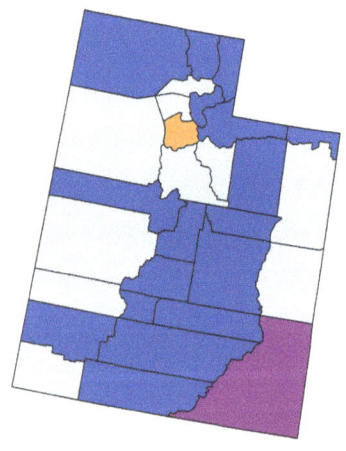

Industry Overconcentration Risk Map
Created with Mapchart.net, data—US Census

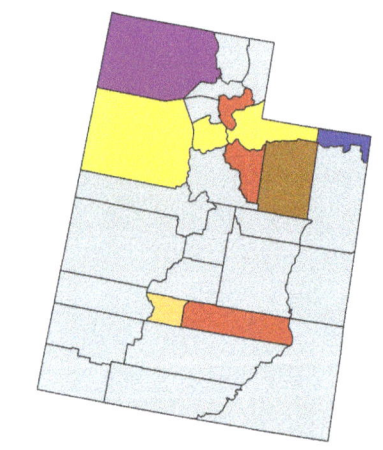

Real Estate Risk Map; G. Brian Davis, SparkRental,
ATTOM Data Solutions, Created with Datawrapper

Density Risk Map
Source: US Census

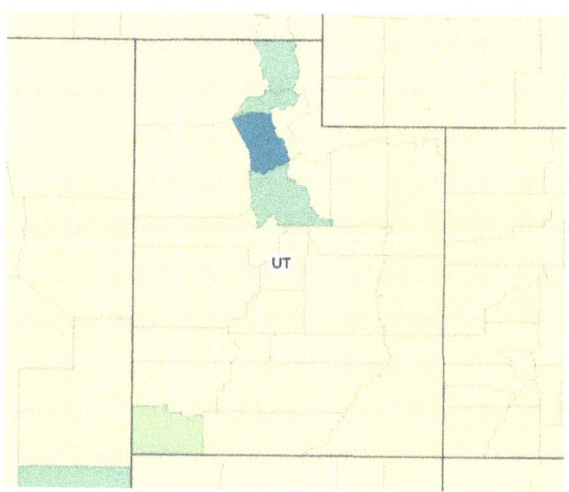

Poverty Risk Map
Source: US Census

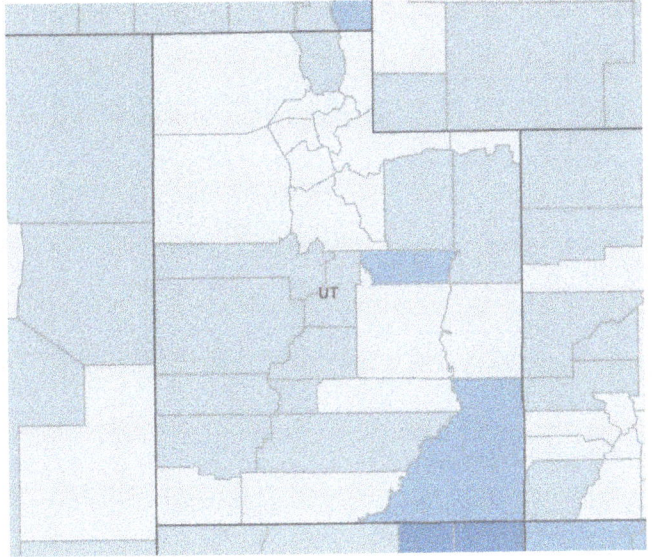

Unemployment Risk Map
Source: SparkRental & BLS

Economic & Crime Risk Map

Main Summaries of Risk Maps

- The percentage of the White population is not desirable enough.
- Industry overconcentration is present in the Northern areas of Utah.
- Metro-area risk is present in the Salt Lake City area.
- High real estate risk is present near the Salt Lake City area.
- High poverty and unemployment rates in south and southeastern counties.

Conclusions

First, racial demographics are not satisfactory. The northern area has industry concentration, while the southeastern area has high unemployment or poverty. The state is mountainous. Utah is not safe in my opinion.

State	New Mexico
Population	2,118 thous.
Land Area	121,298 sq mile
Density/mi2	17.5 people
Percent White	36.5%
Poverty Rate	18.3%
Unempl. Rate	4.0%

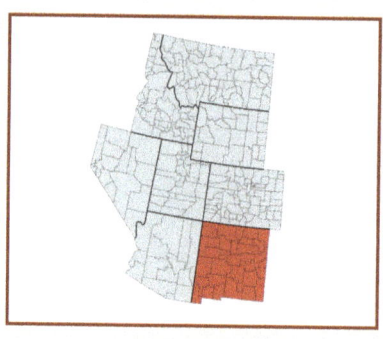

State Location Map
Created with Mapchart.net

New Mexico - Shaded Relief Image
Credit: National Elevation Dataset, compiled
by the U.S. Geological Survey
Visit the USGS at https://usgs.gov.

Racial Risk Map
Created with Mapchart.net, data—US Census

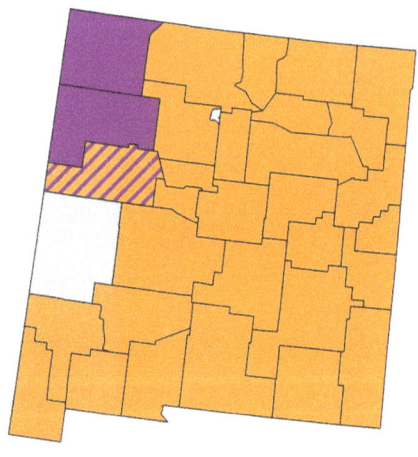

Industry Overconcentration Risk Map
Created with Mapchart.net, data—US Census

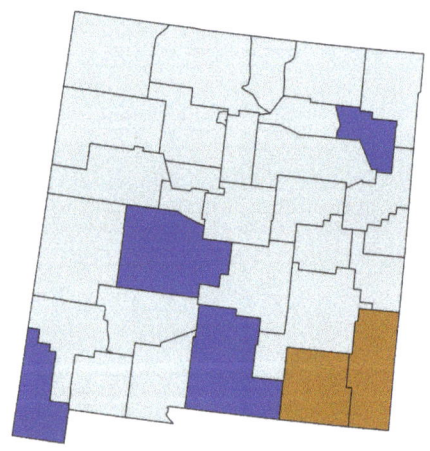

Real Estate Risk Map; G. Brian Davis, SparkRental,
ATTOM Data Solutions, Created with Datawrapper

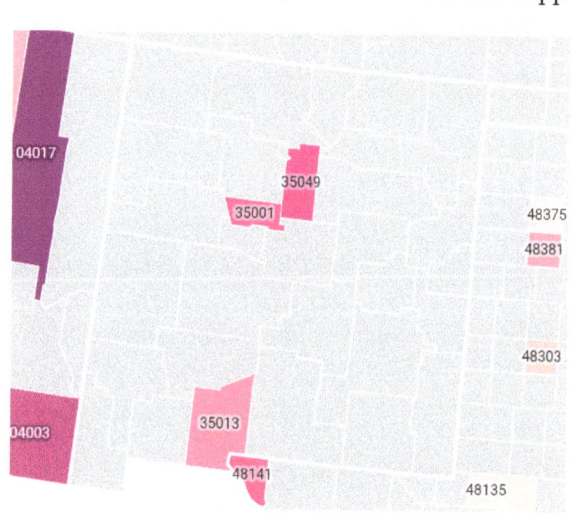

Density Risk Map
Source: US Census

Poverty Risk Map
Source: US Census

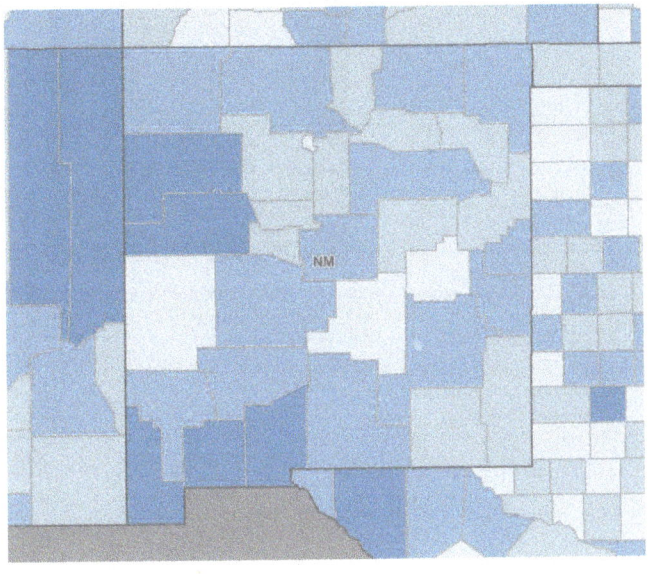

Unemployment Risk Map
Source: SparkRental & BLS

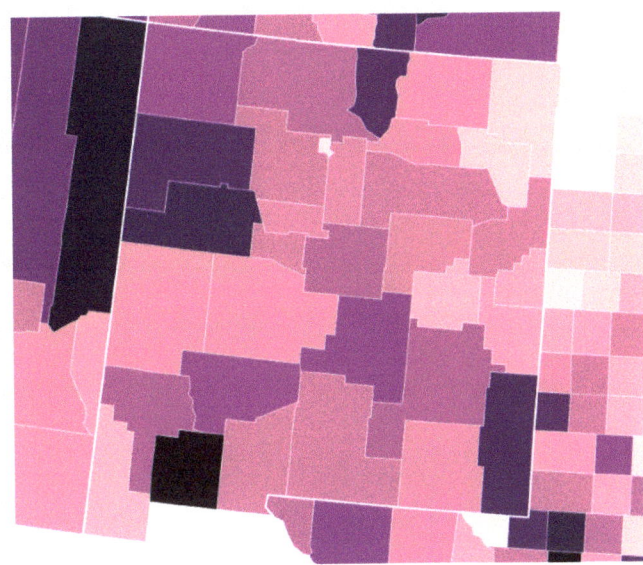

Economic & Crime Risk Map

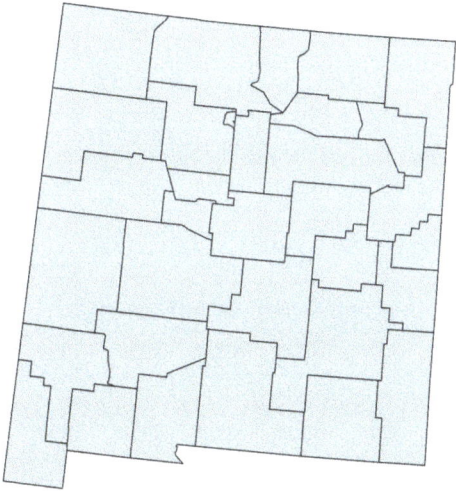

Main Summaries of Risk Maps

- The percentage of the White population is very low.
- High poverty and unemployment rates in many counties.

Conclusions

The race demographics are terrible in New Mexico. There is no need to say anything else besides that the state is poor. New Mexico will be an extremely risky state economically and in terms of crime.

State	Arizona
Population	7,152 thous.
Land Area	113,594 sq mile
Density/mi2	62.9 people
Percent White	53.4%
Poverty Rate	13.1%
Unempl. Rate	3.8%

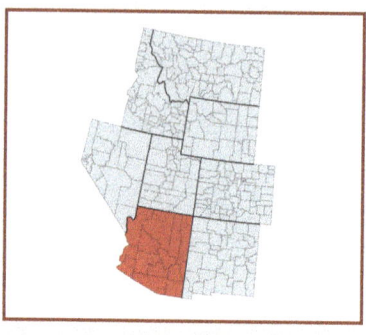

State Location Map
Created with Mapchart.net

Arizona - Shaded Relief Image
Credit: National Elevation Dataset, compiled
by the U.S. Geological Survey
Visit the USGS at https://usgs.gov.

Racial Risk Map
Created with Mapchart.net, data—US Census

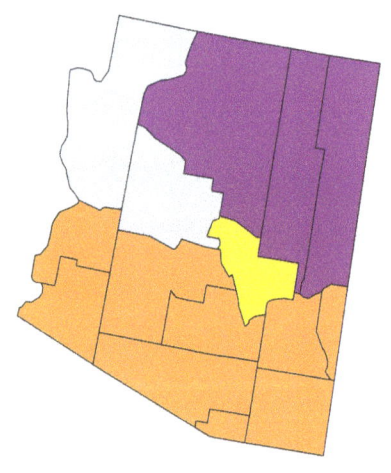

Industry Overconcentration Risk Map
Created with Mapchart.net, data—US Census

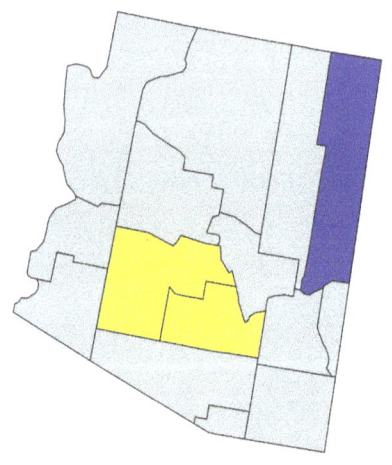

Real Estate Risk Map; G. Brian Davis, SparkRental,
ATTOM Data Solutions, Created with Datawrapper

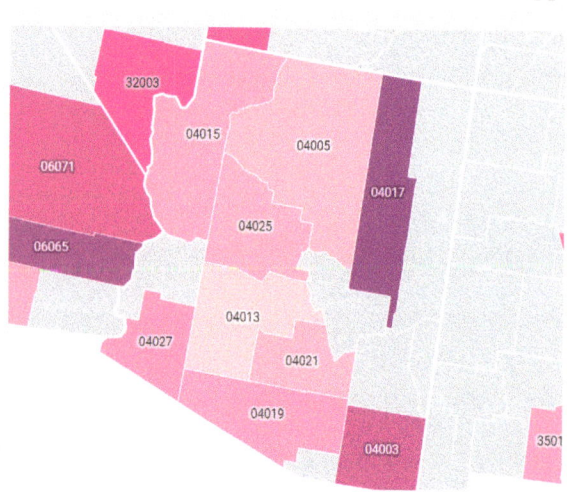

Density Risk Map
Source: US Census

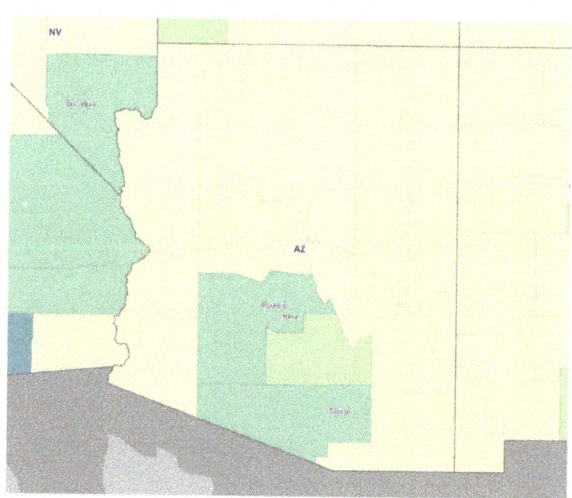

Poverty Risk Map
Source: US Census

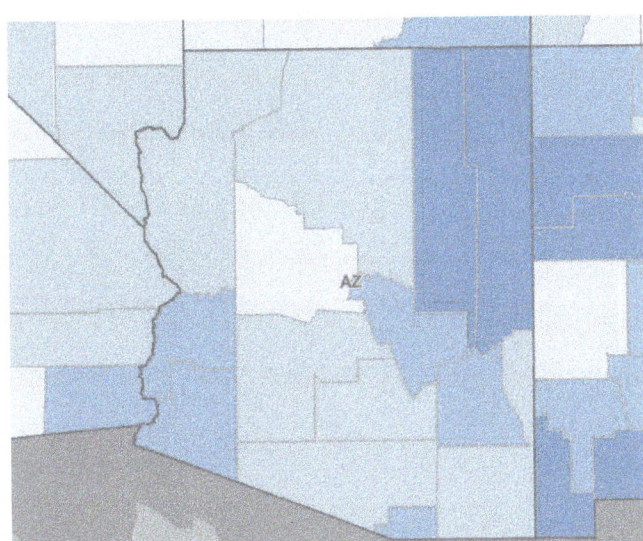

Unemployment Risk Map
Source: SparkRental & BLS

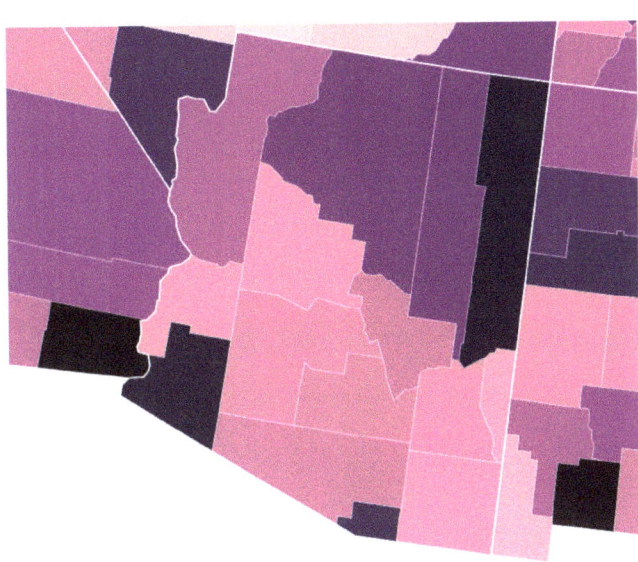

Economic & Crime Risk Map

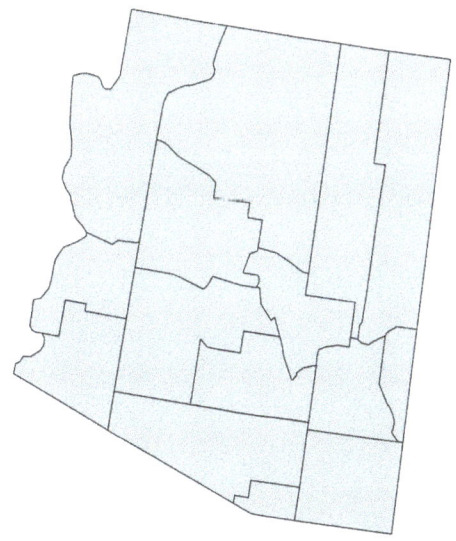

Main Summaries of Risk Maps

- The percentage of the White population is low.
- Arizona is subject to high real estate risk.
- High poverty and unemployment rates in many counties.

Conclusions

No counties with predominantly White people. Nothing else to say. This state is extremely risky in terms of crime and economy.

State	Nevada
Population	3,105 thous.
Land Area	109,781 sq mile
Density/mi2	28.3 people
Percent White	45.9%
Poverty Rate	12.7%
Unempl. Rate	5.4%

State Location Map
Created with Mapchart.net

Nevada - Shaded Relief Image
Credit: National Elevation Dataset, compiled
by the U.S. Geological Survey
Visit the USGS at https://usgs.gov.

Racial Risk Map
Created with Mapchart.net, data—US Census

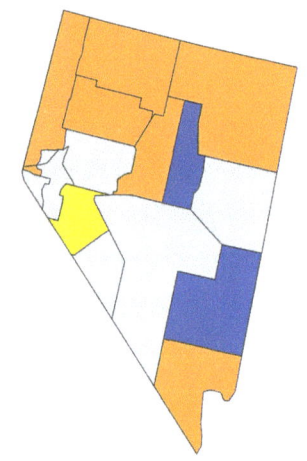

Industry Overconcentration Risk Map
Created with Mapchart.net, data—US Census

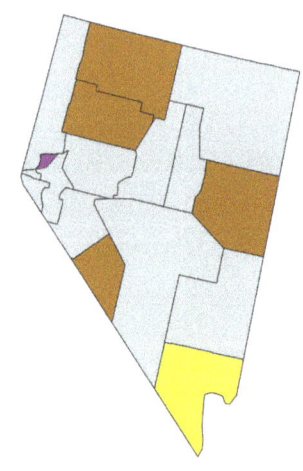

Real Estate Risk Map; G. Brian Davis, SparkRental,
ATTOM Data Solutions, Created with Datawrapper

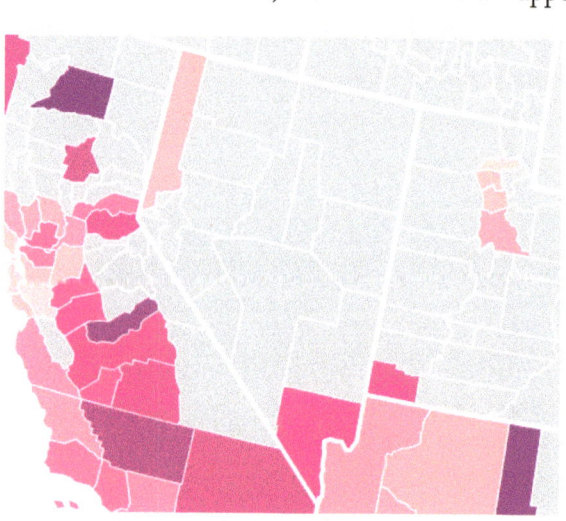

Density Risk Map
Source: US Census

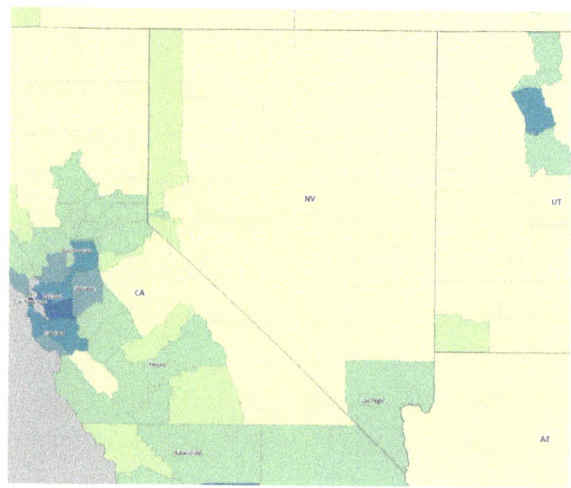

Poverty Risk Map
Source: US Census

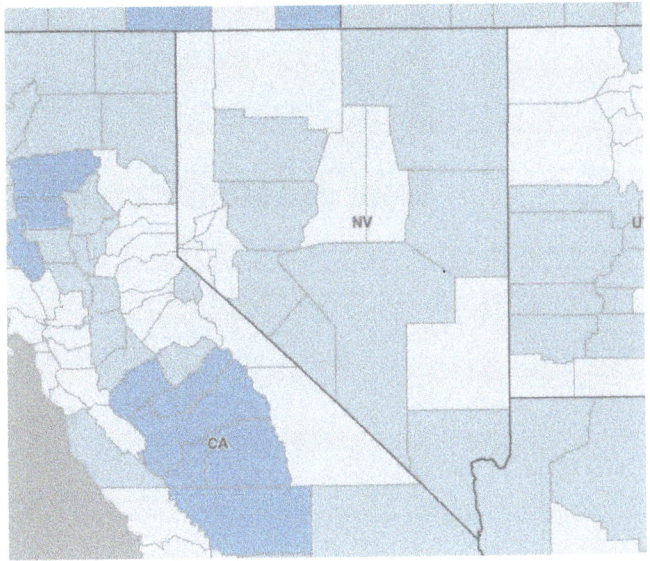

Unemployment Risk Map
Source: SparkRental & BLS

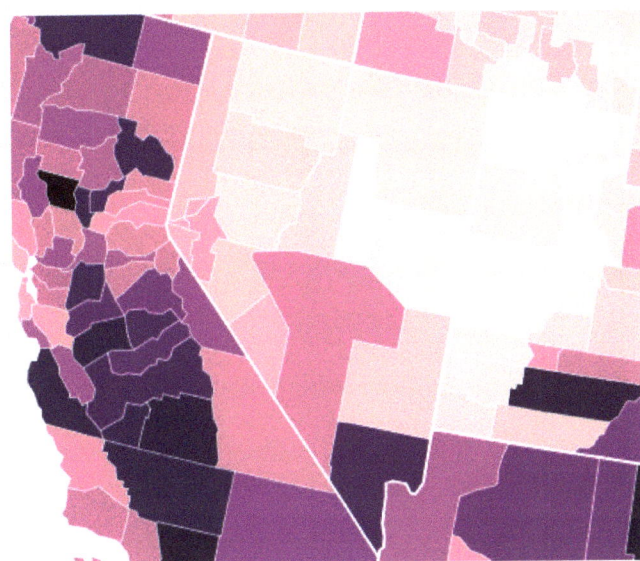

Economic & Crime Risk Map

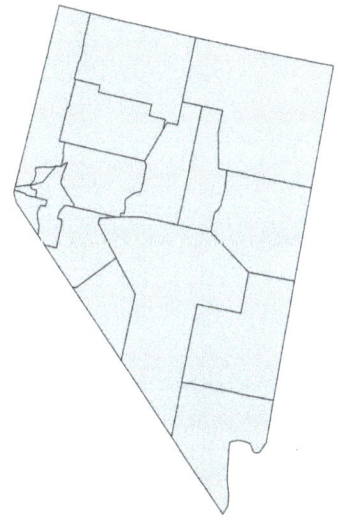

Main Summaries of Risk Maps

- The percentage of the White population is very low.
- Mining industry overconcentration is present.
- The Las Vegas area in the Southern portion of the state is subject to metro-area risk.
- The Las Vegas area is subject to very high real estate risk.

Conclusions

Las Vegas was fueled by the booming economy and has become a symbol of luxurious lifestyle. When tough times come, Las Vegas will be one of the epicenters of economic downturn. The rest of the state has low percentage of White population and high exposure to mining industry. This state will be risky during the downturn.

State	Washington
Population	7,705 thous.
Land Area	66,456 sq mile
Density/mi2	115.9 people
Percent White	63.8%
Poverty Rate	9.9%
Unempl. Rate	4.2%

State Location Map
Created with Mapchart.net

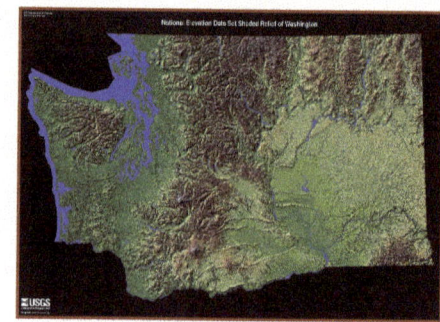

Washington - Shaded Relief Image
Credit: National Elevation Dataset, compiled
by the U.S. Geological Survey
Visit the USGS at https://usgs.gov.

Racial Risk Map
Created with Mapchart.net, data—US Census

Industry Overconcentration Risk Map
Created with Mapchart.net, data—US Census

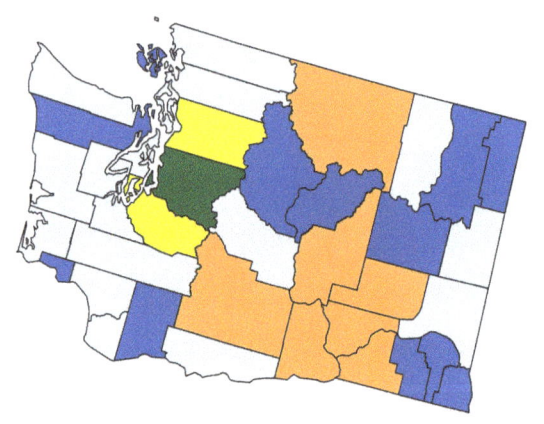

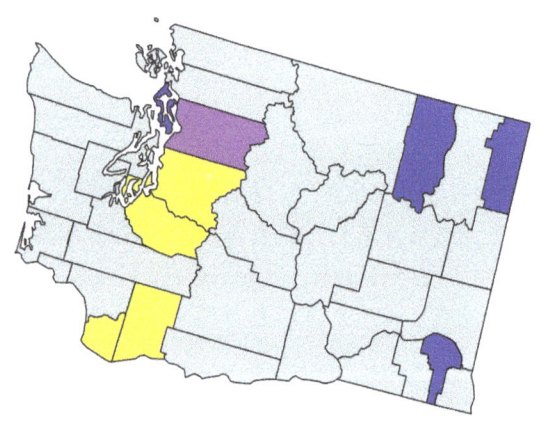

Real Estate Risk Map; G. Brian Davis, SparkRental,
ATTOM Data Solutions, Created with Datawrapper

Density Risk Map
Source: US Census

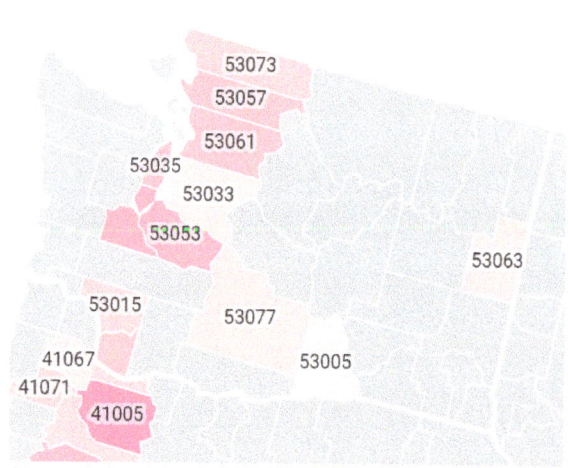

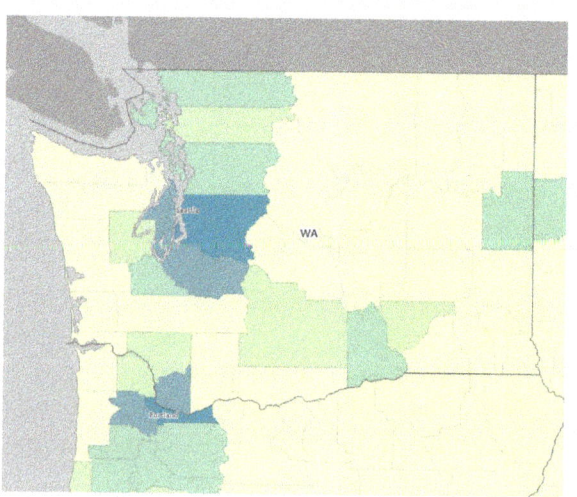

Poverty Risk Map
Source: US Census

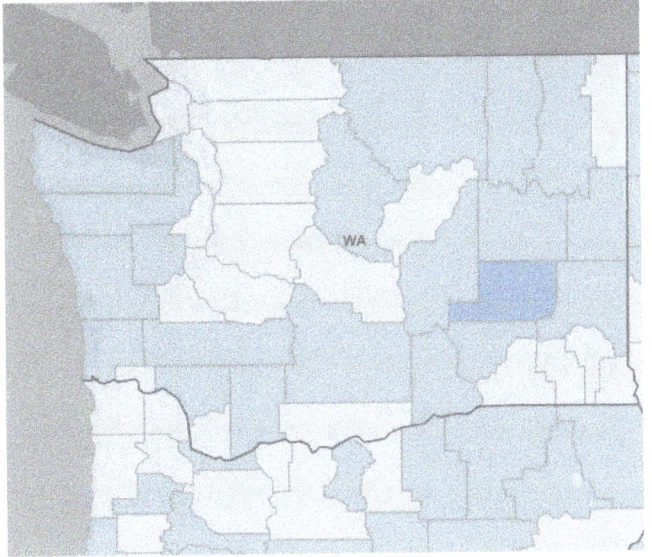

Unemployment Risk Map
Source: SparkRental & BLS

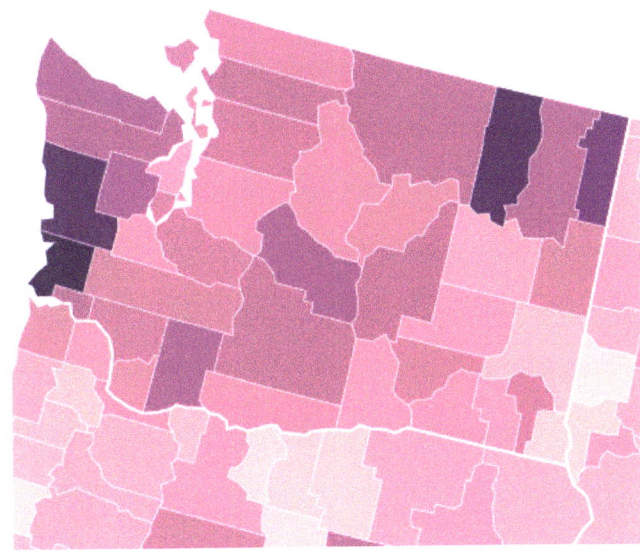

Economic & Crime Risk Map

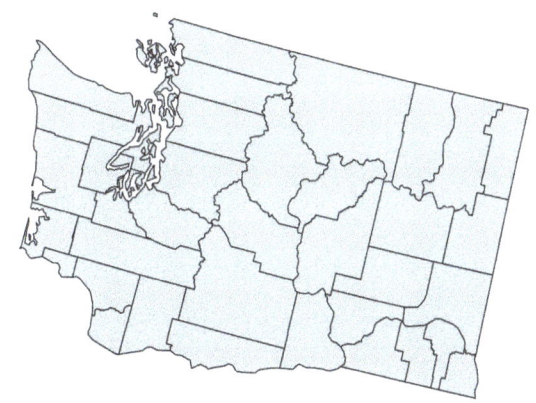

Main Summaries of Risk Maps

- The percentage of the White population is not enough.
- Metro-area risk is present in Seattle-Tacoma-Bellevue metropolitan area and Portland-Vancouver-Hillsboro metropolitan area.
- High real estate risk is present in metropolitan areas and their few adjacent counties.
- Population density is low on the East.
- High unemployment rate in many counties.

Conclusions

Washington's metro areas have typical metropolitan area risks. They are exposed to high real estate risk, and I expect them not to be safe in terms of crime rate. There are few predominantly White counties in the northeast. However, the unemployment rate is high there. The state overall is risky. I do not see safe haven counties.

State	Oregon
Population	4,237 thous.
Land Area	95,988 sq mile
Density/mi2	44.1 people
Percent White	71.7%
Poverty Rate	11.9%
Unempl. Rate	4.2%

State Location Map
Created with Mapchart.net

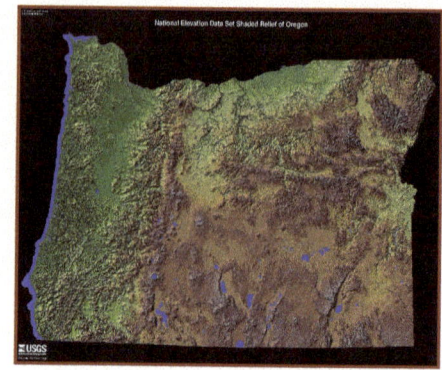

Oregon - Shaded Relief Image
Credit: National Elevation Dataset, compiled
by the U.S. Geological Survey
Visit the USGS at https://usgs.gov.

Racial Risk Map
Created with Mapchart.net, data—US Census

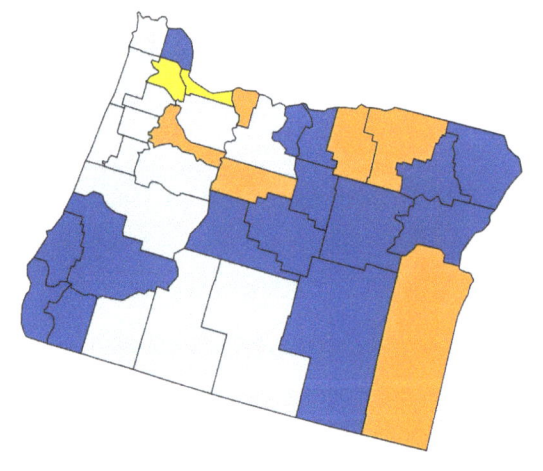

Industry Overconcentration Risk Map
Created with Mapchart.net, data—US Census

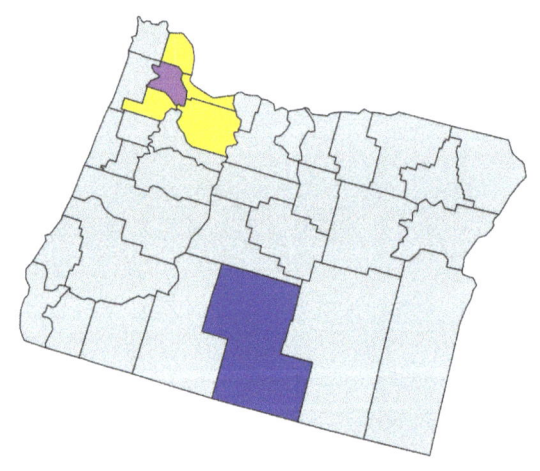

Real Estate Risk Map; G. Brian Davis, SparkRental,
ATTOM Data Solutions, Created with Datawrapper

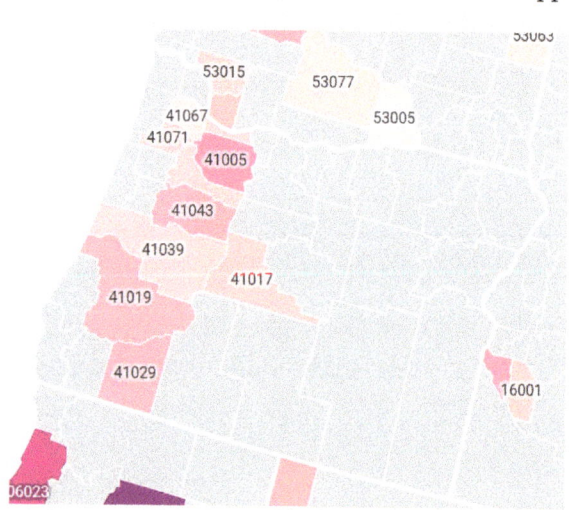

Density Risk Map
Source: US Census

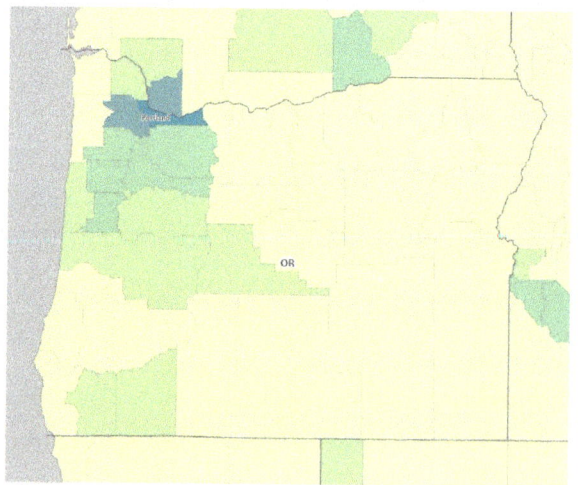

Poverty Risk Map
Source: US Census

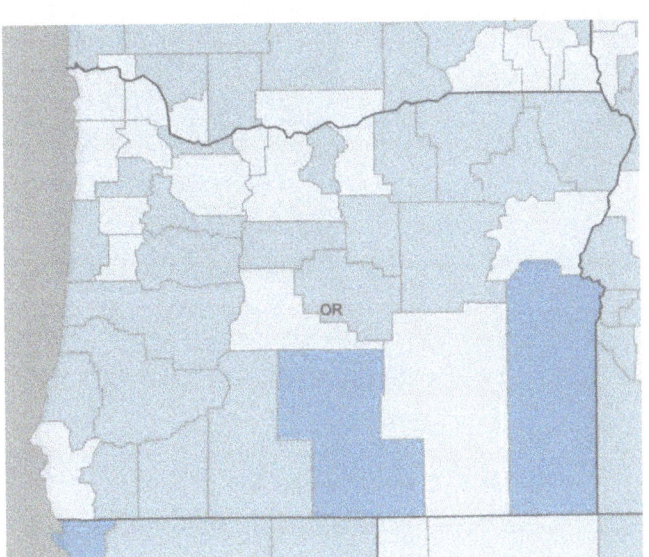

Unemployment Risk Map
Source: SparkRental & BLS

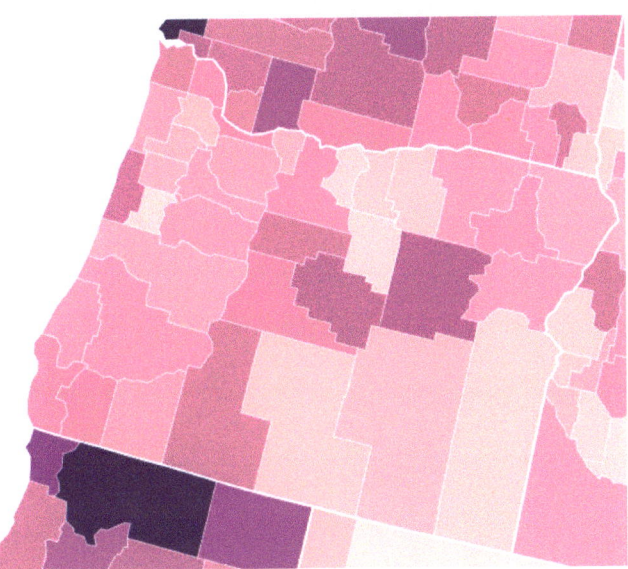

Economic & Crime Risk Map

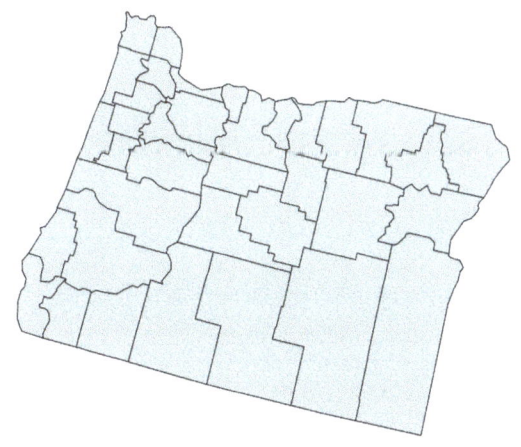

Main Summaries of Risk Maps

- The percentage of the White population is not enough.
- High real estate risk is present on the West Coast of Oregon.
- Population density is low on the East.
- High poverty and unemployment rates in some counties.

Conclusions

Conclusions similar to the state of Washington. Observe risks on all maps and see that there is no cluster of predominantly White counties without any risks. I consider this state to be risky.

State	California
Population	39,538 thous.
Land Area	155,779 sq mile
Density/mi2	253.7 people
Percent White	34.7%
Poverty Rate	12.1%
Unempl. Rate	4.2%

State Location Map
Created with Mapchart.net

California - Shaded Relief Image
Credit: National Elevation Dataset, compiled
by the U.S. Geological Survey
Visit the USGS at https://usgs.gov.

Racial Risk Map
Created with Mapchart.net, data—US Census

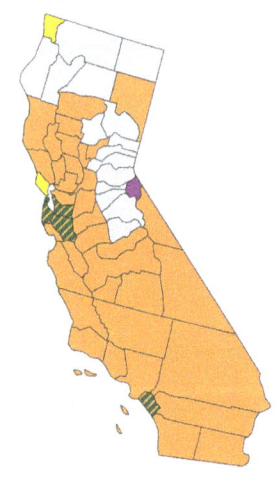

Industry Overconcentration Risk Map
Created with Mapchart.net, data—US Census

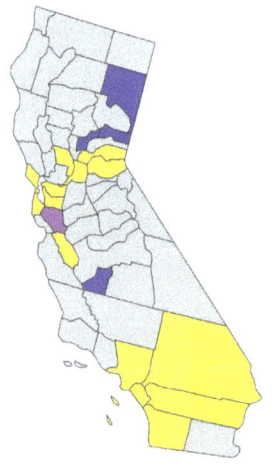

Real Estate Risk Map; G. Brian Davis, SparkRental,
ATTOM Data Solutions, Created with Datawrapper

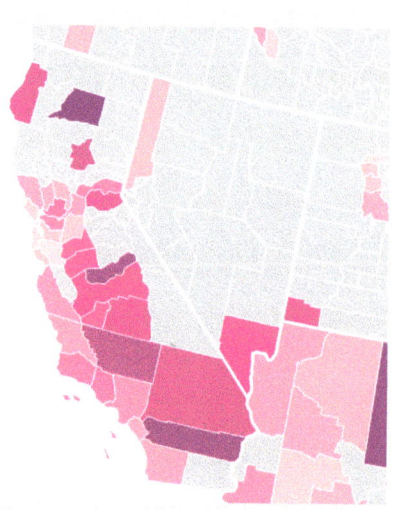

Density Risk Map
Source: US Census

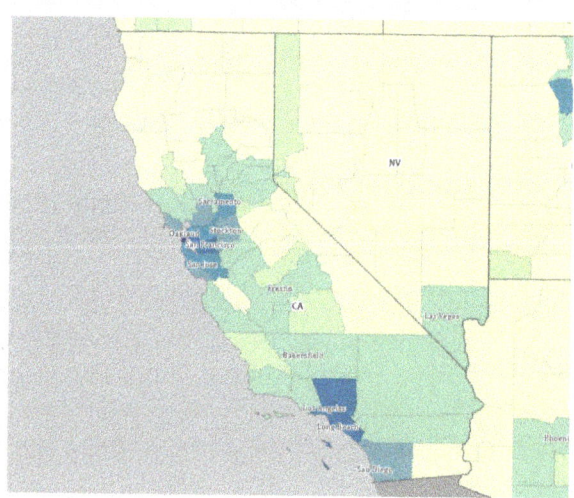

Poverty Risk Map
Source: US Census

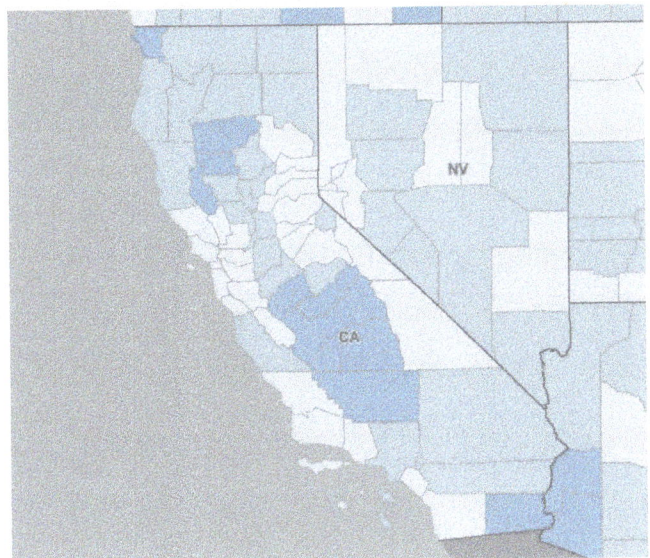

Unemployment Risk Map
Source: SparkRental & BLS

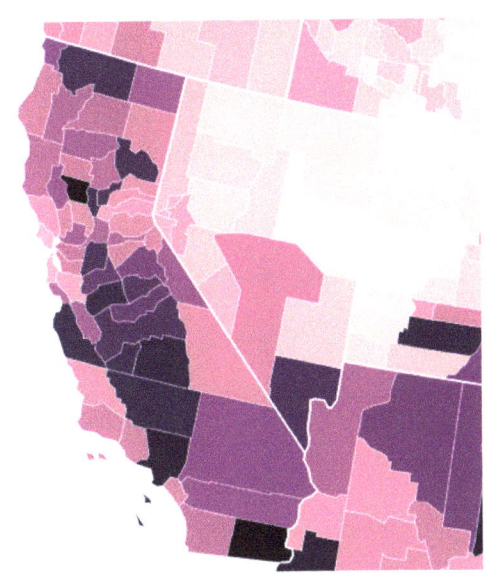

Economic & Crime Risk Map

Main Summaries of Risk Maps

- The percentage of the White population is very low.
- Metro-area risk is very high in Los Angeles and San Francisco.
- California is subject to very high real estate risk.
- High poverty and unemployment rates in many counties.

Conclusions

The percentage of White (non-Hispanic or Latino) people is only 34.7% in California. No more words are needed, especially because you know the issues with California. Los Angeles and San Francisco areas will become devastated by the economic downturn and high crime rate. Well, they are already being hurt by the high crime rate, but it is almost heaven compared to what it will be like in the coming depression.

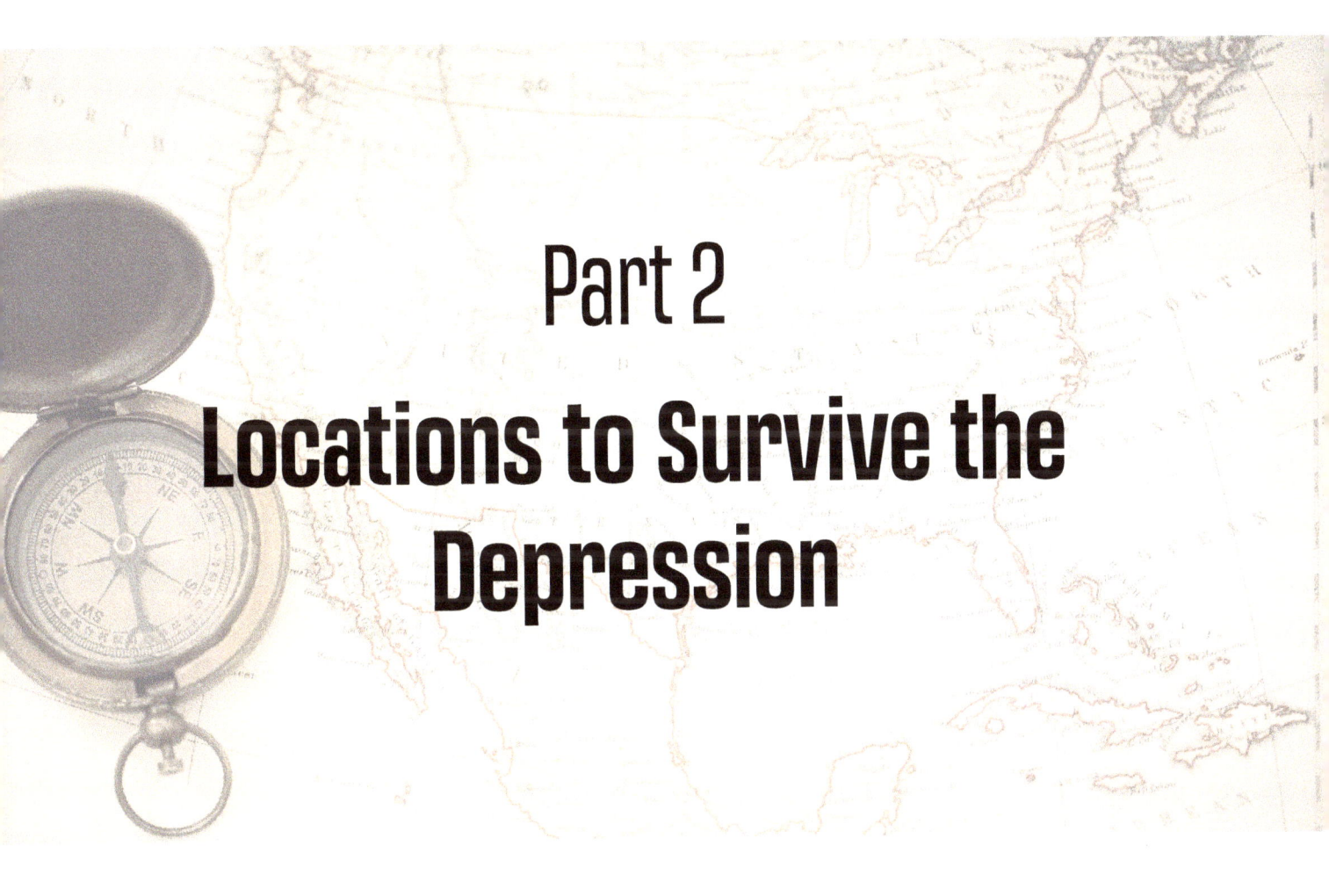

Part 2

Locations to Survive the Depression

CHAPTER 7

Agricultural Self-Sufficiency

A depression starts with an economic downturn. However, the consequences of the downturn will persist for many years, likely decades. The same is true for crime risk. Nevertheless, I will not consider it inappropriate to live through a depression in every location that was deemed unsafe in the previous chapter. Crime and economic risks are probably the most critical factors and if forced to choose between them, I recommend you to live even in areas that will be relatively more hurt economically.

Partly based on prior findings, the characteristics of the "ideal" location to live through a depression are a high percentage of White population; a low crime rate, especially a violent crime; a location not extremely economically devastated; a nonmetropolitan area; agricultural self-sufficiency; no authoritarian state government; and not an extremely miserable quality of life in terms of poverty and unemployment. Also, I think the location should have civilized or relatively civilized people (in depressions so few remain civilized); a reasonable geographic location; reasonable safety from extreme natural risks; and a temperate climate.

This chapter will discuss agriculturally self-sufficient areas. Agricultural self-sufficiency is very important because food and agriculture will be more accessible in a region with high agricultural income and employment. Apparently, it is also the issue of money. If you preserve your wealth through the crisis, the food will most likely be accessible to you. However, your financial well-being cannot be guaranteed. Besides, food and livestock prices would likely be lower and more accessible in the agriculturally prone states. Also, if government interference occurs, some states secede, or interstate and international protectionist measures are imposed, the accessibility and the price of food and livestock may increase.

Overall, the United States is one of the most agriculturally self-sufficient countries. The United States will likely weather a depression in this regard better than most countries. However, there will be individual state variation in agricultural production. Agriculture primarily includes cropland and livestock. Maps will illustrate the relative agricultural self-sufficiency of U.S. states.

The United States Department of Agriculture (USDA) defines croplands as "Cropland includes areas used for the production of adapted crops for harvest." Figure 7.1 shows that a high degree of cropland is concentrated in the Midwestern area, covering most of its states. Despite the heavy concentration of durable goods manufacturing in the East North Central division of the Midwest, that area is also agriculturally sufficient. The South is also rich with cropland (e.g., the southern part of the Mississippi River; see Figure 7.2). The Atlantic and Pacific coasts have some concentration of cropland.

Figure 7.3 from the USDA shows the distribution of corn for grain in harvested acres. Corn-harvested lands are primarily in the Midwest. There is also a distribution of some cropland for corn in Texas and around the southern area of the Mississippi River, near the borders of Louisiana, Mississippi, Arkansas, Tennessee, Missouri, and Kentucky. I will be referring to this area simply as the southern Mississippi River area. Also, the South Atlantic and Middle Atlantic have some land harvested by crops.

Figure 7.4 depicts all wheat for grain in harvested acres. Wheat-harvested areas are distributed in a few Midwestern states (i.e., North Dakota, South Dakota, and Kansas), and to a lesser extent in other Midwestern states including Texas, Oklahoma, the Mountain division's Montana, Idaho, Colorado, and the Pacific division's state of Washington.

Figure 7.2

Mississippi River

Image Source: Pearson Scott Foresman.

Source: Wikimedia Commons

Figure 7.5 illustrates the acres harvested of soybeans for beans. The Midwestern area and southern Mississippi River have the primary concentrations of soybeans. There are also certain acres of land in the South Atlantic.

Figure 7.6 shares the distribution of rice harvested acres. Acres are concentrated around the southern Mississippi River, California, and Texas.

The general picture regarding the croplands is clear. The midwestern area is the richest area, followed by the South Mississippi River basin, and Texas and the South Atlantic. California has some concentration of rice, vegetables, and fruits. Idaho and Washington produce potatoes, and Idaho, Washington, and Montana grow wheat. The only areas with little to no cropland are New England and mountainous states such as Nevada, Utah, Arizona, New Mexico, Wyoming, the western part of Colorado, and West Virginia. As a note, New England states such as Vermont, New Hampshire, and Maine have areas with high elevation. Similarly, the Appalachian Mountain trail, which includes West Virginia, is not very rich in farmland.

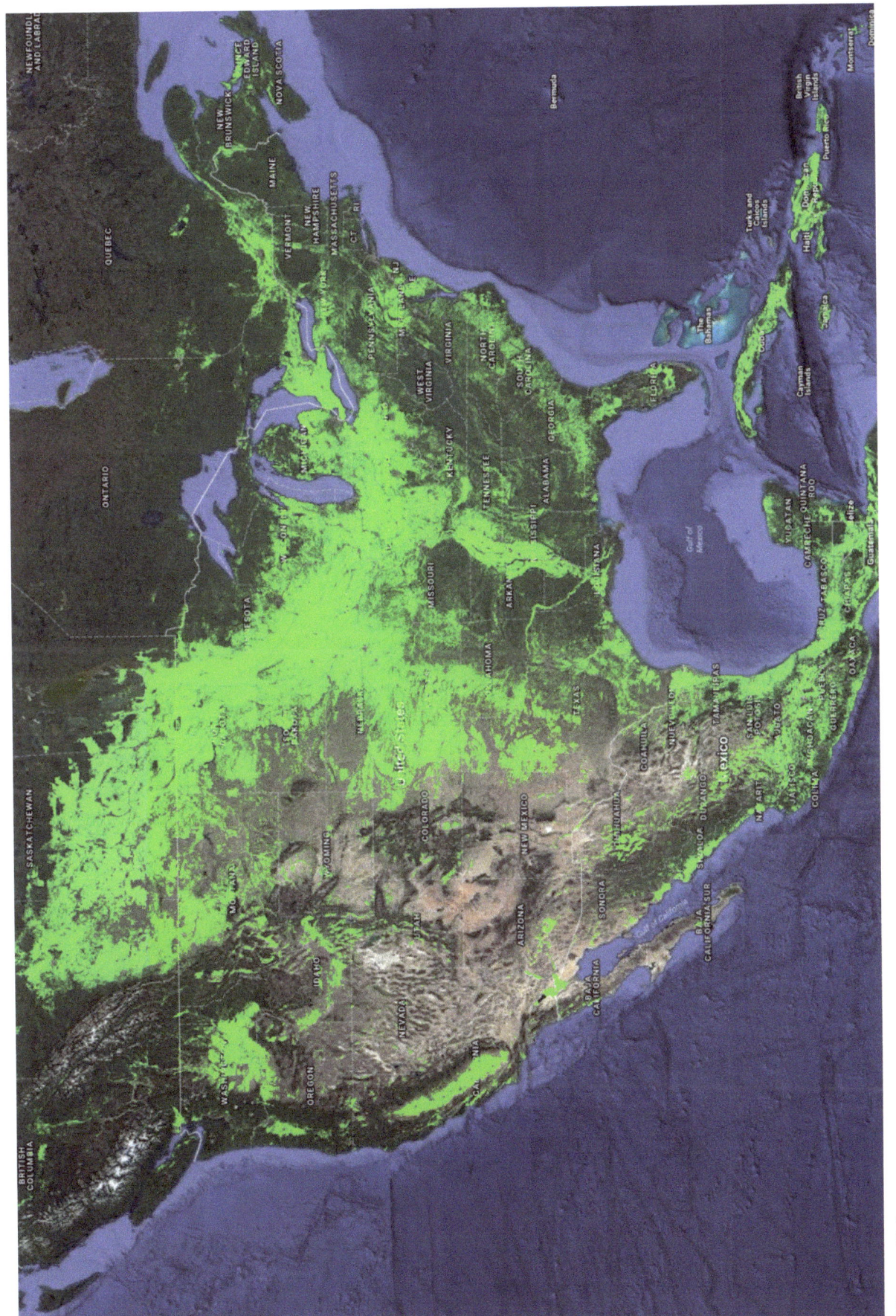

Figure 7.1

Map of Croplands in the United States

Image Source: U.S. Geological Survey, Communications and Publishing department, https://usgs.gov

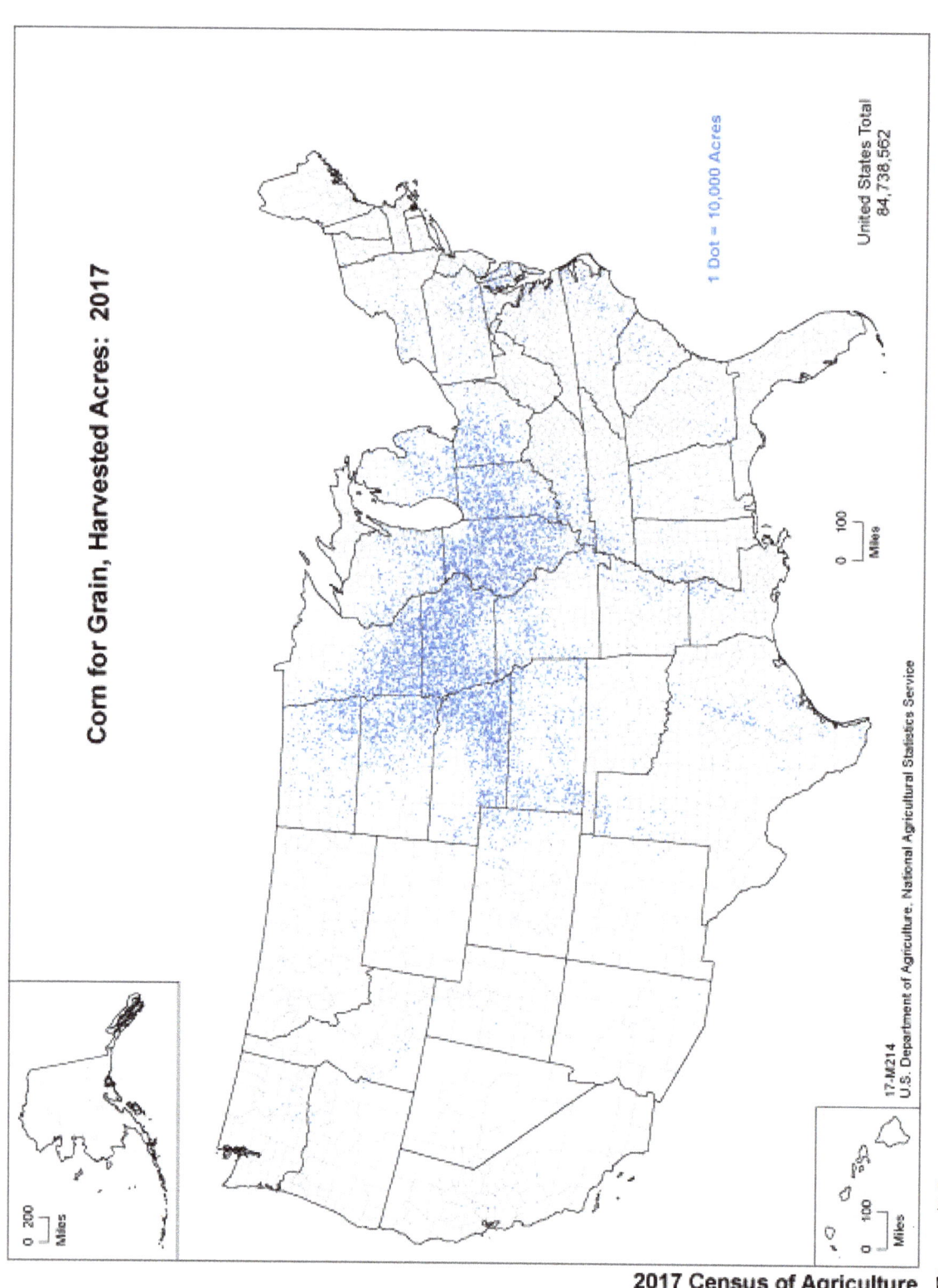

Figure 7.3

Corn for Grain, Harvested Acres: 2017

Image Source: USDA NASS, 2017 Census of Agriculture, Ag Census Web Maps, https://www.nass.usda.gov/Publications/
AgCensus/2017/Online_Resources/Ag_Atlas_Maps/

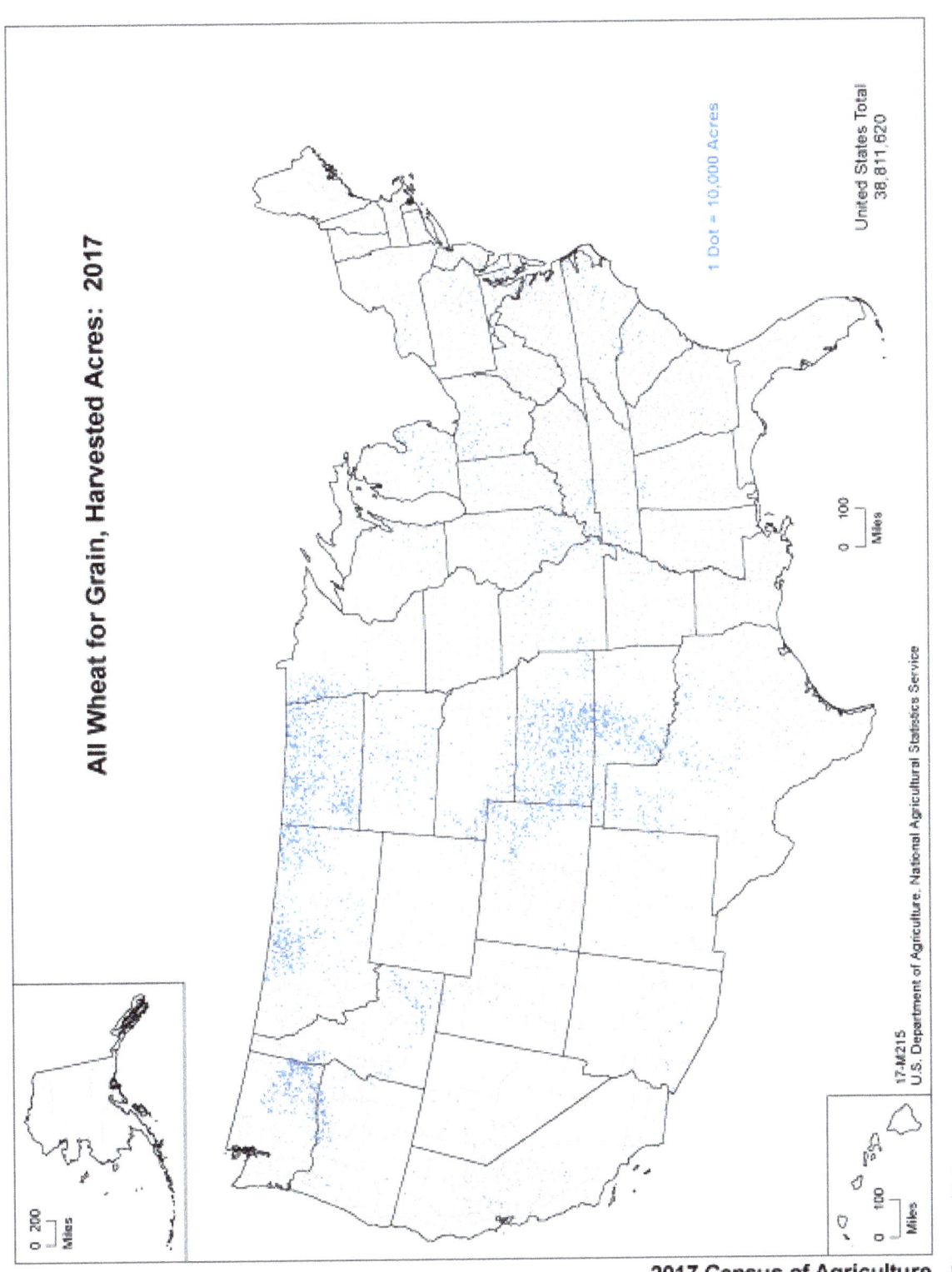

All Wheat for Grain, Harvested Acres: 2017

1 Dot = 10,000 Acres

United States Total
38,811,620

0   100
Miles

17-M215
U.S. Department of Agriculture, National Agricultural Statistics Service

0   200
Miles

0   100
Miles

2017 Census of Agriculture

Figure 7.4

All Wheat for Grain, Harvested Acres: 2017

Image Source: USDA NASS, 2017 Census of Agriculture, Ag Census Web Maps, https://www.nass.usda.gov/Publications/
AgCensus/2017/Online_Resources/Ag_Atlas_Maps/

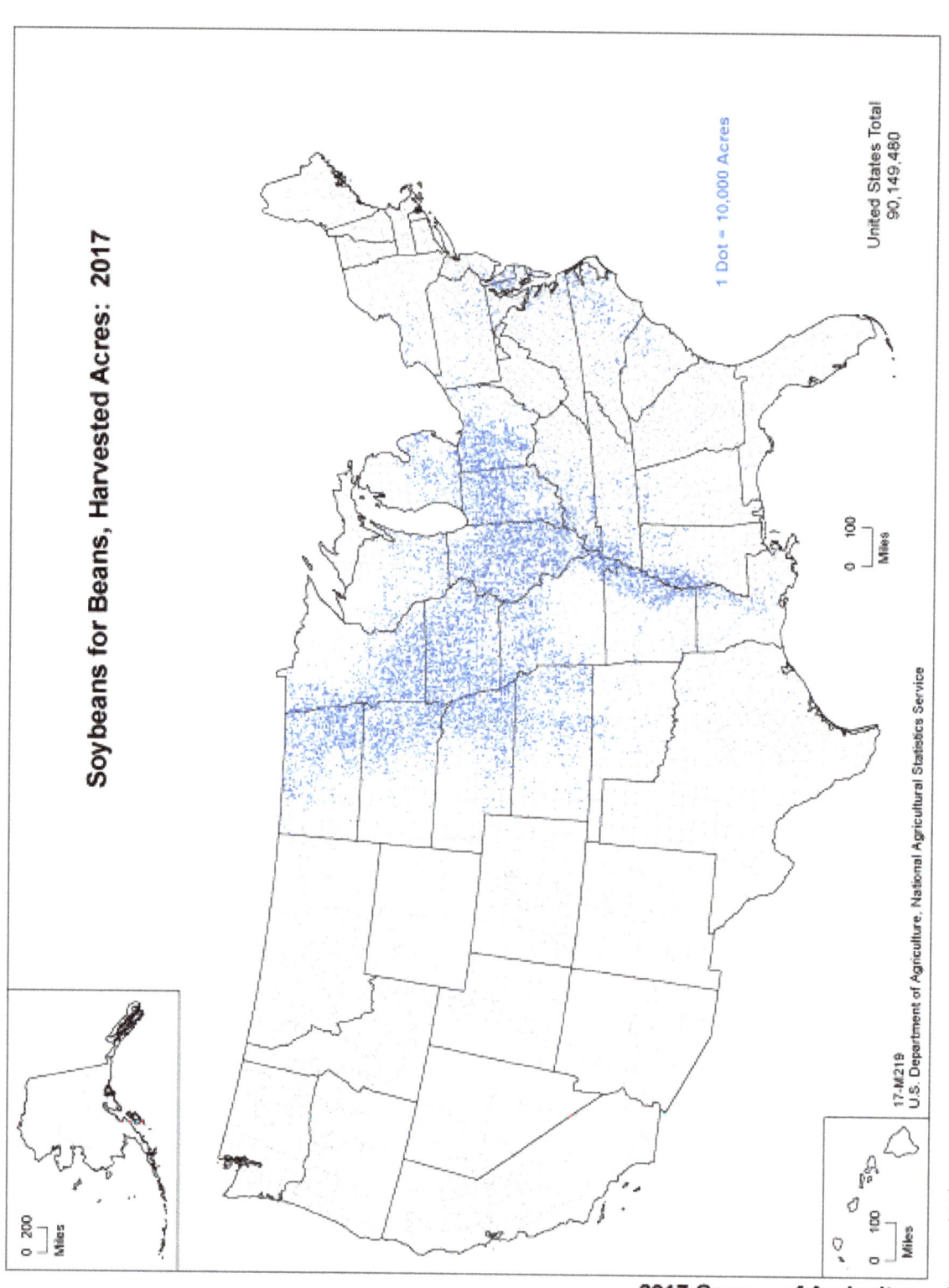

Figure 7.5

Soybeans for Beans, Harvested Acres: 2017

Image Source: USDA NASS, 2017 Census of Agriculture, Ag Census Web Maps, https://www.nass.usda.gov/Publications/AgCensus/2017/Online_Resources/Ag_Atlas_Maps/

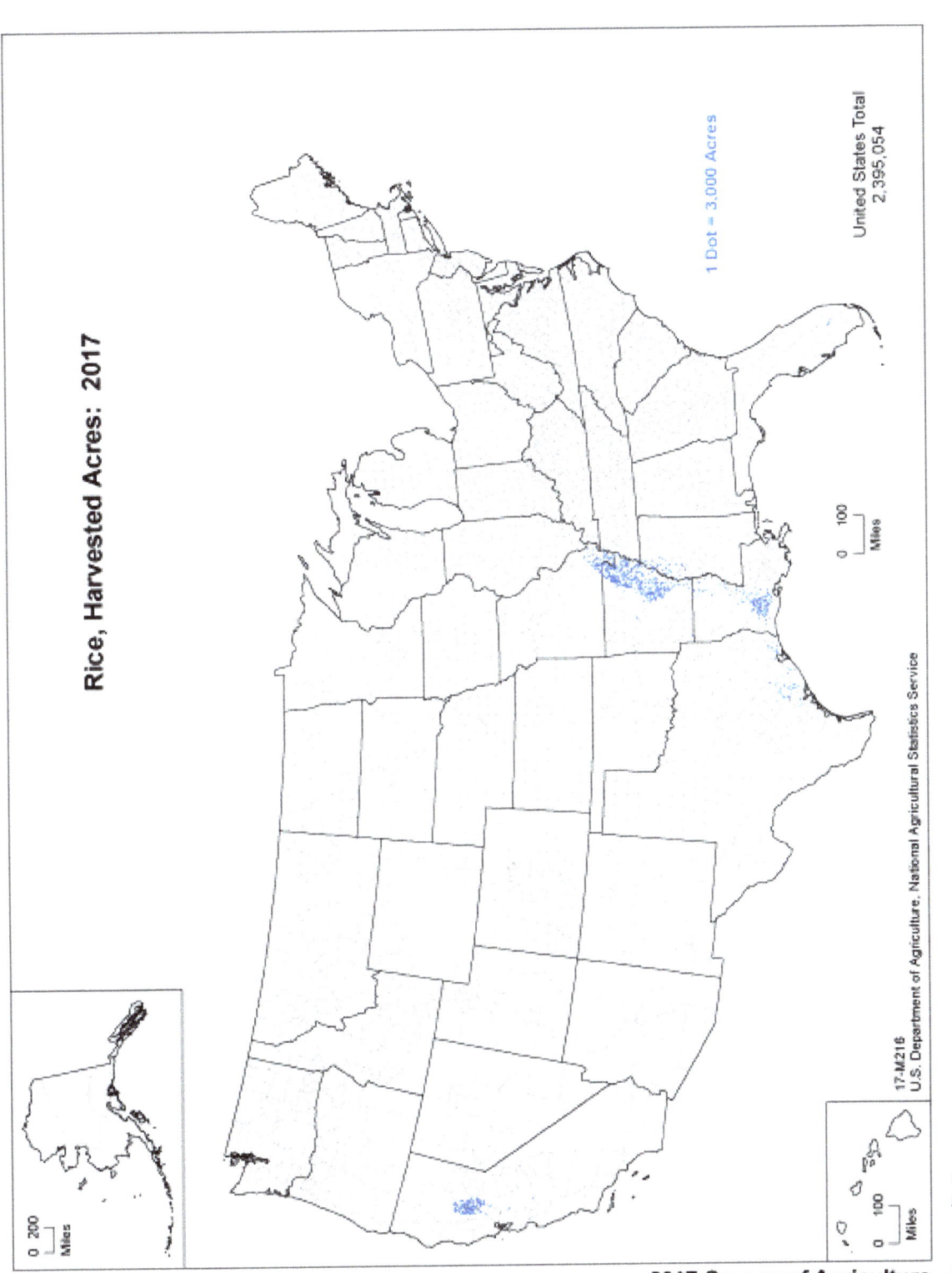

Figure 7.6

Rice, Harvested Acres: 2017

Image Source: USDA NASS, 2017 Census of Agriculture, Ag Census Web Maps, https://www.nass.usda.gov/Publications/

AgCensus/2017/Online_Resources/Ag_Atlas_Maps/

Let us now see the distribution of other critical agricultural goods: meat and milk. Figures 7.7 to 7.11 illustrate the inventory distribution of cattle and calves; milk cows; beef cows; hogs and pigs; and sheep and lambs. Figure 7.12 shows the distribution of broilers and other meat-type chickens sold. These maps illustrate that most of the United States is sufficient in terms of animal products. The Midwestern area is this country's dominant agricultural force. If East North Central (mostly the Rust Belt) part of the Midwest is the most powerful durable goods industrial manufacturing area, then West North Central is the most important agricultural force. At the same time, East North Central is agriculturally moderately sufficient. The South Mississippi River basin is also very well-sufficient in terms of crop products. And the South Atlantic is well-sufficient in terms of food. In the Pacific region, California is well-sufficient. The West South Central is also reasonably sufficient. And the Mountain division in the west, the Northeast region in the east, and the state of West Virginia are much less sufficient for various agricultural goods. The colder climate of the Northeast region and the Mountain area are not ideally suitable for complete self-sufficiency. However, it is not as if Northeast is entirely non-self-sufficient. The New England region's lifestyle is not identical to that of the Midwestern region. However, in the rural parts of Vermont, New Hampshire, and Maine, some people have a lifestyle where their primary work is related to agriculture. New England is not necessarily a highly disadvantageous agricultural area. The summers are warm, even hot. Winters are cold. For people who live in the very southern areas of the United States, it might be cold to an extent. However, New England is not very cold compared to places like Northern Europe or the north of Russia.

Of course, regional variations exist. Besides mountainous areas, there are no significantly large regions with very poor food self-sufficiency. Take highly populated states such as Maryland, Delaware, New Jersey, Connecticut, and Massachusetts. These areas might have certain food deficiencies in a future depression. Nevertheless, I think the leading cause of hunger will be a lack of money and income rather than food. If people manage to retain savings in a depression, they more or less will be fine. Despite that, remember that someday, we might have to supply our own food. This is another reason to avoid metropolitan areas. If someday, the consequences of a depression are an awful federal government economic policy, local social conflict, or military conflict within the United States, then there will be a risk of a shortage of certain types of food.

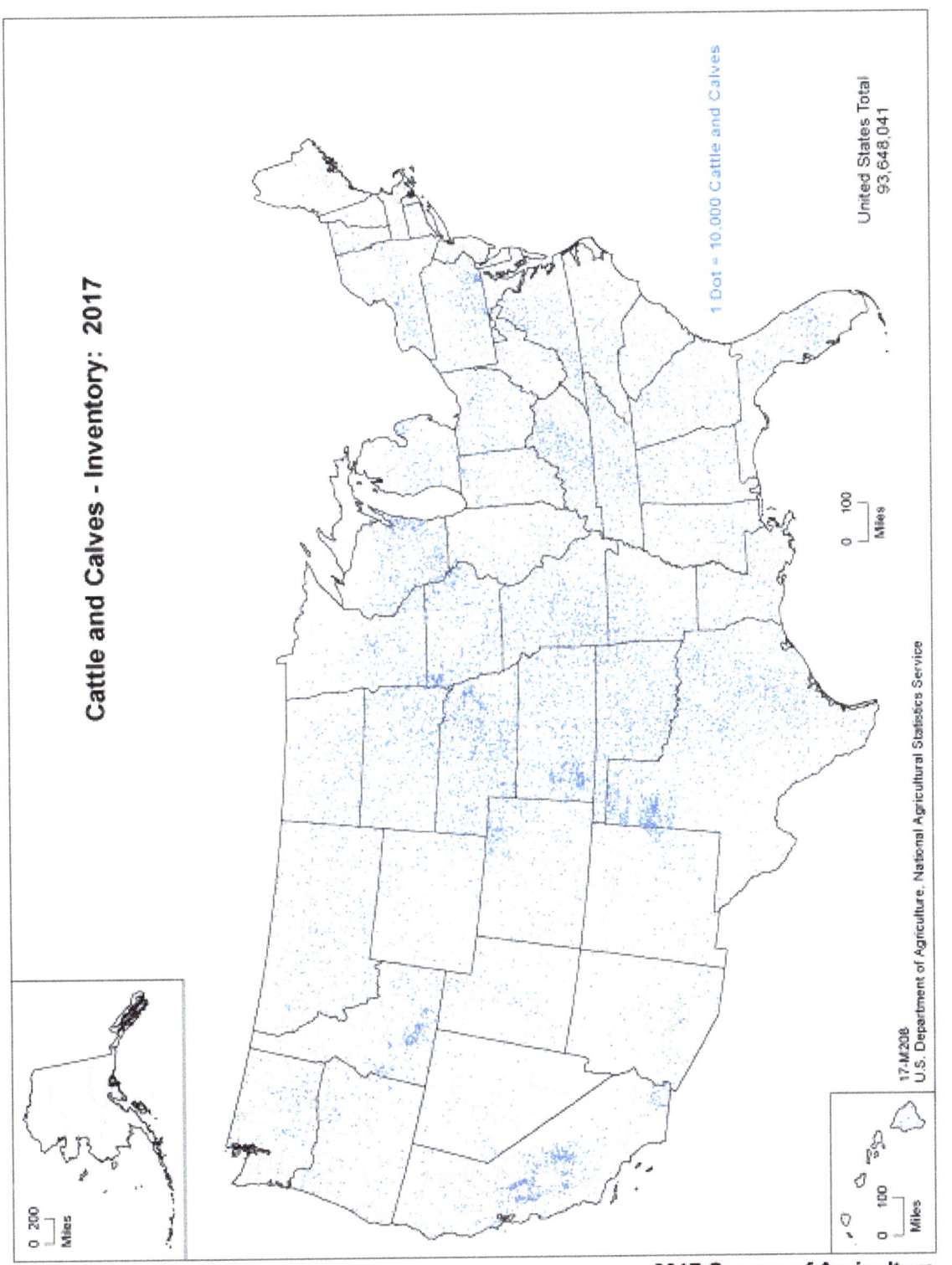

Figure 7.7

Cattle and Calves Inventory: 2017

Image Source: USDA NASS, 2017 Census of Agriculture, Ag Census Web Maps, https://www.nass.usda.gov/Publications/ AgCensus/2017/Online_Resources/Ag_Atlas_Maps/

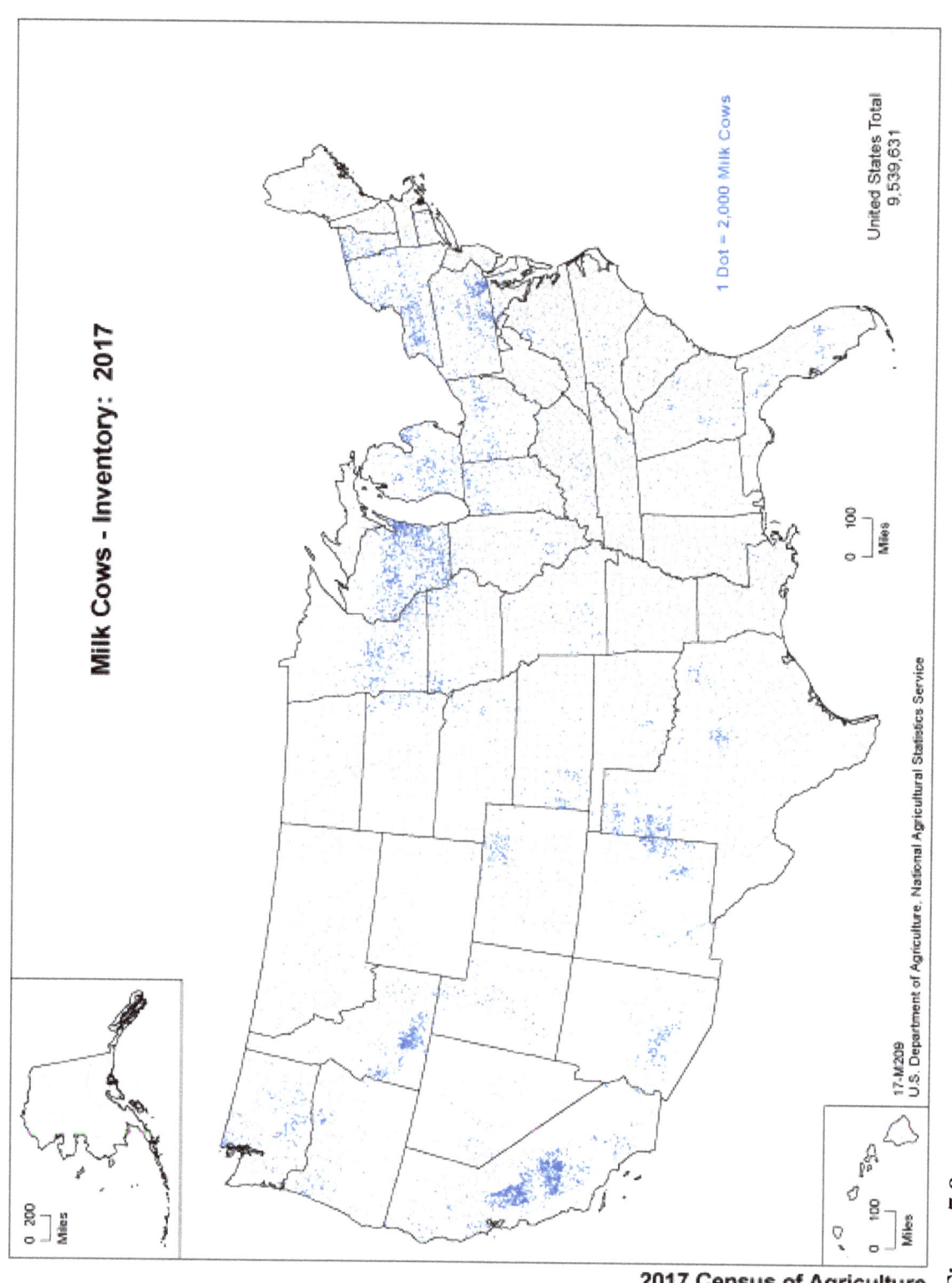

Figure 7.8

Milk Cows Inventory: 2017

Image Source: USDA NASS, 2017 Census of Agriculture, Ag Census Web Maps, https://www.nass.usda.gov/Publications/AgCensus/2017/Online_Resources/Ag_Atlas_Maps/

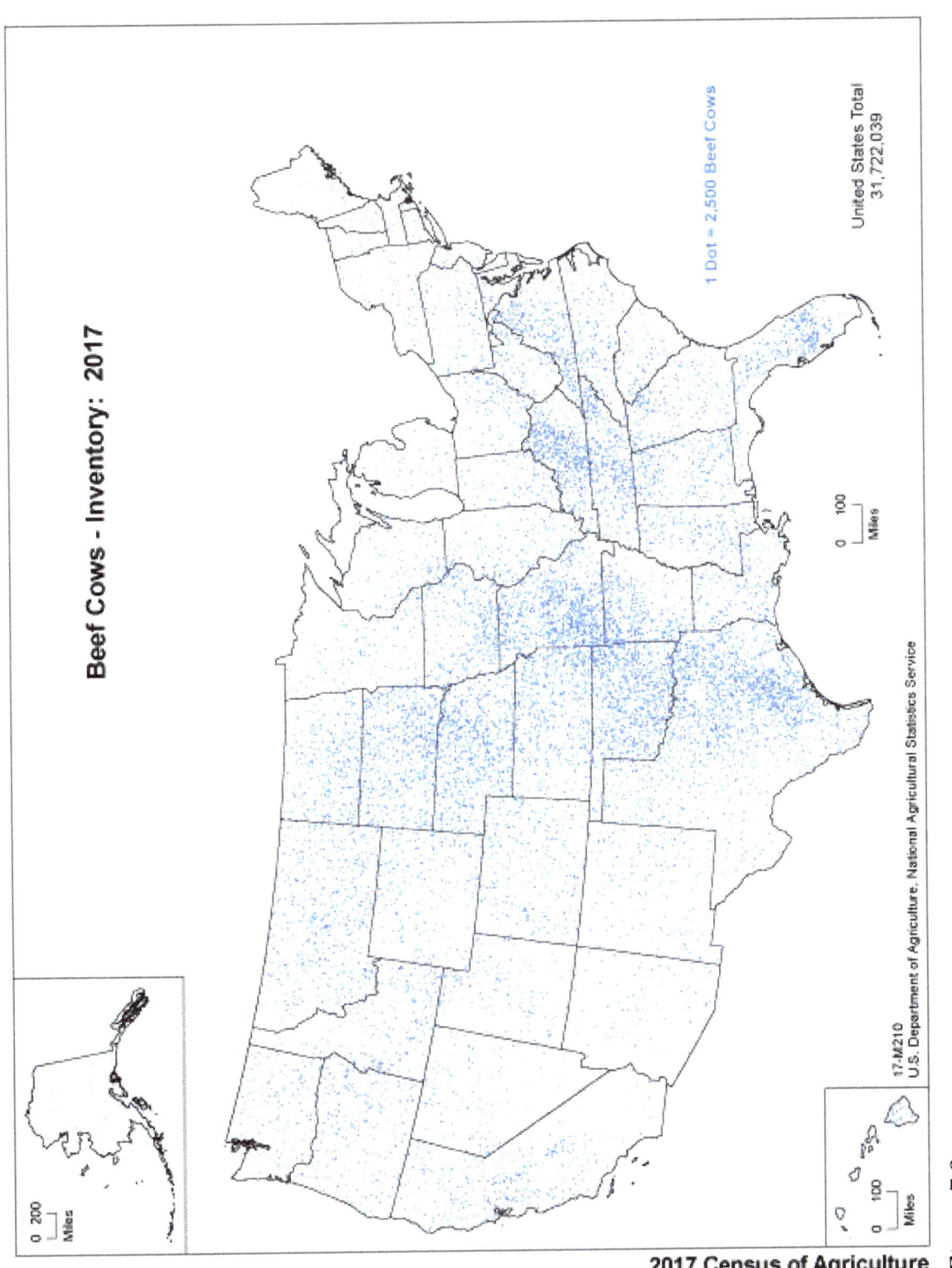

Figure 7.9

Beef Cows Inventory: 2017

Image Source: USDA NASS, 2017 Census of Agriculture, Ag Census Web Maps, https://www.nass.usda.gov/Publications/

AgCensus/2017/Online_Resources/Ag_Atlas_Maps/

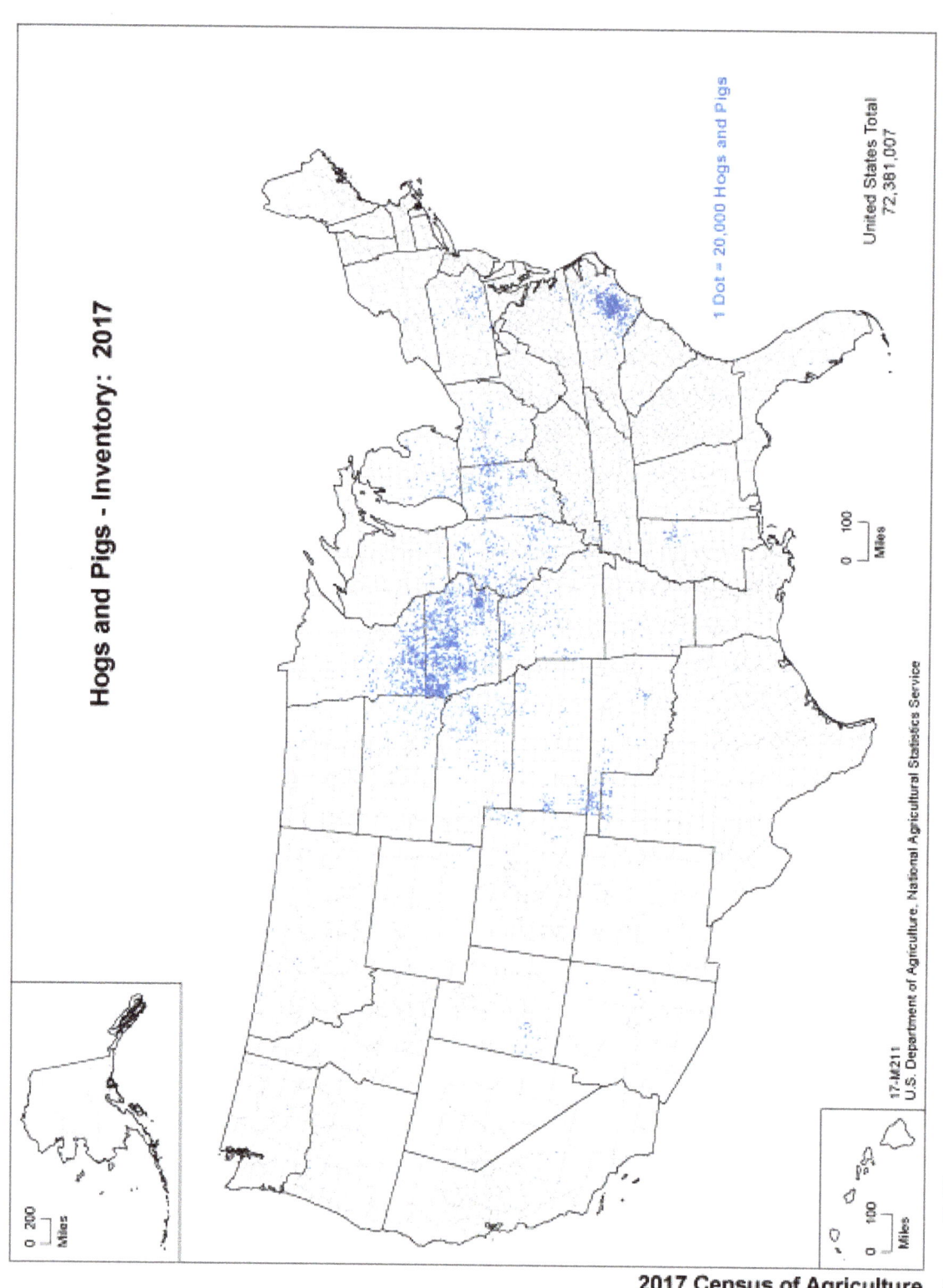

Figure 7.10

Hogs and Pigs Inventory: 2017

Image Source: USDA NASS, 2017 Census of Agriculture, Ag Census Web Maps, https://www.nass.usda.gov/Publications/
AgCensus/2017/Online_Resources/Ag_Atlas_Maps/

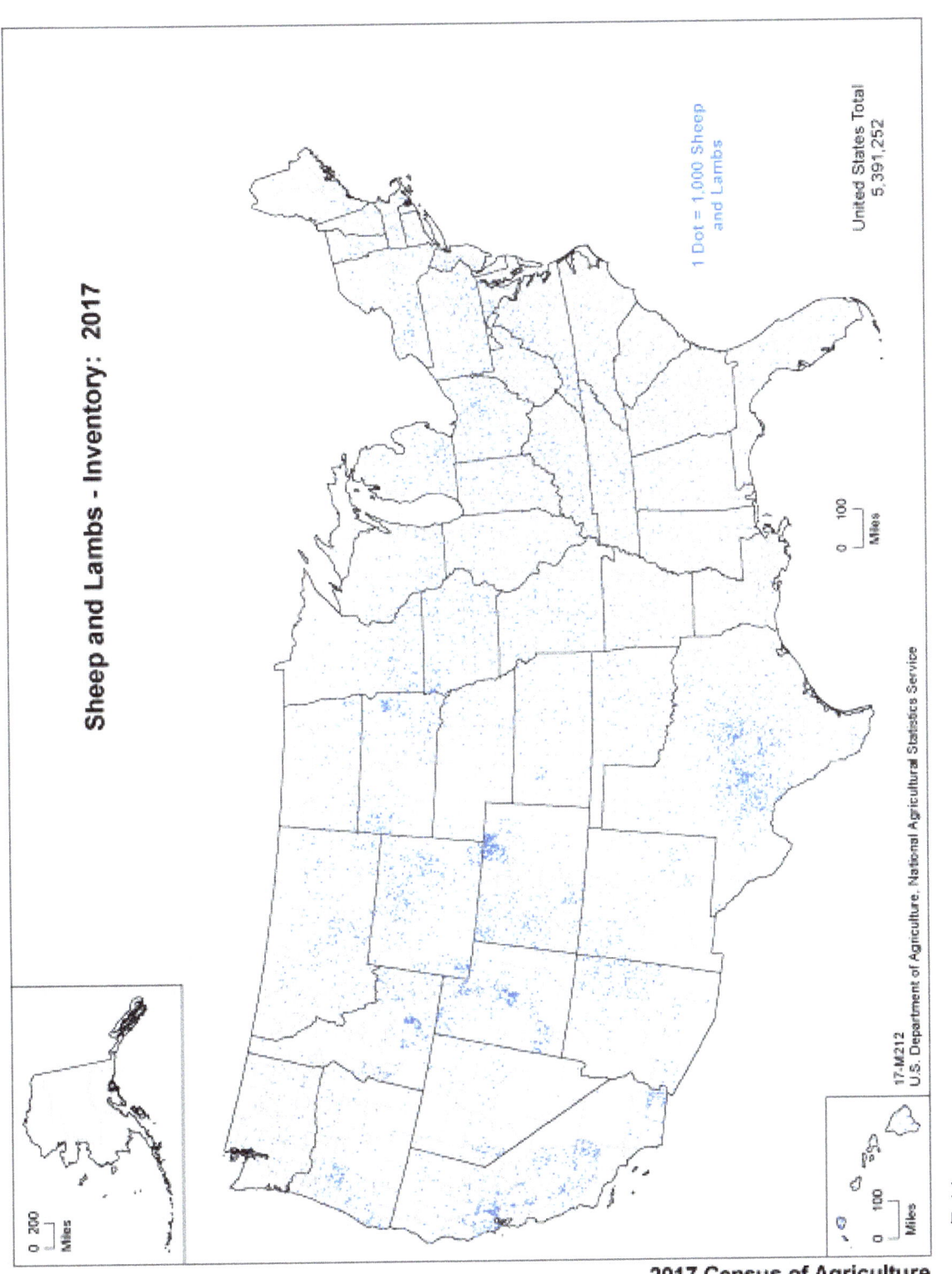

Figure 7.11

Sheep and Lambs Inventory: 2017

Image Source: USDA NASS, 2017 Census of Agriculture, Ag Census Web Maps, https://www.nass.usda.gov/Publications/ AgCensus/2017/Online_Resources/Ag_Atlas_Maps/

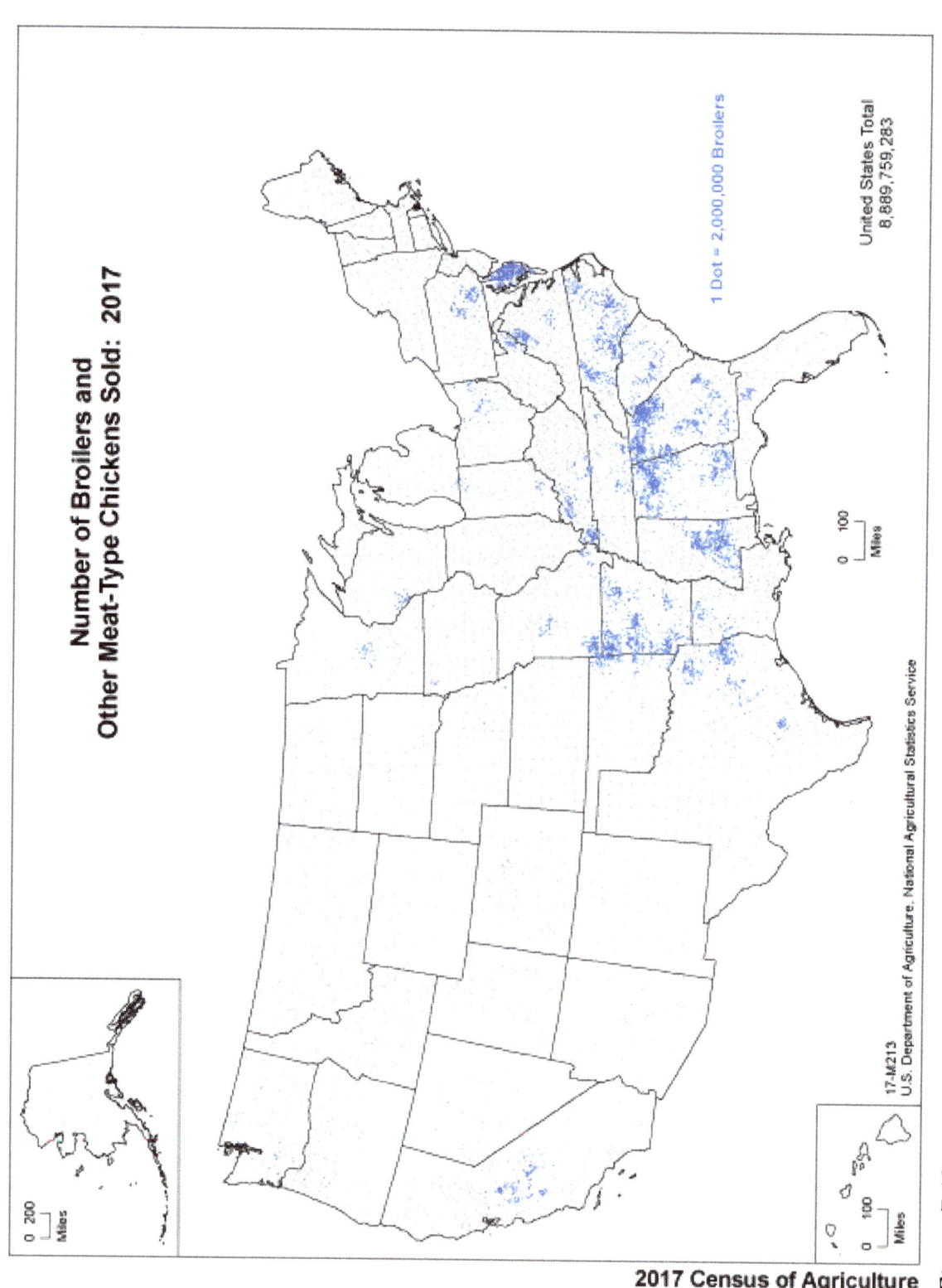

2017 Census of Agriculture

Figure 7.12

Number of Broilers and Other Meat-Type Chickens Sold: 2017

Image Source: USDA NASS, 2017 Census of Agriculture, Ag Census Web Maps, https://www.nass.usda.gov/Publications/AgCensus/2017/Online_Resources/Ag_Atlas_Maps/

CHAPTER 8

Additional Risk Factors to Consider

This chapter will briefly consider other important factors such as epidemics, state authoritarianism (taxes and collectivism), and quality of health care, among others.

Epidemics

Metropolitan areas are dangerous for many previously discussed reasons and include the low percentage of the White population, economic risk, potential future social unrest. Additionally, large metropolitan areas could also be at higher risk of epidemic contagions because they are denser. People constantly interact and live next to each other. On average, spreading diseases and epidemics will be less common in nonmetro areas. During uncertainty, there is a likelihood that outbreaks will become more common. People are poorer, less hygienic, and psychologically distressed. Besides, White people are, on average, much more sanitary and cleaner than non-White people, be they Black Americans or Hispanics. The consequences could be dire because the population of White Americans is lowest in the metropolitan areas. Review Figure 3.2 to see the areas with the highest population density. I would recommend avoiding them or at least relocating to the metro's less dense regions.

State Authoritarianism and Collectivism

Collectivism has increased in popularity during "uncertain" times (e.g., the 1910s, 1930s, 1970s, and post 2008 recession to around 2012). Collectivism manifests itself in anti-capitalistic, anti-individual, and anti-freedom sentiments. Anti-individual sentiment leads to public actions that call against individual rights, such as against the right to life, liberty, and property. Jealousy is so common in almost every individual. Imagine a collapsed economy with all the have-nots in poverty, misery, and despair. They must blame someone. They can never say it is their fault they lost their mortgage, investments, etc. This is not happening. Who is at fault? For them it is rich people, successful people, intelligent people, talented people, decent people, wealthy businessmen, bankers, directors, people in finance, politicians, social elites, or political elites. Obviously, some politicians have committed certain crimes. However, the angry crowd will not determine who is to blame. They will attack all the people mentioned above, even if they are not at fault. Think of Bolshevik actions after their government overthrow in Russia. They publicly attacked successful businessmen just because they were better than anyone else. Why? Simply because the people were jealous and angry. For more, read the history of the South Sea bubble collapse in Great Britain in 1720 in Charles Mackay's *Extraordinary Popular Delusions and the Madness of Crowds.*

The government commonly expresses public mood through its actions. Study the Great Depression. The masses directed their sentiment through the government. The government regulated the economy and raised taxes for the rich. The government redistributed money from producers to consumers—from working people to those who did not work. In the 1930s, socialistic sentiment proliferated, and consequently, people elected socialist president and socialist members of the Congress. The consequence was simple, textbook authoritarianism. The collectivist mentality has been engraved in the United States even post-Great Depression. Individual values still existed in the 1920s. Sadly, since the Great Depression, things changed radically. Of course, most people are collectivist by nature, yet collectivist culture was not so deeply ingrained. Today, many are eager to claim their share of someone else's wealth, and government entitlement programs seem endless, while envy of the successful knows no bounds. Therefore, we know that this time, standing right before the beginning of an economic depression, we are already so collectivist. Unfortunately, the remains of American republicanism will be gone for a long time. Not only politically but philosophically and culturally.

Of course, people might direct their hate against the government and politicians. Something strange might happen, such as a government overthrow, chaotic conflict between Democrats and Republicans, conflict between Blacks and Whites, or state succession. Or it can happen all at the same time, which I think is very likely. Previous tough times led to events like the Civil War or the rise of collectivism during the Great Depression, which were very straightforward. This time, it is very uncertain. Perhaps it will be more predictable several years into the next depression. However, what is predictable is that uncertainty will rise. Therefore, we must work with what evidence we have: Some states are more authoritarian and left-leaning than others. I do not claim that Republican states are heavenly. Many so-called Republicans today are very much collectivist either. Besides, many Republican states have a high percentage of non-White population and many other problems like higher poverty, on average. So, it cannot be concluded that the average Republican state would end up better than the average democrat state or vice versa. However, the extreme democrat-leaning states have social and authoritarian issues.

I have found beneficial research created by the authors William P. Ruger and Jason Sorens, who have published a new book called *Freedom in the 50 States: An Index of Personal and Economic Freedom Seventh Edition*. This book includes the freedom index by state. Their research is beneficial and relatively objective compared to other attempts to estimate the freedom index by state. This project was published by the Cato Institute and accompanied by demographic and economic data on each state. "It is an essential reference for anyone interested in state policy and in advancing a better understanding of a free society."[1] It may be accessed on www.freedominthe50states.org, which also presents the overall freedom rankings as of year-end 2022.[2]

"This study ranks the American states according to how their public policies affect individual freedoms in the economic, social, and personal spheres."[3] Their study subdivides overall freedom into personal and economic freedom and then subdivides the economic freedom on fiscal policy and regulatory policy.

Economic Freedom

Regarding the overall economic freedom ranking, the top 5 freest states are New Hampshire, Florida, South Dakota, Tennessee, and Georgia. The least economically free states are New Jersey, Oregon, California, Hawaii, and New York.

Personal Freedom

When it comes to personal freedom, the top 5 freest states are Nevada, Arizona, Maine, New Hampshire, and New Mexico. The states with the least personal freedom are South Carolina, Kentucky, Wyoming, Idaho, and Texas.

Overall Freedom

The following are the overall freedom rankings that are based on both economic and personal freedom. The top 5 are New Hampshire, Florida, South Dakota, Nevada, and Arizona. And the bottom are Oregon, New Jersey, California, Hawaii, and New York.

While Texas may be ranked in the bottom in terms of personal freedom, based on overall freedom, Texas is ranked 17, much above states such as California, New York, Oregon, and others famous for their authoritarian policies. Unsurprisingly, California, New York, and Oregon are within the five least free states. It is also known that New Hampshire and Florida are relatively free states. (see Figures 8.1 and 8.2) This data will be influential when making final conclusions.

Figures 8.1 and 8.2

Top 5 Freest and Least Free States

Data Source: Cato Institute, 2023 edition of Freedom in the 50 States, William Ruger and Jason Sorens

Top 5 freest states	
1	New Hampshire
2	Florida
3	South Dakota
4	Nevada
5	Arizona

Top 5 least free states	
1	Oregon
2	New Jersey
3	California
4	Hawaii
5	New York

Quality of Healthcare

The quality of medicine and healthcare will be essential during the economic depression. Healthcare is not a primary factor when considering a safe location to survive a depression, but it is crucial when dealing with epidemics or serious diseases.

Because I am not a medical expert, I reviewed individual sources of quality of medicine by state ranking and aimed to find a specific pattern in healthcare quality among states. Most of the studies considered affordability and healthcare quality.

I found that states in the South Atlantic (except Maryland, Virginia, and Delaware), East South Central, and West South Central have the poorest quality of medicine. Meanwhile, states in New England, Minnesota, Wisconsin, Iowa, North Dakota, and South Dakota have a high ranking.

Other Considerations

A few things must be discussed before drawing the final conclusions. First, White people are, on average, much more civilized than people of color. Obviously, it is much better to survive a depression among the civilized people. Also, non-White people are more collectivist and more likely to support socialist ideas. Please refer to the U.S. racial map, Figure 4.5.

Consider again the natural disaster risk map before moving to a particular location. I am not an expert in the field of natural disasters. Therefore, research locations that are less prone to extreme natural disasters.

Another important point is the potential secession of some states from the United States. The secessionist movement might gain attention during difficult times, as happened after 2008. It is hard to predict which states will most likely succeed. Many preconditions may cause several states to secede individually or in groups. One thing to do is to look at the history of secession movements or secession sentiment in certain states. Also, if a state has a high percentage of people who, even in good times like today, hold certain secessionist feelings, that state might act upon those feelings during bad times.

It is no secret that the secessionist movement has been quite popular in the South. It is like a smoldering fire in Texas. However, the typical Southern identity has declined over the years. Besides, the Black population of the Southern states might not share philosophical ideas with secessionists. That is why it will be very chaotic and complex to predict which states would be willing to secede and where the secession will succeed. Perhaps only regions or individuals of the states will want to secede instead of states as a whole.

If Texas hypothetically secedes, it implies that one must choose to live in Texas or the United States during the next depression. If there are certain economic barriers imposed on mutual trade, it will harm both parties. Many in Texas advocate for ideas of freedom and individual liberty. Nevertheless, Texas has many regulations and business restrictions, and, today, it hardly embodies the ideal of liberty. Texas also has a very low White (non-Hispanic or Latino) population and it is quite a rural state and embodies the rural mentality. The standard of living is low in certain areas. Choosing to survive a depression in Texas means that life experience, personality, and philosophical ideas must correspond with a future life in Texas, not only philosophically but also in terms of future employment and lifestyle.

References

1. Freedominthe50states.org (2024). Retrieved from https://www.freedominthe50states.org/about

2. Freedominthe50states.org (2024). Retrieved from https://www.freedominthe50states.org/

3. Freedominthe50states.org (2024). Retrieved from https://www.freedominthe50states.org/about

CHAPTER 9

Locations to Survive the Depression

Figure 9.1 shows the map of colored counties, which would likely be the safest to live in during the coming Depression. Orange indicates the counties I am relatively confident in; pale orange indicates the approximate area because those areas are overall relatively safer, but some individual counties may carry risks. Figures 9.2, 9.3, 9.4, and 9.5 show a closer picture of the safest states of Figure 9.1. A few paragraphs explain each region's selection. I spend the most amount of time explaining my choice for New England because I have researched that region in specifics, while for other areas, my explanation will be more general.

Safest Areas to Survive a Depression

Note: Whenever I mention the White population, I imply White (non-Hispanic or Latino).

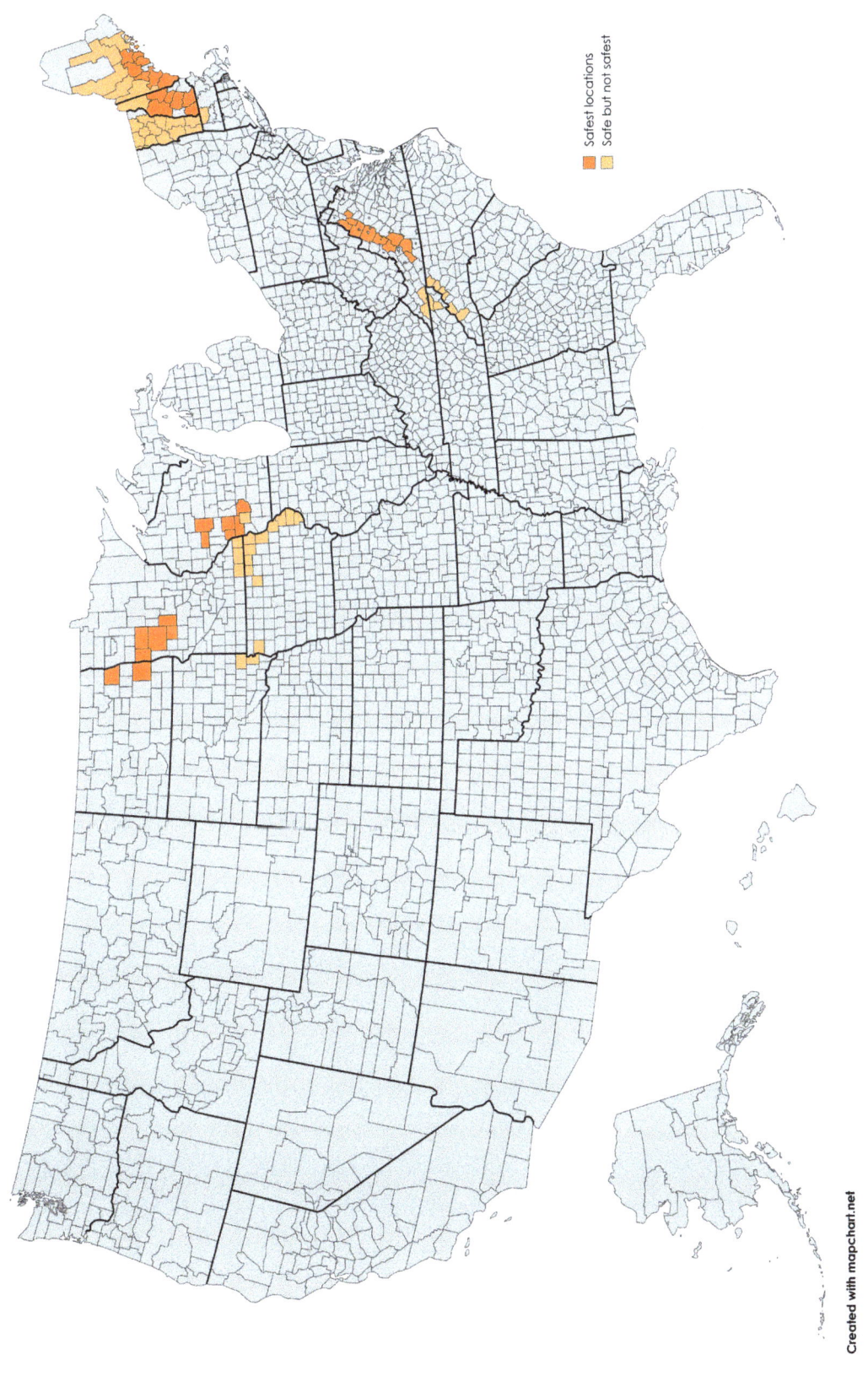

Safest locations

Safe but not safest

Figure 9.1

Locations to Survive the Depression

Note. Created with mapchart.net

New England: New Hampshire; Maine; Vermont; and One County in Massachusetts (see Figures 9.2 and 9.3)

The New Hampshire area is very attractive because the percentage of White people is very high. The state is not extremely exposed to industry risks, except for Sullivan County. The state is not very dense and does not have large metropolitan areas. There is quite a high real estate risk in the southern areas of New Hampshire. In New Hampshire, people seem relatively civilized, peaceful, and not aggressive. The state has the lowest poverty rate in the country and the second-lowest crime rate. The unemployment rate is low.

An attractive location is Merrimack County in New Hampshire. Merrimack County has a 91.4% White population[1] and includes the city of Concord. Concord is quite an old city with a population of around 44,000 to 45,000.[2] Concord is 85.7% White.[3] It is a very simple, nice-looking town without over-concentration of any economic industry.

Another reasonable city is Manchester, within the northern area of Hillsborough County, bordering Merrimack County. The percentage of Whites in Hillsborough County is 82%, while the percentage of White (including Hispanic or Latino) is 88.9%.[4] Manchester has a population of 115,000.[5]

The percentage of White people in the city of Manchester is 72.8%, while the percentage of White (including Hispanic or Latino) is 77.4%.[6] Another city in the south of Hillsborough County is Nashua. The population of Nashua is 91,000,[7] with 73% White, while the percentage of White (including Hispanic or Latino) is 77.8%.[8] Both cities are included in the larger Manchester-Nashua metro area. It is a medium-sized metropolis with a population of 420,000 and a percentage of White people (non-Hispanic or Latino) of around 80%. This is a high number for a medium-sized metro in the United States. Manchester and Nashua, for their respective sizes, will be much safer in terms of crime than comparable cities in other states. However, Manchester and Nashua are cities with one of the lowest, if not the lowest, White populations in New Hampshire. This means that non-White people usually choose to live in bigger cities. Secondly, the White population (non-Hispanic or Latino) in New Hampshire is 87.2%,[9] which means that the rest of the state's population consists of smaller cities with a higher population of White people. In New Hampshire, there are many smaller towns with a percentage of White population at least above 85% or 90%, which will provide much more physical safety than cities and towns in most other states.[10] This is the most important reason why New Hampshire is one of the first states on my list. Moreover, you do not need to live specifically in the centers of these bigger cities, mentioned earlier. You may choose to live in areas next to them where the population of Whites is higher. Obviously, cities like Manchester and Nashua will suffer a lot from an economic downturn and real estate price collapse, but in terms of violent crime risk, they will be safer than most comparable cities. Personally, I would prioritize smaller cities than Nashua or Manchester, located either individually or near bigger ones.

There are places to avoid in New England. Avoid cities that have high employment in a few industries or few companies, such as the city of Keene, located in Sullivan County. Similarly, avoid small mill towns. Towns that have very high employment not only in industries like durable goods manufacturing but even nondurable goods manufacturing. Of course, it is not as risky as other industries we discussed, but in the years of the Great Depression, many small towns were very hurt because of overexposure to a few textile factories (nondurable goods manufacturing). Also, avoid college-based towns because employees will be out of work if certain colleges go bankrupt or lose funding. Moreover, port cities in New Hampshire and Maine probably should be avoided because port cities are quite economically sensitive.

Figure 9.2

Safety Map of New Hampshire, Maine, Vermont, Massachusetts

Note. Created with mapchart.net

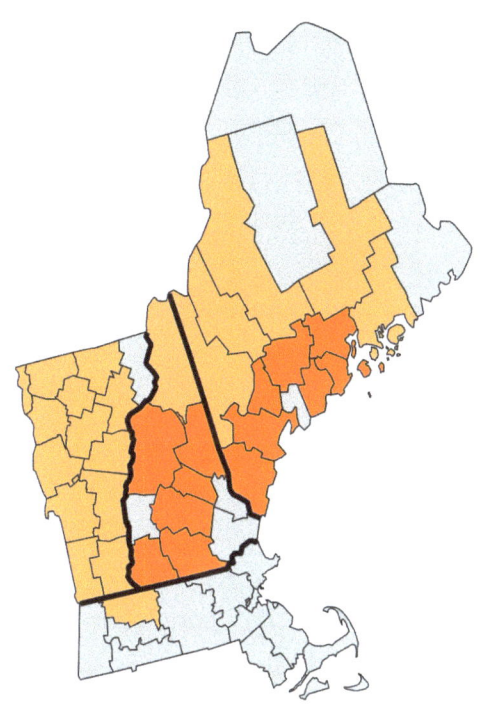

Figure 9.3

Safety Map of New Hampshire

Note. Created with mapchart.net.

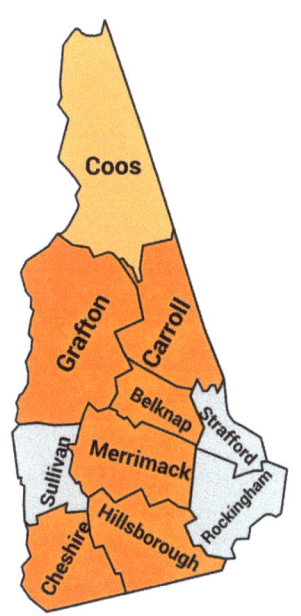

New Hampshire has a relatively decent income, a standard of living, and very civilized people. Also, New Hampshire provides areas with lower density, so it will be possible to move to smaller towns in case of social protests, conflicts, or epidemics. The region's benefit is that it allows one to live near a medium-sized city and have an opportunity to move to much less dense areas located nearby. At the same time, Boston is about an hour's drive from Manchester, which is very close. The great thing is that the high density does not extend as much to New Hampshire as it is in Boston and its nearby areas. Thus, it allows you to live in a freedom-like environment while allowing you a certain connection with the metro area. As I said, metros are not safe during a depression, but perhaps you might need to purchase something, or maybe you will find employment there while living an hour's drive from Boston. So, New Hampshire gives you the flexibility of choice while being relatively devoid of extreme risks. The opportunity to choose will be very limited in a depression. I have advocated many times to avoid large metro areas. That recommendation applies, in general, to most people. At the same time, I encourage people to pursue their dreams and goals, and for people who live for their work and passion, abandoning metro areas where they live and work will be equivalent to death. Thus, the relative closeness of New Hampshire to Boston, which is not one of the worst metro areas, will perhaps provide employment to people who solely live to pursue their intellectual dreams.

Manchester is surrounded by many smaller, very attractive areas where people live near the city. Usually, areas surrounding cities tend to have a higher White population than within those cities. One can live in areas near cities in one's own house, with a high degree of privacy, and move to the city within 15 minutes. There are many houses that are located at a relatively attractive distance from each other. Each house might have its own land. The degree of privacy and distance from other people also provides relative protection from epidemics. Bedford, west of Manchester, is a good example. Of course, it is quite a rich and fancy place to live. However, if you prepare for a depression and save enough money, you will be able to purchase housing in areas similar to Bedford. As I mentioned, Concord is another choice if you prefer smaller towns. There are so many examples. Similarly, if you have saved a lot of money before a depression and do not need to deal with other people, you can purchase a house in a nice forestlike environment within a 15 to 20 minute drive from towns and cities. Moreover, because many small towns with comparable characteristics are located nearby, there is flexibility and optionality to move to other ones if your town experiences problems. In addition, New Hampshire is considered the #1 freedom state in terms of overall freedom rating that considers economic and personal freedoms based on the Cato Institute Freedom in the 50 States Index.

The era of the coming depression will be very difficult, especially for people of science, intelligence, and reason. For more rural people who are used to living in difficulties, it will not be as catastrophic as for people who are not used to rural life. It will be extremely difficult for many people of intellectual achievement and intelligence to get accustomed to life that they have never experienced. Thus, it will be easier for them to survive in New Hampshire, where people are different from the South and very rural areas. Surely, they will need to make their living and get used to the reality of the moment. However, the relative closeness to Boston will allow them to drive there to work if they find one. Thus, if you are philosophically incompatible with rural life and will never be able to endure it, and living in a very rural area equals death for you, I would recommend moving to New Hampshire to outlive the depression. That area will suit you the most.

There are a few warning notes. I do not recommend moving to Boston, but you need to know that the unemployment rate in Boston might reach up to 40 percent. It will be similarly high in other metro areas. There are two cities under New Hampshire, located in Massachusetts near the border with New Hampshire, Lawrence and Lowell, that have a much lower percentage of White population (non-Hispanic or Latino). These are risky cities. The area of northern Massachusetts is less unique than New Hampshire in a racial demographic sense. Thus, use U.S. census services to see the racial demographics of each city you plan to move to, even the ones in New Hampshire.

New Hampshire's colder climate is not ideal for agriculture, making food growing difficult. However, the summers are hot, and the state has plenty of available land. Therefore, many people can own their land and produce food for themselves. Some southern people might be afraid of the northern weather. This is not Scandinavia or Siberia. A little cold can be manageable. Surely, it is not perfect agriculturally, yet as I said, the state is not an urbanized megalopolis. If it comes down to supply chain issues, there is always an option to produce food in New Hampshire, with a degree of difficulty, but it is possible.

To conclude, I recommend moving to New Hampshire and, with less confidence, to Maine and Vermont in that order. I do not recommend moving to Massachusetts except for one county I selected, though I am not as completely confident about it as I am about New Hampshire.

Midwest: Wisconsin; Iowa; Minnesota; small parts of North Dakota and South Dakota. (see Figure 9.4)

I selected parts of the West North Central division of the Midwest, which are a relatively decent area to survive a depression. Obviously, there are dangerous areas, too, which is why I aimed to choose only the safest areas. When it comes to the pale orange regions that I chose, I think that approximate area of those counties overall would be suitable for surviving a depression, though I am not sure for 100% about every specific county, as some of them may be risky. The answer will likely be simpler after the crash phase of the economic depression.

The first reason for choosing those Midwestern areas is the low future crime, as the percentage of White people is high. This area is more rural. It is not very urbanized or dense, making it less susceptible to social upheavals, conflicts between races, and epidemics. This part of the Midwest will be more peaceful and detached from the chaos. Most importantly, West North Central part of the Midwest is an agricultural powerhouse, which means the food will be more accessible. Because agriculture and farming are some of the industries that will not decline by 100%, some employment will be present. People may engage in self-sustenance farming. Farm employment will collapse, though not entirely, perhaps by 50% or more. Therefore, I do not think most of the farming areas will be entirely abandoned, as it might happen in some areas with overconcentration of durable goods manufacturing in the Rust Belt states. Also, the quality of healthcare in some of its states is reasonable.

When it comes to real estate risk, except for the large metro areas, selected counties are not extremely susceptible to real estate price decline. Prices will collapse, but less than in metro areas. Similarly, the metro area risk is low, which is very good.

Midwestern states are more Republican than Democrat. However, even Republicans might and will become collectivist and pass collectivist laws, even though they bear the name "Republican." During the Great Depression, many Midwestern states, at least temporarily, elected Democrat officials,[11] which indicated a growing tendency toward collectivism. However, it is better that there are relatively fewer anti-freedom regulations today than in most extreme left-leaning states, which means those states might be relatively less authoritarian during the depression.

Economic risks are present, and the area is not immune to it, which is a significant downside. Apparently, because of very low density and the geography of towns located in mostly farming land areas, it is hard to tell which towns and counties will be affected more or less. Some of those towns may become highly affected. You may move to a relatively medium-sized town or city nearby, see what happens when the economic downturn is taking its toll, and have time to think. Some West North Central states of the Midwest might secede from the United States. However, the area is relatively large, and you will have an opportunity to choose whether you want to live in the United States or the seceded state. Also, avoid very high-poverty areas.

Overall, these parts of the Midwest (Figure 9.4) will be relatively safer than most other U.S. areas, most importantly in terms of crime risk.

Figure 9.4
Safety Map of West North Central States
Note. Created with mapchart.net.

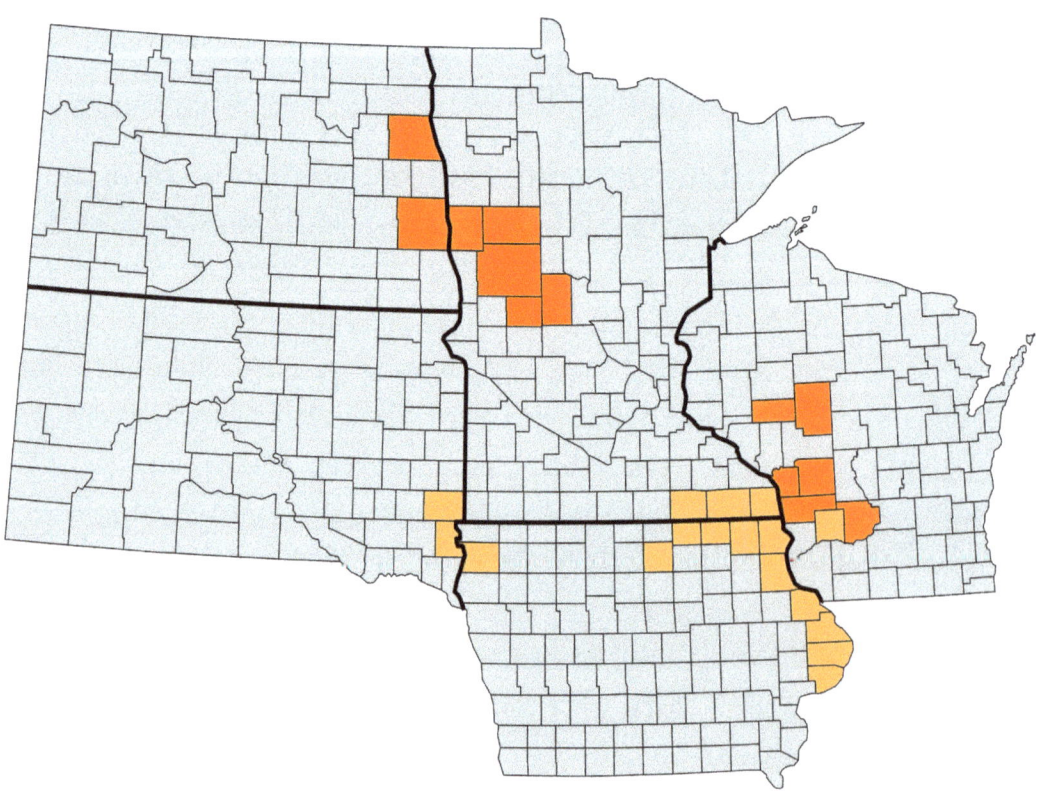

Western areas of Virginia, North Carolina, and Two Counties in Northeast Tennessee (see Figure 9.5)

The primary benefit of this area is safety from violent crime risk because the majority of the population is White. The area is not highly economically risky. Real estate risk is not extreme. This area is more rural (see Figure 9.5). It is relatively detached from reality, though more by its geography and demographics rather than by its physical distance. Agricultural self-sufficiency is not ideal, though nearby areas are agriculturally decent. The eastern part of Virginia is nearby. Thus, the distance is reasonable if someone needs access to large cities. The western areas of Virginia have a low poverty rate. Overall, poverty and unemployment are not extremely high, though the poverty rate might be above average in several counties of North Carolina.

I do not think many words are needed. This area is primarily attractive because of its race demographics, less exposure to real estate risk, and less industry overconcentration. Agricultural self-sufficiency is reasonable but not ideal. And the area is less susceptible to metro area risks. Also, avoid high-poverty cities in this region and small factory or manufacturing towns.

Figure 9.5

Safety Map of Virginia, North Carolina, Tennessee

Note. Created with mapchart.net,

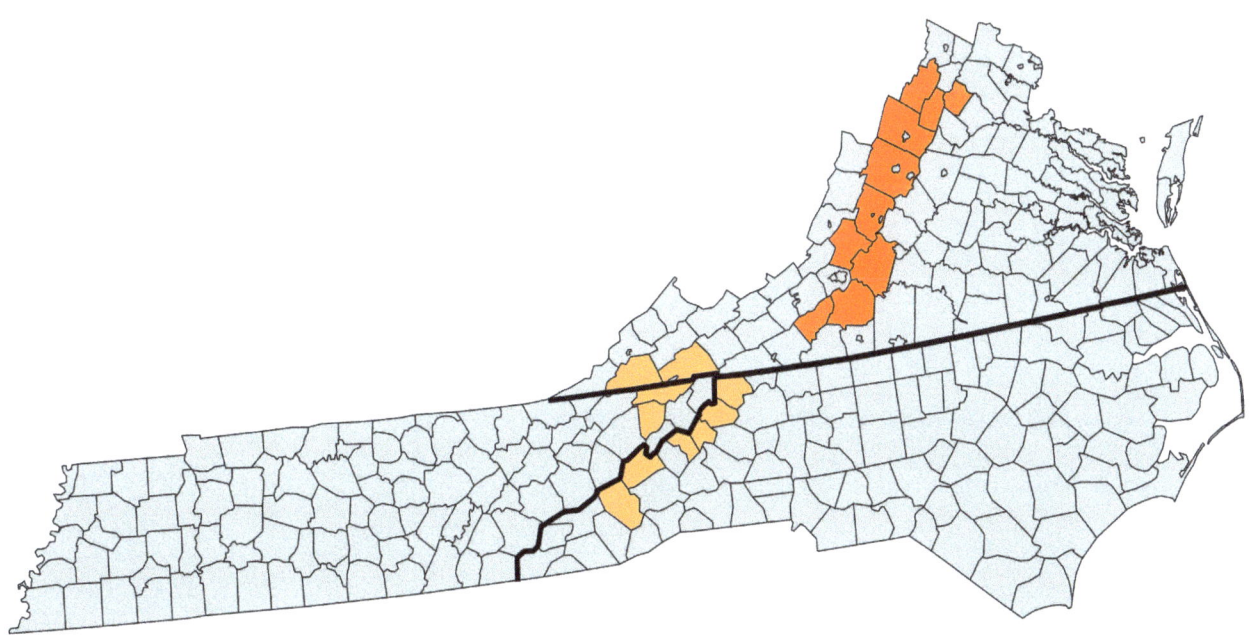

Conclusions

The primary danger in this coming depression is racial demographic differences between regions. So many different issues arise from it. Most importantly, the issue of violent crime. White Americans are statistically and probabilistically much less violent, less dangerous, and less prone to crime than Black Americans or Hispanics. Also, White Americans are more civilized and hygienic. Living among White people during the depression will be much safer. Some of the areas where White people are the majority are quite rural. Though poverty is much less common among White Americans, there are areas where the poverty rate might be above average among White people. Perhaps incomes would be much lower in those towns than in some big cities. Do not be distracted by those things. Slightly higher poverty and lower incomes will be much less an issue than violent crime, which has a cause—racial demographics. Sacrificing physical safety would be justified if you pursue a passion and are tied to a certain area where you can work or turn your dreams into reality. Perhaps you love your town and would want to live there no matter what. In any case, this book gave you invaluable probabilistic knowledge that you may use in case you must and want to move to a location that will more likely be safer.

Moreover, psychological preparedness is critical. Aim to make rational decisions and avoid acting under emotions. I understand how difficult it will be to live through a depression, even for many wealthy people. Personally, I do not want to experience living through an economic depression, though the evidence tells that likely I will. I would always choose to live in happy rather than sad times, though being prepared is very important, even for something we do not want ever to experience.

References

1. U.S. Census Bureau. *QuickFacts: Merrimack County, New Hampshire. Vintage 2022 Population Estimates Program*. Retrieved from https://www.census.gov/quickfacts/fact/table/merrimackcountynewhampshire/POP010220

2. U.S. Census Bureau. *QuickFacts: Concord city, New Hampshire. Vintage 2022 Population Estimates Program*. Retrieved from https://www.census.gov/quickfacts/fact/table/concordcitynewhampshire/PST045222

3. U.S. Census Bureau. *QuickFacts: Concord city, New Hampshire. 2022 ACS 5-year estimates*. Retrieved from https://www.census.gov/quickfacts/fact/table/concordcitynewhampshire/PST045222

4. U.S. Census Bureau. *QuickFacts: Hillsborough County, New Hampshire. Vintage 2022 Population Estimates Program*. Retrieved from https://www.census.gov/quickfacts/fact/table/hillsboroughcountynewhampshire/PST045222

5. U.S. Census Bureau. *QuickFacts: Manchester city, New Hampshire. Vintage 2022 Population Estimates Program*. Retrieved from https://www.census.gov/quickfacts/fact/table/manchestercitynewhampshire/PST045222

6. U.S. Census Bureau. *QuickFacts: Manchester city, New Hampshire. 2022 ACS 5-year estimates*. Retrieved from https://www.census.gov/quickfacts/fact/table/manchestercitynewhampshire/PST045222

7. U.S. Census Bureau. *QuickFacts: Nashua city, New Hampshire. Vintage 2022 Population Estimates Program*. Retrieved from https://www.census.gov/quickfacts/fact/table/nashuacitynewhampshire/PST045222

8. U.S. Census Bureau. *QuickFacts: Nashua city, New Hampshire. 2022 ACS 5-year estimates*. Retrieved from https://www.census.gov/quickfacts/fact/table/nashuacitynewhampshire/PST045222

9. U.S. Census Bureau. *2020 Census Demographic Data Map Viewer*. Retrieved from https://maps.geo.census.gov/ddmv/map.html

10. Ibid.

11. Robert S. McElvaine (2004). *Encyclopedia of The Great Depression*. New York. Thomson Gale. Volume 2, pages 619—624

Chapter 1: Durable Goods Manufacturing

Figure A.1

Durable Goods Manufacturing as a Percentage of Total Gross Domestic Product (GDP) by States, Regions, and Total U.S. GDP

United States	**5.59%**
New England	**5.82%**
Connecticut	8.82%
Maine	4.73%
Massachusetts	4.43%
New Hampshire	7.20%
Rhode Island	5.26%
Vermont	5.64%
Mideast	**2.66%**
Delaware	1.79%
District of Columbia	0.09%
Maryland	2.29%
New Jersey	2.65%
New York	1.81%
Pennsylvania	5.34%
Great Lakes	**9.16%**
Illinois	5.57%
Indiana	14.93%
Michigan	12.20%
Ohio	7.96%
Wisconsin	9.33%
Plains	**6.81%**
Iowa	8.92%
Kansas	7.06%
Minnesota	7.71%
Missouri	6.06%
Nebraska	4.37%
North Dakota	5.23%
South Dakota	4.74%
Southeast	**5.20%**
Alabama	10.93%
Arkansas	8.36%
Florida	2.55%
Georgia	4.87%
Kentucky	8.60%
Louisiana	3.22%
Mississippi	8.63%
North Carolina	6.01%
South Carolina	7.66%
Tennessee	7.42%
Virginia	3.51%
West Virginia	4.76%

Southwest	**5.05%**
Arizona	6.57%
New Mexico	1.67%
Oklahoma	4.80%
Texas	4.94%
Rocky Mountain	**4.35%**
Colorado	3.56%
Idaho	5.96%
Montana	2.23%
Utah	6.28%
Wyoming	1.22%
Far West	**6.36%**
Alaska	0.41%
California	6.69%
Hawaii	0.48%
Nevada	3.13%
Oregon	9.12%
Washington	5.94%

Note. Data is for Q2 2023. Source: U.S. Bureau of Economic Analysis. For District of Columbia, data last updated: September 29, 2023, revised statistics for 2017–2022.

Figure A.2

Durable Goods Employment as a Percentage of Total Employment by States, Regions, and Total U.S. Employment

United States	**3.75%**
New England	**3.90%**
Connecticut	5.14%
Maine	3.50%
Massachusetts	3.06%
New Hampshire	5.58%
Rhode Island	3.76%
Vermont	4.05%
Mideast	**2.35%**
Delaware	1.46%
District of Columbia	0.06%
Maryland	1.50%
New Jersey	1.94%
New York	1.87%
Pennsylvania	4.18%
Great Lakes	**6.53%**
Illinois	4.03%
Indiana	9.29%
Michigan	7.83%
Ohio	6.20%
Wisconsin	7.46%
Plains	**4.79%**
Iowa	5.93%
Kansas	4.94%
Minnesota	5.42%
Missouri	4.32%
Nebraska	3.33%
North Dakota	3.07%
South Dakota	4.39%
Southeast	**3.54%**
Alabama	6.34%
Arkansas	4.51%
Florida	1.97%
Georgia	3.03%
Kentucky	6.15%
Louisiana	2.24%
Mississippi	5.84%
North Carolina	3.88%
South Carolina	5.11%
Tennessee	5.17%
Virginia	2.59%
West Virginia	3.12%

Southwest	**3.01%**
Arizona	3.33%
New Mexico	1.39%
Oklahoma	3.45%
Texas	2.98%
Rocky Mountain	**2.79%**
Colorado	2.25%
Idaho	3.53%
Montana	1.78%
Utah	4.04%
Wyoming	0.82%
Far West	**3.38%**
Alaska	0.42%
California	3.39%
Hawaii	0.36%
Nevada	2.09%
Oregon	5.10%
Washington	3.78%

Note. Data last updated September 29, 2023, new statistics for 2022. Source: U.S. Bureau of Economic Analysis. Data for the District of Columbia and Wyoming are my approximate estimates.

Figure A.3

Durable Goods Manufacturing Private Nonfarm Earnings as a Percentage of Total Nonfarm Earnings by County

Counties (223)	> 25%
Butler, AL	
Clay, AL	✔
DeKalb, AL	
Fayette, AL	
Franklin, AL	✔
Hale, AL	
Lamar, AL	✔
Marion, AL	✔
Talladega, AL	✔
Winston, AL	✔
Arkansas, AR	
Calhoun, AR	✔
Grant, AR	✔
Greene, AR	✔
Howard, AR	
Marion, AR	✔
Mississippi, AR	✔
Santa Clara, CA	
Atkinson, GA	✔
Berrien, GA	✔
Clinch, GA	✔
Dade, GA	✔
Elbert, GA	
Haralson, GA	
Jeff Davis, GA	
Peach, GA	✔
Polk, GA	
Troup, GA	
Walker, GA	
Warren, GA	✔
Boone, IL	✔
Clark, IL	✔
Clay, IL	✔
Cumberland, IL	✔
Douglas, IL	✔
Edgar, IL	✔
Edwards, IL	✔
Lawrence, IL	

	>25%
Logan, IL	
Moultrie, IL	✔
Peoria, IL	
Washington, IL	
Adams, IN	
Bartholomew, IN	✔
Clay, IN	✔
Decatur, IN	✔
DeKalb, IN	✔
Dubois, IN	✔
Elkhart, IN	✔
Fayette, IN	
Fountain, IN	✔
Fulton, IN	
Gibson, IN	✔
Howard, IN	✔
Jackson, IN	✔
Jay, IN	✔
Jefferson, IN	
Kosciusko, IN	✔
Lagrange, IN	✔
Lawrence, IN	
Marshall, IN	
Montgomery, IN	
Noble, IN	✔
Owen, IN	✔
Perry, IN	✔
Pulaski, IN	✔
Randolph, IN	
Shelby, IN	
Steuben, IN	
Tipton, IN	✔
Wabash, IN	
White, IN	
Whitley, IN	✔
Black Hawk, IA	
Delaware, IA	
Des Moines, IA	✔

	>25%
Franklin, IA	
Fremont, IA	
Greene, IA	
Hancock, IA	✔
Ida, IA	✔
Iowa, IA	✔
Mahaska, IA	✔
Marion, IA	✔
Muscatine, IA	
Van Buren, IA	
Allen, KS	
Harvey, KS	✔
Marshall, KS	
Neosho, KS	
Wilson, KS	✔
Carroll, KY	✔
Casey, KY	
Crittenden, KY	
Gallatin, KY	✔
Hancock, KY	✔
Henderson, KY	
Logan, KY	✔
Marion, KY	✔
Mercer, KY	✔
Metcalfe, KY	
Russell, KY	✔
Scott, KY	✔
Simpson, KY	
Todd, KY	
Washington, KY	✔
Sagadahoc, ME	✔
Baraga, MI	
Barry, MI	
Berrien, MI	✔
Hillsdale, MI	✔
Menominee, MI	✔
Missaukee, MI	
Montmorency, MI	

Continued on the next page

Counties (223)	> 25%
Muskegon, MI	
Ottawa, MI	✔
St. Joseph, MI	✔
Jackson, MN	✔
Le Sueur, MN	
Meeker, MN	
Roseau, MN	✔
Steele, MN	
Calhoun, MS	
Chickasaw, MS	
Grenada, MS	
Itawamba, MS	✔
Jackson, MS	✔
Monroe, MS	
Pontotoc, MS	✔
Smith, MS	✔
Tippah, MS	✔
Tishomingo, MS	✔
Union, MS	✔
Winston, MS	
Barry, MO	
Douglas, MO	
Laclede, MO	✔
Osage, MO	✔
Ralls, MO	
Ste. Genevieve, MO	
Webster, MO	✔
Butler, NE	
Platte, NE	✔
Stanton, NE	✔
Thayer, NE	
Storey, NV	✔
Sullivan, NH	
Tioga, NY	✔
Wayne, NY	
Alexander, NC	✔
Montgomery, NC	✔
Yancey, NC	
Sargent, ND	✔
Auglaize, OH	✔
Champaign, OH	✔
Darke, OH	
Defiance, OH	
Fulton, OH	✔
Holmes, OH	

	>25%
Knox, OH	
Logan, OH	✔
Miami, OH	
Preble, OH	✔
Putnam, OH	✔
Sandusky, OH	✔
Shelby, OH	✔
Union, OH	
Van Wert, OH	
Wayne, OH	
Williams, OH	✔
Wyandot, OH	
Marshall, OK	✔
Noble, OK	✔
Washington, OR	
Elk, PA	✔
Fulton, PA	✔
Jefferson, PA	
Abbeville, SC	
Allendale, SC	✔
Chesterfield, SC	✔
Laurens, SC	
Newberry, SC	✔
Union, SC	
Brookings, SD	
Marshall, SD	✔
Anderson, TN	✔
Cheatham, TN	
DeKalb, TN	✔
Grainger, TN	✔
Hardeman, TN	
Loudon, TN	✔
McMinn, TN	✔
Marshall, TN	✔
Meigs, TN	✔
Monroe, TN	✔
Robertson, TN	
Carson, TX	✔
Hunt, TX	
Leon, TX	
Morris, TX	✔
Sabine, TX	
Washington, TX	✔
Young, TX	✔
Box Elder, UT	✔

	>25%
Bland, VA	✔
Northumberland, VA	
Pulaski, VA	✔
Smyth, VA	
Newport News (Independent City), VA	✔
Snohomish, WA	
Hancock, WV	
Jackson, WV	
Mineral, WV	✔
Calumet, WI	
Fond du Lac, WI	
Jefferson, WI	
Manitowoc, WI	
Marinette, WI	✔
Price, WI	✔
Rusk, WI	
Sheboygan, WI	
Trempealeau, WI	✔
Waupaca, WI	

Note.

- Counties checked are above 25%, not checked are 20% to 25%.
- Counties in alphabetical order of states they belong to.
- Data last updated November 16, 2023, new statistics for 2022, Source: U.S. Bureau of Economic Analysis

Chapter 2: Industry Overconcentration

Figure B.1

Counties with Construction Private Nonfarm Earnings above 20% of Total Private Nonfarm Earnings

Counties (52)
Bibb, AL
Cleburne, AL
Custer, CO
Elbert, CO
Burke, GA
Lincoln, GA
Oglethorpe, GA
Pike, GA
Talbot, GA
Teton, ID
Daviess, IN
Vermillion, IN
Grundy, IA
Jefferson, KS
Bath, KY
Garrard, KY
Livingston, KY
Webster, KY
Ascension, LA
Cameron, LA
Grant, LA
Nantucket, MA
Osceola, MI
Benton, MN
Clearwater, MN
Jefferson Davis, MS
Marion, MS
Moniteau, MO
Graham, NC
Holmes, OH
Perry, OH
Jasper, SC
Hamlin, SD
Hanson, SD
Sanborn, SD
Stanley, SD
Blanco, TX
Callahan, TX

Gaines, TX
Hansford, TX
Hartley, TX
Lee, TX
Milam, TX
San Patricio, TX
Throckmorton, TX
Morgan, UT
Wasatch, UT
Wayne, UT
Charles City, VA
Fluvanna, VA
Powhatan, VA
Calhoun, WV

Note. Source: U.S. Bureau of Economic Analysis. Last updated November 16, 2023, new statistics for 2022.

Figure B.2

Counties with Farm Private Earnings Above 45% of Total Private Nonfarm and Farm Earnings Combined

Counties (57)
Gooding, ID
Cumberland, IL
Henderson, IL
Audubon, IA
Greeley, KS
Hamilton, KS
Hickman, KY
Traverse, MN
Chouteau, MT
Liberty, MT
Treasure, MT
Banner, NE
Blaine, NE
Boyd, NE
Dundy, NE
Hayes, NE
Keya Paha, NE
Loup, NE
Sioux, NE
Wheeler, NE
Benson, ND
Burke, ND
Cavalier, ND
Dickey, ND
Eddy, ND
Emmons, ND
Griggs, ND
Kidder, ND
LaMoure, ND
Logan, ND
Nelson, ND
Renville, ND
Sheridan, ND
Steele, ND
Towner, ND
Wells, ND
Cimarron, OK
Harper, OK

Hughes, OK
Campbell, SD
Clark, SD
Edmunds, SD
Faulk, SD
Hutchinson, SD
McCook, SD
McPherson, SD
Marshall, SD
Miner, SD
Sanborn, SD
Sully, SD
Turner, SD
Castro, TX
Hartley, TX
King, TX
Sherman, TX
Swisher, TX
Piute, UT

Note. Source: U.S. Bureau of Economic Analysis. Last updated November 16, 2023, new statistics for 2022.

Figure B.3

Counties with Government and Government Enterprises Private Nonfarm Earnings Above 50% of Total Private Nonfarm Earnings

Counties (80)
Macon, AL
Kusilvak Census Area, AK*
Yukon-Koyukuk Census Area, AK
Apache, AZ
Kings, CA
Lassen, CA
Sierra, CA
Yuba, CA
Union, FL
Camden, GA
Chattahoochee, GA
Houston, GA
Liberty, GA
Long, GA
Miller, GA
Taliaferro, GA
Elmore, ID
Pulaski, IL
Martin, IN
Geary, KS
Leavenworth, KS
Christian, KY
Elliott, KY
McCreary, KY
Martin, KY
East Feliciana, LA
Vernon, LA
Chippewa, MI
Johnson, MO
Pulaski, MO
Blaine, MT
Glacier, MT
Prairie, MT
Blaine, NE
Johnson, NE
Nemaha, NE
Thurston, NE
Harding, NM
Hidalgo, NM
Otero, NM
Socorro, NM

Franklin, NY
Hamilton, NY
Jefferson, NY
Cumberland, NC
Onslow, NC
Benson, ND
Rolette, ND
Sioux, ND
Cherokee, OK
Comanche, OK
Cotton, OK
Greer, OK
Love, OK
Lake, OR
Forest, PA
Buffalo, SD
Corson, SD
Dewey, SD
Oglala Lakota, SD
Todd, SD
Brooks, TX
Hudspeth, TX
Jim Hogg, TX
Kinney, TX
Presidio, TX
Starr, TX
Terrell, TX
Walker, TX
Daggett, UT
King George, VA
Portsmouth (Independent City), VA
Prince George + Hopewell, VA*
Ferry, WA
Garfield, WA
Island, WA
Pend Oreille, WA
Gilmer, WV
Forest, WI
Menominee, WI

Note. Source: U.S. Bureau of Economic Analysis. Last updated November 16, 2023, new statistics for 2022.

Figure B.4

Counties with Mining, Quarrying, and Oil and Gas Extraction Private Nonfarm Earnings Above 20% of Total Private Nonfarm Earnings

Counties (69)
North Slope Borough, AK
Southeast Fairbanks Census Area, AK
Rio Blanco, CO
Wilkinson, GA
Caribou, ID
Shoshone, ID
Graham, KS
Livingston, KY
De Soto, LA
Iron, MO
Fallon, MT
Esmeralda, NV
Humboldt, NV
Pershing, NV
White Pine, NV
Eddy, NM
Lea, NM
Dunn, ND
McKenzie, ND
Mercer, ND
Mountrail, ND
Williams, ND
Beckham, OK
Dewey, OK
Washington, OK
Armstrong, PA
Andrews, TX
Crane, TX
Crockett, TX
Dimmit, TX
Ector, TX
Frio, TX
Garza, TX
Glasscock, TX
Hemphill, TX
Hockley, TX
Hutchinson, TX
Irion, TX
Jack, TX

Jim Wells, TX
Karnes, TX
La Salle, TX
Loving, TX
McMullen, TX
Midland, TX
Mitchell, TX
Ochiltree, TX
Reagan, TX
Reeves, TX
San Augustine, TX
Scurry, TX
Shackelford, TX
Smith, TX
Stephens, TX
Sutton, TX
Upton, TX
Winkler, TX
Yoakum, TX
Zapata, TX
Duchesne, UT
Dickenson, VA
Boone, WV
McDowell, WV
Wood, WV
Wyoming, WV
Campbell, WY
Converse, WY
Sublette, WY
Sweetwater, WY

Note. Source: U.S. Bureau of Economic Analysis. Last updated November 16, 2023, new statistics for 2022.

Figure B.5

Counties with Healthcare and Social Assistance Private Nonfarm Earnings Above 25% of
Total Private Nonfarm Earnings

Counties (28)	
Dillingham Census Area, AK	Otsego, NY
Baxter, AR	Moore, NC
Floyd, GA	Adams, ND
Pulaski, GA	Scioto, OH
Boyd, KY	Nowata, OK
Cumberland, KY	Montour, PA
Floyd, KY	Wayne, TN
Pike, KY	Franklin, TX
Alcona, MI	Stonewall, TX
Olmsted, MN	Cabell, WV
Cape Girardeau, MO	Monongalia, WV
Newton, MO	Webster, WV
Deer Lodge, MT	Wirt, WV
Bronx, NY	Wood, WI

Figure B.6

Counties with Finance and Insurance or Real Estate and Rental and Leasing Private Nonfarm Earnings
Above 30% of Total Private Nonfarm Earnings

Counties (4)	
New York, NY	Dallas, IA
McLean, IL	Sully, SD

Figure B.7

Counties with Transportation and Warehousing Private Nonfarm Earnings Above 25% of Total Private
Nonfarm Earnings

Counties (10)	
Clayton, GA	Boyd, NE
Twiggs, GA	Clinton, OH
Lafourche, LA	Madison, OH
Iosco, MI	Franklin, TX
Marshall, MS	Hot Springs, WY

Note. Source for Figures B-5; B-6; B-7: U.S. Bureau of
Economic Analysis. Last updated November 16, 2023, new
statistics for 2022.

Chapter 4: Crime

Figure C.1

Linear Regression Between Percentage Black and Homicide Rate per 100,000
Correlation Coefficient: 0.85

SUMMARY OUTPUT

Regression Statistics	
Multiple R	0.845808
R Square	0.715392
Adjusted R	0.709584
Standard E	3.255442
Observatic	51

ANOVA

	df	SS	MS	F	ignificance F
Regression	1	1305.307	1305.307	123.1666	5.66E-15
Residual	49	519.2972	10.5979		
Total	50	1824.604			

	Coefficients	andard Err	t Stat	P-value	Lower 95%	Upper 95%	ower 95.0%	Jpper 95.0%
Intercept	2.293888	0.701585	3.26958	0.001974	0.884	3.703776	0.884	3.703776
X Variable	47.9594	4.321429	11.09804	5.66E-15	39.27517	56.64364	39.27517	56.64364

Figure C.2

States by Percentage of Individuals in Poverty and Homicide Mortality Rate per 100,000

Note. Homicide mortality source: Source for homicide mortality (2021): cdc.gov, for DC, NH, VT, and WY: number of homicides divided by population and multiplied by 100,000. Poverty rate source: data.census.gov, 2022: ACS 5-year estimates subject tables.

State	Poverty %	Homicide mortality per 100,000
Alabama	15.7	15.9
Alaska	10.5	6.4
Arizona	13.1	8.1
Arkansas	16.2	11.7
California	12.1	6.4
Colorado	9.6	6.3
Connecticut	10.1	4.8
Delaware	11.1	11.3
District of Columbia	15.1	33.9
Florida	12.9	7.4
Georgia	13.5	11.4
Hawaii	9.6	2.7
Idaho	11.0	2.2
Illinois	11.8	12.3
Indiana	12.3	9.6
Iowa	11.1	3.2
Kansas	11.6	6.4
Kentucky	16.1	9.6
Louisiana	18.7	21.3
Maine	10.9	1.7
Maryland	9.3	12.2
Massachusetts	9.9	2.3
Michigan	13.1	8.7
Minnesota	9.3	4.3
Mississippi	19.2	23.7
Missouri	12.8	12.4
Montana	12.4	4.4
Nebraska	10.4	3.6
Nevada	12.7	8.5
New Hampshire	7.3	1.1
New Jersey	9.7	4.8
New Mexico	18.3	15.3
New York	13.6	4.8
North Carolina	13.3	9.7
North Dakota	10.8	3.4
Ohio	13.3	9.3
Oklahoma	15.2	8.9
Oregon	11.9	4.9

Pennsylvania	11.8	9.2
Rhode Island	11.2	3.6
South Carolina	14.4	13.4
South Dakota	12.3	5.3
Tennessee	14.0	12.2
Texas	13.9	8.2
Utah	8.5	2.7
Vermont	10.4	1.5
Virginia	10.0	7.2
Washington	9.9	4.5
West Virginia	16.8	6.9
Wisconsin	10.7	6.4
Wyoming	10.7	2.8

Figure C.3

Linear Regression Between Poverty and Crime Based on the Data on Appendix Figure C.2 with Correlation Coefficient 0.7

SUMMARY OUTPUT

Regression Statistics	
Multiple R	0.696857
R Square	0.485609
Adjusted R	0.475111
Standard E	4.376561
Observatic	51

ANOVA

	df	SS	MS	F	ignificance F
Regression	1	886.0446	886.0446	46.2583	1.35E-08
Residual	49	938.5599	19.15428		
Total	50	1824.604			

	Coefficients	andard Err	t Stat	P-value	Lower 95%	Upper 95%	ower 95.0%	lpper 95.0%
Intercept	-11.548	2.969321	-3.8891	0.000303	-17.5151	-5.5809	-17.5151	-5.5809
X Variable	1.599411	0.235161	6.801346	1.35E-08	1.126837	2.071984	1.126837	2.071984